THE KEY TO UNDERSTANDING
GLOBAL HISTORY

JAMES KILLORAN
STUART ZIMMER
MARK JARRETT, Ph.D.

JARRETT PUBLISHING COMPANY

East Coast Office:
P.O. Box 1460
Ronkonkoma, NY 11779
631-981-4248

West Coast Office:
10 Folin Lane
Lafayette, CA 94549
925-906-9742

1-800-859-7679   Fax: 631-588-4722

www.jarrettpub.com

ISBN 1-882422-40-6
Copyright 2011 Jarrett Publishing Company
Printed in the United States of America
10 9 8 7 6 5 4 3 2 1   12 11

ACKNOWLEDGMENTS

The authors would like to thank the following educators who reviewed the manuscript, and whose comments, suggestions, and recommendations proved invaluable: **D. Joe Corr,** Shaker High School, Latham, NY; **Steve Goldberg,** New Rochelle High School, New Rochelle, NY; **Theresa Noonan,** West Irondequoit High School, Rochester, NY; **Kevin Sheehan,** Oceanside High School, Oceanside, NY; **Al Sive,** Walton High School, Walton, NY; and **Rhoda Weinstein,** Franklin K. Lane High School, Brooklyn, NY.

Layout, graphics and typesetting by Maple Hill Press, Huntington, NY.

ILLUSTRATION CREDITS

Cover: The gold funerary mask of Pharaoh Tutankhamen, Egyptian National Museum, Cairo; © Superstock, Inc.; Page 13, Library of Congress; page 38, Jarrett Archives; page 57, United Nations; page 70, Israeli Department of Tourism; page 77, Library of Congress; page 99, Pitlik Collection; page 107, Israeli Department of Tourism; page 110, Library of Congress; page 119, Alex Gardega; page 134, Library of Congress; page 136 (t and b), Jarrett Archives; page 137 (t, m, and b), Jarrett Archives; page 138, (t) Jarrett Archives, (m) National Museum of African Art, (b) Mexican Government Tourist Office; page 139, (t) Indian National Tourist Office, (m) Smithsonian Museum, (b) Japanese National Tourist Office; page 145, Library of Congress; page 147, Japanese National Tourist Office; page 158, Jarrett Archives; page 159, Mexican Government Tourist Office; page 166, Jarrett Archives; page 176, Library of Congress; page 177, Jarrett Archives; page 178, Library of Congress; page 185, Asian Museum, San Francisco; page 193, Library of Congress; page 194, Library of Congress; page 221, Japanese National Tourist Office; page 231, Library of Congress; page 232, Library of Congress; page 238, Library of Congress; page 246, Library of Congress; page 258, Embassy of Poland; page 277, United Nations; page 312, Jarrett Archives; page 324, Library of Congress; page 325, Library of Congress; page 327, United Nations; page 347, Corbis: Gary Conover.

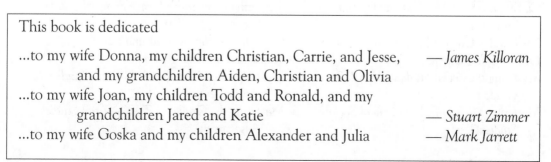

This book is dedicated

...to my wife Donna, my children Christian, Carrie, and Jesse,   — *James Killoran*
      and my grandchildren Aiden, Christian and Olivia
...to my wife Joan, my children Todd and Ronald, and my
      grandchildren Jared and Katie   — *Stuart Zimmer*
...to my wife Goska and my children Alexander and Julia   — *Mark Jarrett*

ABOUT THE AUTHORS

James Killoran is a retired New York Assistant Principal. He has written *Government and You*, and *Economics and You*. Mr. Killoran has extensive experience in test writing for the New York State Board of Regents in Social Studies and has served on the Committee for Testing of the National Council of Social Studies. His article on social studies testing has been published in *Social Education*, the country's leading social studies journal. In addition, Mr. Killoran has won a number of awards for outstanding teaching and curriculum development, including "Outstanding Social Studies Teacher" and "Outstanding Social Studies Supervisor" in New York City. In 1993, he was awarded an Advanced Certificate for Teachers of Social Studies by the N.C.S.S. In 1997, he became Chairman of the N.C.S.S. Committee on Awarding Advanced Certificates for Teachers of Social Studies.

Stuart Zimmer is a retired New York Social Studies teacher. He has written *Government and You*, and *Economics and You*. He served as a test writer for the New York State Board of Regents in Social Studies, and has written for the National Merit Scholarship Examination. In addition, he has published numerous articles on teaching and testing in Social Studies journals. He has presented many demonstrations and educational workshops at state and national teachers' conferences. In 1989, Mr. Zimmer's achievements were recognized by the New York State Legislature with a Special Legislative Resolution in his honor.

Mark Jarrett is a former Social Studies teacher who served as a test writer for the New York State Board of Regents and taught at Hofstra University. He was educated at Columbia University, the London School of Economics and Stanford University, and has a law degree from the University of California at Berkeley. Dr. Jarrett has received several academic awards including the Order of the Coif at Berkeley and the David and Christina Phelps Harris Fellowship at Stanford, where he earned a doctorate in history.

ALSO BY KILLORAN, ZIMMER, AND JARRETT

The Key To Understanding U.S. History
Mastering Global History
Mastering U.S. History and Government
A Quick Review of Global History
A Quick Review of U.S. History and Govt.
Claves para la comprensión de historia universal
Los Estados Unidos: Su historia, su gobierno
Principios de economía
Mastering the Social Studies MEAP Test: Grade 8
Mastering Michigan's High School Social Studies Test

Michigan: Its Land and Its People
Mastering Ohio's Grade 8 Social Studies Achievement Test
Mastering the Ohio Graduation Test in Social Studies
Learning About New York
Mastering New York's Grade 8 Intermeditate Social Studies Test
Ohio: Its Neighbors Near and Far
Texas: Its Land and Its People
Mastering the Grade 8 TAKS Social Studies Assessment
Mastering the Grade 11 TAKS Social Studies Assessment

TABLE OF CONTENTS

PART 1: TEST-TAKING STRATEGIES

PART 2: CONTENT REVIEWS

CHAPTER 1

HOW TO REMEMBER IMPORTANT INFORMATION

The Global History Regents Examination tests your knowledge of important terms, concepts, and people. To learn and remember this information well, you need to engage your mind actively in the learning process. This chapter discusses one way of studying that will make it easier for you to remember important information.

REMEMBERING IMPORTANT TERMS

There are many different types of important **terms** to remember in global history:

- *document* — U.N. Charter
- *time period* — Ming dynasty
- *religion* — Hinduism
- *group* — serfs

- *event* — attack on Pearl Harbor
- *policy* — Russification
- *organization* — OPEC
- *war* — World War II

All these terms refer to a *specific* thing that happened or existed — a document signed, a group formed, or a war fought. Questions about a term generally require you to know:

- what it is or was
- its causes and effects
- its significance

It is easier to remember a term if you jot down the main information and add a simple drawing. Every time you read about an important term, concept or person, you should complete a study card similar to the one shown at right:

MAGNA CARTA

WHAT IS IT? A document signed by King John of England in 1215 that forced the king to share power with his nobles.

MAJOR CAUSE: The nobles objected to the excessive power of the king.

MAJOR EFFECT: The Magna Carta became the cornerstone of English law by stating the king's subjects had basic rights.

(Drawing may be on the front or back of the card.)

REMEMBERING KEY CONCEPTS

Concepts are the building blocks of knowledge. They are words or phrases that denote **categories of information**. Concepts allow us to organize vast amounts of information. Unlike terms — which identify specific things — concepts are ideas that identify relationships in **groups** of things. At the right is an example of a study card about a concept.

REPRESENTATIVE DEMOCRACY

DEFINITION: A system of government in which people rule themselves through elected representatives.

EXAMPLE: The system of government by elected officials that exists in the United States.

Ballot Box

REMEMBERING FAMOUS PEOPLE

In global history you will also learn about many famous people. Questions about these individuals will usually ask *who they are* and *why they are famous*. You will need to know the place and time in which they lived, their position in society, and their accomplishments and impact on history. At the right is an example of a study card about a famous person.

MOHANDAS GANDHI

PLACE/TIME: India, 20th century.

BACKGROUND: Political leader in India's struggle for independence from British rule.

ACCOMPLISHMENTS/IMPACT: His non-violent methods of "civil disobedience" won India independence in 1947. He inspired leaders in other Asian and African colonies by his example.

BOYCOTT

In each content chapter the key *terms, concepts,* and *people* appear in a box on the first page. At the end of each content chapter review are **study cards** you can photocopy for your personal use or hand-copy onto your own cards. You can study with these cards by blocking out everything but the card title to see how much you can recall. These study cards, and others you make while reading each chapter, will help you during your final review before the Regents Examination.

CHAPTER 2

INTERPRETING DIFFERENT TYPES OF DATA

The Global History Regents Examination will have several questions based on interpreting information provided in the question itself. Such information, or *data*, may appear in the form of a map, table, political cartoon, line graph, pie chart, outline, bar graph, timeline, speaker question, or reading passage.

Having experience with these types of data and knowing **how** to interpret them is therefore crucial to performing well on this form of test question. In this chapter, you will review the ten types of data most often used by Regents testmakers:

- Maps
- Bar Graphs
- Line Graphs
- Pie Charts
- Tables

- Timelines
- Political Cartoons
- Outlines
- Speaker Questions
- Reading Passages

MAPS

WHAT IS A MAP?

A map is a diagram or representation of an area. Different kinds of information can be shown on a map:

✦ **Political maps** usually show the major boundaries between countries or states.

✦ **Physical maps** show the physical characteristics of a region, such as its rivers, mountains, vegetation, and elevation (*height above sea level*).

✦ **Product maps** show the major natural resources and agricultural and industrial products of an area.

✦ **Theme maps** can provide information on almost any theme, such as rainfall, population density, languages spoken, or main points of interest.

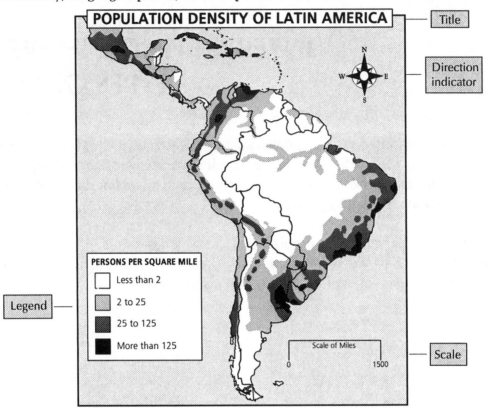

KEYS TO UNDERSTANDING A MAP

Title. The title of a map usually identifies the area shown and any special information that is presented. For example, the title of the above map is: *Population Density of Latin America*. The map shows the number of people living per square mile in Latin America.

Legend. The legend (or **key**) unlocks the information on a map. The legend shows the symbols used and identifies what each one represents. For example, in this map legend:

- the *white box* shows areas where the density is less than 2 people per square mile
- the *light gray box* shows areas where the density is from 2 to 25 people per square mile
- the *dark gray box* shows areas where the density is from 25 to 125 people per square mile
- the *black box* shows areas where the density is more than 125 people per square mile.

Direction. To find directions on a map, look at its **direction indicator** (*compass rose*). It is used to indicate the four basic directions: north, south, east, and west. If no indicator is shown, assume that north is at the top.

Scale. A map would be impossible to use if it were the same size as the area it represents. Mapmakers use a scale to show how much the distances have been reduced. A map scale is often a line marked in miles or kilometers. On this map, one inch equals 1,500 miles. The scale is used to find the actual distance between two points on the map.

CHECKING YOUR UNDERSTANDING

Use the map on page 4 to answer the following questions:

1. What area of Latin America has the lowest population density?_____

2. What areas on the map have the highest concentrations of people?_____

BAR GRAPHS

WHAT IS A BAR GRAPH?

A bar graph is a chart made up of parallel bars with different lengths. A bar graph is used to compare two or more items. It can also show how items have changed over time.

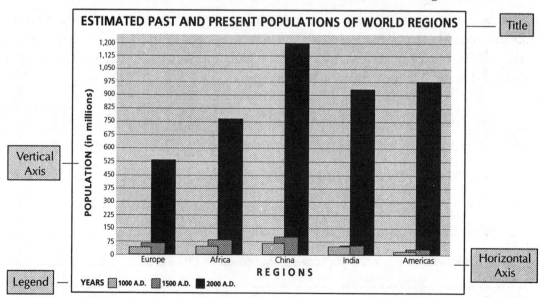

KEYS TO UNDERSTANDING A BAR GRAPH

Title. The title identifies the general topic of the graph. For example, the title of this bar graph is: *Estimated Past and Present Populations of World Regions.* It shows the estimated population of five world regions at different time periods.

Legend. The legend shows what each bar represents:

- the light gray bars represent estimated populations in 1000 A.D.
- the dark gray bars represent estimated populations in 1500 A.D.
- the black bars represent estimated populations in 2000 A.D.

Vertical and Horizontal Axes. Every bar graph has a vertical and a horizontal axis.

- The **vertical axis** runs from the bottom to the top. It allows the reader to measure the length of the bars. Here, the vertical axis lists the estimated population in millions. Thus, the first light gray bar for Europe (1000 A.D.) represents a population of about 40 million (*slightly more than halfway between 0 and 75*).

- The **horizontal axis** runs from left to right. It identifies what each individual bar represents. Here, the horizontal axis indicates five world regions: Europe, Africa, China, India, and the Americas.

Trends. Sometimes a bar graph will reveal a **trend** — a general direction in which events are moving. We can often identify a trend from the height of the bars. For example, one trend shown in this graph is that the rate of population growth in each world region has increased dramatically in the past 500 years.

CHECKING YOUR UNDERSTANDING

Use the bar graph on page 5 to answer the following:

1. What was the population of the Americas in the year 1000? _____

2. What was the population of Africa in the year 1500? _____

3. In which region has the population increased the most? _____

LINE GRAPHS

WHAT IS A LINE GRAPH?

A line graph is a chart made up of points connected in a line. It is often used to show how something has changed over time. Some graphs have more than one line.

KEYS TO UNDERSTANDING A LINE GRAPH

Title. The title identifies the topic. For example, the title of the line graph below is *Estimated Native American Population of Mexico, 1518 to 1593*. This means the graph shows changes in Mexico's Native American population for 75 years, from 1518 to 1593.

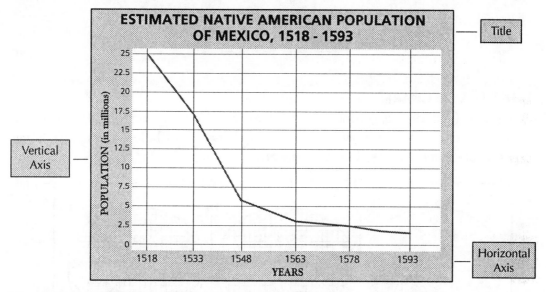

Vertical and Horizontal Axis. Each line graph has a vertical and a horizontal axis.

- **Vertical Axis.** The vertical axis runs from bottom to top. It usually measures the size of items. Notice that as you move up the vertical axis the numbers increase. Since the population is shown in millions, "25" means 25 *million* Native Americans.

- **Horizontal Axis.** The horizontal axis runs from left to right. Often it measures the passage of time. In this line graph, the horizontal axis shows years. The first year is 1518, and the dates continue in fifteen-year intervals until 1593.

Legend. If the graph has many lines, a legend explains what each line represents. If it has only one or two lines, as in this graph, the information is printed directly on the graph.

Trends. Often a line graph will reveal a trend or pattern. One trend shown in this graph is the sharp decrease in Mexico's Native American population after 1518.

CHECKING YOUR UNDERSTANDING

Use the line graph on page 7 to answer the following:

1. What was Mexico's Native American population in 1533? _____

2. What does the vertical axis show? _____

PIE CHARTS

WHAT IS A PIE CHART?

A pie chart (*or circle graph*) consists of a circle divided into sections of different sizes. A pie chart is often used to show the relationship between a whole and its parts. Sometimes several circles are used for comparisons.

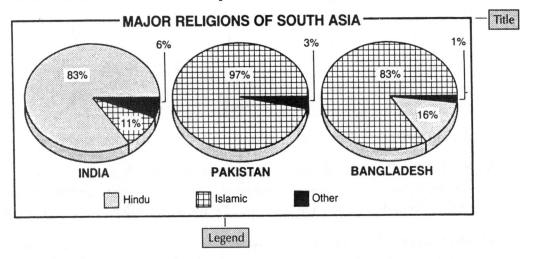

KEYS TO UNDERSTANDING A PIE CHART

Title. The title identifies the overall topic of the chart. In this example, the title is *Major Religions of South Asia.* The three "pies" show the major religious groups of South Asia and the relative sizes of these groups.

Slices of the Pie. Each slice of the pie shows the size or relationship of one of the parts to the whole pie. Think of the pie as 100% of something. If you add all the slices together, they total 100%. Each of the pies in the chart on page 8 has three slices. Two of the slices represent Hinduism and Islam. The third slice represents other religions.

Size of each Slice. The size of each slice tells you the relative size of each religious group. For example, you can see that the largest group in India is Hindu, while Pakistan and Bangladesh are predominantly Muslim (*followers of the Islamic faith*).

Legend. A pie chart may include a legend, as this one does. In many pie charts a legend is not necessary because the information is displayed on the slices themselves.

CHECKING YOUR UNDERSTANDING

Use the pie chart on page 8 to answer the following questions:

1. What percentage of Bangladesh's population follow the Hindu religion?_____

2. Which of the three countries has the largest percentage of Muslims?_____

TABLES

WHAT IS A TABLE?

A table is an arrangement of words or numbers in columns and rows. A table is often used to organize many facts so that they can be easily located and compared.

ECONOMIC CONDITIONS IN LATIN AMERICA, 1997 — Title

Nations	Population (in millions)	Per Capita GDP (in dollars)	Infant Mortality (per 1,000)	Literacy (percent)	Life Expectancy (years)
Bolivia	7.1	2,370	68	80	60
Brazil	162.6	5,580	55	83	62
Costa Rica	3.4	5,050	14	95	76
Haiti	6.7	870	104	45	49
Mexico	95.7	7,900	25	90	74
Venezuela	21.9	8,670	30	91	72

KEYS TO UNDERSTANDING A TABLE

Title. The title identifies the overall topic. The title of the table on page 9 is *Economic Conditions In Latin America, 1997.* The table provides various economic data for six Latin American nations in 1997.

Categories. A table is made up of various categories of information. Each column represents a category named in the headings found across the top of the table. In this table, there are six different categories: *nation, population, Gross Domestic Product per capita, infant mortality, literacy,* and *life expectancy.* Each row represents a different nation in Latin America. To find a particular piece of information, choose a category and look down that column until you reach the row of the country that is of interest.

Inferring from the Data. By examining a table, it is often possible to identify trends or draw conclusions. For example, Haiti's high infant mortality and low life expectancy seem to indicate problems in the area of public health.

CHECKING YOUR UNDERSTANDING

Use the table on page 9 to answer the following questions:

1. Which country in the table has the largest population? —————————

2. Which country has the highest literacy rate? —————————

3. Which country do you think is the poorest? Explain. —————————

TIMELINES

WHAT IS A TIMELINE?

A timeline presents a series of events arranged in chronological order along a line. **Chronological order** is the sequence in which the events actually occurred. Thus the event that occurred earliest is the first event on the timeline. The distances between events on a timeline are usually in proportion to the actual time between the events they represent. A timeline can span anything from a short period of time to thousands of years. The purpose of a timeline is to show how events are related to each other.

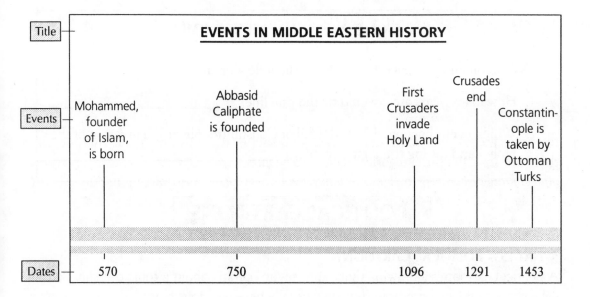

KEYS TO UNDERSTANDING A TIMELINE

Title. The title states the topic. For example, the title of this timeline is *Events in Middle Eastern History*. The timeline lists some milestones in the history of the Middle East.

Events. All of the events on the timeline are related in some way to its title.

Dates. Events on a timeline are in chronological order. This timeline starts with the birth of Mohammed in 570 and ends in 1453, when the Ottoman Turks took Constantinople.

If you add a new event, the date of the event should fall between two dates on the timeline. For example, if you wanted to add the Arab reconquest of Jerusalem by Saladin in 1187, where on the timeline would it go? Since 1187 is closer to 1096 (*91 years*) than to 1291 (*104 years*), you would place it a bit closer to 1096 than to 1291.

Special Terms. To understand questions about timelines or time periods, you should be familiar with several special terms:

  • **Decade:** 10 years   • **Century:** 100 years   • **Millennium:** 1,000 years

Division Between B.C. and A.D.:
B.C. (or B.C.E. — Before the Common Era) refers to the period before Christ was born, and A.D. (or C.E. — the Common Era) means the years since the birth of Christ.

Use the timeline on page 11 to answer the following questions:

1. How many years are covered by the timeline?_____

2. Which event happened first: the fall of Constantinople or the invasion of the Holy Land during the First Crusade? _____

POLITICAL CARTOONS

WHAT IS A POLITICAL CARTOON?

A political cartoon is a drawing that expresses an opinion about a topic or issue. Political cartoons may be humorous, but they usually have a serious point.

KEYS TO UNDERSTANDING A POLITICAL CARTOON

Title or Caption. Most political cartoons have a title or caption that helps explain the message the cartoonist is trying to get across.

Medium. Cartoonists want to persuade readers to support their point of view. To achieve this, the cartoonist will often use the size of objects, facial expressions, exaggerations or words spoken by the cartoon characters to satirize (*poke fun at*) some positions and to support others.

The Future of World Oil Prices? — Caption

Symbols. Cartoonists often use symbols. A **symbol** is any object that *represents* or stands for something else.

People. A cartoonist often draws attention to an issue by drawing a caricature of a famous person associated with the issue. A **caricature** is a drawing in which a person's features are exaggerated for comic effect.

CHECKING YOUR UNDERSTANDING

Use the cartoon on page 12 to answer the following questions:

1. What objects, people, or symbols are used by the cartoonist? _____

2. Which elements has the cartoonist exaggerated? _____

3. What situation is taking place in the cartoon? _____

4. What is the main idea of the cartoon? _____

OTHER VISUALS

Other types of visuals that may appear on the Global History Regents Examination are photos, illustrations, and diagrams. Unlike cartoons, these do not usually express an opinion, but depict a scene, person, situation, or process.

Photographs and Illustrations. Photographs and illustrations are especially useful for understanding the past. They show how people once looked, dressed, and lived. A photograph gives us a feeling for an earlier time or a different place. Since photography was not invented until the mid-1800s, we rely on drawings and paintings for a glimpse of what life was like before that time.

Examine this photograph of Jewish prisoners in a Nazi concentration camp in 1945. What do the details in the photo tell us about the kind of treatment that was endured by prisoners in Nazi concentration camps during World War II?

CHECKING YOUR UNDERSTANDING

Use the photograph on page 13 to answer the following questions:

1. What conclusion can you draw from the number of people assigned per bunk?
   _____

2. What conclusions can you draw about conditions in Nazi concentration camps from the appearance of the standing prisoner and the prisoner whose head sticks out from the bunk? _____

DIAGRAMS

A **diagram** is a symbolic drawing that shows how something is organized or how a particular process works.

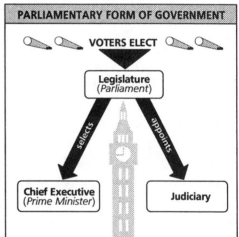

Unlike the United States, most democratic countries have parliamentary systems. Examine the diagram at the right, showing how the parliamentary form of government is structured.

The diagram shows the branches of parliamentary government and what each branch is called. It also indicates which officials are directly elected by the citizens and which are appointed to their positions.

CHECKING YOUR UNDERSTANDING

Use the diagram above to answer the following questions:

1. Who elects the members of parliament? _____

2. Who chooses the chief executive (*Prime Minister*)? _____

3. Who selects the judiciary in a parliamentary government? _____

OUTLINES

WHAT IS AN OUTLINE?

An outline is a brief plan in which a topic or major idea is divided up into smaller units. The purpose of an outline is to show the relationships between a topic (*major idea*) and its parts. This serves as a "blueprint" to help organize the writer's thoughts.

KEYS TO UNDERSTANDING AN OUTLINE

Title. The title identifies the general topic of the outline.

Format. Most outlines follow a format that allows you to easily understand how the main topic is divided into subsections.

- **Roman Numerals.** The first major divisions of the topic are given Roman numerals (I, II, III, etc.).

- **Capital Letters.** If the topic needs to be further divided, its sub-topics are listed by capital letters (A, B, C, etc.).

- **Arabic Numbers.** If the sub-topics are divided further, Arabic numerals (1, 2, 3) are used. To illustrate this process, assume you want to write an essay about 20th-century wars. It might be outlined as shown at the right.

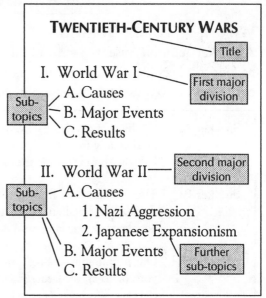

Outlines go from the *general* to the *specific*: they break down a larger idea into smaller and smaller units. In this example, each smaller unit (*sub-topic*) helps to develop the larger concept. For example, information about the causes, events, and results of World War I helps explain what the war was all about. The outline might then go into further detail on each of these sub-topics.

Outlining provides a useful tool for taking notes or for organizing your thoughts when answering essay questions on the Regents Examination.

CHECKING YOUR UNDERSTANDING

Use the outline on page 15 to answer the following questions:

1. What are the main units that make up the topic "Twentieth-Century Wars"?
   _____

2. What units make up the topic "World War II"? _____

3. If you were to add details about the "Results" of World War II, which would
   you use: Roman numerals, letters, or Arabic numerals? _____

SPEAKER QUESTIONS

WHAT IS A SPEAKER QUESTION?

A speaker question presents a series of statements by different speakers. There will usually
be four speakers identified by the letters A, B, C, and D. The main function of this type
of question is to present a discussion in which different viewpoints are expressed.

Speaker A:	We have given this backward colony a bright future. These people have benefited greatly from the introduction of our system of government and our laws. All we ask in return is the right to sell our finished goods to these people.
Speaker B:	The problems we find today in the homeland of our ancestors are not our doing. We lived in peace for centuries. Foreigners enslaved many of our people, took our land, and destroyed our heritage.
Speaker C:	Our people must unite. Our rights have been abused. We are not allowed to vote or to speak freely in our own land. Europeans treat us as second-class citizens. We must persuade these foreigners to leave our homeland through civil disobedience.
Speaker D:	We must think ahead to the day when we have our independence. We will be in desperate need of foreign investments and technology. We must maintain friendly ties with all nations, including our present rulers.

KEYS TO UNDERSTANDING A SPEAKER QUESTION

Each speaker's statement usually expresses an opinion about a social studies term, concept, or situation. Start by asking yourself the following questions about each speaker:

- What term, concept, or situation is being described or discussed by the speaker? For example, Speaker A is describing imperialism, the control of one country by another.
- What is Speaker A saying about imperialism?
- Note how some of the speakers have contrasting opinions. Why do they disagree?

CHECKING YOUR UNDERSTANDING

Use the speakers' comments on page 16 to answer the following questions:

1. What concept is being discussed by Speaker C? _____

2. Which speaker's views are most similar to those of Mohandas Gandhi?_____

READING PASSAGES

WHAT IS A READING PASSAGE?
The main function of a reading is usually to present someone's views about a topic.

KEYS TO UNDERSTANDING A READING PASSAGE
Ask yourself the following questions about a reading selection:

1. What do you know about the writer?
2. What term, concept, or situation is being discussed by the writer?
3. What is the main idea of the passage?
4. What facts does the writer present to support his/her views?

No one in France ... doubts the benefits of colonization ... Everyone agrees that colonies offer markets for raw materials, the means of production, the products lacking to the mother country; that they open markets to all the commerce and all the industries of an old country, by the wants, by the new needs of the people with whom they are in relation ...

— Paul Leroy-Beaulieu
The Ideology of French Imperialism, 1871-1881

CHECKING YOUR UNDERSTANDING

Answer the following questions based on the reading passage above:

1. What is the main idea of the passage?_____

2. What term or concept is the writer discussing?_____

CHAPTER 3

HOW TO ANSWER MULTIPLE-CHOICE QUESTIONS

The purpose of this chapter is to familiarize you with answering multiple-choice questions. Let's begin by examining the types and structures of multiple-choice questions.

ANSWERING MULTIPLE-CHOICE QUESTIONS

Multiple-choice questions on the New York State Regents in Global History can be grouped into two major types:

✦ **Statement Questions** begin with a question or an incomplete statement. This is followed by either a list of four possible answers to the question or four ways in which the statement can be completed.

✦ **Data-based Questions** present some type of data or information to introduce the question. You are then asked to select the correct answer from a list of four choices.

Multiple-choice questions test your mastery of both the content of global history and of fundamental social studies thinking processes (*analysis, synthesis and hypothesis*). Testmakers do this with a variety of question structures, many of which are identified on the following pages.

KNOWLEDGE OF IMPORTANT INFORMATION
Statement questions usually test your knowledge of important terms, concepts, and people. The examples below illustrate some of the ways in which these questions may be phrased:

- An example of [*economic interdependence*] is ...
- Which statement about the [*French Revolution*] is most accurate?
- Two beliefs of [*Buddhism*] are ...

To help you recognize major terms, concepts, and people, these will be in **bold type** in each content chapter.

COMPREHENSION

"Comprehension" applies to data-based questions. Such questions test whether you understand information or data presented as part of the question. A comprehension question may take any of the following forms:

- In the cartoon, which system is represented by the [*hammer and sickle*]?
- According to the table, in which time period was [*rice production*] the greatest?
- The diagram represents the [*rigid class system*] of ...

The crucial factor in answering comprehension questions is being able to identify and understand the specific information given in the data. Data-based questions appear frequently throughout this book, allowing you to practice answering this type of question.

CONCLUSION OR GENERALIZATION

Some questions will ask you to make a generalization or draw a conclusion based on your knowledge of global history. The following are typical examples of conclusion or generalization questions:

- Which conclusion can be drawn from information provided by the map?
- The idea that [*a nation's geography can greatly influence its economy*] is best illustrated by ...
- In an outline, one of these is a main topic, and the other three are sub-topics. Which is the main topic?

To help you succeed in answering this type of question, generalizations are used throughout this book. They summarize the "big idea" or main theme found in each chapter. Generalizations are also explained in detail in Chapter 4.

COMPARE AND CONTRAST

The act of comparing and contrasting allows us to highlight and separate particular events, ideas, and concepts, placing them in sharper relief. Compare-and-contrast questions might appear as follows:

- The [*Magna Carta*] and the [*English Bill of Rights*] are similar in that they both ...
- A major difference between [*ancient Egypt*] and [*Mesopotamia*] was that ...
- A study of [*World War I*] and [*World War II*] shows that both events ...

As you read through each content chapter, test yourself by comparing and contrasting **new** names and terms with those you already know. It is important to understand what things have in common and how they differ.

CAUSE AND EFFECT

History consists of a series of events leading to other events. Cause-and-effect questions test your understanding of the relationship between an action or event and its corresponding effects. In answering these questions, be careful to understand what is being asked for — the *cause* or the *effect*. These types of questions might appear as follows:

- Which was a significant cause of [*colonialism*]? (asks for a *cause*)
- The [*Byzantine Empire*] made its most important contributions to later civilizations by ... (asks for an *effect*)
- Which situation is considered a cause of the other three? (asks for a *cause*)

To help you answer these types of questions, important cause-and-effect relationships are identified in each content chapter, often with graphic organizers.

CHRONOLOGY

Chronology refers to the order in which events occurred. A list of events in chronological order starts from the earliest event and progresses to the latest one. This arrangement allows us to see patterns and sequences among events. Questions related to chronology might appear as follows:

- Which sequence of events best describes the historical development of [*Mesoamerica*]?
- Which group of events is in the correct chronological order?

To help you with these types of questions, timelines are presented at the beginning of each content chapter and in a separate section in the back of this book. In addition, to help bolster your understanding of chronology, most *Testing Your Understanding* sections have a least one multiple-choice question dealing with chronology.

FACT AND OPINION

Certain questions will ask you to distinguish between facts and opinions.

✦ A **fact** is a statement that can be verified to be true. For example, the following is a factual statement:

"World War II began in Europe in 1939."

We frequently check the accuracy of factual statements by looking at other sources.

✦ An **opinion** is an expression of someone's belief and cannot be verified. An example of an opinion is:

"The greatest person ever to rule France was Napoleon Bonaparte."

Questions asking you to distinguish fact from opinion could be phrased as follows:

- Which statement about the [*T'ang dynasty*] would be the most difficult to prove?
- Which statement about the [*Code of Hammurabi*] expresses an opinion rather than a fact?

The crucial factor is to know the difference between a fact and an opinion. To help you understand these questions, several *Testing Your Understanding* sections have multiple-choice questions asking you to distinguish facts from opinions.

CHAPTER 4

HOW TO ANSWER
THEMATIC ESSAY QUESTIONS

An **essay question** tests your ability to present information in written form. This chapter focuses on how to write thematic essay questions, one of the two types of essay questions you will be required to write on the Global History Regents Examination.

WHAT IS A THEMATIC ESSAY?

Essay questions requiring you to focus on a particular theme or generalization are known as **thematic essay questions**. Let's look at a typical example.

Directions: Write a well-organized essay that includes an introduction, several paragraphs addressing the task below, and a conclusion.

Theme: Change

> Revolutions are great events that not only change conditions within a country, but may also have a regional or worldwide impact.

Task:

> Select *two* different revolutions that changed conditions within a country and for *each*
> - Describe one major cause of the revolution
> - Explain how the revolution had a regional or worldwide impact

You may use any examples from your study of global history. Some suggestions you might wish to consider include the French Revolution, Russian Revolution, Chinese Revolution, Cuban Revolution, and Iranian Revolution.

You are *not* limited to these suggestions.

In your essay, be sure to:

- Address all aspects of the *Task*
- Support the theme with relevant facts, examples, and details
- Use a logical and clear plan of organization
- Introduce the theme by establishing a framework that is beyond a simple restatement of the *Task* and conclude with a summation of the theme

Notice that a thematic essay question opens with **directions** that tell you the form in which your answer must be written. Next, you are given a **Theme** in the form of a **generalization**. Here the generalization is about revolutions. The question then provides you with a **Task** to complete. Examples you might use to support the generalization are suggested.

WHAT IS A GENERALIZATION?

Since the "Theme" of the question is stated as a generalization, you should understand what it is and how to support it. A **generalization** is a powerful organizing tool used to summarize large amounts of information in simpler form. First, read the following list of facts:

- ✦ Ancient Egyptian civilization emerged along the banks of the Nile River.
- ✦ Mesopotamian civilizations arose between the Tigris and Euphrates Rivers.
- ✦ Chinese civilization started along the banks of the Huang He.
- ✦ The Indus civilization originated in the Indus River Valley.

The following generalization shows what these four facts have in common: *All of these ancient civilizations began in river valleys.* Let's see how this generalization and its supporting facts might be presented in a diagram:

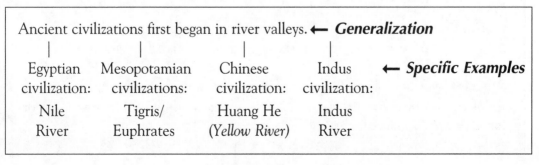

THE "ACTION WORDS"

Thematic essay questions require you to understand certain key words. The exact instructions for what you are supposed to do in writing your answer are contained in the "action words" in the Task. The most common action words are:

Describe or Discuss   Explain *How* or *Why*   Compare and Contrast   Evaluate

DESCRIBE OR DISCUSS

Describe means "to illustrate something in words, or to tell about it." **Discuss** means "to make observations about something using facts, reasoning and argument; to present in some detail." In essay questions, the word *describe* is used when you are asked for the *who*, *what*, *when* and *where* of something. The word *discuss* includes these four elements, and may also expect you to consider *how* and *why*. Not every "describe" or "discuss" question requires all of these elements, but when you describe or discuss something you should also tell about its *importance*. The following are examples of "describe" and "discuss" questions:

- *Describe* a scientific achievement of the Renaissance.

- *Discuss* the religious differences between Hindus and Muslims.

- *Discuss* the problems caused by international terrorism.

Assume you chose to answer the first *describe* question above and selected the work of Nicholas Copernicus as the scientific achievement to *describe*. To achieve a high score, your answer should create a verbal picture of his achievement. Tell about the **who** (*Nicholas Copernicus*), **what** (*he challenged the teachings of the Roman Catholic Church by stating that the earth revolved around the sun*), **when** (*during the Renaissance*), and **where** (*Europe*); include the importance of this achievement (*Copernicus used reason and observation rather then relying on traditional authority*). **Helpful hint**: Whenever you *describe* or *discuss* something, go through your own mental checklist of *who*, *what*, *when* and *where*, add *why* and *how* if needed, and state the importance of what you are discussing or describing.

EXPLAIN

Explain means "to make plain or understandable; to give reasons for or causes of; to show the logical development or relationships of things." *Explain* is often linked to the words *how* or *why*. The key to approaching any *explain question* is to determine whether the question requires you to tell *how* something happened or *why* it happened.

Explain How

Explain how questions ask you to show a logical development or relationship. The phrase "explain how" is followed by a generalization. The question may ask you to explain "how" something works or "how" it relates to something else. Let's look at three examples:

- *Explain how* feudalism created a new system of government in Western Europe during the Middle Ages.

- *Explain how* improvements in technology can affect a country's social and economic development.

- *Explain how* nations are responding to the threat of terrorism in the 21st century.

Assume you chose to answer the first *explain how* question above. Begin by giving background information about feudalism — **what** it was, **where** it developed and **when**. Then provide facts, examples and details to fully explain how feudalism provided a new system of government in Western Europe. **Helpful Hint**: To explain *how*, provide facts, examples and details that tell about a relationship or that explain how a generalization is true.

Explain Why

Explain why questions ask you to give reasons why an event took place or to show why a relationship identified in the question occurred. *Explain why* questions focus on causes. Your answer should identify the reasons why the event or relationship took place, and briefly describe each cause. Two examples of such questions are:

- *Explain why* the first civilizations emerged in river valleys.

- *Explain why* the Scientific Revolution first started in Europe.

To answer the first *explain why* question on page 25, begin by identifying the earliest civilizations. Then present reasons that *explain why* these civilizations first emerged six thousand years ago. For example, you might explain that these civilizations arose in river valleys where yearly flooding of the river deposited very fertile soil on the land. You would then provide specific facts and details based on what you recall about Mesopotamia, Egypt, the Indus River Valley civilization and the Huang He civilization in China. **Helpful Hint:** Go through a checklist of reasons or causes that *explain why* the event occurred.

COMPARE AND CONTRAST

Compare and contrast means "to discuss similarities and differences." *Compare-and-contrast questions* ask you to identify the similarities and differences between two or more items. Here are two examples of this type of question:

- *Compare and contrast* the response of two countries to European imperialism.

- *Compare and contrast* two political revolutions that occurred in the 20th century.

To answer a *compare-and-contrast question*, first identify the items you are comparing. Then identify and describe important similarities. Finally, identify and describe important differences. For example, to answer the first compare-and-contrast question above, begin by selecting two countries, such as India and China. Provide background information by describing European imperialism in each country. Then identify similarities and differences. In both India and China, there was resistance to European intervention: the Sepoy Mutiny in India and the Boxer Rebellion in China. A major difference was that Great Britain took direct control of India, but European powers never established more than "spheres of influence" in China. **Helpful Hint:** Create a Venn diagram to plan your answer.

EVALUATE

Evaluate means "to examine and judge the significance, worth or condition; to determine the value of." *Evaluate questions* ask you to make a judgment. Before writing your answer, you must consider the criteria by which the things in the question are to be judged. Then you must weigh the facts using these criteria. Here are two examples of *evaluate questions*:

- *Evaluate* the impact of imperialism on the people of Africa.

- Identify one system of government you have studied and *evaluate* how successful it has been in meeting the needs of its people.

In order to answer an *evaluate question*, you must:

1. describe the good *and* bad effects of what you are evaluating; then

2. make a judgment as to whether the overall impact was positive *or* negative.

> To answer the first *evaluate question*, begin by giving background information about European imperialism in Africa. You might tell **which** nations established colonies in Africa, **what** caused them to do so, and **when.** Then you would describe some good and bad effects of imperialism on the people of Africa. In the conclusion of your essay, you would make a final judgment or evaluation. If you thought the overall impact was negative, tell why its disadvantages outweighed its advantages. If you felt the overall impact was positive, tell why the advantages were more important. **Helpful Hint**: When you evaluate, you must tell about the overall impact.

Note how the answer in each case (*describe, discuss, explain how* or *why, compare and contrast,* and *evaluate*) follows a similar pattern. A diagram of this pattern might look like this:

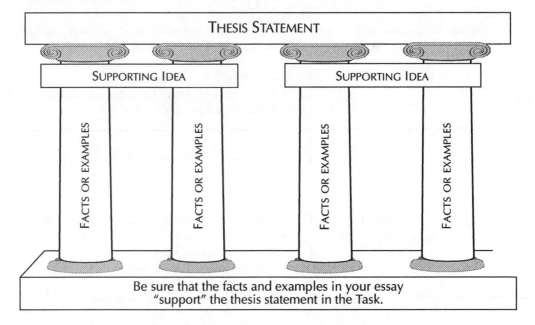

THESIS STATEMENT

SUPPORTING IDEA   SUPPORTING IDEA

FACTS OR EXAMPLES   FACTS OR EXAMPLES   FACTS OR EXAMPLES   FACTS OR EXAMPLES

Be sure that the facts and examples in your essay "support" the thesis statement in the Task.

PLANNING YOUR THEMATIC ESSAY

Now that you understand the "action words," you should be ready to write a thematic essay. Start by reading the *Task*. Think about how you will approach the question by writing a *thesis statement*. Next, decide which historical examples you know the most about that are related to the *Task*. Take notes for your essay, including facts like names and dates, in response to the *Task*. Below is one approach for planning your essay. (These notes refer to the thematic essay question about revolutions on page 22.)

> The Task requires two examples. Your introduction should provide the historical context to both your examples.

> The *thesis statement* is the main generalization of your essay. It provides a theme related to the *Task*.

Historical Context (Framework): The Russian Revolution occurred in 1917. Russians overthrew the Tsar and their political and social systems. Iran had a revolutionary change in 1979, overthrowing its secular ruler and establishing a religious regime. Both the Russian and Iranian Revolutions had effects beyond their borders.

Thesis: A revolution in one country can have a regional or worldwide impact.

Example/Action Word	Facts and Details
Russian Revolution *Explain* its regional or worldwide impact	• Under the Tsar, most Russians lived in poverty • Heavy Russian casualties in World War I led to strikes and mutinies; Tsar overthrown in 1917 • Lenin and Bolsheviks came to power, pledging to provide "Peace, Bread, and Land" • Bolsheviks took Russia out of the war and established a Communist society • Soviet Union spread Communism abroad — Eastern Europe, China, Cuba
Iranian Revolution *Explain* its regional or worldwide impact	• Mass protests against Shah for being pro-West; he had to flee country • Islamic Revolutionaries set up religious republic under Khomeini • Iran cut ties with U.S., held Americans hostage • Iranian Revolution led to worldwide spread of Islamic Fundamentalism • Iran went to war with Iraq

WRITING YOUR THEMATIC ESSAY

Now use the information from your notes to write your essay.

✦ Be sure to include an introduction that goes beyond a mere restatement of the *Task* by providing the historical context. Then write a **thesis statement** that responds to the *Task*.

✦ In the body of your essay, be sure to provide the correct number of examples required by the *Task* (*in this case, it is two examples*).

✦ Be sure to include specific names, details, and other facts. You will receive a higher score if you provide more relevant details and examples to support your main ideas. To obtain the highest score, you must analyze, evaluate, or present information in a new and original form.

✦ Organize the main body of your answer in some logical order. Often it helps to introduce the facts in your essay chronologically — in the order in which they occurred. Another way is to organize your essay by cause and effect, discussing each cause or effect in a separate paragraph.

✦ Finish your essay with a conclusion that relates the information in the body of your essay to your opening thesis statement.

✦ After you complete your essay, read it over carefully. Add information you may have left out and eliminate information that does not relate to the *Task*.

Notice how the opening paragraph provides the **historical context** (framework) for the essay.

The last sentence of the introduction provides the **thesis statement**, and also serves as a transition to the body of the essay.

Revolutions are great events that affect a country's political and social order. Revolutionary changes often have effects well beyond a nation's borders. Although they were almost 60 years apart, this was the case for both the Russian Revolution (1917) and the Iranian Revolution (1979). Both revolutions had significant regional and worldwide effects.

This paragraph provides facts and details for the first example of the thesis statement — Russia

The Russian Revolution began while Russia was involved in World War I. Most Russians lived in poverty, while the Tsar and the nobility had immense wealth. With the strains of war, the Russian economy collapsed. Strikes broke out in major cities. Soldiers refused to fire at the strikers. Tsar Nicholas II was forced to abdicate in March 1917. A provisional government was established, but it made the mistake of continuing the war effort. Lenin and his fellow Bolsheviks promised workers and peasants "Peace, Bread, and Land." The Bolsheviks overthrew the government and established the world's first Communist state. The revolution had important effects worldwide. First, Russia withdrew from World War I. More importantly, Russia promoted the spread of Communism. Eastern Europe, China, Cuba and Indochina later became Communist.

The Iranian Revolution introduced sudden and important changes in Iran. The Shah, a pro-Western ruler, had tried to reduce the influence of Muslim religious leaders, and was increasingly unpopular. Mass demonstrations became impossible to put down. Fearing for his life, the Shah fled the country. An Islamic Fundamentalist, Ayatollah Khomeini, took power. He set up an Islamic Republic in which Iranians were forced to follow new ways of life based on Khomeini's view of the Qu'ran. As a protest against Western influence, Iranians seized members of the U.S. embassy in the capital of Iran. They held these hostages for over a year, causing frustration and anger in the United States. Shortly after the Iranian Revolution, Iran also entered into a long war with Iraq.

In the case of both Russia and Iran, national revolutions clearly had regional and worldwide impact. Both nations attempted to export their revolutionary ideas to other countries.

The **conclusion** relates information in the body of the essay to the thesis statement by summarizing the main points of the essay.

REGENTS GUIDELINES FOR THEMATIC ESSAYS

The following **Guidelines for Thematic Essays** will appear on the Global History Regents Examination. Check your essay to be sure that it conforms to these guidelines:

In your essay, be sure to:
- Address all aspects of the Task
- Support the theme with relevant facts, examples, and details
- Use a logical and clear plan of organization
- Introduce the theme by establishing a framework that is beyond a simple restatement of the Task, and conclude with a summation of the theme

---

SCORING YOUR THEMATIC ESSAY

Your answer will receive a score of 0, 1, 2, 3, 4, or 5, based on a scoring rubric. This rubric describes the characteristics of a typical essay for each score. To obtain the highest score, your essay should address all aspects of the *Task*, be well organized, and richly support your main ideas with facts, examples, and details. If your introduction and conclusion merely restate the *Task*, you will limit your overall score to 3.

Carefully review the rubric below, which will be used by teachers to score your essay. Each content chapter of this book has a practice thematic essay for you to write. After you have written each essay, return to this rubric to determine what score your answer should receive.

— THEMATIC ESSAY: GENERIC SCORING RUBRIC —

SCORE OF 5:
- Thoroughly develops all aspects of the task evenly and in depth
- Is more analytical than descriptive (analyzes, evaluates, and/or creates* information)
- Richly supports the theme with many relevant facts, examples, and details
- Demonstrates a logical and clear plan of organization; includes an introduction and a conclusion that are beyond a restatement of the theme

---

* "Create" implies an insightful reorganization of information into a new pattern or whole. (Anderson, Krathwohl, et al., *Bloom's Taxonomy of Educational Objectives*, 2001 revision.)

SCORE OF 4:
- Develops all aspects of the task but may do so somewhat unevenly
- Is both descriptive and analytical (applies, analyzes, evaluates, and/or creates information)
- Supports the theme with relevant facts, examples, and details
- Demonstrates a logical and clear plan of organization; includes an introduction and a conclusion that are beyond a restatement of the theme

SCORE OF 3:
- Develops all aspects of the task with little depth or develops most aspects of the task in some depth
- Is more descriptive than analytical (applies, may analyze, and/or evaluate information)
- Includes some relevant facts, examples, and details; may include some minor inaccuracies
- Demonstrates a satisfactory plan of organization; includes an introduction and a conclusion that may be a restatement of the theme

SCORE OF 2:
- Minimally develops all aspects of the task or develops some aspects of the task in some depth
- Is primarily descriptive; may include faulty, weak, or isolated application or analysis
- Includes few relevant facts, examples, and details; may include some inaccuracies
- Demonstrates a general plan of organization; may lack focus; may contain digressions; may not clearly identify which aspect of the task is being addressed; may lack an introduction and/or a conclusion

SCORE OF 1:
- Minimally develops some aspects of the task
- Is descriptive; may lack understanding, application, or analysis
- Includes few relevant facts, examples, or details; may include inaccuracies
- May demonstrate a weakness in organization; may lack focus; may contain digressions; may not clearly identify which aspect of the task is being addressed; may lack an introduction and/or a conclusion

SCORE OF 0:
Fails to develop the task or may only refer to the theme in a general way; OR includes no relevant facts, examples, or details; OR includes only the theme, task, or suggestions as copied from the test booklet; OR is illegible; OR is a blank paper

CHAPTER 5

HOW TO ANSWER DOCUMENT-BASED ESSAY QUESTIONS

The Global History Regents Examination will require you to answer one **document-based essay question**, sometimes known as a "D.B.Q." This type of question tests your ability to interpret and draw conclusions from as many as eight historical documents.

This chapter is divided into two main sections. In the first section you will learn how to interpret historical documents. In the second section, you will examine a sample document-based essay question and learn one approach for answering this type of question.

INTERPRETING HISTORICAL DOCUMENTS

A *document-based essay question* provides you with actual historical documents you must interpret to help answer the question. Think of yourself as a historian who must use these documents as evidence to guide your conclusions. Some of the documents will be charts, graphs, and timelines. In Chapter 2 you learned how to interpret these different types of data. A large number of the documents, however, will be short original texts. This section will show you how to read and interpret these kinds of original sources.

Most documents in a document-based essay question will be short passages that are excerpts from longer speeches or texts. You will need to take yourself back in time in order to understand someone else's point of view. A writer in the past is likely to have a very different attitude than we have today.

UNDERSTANDING DIFFERENT POINTS OF VIEW

In interpreting a historical document, you must be a critical reader. Sometimes a document in a D.B.Q. will give you information about the writer's background or position. This information will help you understand how the writer's status in society may have affected his or her ideas.

Following are the questions you should ask yourself when reading any historical document.

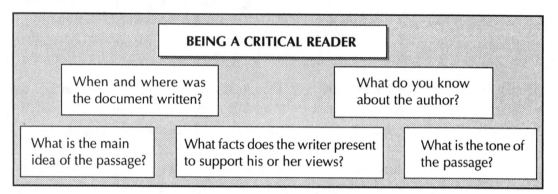

BEING A CRITICAL READER

When and where was the document written?

What do you know about the author?

What is the main idea of the passage?

What facts does the writer present to support his or her views?

What is the tone of the passage?

DETERMINING THE MEANING OF WORDS FROM CONTEXT CLUES

Sometimes you may encounter unfamiliar words or phrases. **Context clues** will help you figure out what they mean. The surrounding words, phrases and sentences often provide clues that help you discover the meaning of the unfamiliar word.

Part of Speech. From the words in the sentence, can you guess what part of speech the unfamiliar word is, such as an adjective, noun, verb, or adverb?

Substitute Words. Can you guess the meaning from the tone or meaning of the passage? Would another word make sense if you substituted it for the unfamiliar word?

USING CONTEXT CLUES TO FIND THE MEANING

Related Familiar Words. Is the word similar to any words you know? Does that help figure out what the word means? Or try breaking the unfamiliar word into parts — a prefix, word stem, or suffix.

Bypass the Word. Can you understand the main idea of the sentence without knowing the meaning of the unfamiliar word? If so, it may not be important to spend time trying to figure out its meaning.

STEPS TO INTERPRETING DOCUMENTS

Let's begin by examining two historical documents about the Industrial Revolution in England.

DOCUMENT 1

"Suddenly cotton mills have appeared everywhere in our town. They billow out endless smoke day and night. The poor souls working in these factories suffer the worst torments imaginable. Young children work from 6 in the morning to 8 at night. They have no schooling and no rest. Many die before the age of 13 by falling into those large merciless machines driven by steam."

—*A Manchester citizen testifying before
the British Parliament (1835)*

Suppose you did not understand the word *mills* in the first sentence. Following is a way of figuring out the meaning of this word.

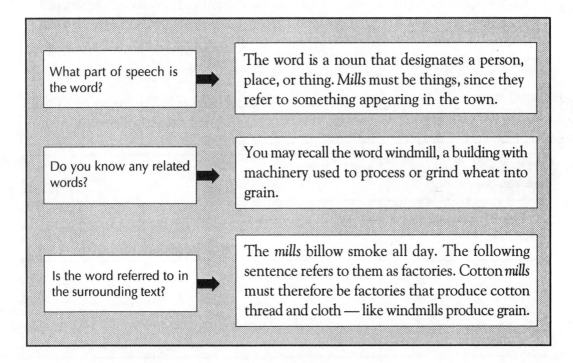

Now consider the background and viewpoint of the author.

When and where was the document written?	Early 19th century England.
What do you know about the author?	The author is a citizen of Manchester, England, providing testimony about industrial conditions.
What is the viewpoint of the author?	The author appears to oppose cotton factories in Manchester. They emit endless amounts of smoke. Even worse, the author believes that workers in the new factories are mistreated — especially the children.

Compare this viewpoint with a second reading passage about the Industrial Revolution.

DOCUMENT 2

"The laborers in our factories are the laziest beings on this earth. Many come from farms where they had no experience with continuous labor. They started and stopped just when they pleased. We have had to introduce stern discipline just to keep them from getting drunk at work. If it were not for the foreman's whip, England's factories would come to a grinding halt."

—*A factory-owner in Manchester testifying before the British Parliament (1835)*

When and where was the document written?	Your Answer:
What do you know about the author?	Your Answer:
What is the viewpoint of the author?	Your Answer:

ANSWERING DOCUMENT-BASED ESSAYS

Let's look at a simplified document-based essay question on the French Revolution.

This question is based on the accompanying documents (1-3). This question is designed to test your ability to work with historical documents. Some of these documents have been edited for the purposes of this question. As you analyze the documents, take into account both the source of each document and any point of view that may be presented in the document.

Historical Context:
During the late 1700s, a revolution occurred in France which greatly affected not only France but the rest of the world.

Task: Using information from the documents and your knowledge of global history, answer the questions that follow each document in Part A. Your answers to the questions will help you write the Part B essay, in which you will be asked to:

Discuss the political and social changes brought about by the French Revolution.

Part A — Short-Answer Questions
Directions: Analyze the documents and answer the question that follows each document.

Note: On many D.B.Q.s there are up to eight pieces of data (documents). To simplify our explanation, this sample question has only three documents.

DOCUMENT 1

1. Men are born and remain free and equal in rights; social distinctions can be established only for the common benefit.
2. The aim of every political association is the conservation of the natural rights of man; these rights are liberty, property, security, and resistance to oppression.
3. The source of all sovereignty is located ... in the nation; no body, no individual, can exercise authority which does not emanate from it expressly."

Declaration of the Rights of Man and of the Citizen
August 20-26, 1789

1 According to the document, what is the purpose of every government? _____

DOCUMENT 2

"The National Assembly decrees that hereditary nobility is forever abolished; in consequence, the titles of prince, duke, count, marquis, viscount, vidame, baron, knight ... and all other similar titles shall neither be taken by anyone nor given to anyone."

Decree of the National Assembly
June 19, 1790

2 What was the effect of this decree on the nobles of France? _____

DOCUMENT 3

3 What was the significance of the King's execution?

_____

_____

The beheading of Louis XVI

Part B — Essay

Directions:

Write a well-organized essay that includes an introduction, several paragraphs, and a conclusion. Use evidence from all **three** documents in the body of your essay. Support your response with relevant facts, examples and details. Include additional outside information.

Historical Context:

During the late 1700s, a revolution occurred in France which greatly affected not only France but the rest of the world.

Task: Using information from the documents and your knowledge of global history and geography, write an essay in which you:

Discuss the political and social changes brought about by the French Revolution.

Notice that document-based essay questions have the following parts:
    (1) directions on how to write the essay;
    (2) a Historical Context setting the stage for the essay question;
    (3) a *Task* you must perform, stated in the form of a question;
    (4) Part A, with up to 8 documents, each followed by one or more questions; and
    (5) Part B, where you write the essay.

To do well on a document-based essay question, you need to focus on three important areas: (1) Look at the task; (2) Analyze the documents and answer the accompanying questions; and (3) Write the essay. An easy way for you to remember this three-pronged approach is to think of the word "L•A•W."

"L" — LOOK AT THE TASK

Let's follow the "L•A•W" approach, to see how it can be used to answer a document-based essay question. First, "Look" at the *Task* in the sample question on page 37:

> **Historical Context:**
> During the late 1700s, a major revolution occurred in France which greatly affected not only France but the rest of the world.
>
> **Task:** Discuss the political and social changes brought about by the French Revolution.

Notice that the *Task* contains two important directions:

(1) An action word for you to follow. These action words will usually be the same as for thematic essays: *describe, discuss, explain how* or *why, compare and contrast,* and *evaluate.*
(2) The areas you must cover.

Action Word:	**Areas to Cover:** You must discuss two types of change:
"Discuss"	(1) political (2) social

This information indicates *how many paragraphs* you should write. All essays must have an introduction and a conclusion. What varies from one essay to the next is the number of paragraphs needed to answer the *requirements in the Task.* In this example, you need at least *two* paragraphs, one for each type of change brought about by the French Revolution. Your final written essay should therefore contain at least four paragraphs:

• **Paragraph 1** should introduce the essay with the historical context, your thesis statement and a transition sentence. The thesis statement must respond to the *Task.*

• **Paragraph 2** should deal with *political* changes brought about by the French Revolution. (This could be more than one paragraph, based on how many examples, facts and references there are in the document[s] you are referring to.)

- **Paragraph 3** should deal with *social* changes brought about by the French Revolution. This could also be one or more paragraphs.)

- **Paragraph 4** is your conclusion, which should relate the body of the essay to your thesis statement.

"A" — ANALYZE THE DOCUMENTS

You are now ready for the second part of the "**L•A•W**" approach — Analyzing the documents and answering the accompanying questions. There may be as many as 8 documents, each followed by a question or questions. Your answer to these questions will be scored. These questions help to pinpoint information in the documents relating to the Task. The questions are called **scaffolding questions** because they help you build a "scaffold" or framework for writing your essay. Use what you learned about interpreting data and historical documents to answer these scaffolding questions.

D.B.Q.s have so much data that an effective way to organize your analysis of the documents is to use a **Document Box.** Fill in each section in *note form* as you read the documents. The scaffolding questions will guide you to what is most important in each document.

SAMPLE DOCUMENT BOX

Document	Main Ideas	Political	Social
1 (Declaration of Rights of Man)	• *People are born free with equal rights* • *Purpose of government is to protect these rights* • *Source of political power is in the nation (the people)*	✓	✓
2 (National Assembly)	• *Abolished hereditary nobility in France.*		✓
3 (Illustration)	• *Louis XVI beheaded in 1793* • *Republican zeal spread throughout France* • *Aristocratic clothing replaced by simple clothes*	✓	✓
Related outside information:			

- *Revolutionaries called each other "citizen"*
- *During Revolution, chaos and violence erupted in France.*
- *Revolutionary France involved in war against monarchies of Europe.*
- *During "Reign of Terror," nobles and priests beheaded by revolutionaries.*

Let's look at the information in the Document Box on page 40:

- In the **Document** column, write the number that identifies each document.

- In the **Main Ideas** column, jot down *in note form* the most important ideas of each document. Refer to your answers to the questions following each document. (*Note:* You can omit the Main Ideas column if you have written enough information in your answers following the documents, and just refer to your answers there instead.)

- The last two columns depend on what you have to cover in your essay. For example, since the first document here deals with both **political** and **social** aspects of the French Revolution, check marks (✓) are placed in both columns.

- Note that the directions asked you to include additional information based on your knowledge of world history. Put this information at the bottom of the Document Box.

- Be sure that you answer every scaffolding question accompanying each document. You will get a separate score for your answers to these **Part A** questions.

"W" — WRITE THE ESSAY

In the last part of the "L•A•W" approach, you Write the essay. You should follow the same general rules as for writing thematic essays, except that your answer must also include references to the documents. Here are two ways to refer to documents when writing a document-based essay.

✦ **Refer to the Document in Parentheses**. Use information from the document, and then add the document number in parentheses. For example, "The Declaration of the Rights of Man announced that all citizens of France had equal rights. (Document 1)."

✦ **Refer Directly to the Document**. A second way is to refer directly to the document in the text of your essay. For example, "Document 2 shows that the French abolished the priviliges of the nobility during the Revolution."

Before studying the following sample essay, read the *Guidelines for Document-Based Essays* on page 43. These *Guidelines* will appear on the Regents Examination to help you conform your essay to Regents requirements and achieve a high score.

The introduction sets the **historical context** and identifies the essay's subject in a **thesis statement**.

A revolution is a rapid change that occurs within a society. The French Revolution (1789) provided a classic example. At the time the revolution broke out, France was a monarchy with a hereditary nobility. The king had almost absolute power, which he claimed through divine right. Nobles enjoyed important privileges, including freedom from many taxes. The French Revolution destroyed the old system, as France underwent drastic political and social changes.

This paragraph addresses the first part of the *Task*: political changes.

The political changes came first. The revolution began when the government needed more funds and the King agreed to call a meeting of the Estates General to raise taxes. Once the Estates General met, members of the Third Estate, made up of the common people, declared themselves to be a National Assembly. The new Assembly issued the Declaration of the Rights of Man (Document 1). It declared that the source of political power was in the people, not the king. Soon the revolution took a more radical turn. In 1793 the King was beheaded by the guillotine. As illustrations from that time show, the King's execution was a public spectacle (Document 3). France became a republic, leading to war with other European nations whose monarchs felt threatened by the events in France.

This paragraph discusses the second part of the *Task*: social changes.

Social changes also took place during the revolution. For centuries, the peasants and the middle class had resented the privileges of nobles and priests. The Declaration of the Rights of Man made it clear that these privileges were no longer justified. The National Assembly quickly abolished feudalism and the nobility (Document 2). People were no longer addressed by titles such as Duke or Prince. Instead, everyone was called "citizen." Aristocratic dress was replaced by simple clothing. Many nobles and priests resisted theses changes. For this reason, they were often considered enemies of the Republic. At the height of the revolution, during the Reign of Terror, many of them were guillotined.

Notice how each document was referred to in the body of the essay to support the thesis statement.

Although the French Revolution was violent, it had a number of important conse-quences. The revolutionaries overthrew the political and economic power of the king, the nobility and the church. They challenged centuries of feudalism and rule by divine right in favor of political and social change, as well as human rights.

The **conclusion** ties the body of the essay to the thesis statement.

REGENTS GUIDELINES FOR DOCUMENT-BASED ESSAYS

The following *Guidelines for Document-Based Essays* will appear on the Regents Examination. Check your essay to be sure that it conforms to these *Guidelines*:

In your essay, be sure to:
- Address all aspects of the *Task* by accurately analyzing and interpreting at least
  *____documents
- Incorporate information from the documents
- Incorporate relevant outside information
- Support the theme with relevant facts, examples, and details
- Use a logical and clear plan of organization
- Introduce the theme by establishing a framework that is beyond a simple restate-ment of the *Task* or *Historical Context*, and conclude with a summation of the theme

* *This number changes depending on the total number of documents in the DBQ*

SCORING YOUR DOCUMENT-BASED ESSAY

Just like your thematic essay, your answer to the document-based essay question will be scored with a rubric. The rubric on the next page is very similar to the one used for themat-ic essays. However, this rubric requires you to analyze and interpret documents as part of your answer.

Throughout the remainder of this book, there are several document-based essay ques-tions. After you have written each essay, you should return to this rubric to determine what score your answer should receive.

(continued on following page)

SCORE OF 5:

- Thoroughly develops all aspects of the task evenly and in depth
- Is more analytical than descriptive (analyzes, evaluates, and/or creates* information)
- Incorporates relevant information from at least [X] documents
- Incorporates substantial relevant outside information
- Richly supports the theme with many relevant facts, examples, and details
- Demonstrates a logical and clear plan of organization; includes an introduction and a conclusion that are beyond a restatement of the theme

SCORE OF 4:

- Develops all aspects of the task but may do so somewhat unevenly
- Is both descriptive and analytical (applies, analyzes, evaluates, and/or creates information)
- Incorporates relevant information from at least [X] documents
- Incorporates relevant outside information
- Supports the theme with relevant facts, examples, and details
- Demonstrates a logical and clear plan of organization; includes an introduction and a conclusion that are beyond a restatement of the theme

SCORE OF 3:

- Develops all aspects of the task with little depth or develops most aspects of the task in some depth
- Is more descriptive than analytical (applies, may analyze, and/or evaluate information)
- Incorporates some relevant information from some of the documents
- Incorporates limited relevant outside information
- Includes some relevant facts, examples, and details; may include some minor inaccuracies
- Demonstrates a satisfactory plan of organization; includes an introduction and a conclusion that may be a restatement of the theme

SCORE OF 2:

- Minimally develops all aspects of the task or develops some aspects of the task in some depth
- Is primarily descriptive; may include faulty, weak, or isolated application or analysis
- Incorporates limited relevant information from the documents or consists primarily of relevant information copied from the documents
- Presents little or no relevant outside informations
- Includes few relevant facts, examples, and details; may include some inaccuracies
- Demonstrates a general plan of organization; may lack focus; may contain digressions; may notclearly identify which aspect of the task is being addressed; may lack an introduction and/or a conclusion

SCORE OF 1:

- Minimally develops some aspects of the task
- Is descriptive; may lack understanding, application, or analysis
- Makes vague, unclear references to the documents or consists primarily of relevant and irrelevant information copied from the documents
- Presents no relevant outside information
- Includes few relevant facts, examples, or details; may include inaccuracies
- May demonstrate a weakness in organization; may lack focus; may contain digressions; may not clearly identify which aspect of the task is being addressed; may lack an introduction and/or a conclusion

SCORE OF 0:

Fails to develop the task or may only refer to the theme in a general way; OR includes no relevant facts, examples, or details; OR includes only the historical context and/or task as copied from the test book-let; OR includes only entire documents copied from the test booklet; OR is illegible; OR is a blank paper.

CHAPTER 6

TOOLS FOR MASTERING GLOBAL HISTORY

Global history has two fundamental characteristics: first, it is a branch of history; and second, it deals with the whole world. In this chapter we will look more closely at the implications of each of these characteristics.

WHAT IS HISTORY?

History is the story of people in the past. People who study and write about history are called **historians.** They are concerned with understanding events that happened in the past, and learning about the ideas, actions and beliefs of people who lived before our time. The study of history helps people to understand who they are and where they are going. Just as your own life would be purposeless if you had no memory of who you were or what you had done, each society looks to its history for a sense of identity.

SOURCES OF HISTORY

In a sense, the historian acts like a detective gathering clues. To find information about the past, historians rely on two kinds of sources:

* **Primary Sources** are original records of an event. They include documents left by eyewitnesses, records written at the time of the event, the texts of speeches and reports, letters by people involved in the event, paintings, photographs, and artifacts.

* **Secondary Sources** are the later writings and interpretations of historians and other writers. Often, secondary sources like textbooks and articles provide convenient summaries of the information found in primary sources.

HAVING A SENSE OF TIME AND PLACE

Global history covers a vast period of time, from the beginning of humankind to the present, touching all four corners of the globe. Thus it is very important to have a sense of time and place — a sense of global chronology and region. Think of these as the foundations for everything else you learn.

First, you need a strong sense of chronology — the basic *time periods* in world history. To help you develop this, in addition to the information below, each review chapter focuses on a particular time period.

HISTORICAL PERIODS

Historians divide the continuous stream of events into **historical periods** — spans of time identified by common characteristics, circumstances, events, or people. There is no agreement on historical periods and their dates. Different periods may begin and end at different times in different places. Traditionally, historical periods have been tied to a particular region or culture. For example, the Middle Ages is a period associated with Europe, while the Ming Dynasty refers to a period in the history of China.

In a broad sense, humankind appears to have passed through several historical periods or **eras**. This book divides the history of the world into eight eras, each with its own distinctive features:

— ERAS OF WORLD HISTORY —

+ The Dawn of Civilization, 3500 B.C. to 500 B.C.
+ The Classical Civilizations, 500 B.C. to 500 A.D.
+ New Centers of Culture in an Age of Turmoil, 500 to 1200
+ Warriors on Horseback and the Revival of Europe, 1200 to 1500
+ The Birth of the Modern World, 1500 to 1770
+ New Currents: Revolution, Nationalism, Imperialism, 1770 to 1900
+ The World at War, 1900 to 1945
+ From the Cold War to Global Interdependence, 1945 to the present

Second, to have a sense of *place*, you must know the *regions* of the world where the important events in global history have unfolded. To help you review the world's major physical regions, they are shown and described on the following pages.

GEOGRAPHY AND GLOBAL HISTORY

The subject matter of global history concerns the history of human activity all around our planet. The diverse physical settings in which these events have taken place is therefore of crucial importance. How people act is often affected by the place in which they live, its location relative to other places and the natural resources it has.

To understand global history, it is essential to have a firm grasp of world geography — the different regions of the world and their physical characteristics. Throughout global history, certain key areas have been centers of development. Let's take a closer look at some of them.

Continents are the major land masses of the world. Geographers have identified seven continents: Asia, Africa, North America, South America, Antarctica, Europe, and Australia.

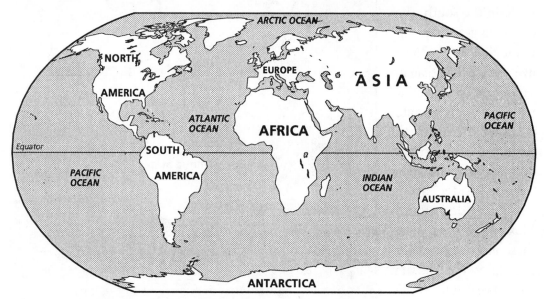

The continents of North America, South America, and part of Antarctica make up the **Western Hemisphere**. Asia, Africa, Europe, Australia, and part of Antarctica are the continents of the **Eastern Hemisphere**.

Most of the Earth's surface is covered by oceans. An **ocean** is an extremely large body of salt water. There are four oceans: (1) the Atlantic, (2) the Pacific, (3) the Indian, and (4) the Arctic.

NORTH AMERICA

North America is the world's third largest continent. It is bordered by three oceans: the Atlantic, Pacific, and Arctic. South of Mexico, the land changes to a narrow strip known as Central America, which is connected to South America.

The Impact of Geography. For much of its history, North America's location separated it from the civilizations of Africa, Asia, and Europe.

North America has a wide range of climates. In the north, it is extremely cold in winter, while in the south, the climate is generally hot. In Mexico, most people live on a high plateau in the center of the country because the climate is cooler there. North America's mountain ranges extend along its western side, from Canada down to Mexico. To the east of these mountain ranges are plains with fertile farmland.

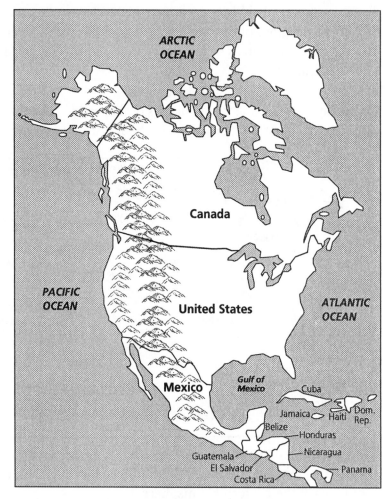

Because of Central America's proximity to North America, the United States exercised special influence over this region in the 19th century. The United States built a canal through Panama to connect the Atlantic and Pacific Oceans.

SOUTH AMERICA

South America is a large continent surrounded by the Pacific and Atlantic Oceans.

> **Note:** The name "Latin America" is often applied to the Americas south of the United States: Mexico, Central America, the West Indies (*Caribbean*), and South America. This region is known as **Latin America** because the people mainly speak Spanish and Portuguese, languages both derived from Latin.

The Impact of Geography. Much of South America is warm because it is located near the **equator**. The most important river in the region is the **Amazon**, the second longest river in the world. The Amazon rain forest occupies most of northeastern South America. Mountains, rain forests, and poor soils make much of South America's land unproductive.

Two important exceptions are the **pampas** and **llanos,** large grassy plains in the southeast and northeast.

The **Andes Mountains** run more than 4,500 miles along western South America, and are among the highest in the world. They once were home to the great Inca empire. In more recent times, the Andes separated people in different parts of South America from one another.

Central America consists mainly of rain forests. One of the earliest Native American civilizations arose there. To the northeast of Central America is the **West Indies**, a large number of islands including Cuba, Haiti joined

with the Dominican Republic, and Jamaica. When they were European colonies, these islands produced most of the world's sugar.

AFRICA

Africa is the second largest continent in area, and is almost three times the size of the United States. Today, this continent contains more than 50 countries. Geographers often divide Africa into two separate regions: North Africa and sub-Saharan Africa.

✦ **North Africa,** whose people are mainly of Arab descent and followers of Islam, is often considered to be more closely tied to the Middle East than to the rest of Africa.

✦ **Sub-Saharan Africa,** the area south of the Sahara Desert, has a very different climate and topography from North Africa. With its non-Arab populations, it is often considered a separate and distinct region.

The Impact of Geography. North Africa has a very warm, dry climate. On its northern border is the Mediterranean Sea. The **Sahara,** the world's largest desert, takes up much of North Africa. For centuries it has been a barrier separating the people north and south of it.

A large part of sub-Saharan Africa is **savanna** (*land where tall, wild grasses grow*). The savanna provides the best land in Africa for growing crops and raising livestock. Africa's mountains and deserts have kept different groups apart, allowing them to develop separate

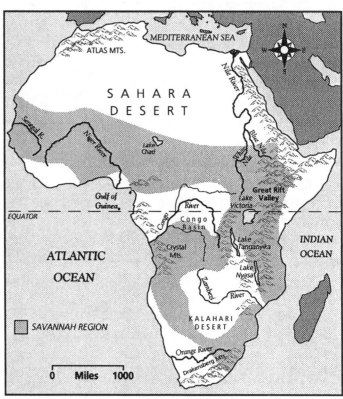

cultures, languages, and traditions. Most of Africa is warm, with hot summers and mild winters. The southern part of West Africa and much of Central Africa consists of **tropical rain forest**. These areas get from 60 to 100 inches of rainfall a year.

EUROPE

Europe and Asia share the same land mass, which is so large that geographers divide it into two continents. The dividing line runs through the center of Russia, along the Ural Mountains to the Caspian Sea and southwest to the Black Sea. On its other sides, Europe is surrounded by water — the Baltic, Arctic Ocean and North Sea to the north, the Atlantic Ocean to the west, and the Mediterranean and Black Sea to the south.

The Impact of Geography. Mountain ranges such as the Pyrenees and Alps separated European peoples, allowing them to develop different languages and cultures. However, Europe's location close to Africa and the Middle East also enabled Europeans to borrow from the cultures of these regions.

Much of Europe consists of a broad, fertile plain. To the east, this flat plain has few defensible frontiers. Thus, throughout its history, the borders of Russia, Poland, and Germany have constantly shifted. Because of Europe's dense population, many different ethnic groups live close to one another. As a result, Europe has been the stage for frequent wars.

ASIA

Asia is the world's largest continent. Today, it is home to more than two-thirds of the world's population. Because of its immense size and diversity of cultures, geographers think of Asia as consisting of several distinct regions.

THE MIDDLE EAST

The Middle East, located in southwest Asia, is the "crossroads of three continents." It connects Africa, Asia, and Europe. Some geographers consider North Africa part of the Middle East.

The Impact of Geography. Much of this region is desert. As a result, the greatest population density is found along the coasts and on major rivers, where water supplies are more plentiful and crops can be grown. In ancient times, the land in these river valleys was extraordinarily fertile.The three major rivers in the area are the **Nile** (*the world's longest river*), the **Tigris**, and the **Euphrates.** The

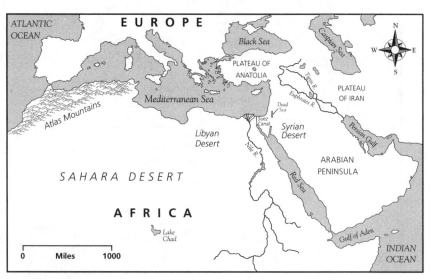

climate of this region is very hot and lacks plentiful water. However, the Middle East provides half of the world's oil.

NORTHERN AND CENTRAL ASIA

Northern Asia is occupied by Russia, which stretches from the borders of Eastern Europe all the way to the Pacific Ocean. Although most of Russia's population, farmland and industry is located on the Russian Plain, most of its land area lies to the east. Siberia, in northeastern Russia, is a cold region with forests, oil and gas deposits, diamonds and gold. **Central Asia** consists of a vast corridor south of Russia and north of India and China. It is mainly an area of deserts and treeless grasslands known as **steppes**, occupied by former Soviet republics such as Uzbekistan, Khazakstan and Turkmenistan (now part of the Commonwealth of Independent States) and Mongolia.

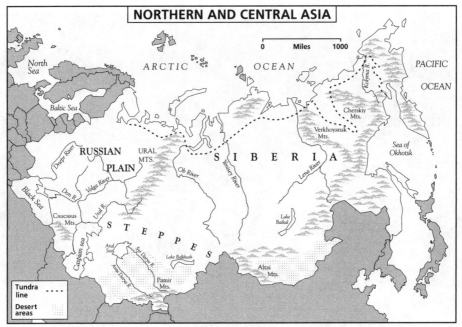

The Impact of Geography. Most of Russia has long, cold winters and short, mild summers. Northernmost Russia is **tundra**, where the ground is frozen much of the year. The Arctic Ocean, north of Russia, is frozen most of the year. To the south, Russia is landlocked (*access to the sea is blocked by other countries*). The need for a warm-water port has been a major problem in Russian history, causing its rulers to expand south and west. Because of Russia's great distance from Western Europe, its culture developed separately. It was greatly influenced by the Byzantine empire and the Mongol conquest. Later, the frigid winters stopped invaders like Napoleon and Hitler from conquering Russia.

Central Asia has long been a crossroads for overland trade routes between China, India, the Middle East, and Europe. Because the **steppes** of Central Asia provide excellent grazing land, its people became cattle herders and excelled at horsemanship. Throughout much of history, warriors on horseback from the Central Asian steppes periodically emerged to conquer people in neighboring lands.

EAST ASIA

East Asia includes three important countries: (1) China, (2) Korea, and (3) Japan.

China, one of the world's most ancient civilizations, is the world's third largest country in area: only Russia and Canada are larger. For most of its history, China has been the world's most populated nation. **Korea** is a peninsula that extends from the northeast coast of China.

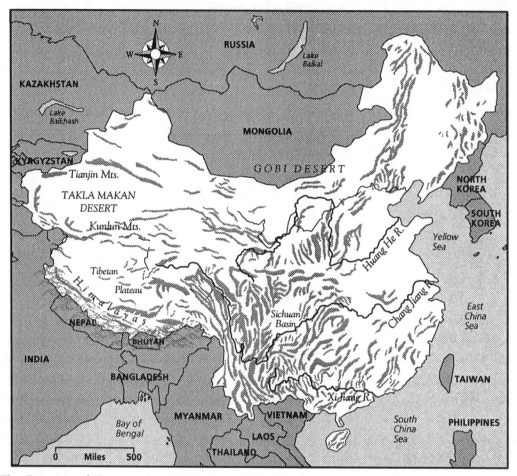

The Impact of Geography. China's southern and western borders are ringed by some of the highest, most rugged mountains in the world: the Himalaya, Kunlun, and Tianjin Mountains. These mountains have often protected and isolated China from the outside world. The **Gobi Desert** to the north and the Pacific Ocean to the east have further isolated China.

The mountains, desert, and seas surrounding China permitted it to develop a uniform culture in isolation from other world centers of civilization. This encouraged a centralization of power and a concentration of resources that made China one of the most advanced civilizations for thousands of years.

Eastern China consists of a vast plain with fertile river valleys. As a result, most of China's population has settled in this area.

Japan lies east of the Asian mainland, separated from Korea and Russia by the Sea of Japan. Japan consists of four main islands and thousands of smaller ones, extending 1,500 miles from its northern tip to its southern end.

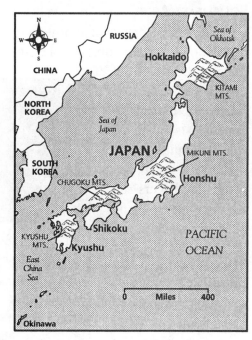

The Impact of Geography. Japan is a small country, and 85% of its land is covered by mountains. Nevertheless, Japan has a relatively large population. Its high population density has led to a social closeness and promoted the ability of its people to work together. Japan lacks many important natural resources necessary for its modern industries, and must import what it needs. In modern times, Japan's scarce natural resources have caused it to seek raw materials from other nations, either through trade or military conquest.

SOUTH ASIA

South Asia consists of a **subcontinent** (*a large land mass that is smaller than a continent*). This subcontinent forms a triangle about half the size of the United States, jutting into the Indian Ocean. It contains India, Pakistan, Bangladesh, and several smaller nations.

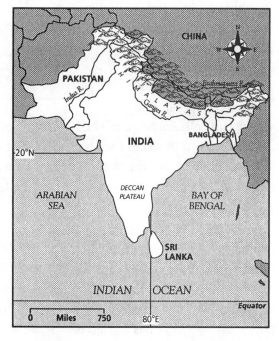

The Impact of Geography. The **Himalaya Mountains** are the highest in the world and separate the Indian subcontinent from the rest of Asia. The main rivers of the Indian subcontinent, the **Indus** and **Ganges**, were the sites of some of the world's earliest civilizations. The subcontinent's nearness to the Middle East led to the spread of Islam in much of the area.

SOUTHEAST ASIA

Southeast Asia consists of another large peninsula on the southeast corner of the Asian mainland and a large number of islands south and east of this peninsula. Some of the major countries of Southeast Asia are Thailand, Vietnam, Indonesia, Malaysia, and the Philippines. The Mekong, Salween, and Irrawaddy Rivers run through the mainland of Southeast Asia.

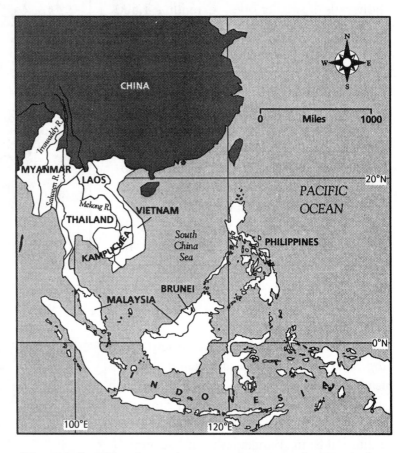

The Impact of Geography

Southeast Asia provides the shortest route between the Pacific and Indian Oceans. As a result, Southeast Asia has been heavily influenced by the mix of different peoples coming into the region, especially Chinese, Indians, Arabs, and European colonial powers. The islands of Southeast Asia, once known as the East Indies, export important spices such as pepper, cinnamon, and nutmeg, used in cooking all over the world. In earlier times, these spices were highly prized in Europe and the Middle East because they provided a way of preserving food that was more flavorful than using only salt.

The most important feature of the climate of Southeast Asia are the **monsoons**, winds that bring heavy summer rains. Rain helps to water the crops and to support life. However, if the monsoons bring too much rain they cause flooding, property damage, and death.

CHAPTER 7

THE DAWN OF CIVILIZATION,
3500 B.C. - 500 B.C.

Pyramid in Giza, Egypt

KEY TERMS, CONCEPTS AND PEOPLE

- Neolithic Revolution
- Culture
- Civilization
- Mesopotamia
- Hammurabi
- Ancient Egypt
- Hieroglyphics
- Indus River Valley
- Huang He
- Sumerians
- Babylonians
- Hebrews
- Moses
- Kush

	3500 BC	3000 BC	2500 BC	2000 BC	1500 BC	1000 BC	500 BC
MIDDLE EAST		MESOPOTAMIAN CIVILIZATIONS:					
		SUMER			BABYLON	HITTITE	ASSYRIAN
					HEBREW CIVILIZATION		
INDIA			INDUS RIVER CIVILIZATION				
CHINA				HUANG HE CIVILIZATION			
NORTH AFRICA		EGYPTIAN CIVILIZATION					
							KUSH

WHAT YOU SHOULD FOCUS ON

In this chapter, you will review how the first human beings emerged hundreds of thousands of years ago, gradually spread around the world, and developed farming and more advanced forms of culture. You will then learn how the earliest civilizations arose in the river valleys of Africa and Asia.

Studying this era will better enable you to appreciate the common past we all share. The study of human origins and ancient civilizations helps us to understand the basic problem that all societies face — how to organize to meet human needs.

When we study the civilizations of the past, we also develop a greater awareness of the tremendous debt we owe to those who came before us. The ancient invention of writing, for example, has allowed a vast amount of human knowledge to be recorded and passed down from one generation to the next.

Even today, our clothing styles, foods, and languages continue to be affected by the legacy of these ancient cultures. This is especially true of our laws, literature, art forms, religious beliefs, and knowledge of science and mathematics — much of which has developed from the accomplishments of ancient cultures.

In preparing for the Regents Examination in Global History, keep in mind that testmakers are likely to ask questions about the following:

- What were the consequences of the Neolithic Revolution?

- What factors led to the rise of the first civilizations?

- What were the most important achievements of early civilizations?

Knowing the answers to these questions can help you to uncover the factors that will promote prosperity, stability, and innovation in our own day just as they did in the past.

LOOKING AT GEOGRAPHY

In this chapter, you will review how humans developed agriculture and how early civilizations arose. Geographical factors played a central role in these events. This introductory section takes a special look at the nature of geography.

THE FIVE THEMES OF GEOGRAPHY

The word *geography* comes from an ancient Greek phrase for writing about the Earth. Geographers have identified five major themes in the study of this subject.

LOCATION

This theme deals with where something is located in relation to other things. For example, where was Mesopotamia in relation to Egypt? To allow us to find any fixed point on the earth, geographers use longitude and latitude.

PLACE

This theme refers to the special features that make one location different from others. For example, what was Babylon like in ancient times? Was it hot or cool? Mountainous or flat? To describe the physical characteristics of a place, geographers look at its **topography** (*surface features*) and **climate** (*weather conditions over a long period*). Each place also has its own special **natural resources** (*minerals, fertile soil, or fresh water*).

REGION

A region is an area that shares common features and whose people have greater contacts within the area than outside it. The concept of region in geography, like that of a time period in history, is flexible. Different regions, such as ancient Egypt, can expand and contract over time. In studying any region in history, ask yourself: What makes this area a region? What are its common features?

HUMAN-ENVIRONMENTAL INTERACTION

This theme describes how the physical features of a place interact with the people who live there. Since ancient times, people have affected the environment in many ways: planting fields, irrigating land, and building cities. Also, the environment often affects what people do: How would the kind of society that develops in a desert be different from one that emerges in a tropical rainforest?

MOVEMENT

Throughout history, some areas have had surpluses of certain resources and goods, while other areas have had shortages of these same items. These differences have stimulated trade and other contacts among peoples. Understanding the movement of goods, services, ideas, and peoples from place to place is another important theme of geography.

ANSWERING QUESTIONS ON GEOGRAPHY

Essay questions on geography often focus on how the physical setting of an area affects the development of its people. When answering such questions, keep in mind that **location** is often crucial in determining interactions with peoples of other areas. Also, the kind of **place** an area is — its topography, climate, and resources — usually determines the number of people who live in the area, where they live, and how they meet their needs for food, water, and shelter. For example, population density is generally greatest along coasts, in river valleys, and on fertile plains.

MAJOR
HISTORICAL DEVELOPMENTS

EARLY HUMAN SOCIETY

Anthropologists study the origins, customs, and beliefs of humankind. Most anthropologists now believe the **Great Rift Valley** in East Africa was the birthplace of humanity. Many scientists believe that human beings as we know them today — **Homo Sapiens** — first appeared between 400,000 and 200,000 years ago.

THE IMPORTANCE OF CULTURE

Human beings had several important advantages over other animals: superior intelligence, the use of hands to make tools, and the ability to communicate through speech. Because human beings had these ways of communicating, remembering and making things, they were able to pass on what they learned to their children and other members of their group. In this way, the first human cultures developed.

> **Culture** refers to a people's way of life. It includes such things as their language, clothes, homes, family organization, rituals, and foods. Culture also includes a people's crafts, arts, and religious beliefs.

People in the earliest human societies were hunter-gatherers. They relied on hunting, fishing, and gathering wild plants for food. They learned to make fires, canoes, and spears with pieces of bone or stone. Because these people made stone tools, historians refer to early human societies as **Stone Age** cultures. Over thousands of years, some Stone Age peoples also learned to make clay pottery and to domesticate dogs.

The primary activity of early humans was obtaining food. They migrated to areas where food was available. The search for food led people to migrate from Africa to other parts of the world, including the Americas and Australia. Wherever people went, they showed great ingenuity in adapting to local conditions.

THE NEOLITHIC REVOLUTION

About 10,000 years ago, one of the great turning points in human history occurred. People began to change from hunter-gatherers to producers of food. Two important developments brought this about: people learned how to grow food and to herd animals.

Anthropologists believe this change may have first occurred in parts of Southwest Asia (*commonly known as the Middle East*), where wild wheat and barley were plentiful. People noticed they could spread the seeds of these plants to grow crops. They also learned how to domesticate animals such as goats, sheep, and cattle. These advances are referred to as the **Neolithic Revolution**.

Wherever agriculture was introduced, people no longer had to lead a nomadic life — wandering in search of food. Instead, they could build permanent homes and villages. Populations grew. Although the emergence of agricultural societies is believed to have first occurred in Southwest Asia, it also took place independently at later times in Southeast Asia, China, Africa, and the Americas.

The Neolithic Revolution brought both benefits and problems. People could grow more food than they had been able to gather or hunt, but they were also more vulnerable to attacks by other groups because they settled in one area. As settlements developed, two new social classes emerged: warriors and priests. Because the village had to be defended, a warrior class was necessary. A separate priesthood emerged to conduct religious rituals to protect the crops and village from danger.

THE RISE OF RIVER VALLEY CIVILIZATIONS

As agricultural societies developed and grew, their way of life continued to change. Around 4000 B.C., the world's first civilizations arose.

A **civilization** is an advanced form of human culture in which people build cities, have complex social institutions, use some form of writing, and are skilled in science and technology.

The first civilizations developed in four separate **river valleys**. Each of these river valleys offered a mild climate and a water highway to other places. Most important, each of these valleys occupied a flood plain where the river overflowed every year, depositing fertile soil. People introducing agriculture to these regions were able to grow abundant crops that could support large populations and advanced cultures. Following is a brief overview of these four early civilizations.

MESOPOTAMIA (3500 B.C. - 1700 B.C.)

Archaeologists study the artifacts of past civilizations. Archaeologists believe that between 5,000 and 6,000 years ago the first river valley civilization developed in Mesopotamia, the region located between the **Tigris** and **Euphrates** Rivers *(in present-day Iraq)*. This area is part of a larger region historians call the **Fertile Crescent**, a band of land that arches from the Mediterranean to the Persian Gulf.

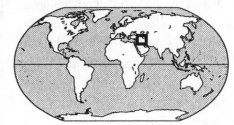

Although the area was hot and dry, people learned how to irrigate the land by diverting water from the Tigris and Euphrates Rivers. Irrigation allowed farming settlements to flourish and food supplies to increase. Since people could produce more food, some people began to specialize in activities such as pottery, weaving, and metal working.

The people of southern Mesopotamia, known as **Sumerians**, built a number of cities. At first, each city had its own ruler and local gods. Later, these states were united under a single ruler. By 2000 B.C., the city of Ur probably had a population of more than 10,000 people. But because the Sumerians lived on a flat plain, they were vulnerable to invasion by neighboring peoples.

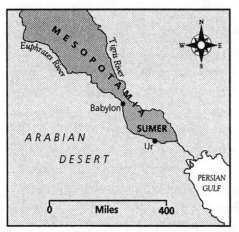

Around 1800 B.C., nomadic *(wandering)* warriors known as the Amorites conquered the Sumerians and made Babylon their capital. Later the area was conquered by the Hittites, Assyrians, Chaldeans, and Persians.

INVENTIONS, SCIENCE AND MATHEMATICS

Some of the most important inventions in human history were made in ancient Mesopotamia. The Sumerians probably invented the wheel and the sailboat. They developed tools and weapons of copper and bronze. They also devised the world's earliest known writing, **cuneiform** — a type of symbol-writing on clay tablets. The Sumerian calendar divided the year into 12 months. The Babylonian number system was based on 60, which still provides the basis for our clock time: seconds and minutes.

BUILDING

The Sumerians were the world's first city-builders. They lacked stone and timber, so they made their buildings from mud bricks and crushed reeds. They constructed walled cities, temples with arches, and stepped pyramids known as **ziggurats**.

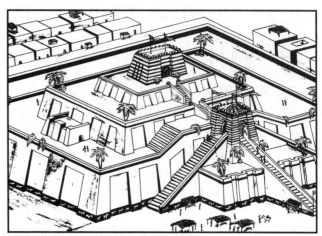
Sumerian ziggurat

SYSTEM OF LAW

Mesopotamian peoples developed elaborate legal systems. When Hammurabi, a Babylonian ruler, conquered all of Mesopotamia, he developed the earliest known written law code— the **Code of Hammurabi**. It covered almost every occurrence in daily life. Hammurabi's aim was to ensure order, protect the weak, and fight evil. Some of the code's provisions punished criminals quite harshly, stressing the idea of "an eye for an eye, and a tooth for a tooth."

ANCIENT EGYPT (3200 B.C. - 500 B.C.)

Egypt is located in North Africa, and the world's longest river, the **Nile**, runs through it. Each year the Nile floods the lands along its banks, depositing fertile soil. With this rich soil and ample fresh water, Egyptian farmers grew large amounts of food. Farmers supported a large number of crafts-

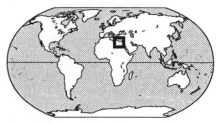

men, warriors, priests, and nobles. Ease of communication along the river encouraged the development of a highly centralized government. At the same time, Egypt was less prone to foreign invasion than Mesopotamia because it was surrounded by desert.

SOCIAL SYSTEM

The **pharaoh** (*king*) governed Egypt as an absolute ruler. He commanded the army and controlled irrigation and grain supplies. Egyptians considered the pharaoh to be a god. Next in the social order came priests, nobles, warriors, scribes, merchants, and craftsmen. At the bottom of Egyptian society were peasants and slaves. They spent their time farming, herding cattle, and working on massive building projects for the pharoah.

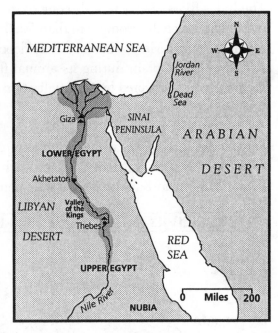

RELIGIOUS BELIEFS

The Egyptians believed that a person's body should be preserved after death, in preparation for the afterlife. When pharaohs died, their bodies were embalmed and buried in a special room inside a huge triangular stone tomb called a **pyramid**. Here they were surrounded with gold, jewels, and other precious objects for use in the afterlife, which Egyptians believed would be much like life on earth.

Biology. Egyptians obtained knowledge of the human body through embalming. They performed surgery, such as setting bone fractures.

Hieroglyphics. One of the earliest forms of writing, based on picture symbols, hieroglyphics appeared on buildings and on scrolls of paper known as **papyrus**.

ACCOMPLISHMENTS OF THE ANCIENT EGYPTIANS

Building. Egyptian architects and engineers built magnificent stone pyramids, palaces, temples, and statues.

Geometry and Astronomy. They used geometric principles to build pyramids and other structures. By observing the stars, they developed a 365-day calendar.

INDUS RIVER VALLEY (2500 B.C. - 1500 B.C.)

The Indus River Valley was also one of the first centers of human civilization, more than 5000 years ago. As in Egypt and Mesopotamia, a river deposited rich soil all over the plain during its annual flood. The geographic area covered by this civilization exceeded both Mesopotamia and Egypt.

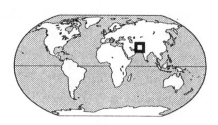

Farmers grew barley, wheat, dates, and melons. Food surpluses allowed people to build large cities like Harappa and Mohenjo-Daro. Each of these cities had more than 30,000 people. Remarkably, almost all the houses were connected to public sewers and a water supply.

The Harappans were also the first people known to make cotton cloth.

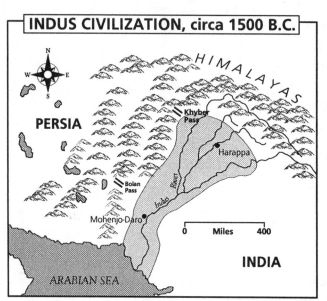

INDUS CIVILIZATION, circa 1500 B.C.

HIMALAYAS

PERSIA

Khyber Pass

Harappa

Bolan Pass

Indus River

Mohenjo-Daro

0   Miles   400

INDIA

ARABIAN SEA

Trade was an important part of the economy. Many small clay containers, probably used for trading purposes, have been discovered by archaeologists. They also have found pottery kilns and evidence of the use of metals. The Harappans developed their own form of writing, although scholars still cannot decipher it. No one knows exactly why this civilization collapsed, but it happened suddenly. Some scholars believe that Aryan tribes from Central Asia came through the Khyber Pass and conquered the Indus River peoples.

THE HUANG HE (2000 B.C.- 1027 B.C.)

Some 500 years after the Harappans settled in the Indus River Valley, China's first civilization emerged in the fertile plains along the Huang He (*the Yellow River*).

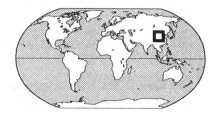

> **NOTE**: Traditional Chinese writing uses a system of pictographs *(picture symbols)*. In 1979, the Chinese government adopted a system called Pinyin for spelling Chinese names and places in English. This book, with some exceptions, uses Pinyin spelling. For example: Mao Tse Tung appears as Mao Zedong, the Chou Dynasty as the Zhou Dynasy, and Taoism as Daoism.

As along the Nile and Indus Rivers, the fertility of the soil along the Huang He was increased by the river's occasional overflowing of its banks. Around 4500 B.C., farmers began growing millet *(a type of grain)* in this region. Later, the farming of soybeans and the raising of chickens, dogs, and pigs was introduced. About 1500 B.C., people from the Huang He area migrated south to the Yangtze River, where they learned to grow rice.

THE SHANG DYNASTY

Lake Baikal
Lake Balkhash
Tien Shan Mnts.
Kunlun Mnts.
Himalayas
Anyang
Yellow Sea
Huang He R.
C H I N A
Yangtze R.
East China Sea
Xi Jiang R.
Bay of Bengal
South China Sea

Extent of Shang empire circa 1100 B.C.

0   Miles   500

POLITICAL RULE

Around 1760 B.C., a **dynasty** *(ruling family)* known as the **Shang** took power. They built the first Chinese cities, and made their capital at Anyang. They ruled with the help of powerful nobles until about 1120 B.C.

ACCOMPLISHMENTS

The Chinese were skilled in many crafts. Their special skill in bronze work can be seen in many objects found from this period. They discovered how to make silk from silkworm cocoons, constructed irrigation systems, and developed a precise calendar. The Chinese also developed their own system of writing based on picture symbols, much as the ancient Egyptians and Sumerians had done.

THE SPREAD OF CIVILIZATION

The civilizations of Egypt and Mesopotamia gradually influenced neighboring areas. Civilization spread from Egypt upstream along the Nile into the kingdom of Kush. The ancient Hebrews and Phoenicians were influenced by both Mesopotamia and Egypt.

THE KUSHITE CIVILIZATION (750 B.C. - 350 A.D.)

Kush, also known as Nubia, was an African kingdom located up-river on the Nile, south of Egypt *(in present-day Sudan)*. Although the Kushites were nomadic cattle herders, goods were frequently exchanged between Kush and Egypt. In some periods, Egyptian pharaohs sent administrators, merchants and armies to conquer Kushite territory.

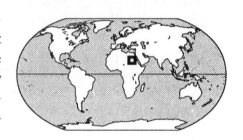

IMPORTANT DEVELOPMENTS
In 750 B.C., Kush conquered Egypt, but the victory was short-lived. The Kushites were

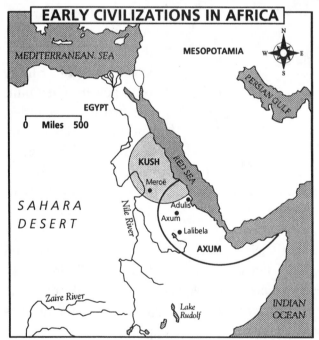

driven out 80 years later by the Assyrians, who invaded from Mesopotamia. Kush itself remained independent and wealthy, however, deriving riches from its trade and iron products. Egypt had an important influence on Kush. The Kushites copied Egyptian art, language and religion. They built pyramids in their capital city of Meroë. Kush suddenly weakened around 300 A.D., when it was conquered by the nearby kingdom of Axum.

PRINCIPAL ACHIEVEMENTS
Kush was known in the ancient world as an iron-producing center.

Caravans traveled to Kush to obtain iron spears and iron plows to till the soil. Kushites also grew rich from the sale of ivory, ebony, wood, animal skins, and slaves. Kush developed its own form of writing. At first this was similar to Egyptian hieroglyphics, but later Kushites created their own alphabet.

THE PHOENICIAN AND HEBREW CIVILIZATIONS

The Hittites defeated the Babylonians around 1600 B.C. The Hittites were able to conquer Mesopotamia because they had iron weapons that were stronger than the bronze weapons of other peoples. After several hundred years, the Hittite empire collapsed. Smaller states emerged, such as those of the Phoenicians and Hebrews.

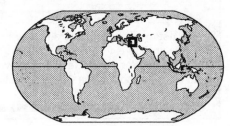

THE PHOENICIANS

Phoenicia was located on the Mediterranean coast, by present-day Lebanon. By 1200 B.C., the Phoenicians had become known as great traders, setting up trading posts in Italy, Spain and North Africa, including the city of Carthage. They invented a new way of writing that used only 22 symbols. This was much simpler than cuneiform, which had 600 symbols. Soon Phoenician writing was being used throughout the Mediterranean world. Four more symbols were added later, resulting in the alphabet used today in most of the Western world. In fact, the word "alphabet" comes from the first two letters of the Phoenician alphabet — *aleph* and *beth*.

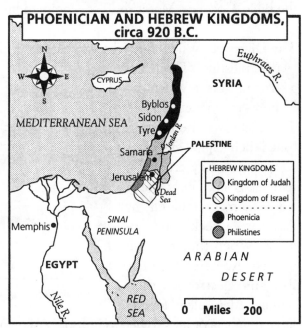

THE HEBREWS

About 2000 B.C., Hebrew (*or Jewish*) civilization arose just south of Phoenicia, in the area occupied by present-day Israel, Lebanon, and Jordan. Because of their location, the ancient Hebrews were deeply influenced by both Mesopotamia and Egypt.

Judaism, the ancient Hebrew religion, had a great influence on later civilizations.

Other peoples in the ancient world were **animists**, believing each object had its own spirit, or **polytheists**, who believed in many gods. The Hebrews believed in one God. **Monotheism**, the belief in one God, became the basis for later religions such as Christianity and Islam.

KEY FEATURES OF JUDAISM

The history of the Hebrews and their relationship with God is told in the first books of the **Bible**, known as the **Old Testament**. Jews refer to the early books of the Old Testament as the **Torah**.

The **Ten Commandments**, which the Hebrews believed were given to Moses by God, forbade immoral conduct such as stealing and murder.

The Exodus. According to Jewish tradition, the ancient Hebrews migrated to Egypt in 1800 B.C. to escape food shortages. They remained in Egypt for hundreds of years, where they became enslaved. Their leader, **Moses**, eventually led the Hebrews out of Egypt and slavery. Their flight from Egypt is known as the **Exodus**. Afterwards, according to the Bible, God gave Moses the Ten Commandments, which he presented to his people.

The Diaspora. When the Hebrews returned to Israel about 1000 B.C., it was occupied by the Philistines. This led to a series of wars in which the Hebrews reconquered Israel. The Hebrews then established their capital at Jerusalem, where they erected a temple to God. The Hebrews were later conquered by Assyrians, Greeks, and Romans. When they rebelled against Roman rule, the Romans destroyed their temple at Jerusalem, forcing

The Wailing Wall — part of ancient Jerusalem's temple wall.

large numbers of Jews to flee to Europe, Asia, and Africa. This period of Jewish history is known as the Diaspora (*dispersion*).

STUDY CARDS: You may photocopy this page. Then cut apart these cards to add to the study cards you made while reading this chapter.

Culture/Civilization

- **Culture:** A people's way of life — their foods, their clothing, their customs and beliefs

- **Civilization:** Advanced form of society; people live in cities, have complex institutions, use some form of writing

Hieroglyphics/Cuneiform

Writing is one of the signposts of civilization. Earliest writing systems were:

- **Hieroglyphics:** Egyptian picture-writing cut in stone or written on papyrus
- **Cuneiform:** Symbol-writing on wet clay, developed by Sumerians and others in Mesopotamia
- **Others:** The Chinese developed pictorial character writing; the Phoenicians developed the first known **alphabet**.

Neolithic Revolution

When: Began about 10,000 years ago. People in Middle East changed from nomadic hunting and gathering food, and learned to grow crops and domesticate animals.

Significance: Resulted in building permanent homes and villages where different social classes emerged, such as warriors and priests.

Judaism

Religion of the Jewish people. Began with the ancient **Hebrews** in lands now known as Israel. **Moses** led the Jews out of Egyptian slavery, gave them the first part of the **Bible** with the **Ten Commandments**.

Significance: Ancient Hebrews developed **monotheism** — belief in one God rather than several gods.

River Valley Civilizations

First civilizations developed in river valleys. Yearly floods deposited fertile soil, allowing people to grow surpluses of food.

- **Mesopotamia:** along the Tigris and Euphrates
- **Egypt:** along the Nile
- **Indus Valley Civilization:** along the Indus
- **First Chinese Civilization:** along the Huang He (*Yellow River*)

Contributions of Early Civilizations

- **Mesopotamia:** sailboat, wheel, sundial, irrigation, earliest known legal system (**Code of Hammurabi**)
- **Ancient Egypt:** mathematics, astronomy, medicine, sculpture, architecture
- **Phoenicians:** first known alphabet
- **Ancient China:** silk-making
- **Ancient Hebrews:** monotheism, Bible, Ten Commandments

SUMMARIZING YOUR UNDERSTANDING

COMPLETING A PARAGRAPH FRAME

The earliest civilizations made important and lasting contributions to human progress. Select **one** ancient civilization from this chapter and **show how** it made an important and lasting contribution to the world. To help you write this essay, a paragraph frame has been provided.

NOTE: Parts of this paragraph frame have been completed for you, using ancient Egypt as the selection. Complete the rest of the paragraph frame.

Selection: [*Ancient Egyptian civilization*] made important and lasting contributions to humankind.

Example(s): Among the major contributions of Egypt was [*its system of writing*]. The Egyptians developed [*hieroglyphics, one of the earliest kinds of writing. Hieroglyphics used pictures to stand for ideas, words and letters*]. **Link:** [*The development of writing helped cultures to pass down their knowledge and values from one generation to the next. This made it possible for later generations to benefit from earlier ideas and technologies.*]

Another Example: A second contribution of ancient Egyptian civilization was

[_____

_____].

Link: [_____

_____].

Closing: From these achievements, we can see that [*ancient Egyptian civilization*] made important and lasting contributions to the advancement of world civilization.

TESTING YOUR UNDERSTANDING

Test your understanding of this chapter by answering the following questions.

MULTIPLE-CHOICE QUESTIONS

1   During the Neolithic Revolution, people learned how to
    (1) create writing systems
    (2) grow food and domesticate animals
    (3) build fires
    (4) make bronze weapons

2   A student's report contains the following topics: Fertile Crescent, Sumer, and Huang He. The report is most likely about
    (1) religious groups
    (2) early forms of writing
    (3) river valley civilizations
    (4) dynastic rulers

3   Recent archaeological studies support the theory that
    (1) the earliest humans evolved in the Great Rift Valley in East Africa
    (2) farming societies developed before hunting and gathering societies
    (3) all the continents were settled at the same time
    (4) the wheel was used by all ancient societies

4   Which heading would be most appropriate on the blank line below?

I. _____	(1) Economic Changes in the Ancient World
A. ziggurats - Sumerians	(2) Buildings of Ancient Civilizations
B. iron tools - Kushites	(3) Achievements of Ancient Civilizations
C. alphabet - Phoenicians	(4) Early Civilizations and Their Reforms

5   The river valleys of the Tigris and Euphrates, the Nile, and the Indus were each centers of civilization because they
    (1) had rich deposits of iron ore and coal
    (2) were isolated from other cultural influences
    (3) had rich soils from annual floods
    (4) were easy to defend from invasion

6   Which group of dates is arranged in correct chronological order?
(1) 567 B.C. → 214 B.C. → 567 A.D. → 1865 A.D.
(2) 123 B.C. → 124 B.C. → 18 B.C. → 1985 A.D.
(3) 37 B.C. → 38 B.C. → 98 A.D. → 1995 A.D.
(4) 557 A.D. → 234 B.C. → 56 A.D. → 22 B.C.

7   Which characteristic was common to the ancient civilizations of Egypt and China?
(1) nomadic lifestyle   (3) monotheistic religion
(2) influence of European cultures   (4) written forms of communication

8   Which statement about ancient Egyptian civilization expresses an opinion rather than a historical fact?
(1) The ancient Egyptians had a written language.
(2) Ancient Egypt was protected from invasion by the surrounding desert.
(3) Egyptians produced the most beautiful art works of the ancient world.
(4) The pyramids were tombs built for the pharaohs.

9   "If a seignior (noble) has knocked out the tooth of a seignior of his own rank, they shall knock out his tooth. But if he has knocked out a commoner's tooth, he shall pay one-third mina of silver."

—*Code of Hammurabi*

Which ancient Babylonian belief does this portion of Hammurabi's law code reflect?
(1) All men are equal under the law.
(2) Physical punishment is preferable to paying a fine.
(3) Differences exist between social classes.
(4) Violence must always be punished with violence.

10 Four events in early global history are listed below.

A. The rise of Egyptian civilization
B. The Neolithic Revolution begins
C. Homo Sapiens make their first appearance
D. The Phoenicians invent the alphabet

Which is the correct chronological order of these events?

(1) A → B → C → D   (3) A → B → D → C
(2) D → C → A → B   (4) C → B → A → D

11 One reason for the rise of civilization along the Huang He was that
    (1) its location protected it from invasion by land
    (2) rich soil along the river was ideal for farming
    (3) it provided a direct route between Europe and Asia
    (4) it flowed into the Mediterranean Sea

12 Archaeologists digging at a site discover hieroglyphics on stone walls, a well-preserved mummy, and gold jewelry. The site was most probably the location of
    (1) an Egyptian pharaoh's tomb   (3) ancient Hebrew ruins
    (2) an early Kushite temple   (4) a tomb of a Chinese ruler

13 Our modern-day alphabet is based in large part on the alphabet of the
    (1) Phoenicians   (3) Egyptians
    (2) Harappans   (4) Sumerians

14 An important characteristic of Judaism is the belief in
    (1) many gods   (3) reincarnation
    (2) monotheism   (4) the New Testament

INTERPRETING DOCUMENTS

1a Identify two ancient civilizations that began in river valleys.

- _____

- _____

b Give **two** reasons that explain the attraction of ancient peoples to river valleys.

- _____

   _____

- _____

   _____

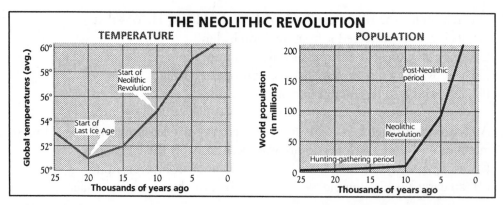

2a What was the world's population at the start of the Neolithic Revolution?

b Explain how the Neolithic Revolution was affected by a change in temperature.

THEMATIC ESSAY QUESTION

In this exercise and similar ones in later chapters, you will get practice in writing thematic essays. For the *Regents Guidelines* for thematic essays, re-read page 31.

Directions: Write a well-organized essay that includes an introduction, several paragraphs addressing the Task below, and a conclusion.

Theme: Change

The contributions and achievements of ancient civilizations have helped to influence and change the world.

Task:

- Identify **two** ancient civilizations that have helped to influence and change the world.
- Describe a contribution or achievement of *each* civilization.
- Explain how that contribution or achievement helped to influence and change the world.

You may choose any ancient civilizations from your study of global history. Some suggestions you might wish to consider include: Mesopotamia, Egypt, the Indus River Valley civilization, and the Huang He civilization.

You are *not* limited to these suggestions.

CHAPTER 8

THE CLASSICAL CIVILIZATIONS, 500 B.C. - 500 A.D.

Alexander the Great

	500 B.C.	300 B.C.	100 B.C.	100 A.D.	300	500
GREECE	CITY-STATES	HELLENISTIC PERIOD				
ROME	ROMAN REPUBLIC			ROMAN EMPIRE		
ASIA	PERSIAN EMPIRE					
	ZHOU DYNASTY	QIN	HAN DYNASTY			
	ARYAN KINGDOMS	MAURYAN EMPIRE			GUPTA EMPIRE	
RELIGIONS AND BELIEF SYSTEMS				CHRISTIANITY		
	CONFUCIANISM					
	HINDUISM					
	BUDDHISM					

WHAT YOU SHOULD FOCUS ON

In this chapter, you will review the classical civilizations of the world. During this era, civilizations spread beyond river valleys. Some societies gained sufficient military power to conquer their neighbors and create giant empires. Civilizations began to reflect more on morality and the purpose of life. As a result, some of the world's major religions emerged.

These same civilizations developed institutions, systems of thought, and cultural styles that still influence us today. Their arts and literature set the standards by which later works would be judged. For these reasons, we refer to them as the *classical* civilizations, meaning that they were of the highest class or rank.

The **Persian empire** was the first to unite many civilizations, establishing a pattern for future empires.

The **Greeks** applied reason to inquire about nature and the human condition, laying the foundation for much of Western culture.

OVERVIEW OF CLASSICAL CIVILIZATIONS IN THIS CHAPTER

The **Romans** spread Greek culture throughout Western Europe, leaving a legacy of language, a system of laws, and Christianity.

China saw the emergence of great philosophers, who set the tone for much of Chinese thought and tradition.

India witnessed a flowering of Hindu and Buddhist cultures, which spread throughout much of South and Southeast Asia.

In reviewing this era, keep in mind that test writers are most likely to ask you:

- What was the importance of military power, technology, and transportation to the development of large empires like Persia, China, and Rome?
- What were the major cultural accomplishments of these civilizations?
- What factors led to the collapse of classical civilizations?
- How were classical civilizations affected by their religions and belief systems?

LOOKING AT
THE WORLD'S RELIGIONS

All societies have some form of religious belief. Because these beliefs involve what people think life itself is about, religion often has a major impact on people's behavior. Thus, religion has been one of the most powerful influences on human history.

WHAT IS RELIGION?

You may be surprised to learn that there is no *precise* definition of "religion." Nonetheless, most definitions of religion list three common elements:

> A set of beliefs about the origin and the nature of the universe, the existence of one God or many gods, and the meaning of life.

CHARACTERISTICS OF A RELIGION

> A set of customs and practices that relate to the worship of one God or several gods, and a set of rules for proper conduct.

> An organization, such as a church, synagogue, mosque or other place of worship, that oversees religious practices.

In studying about a religion, ask yourself the following:

- **BELIEFS:** Do its followers believe in one or several gods? Do they have prophets or holy persons? Do they believe in life after death? What do they believe is the purpose and meaning of life?

- **CUSTOMS/PRACTICES:** Does the religion have rules for leading a moral life? Does it have holy places and holy days? Are certain things prohibited?

- **ORGANIZATION:** Does the religion have a group of priests or clerics? Is there a single religious head, like the Roman Catholic Pope? Does it have houses of worship such as churches, mosques or synagogues?

CLASSIFYING THE WORLD'S MAJOR RELIGIONS

One way to look at the world's major religions is to organize them according to their historical development. For example, Christianity and Islam developed out of Judaism. Catholicism, Eastern Orthodoxy and Protestanism are forms of Christianity.

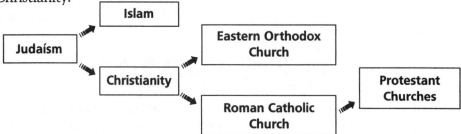

Another family of religions developed in India. Buddhism grew out of Hinduism. Sikhism is a blend of Hindu and Muslim beliefs. Zen Buddhism is a form Buddhism that developed in Japan.

This way of grouping religions is useful because each new religion borrowed ideas and practices from the religion it grew out of.

ANSWERING QUESTIONS ABOUT RELIGION

Questions concerning religion on the Regents Examination will usually focus on two aspects:

- major beliefs of a religion and how these beliefs influenced history or culture

- the social conflicts that sometimes arise out of religious differences.

MAJOR
HISTORICAL DEVELOPMENTS

CLASSICAL CIVILIZATIONS EMERGE

THE PERSIAN EMPIRE (2000 B.C. - 100 B.C.)

The Medes and the Persians lived on the Iranian plateau between the Caspian Sea and the Persian Gulf. In 550 B.C., the Persian ruler **Cyrus the Great** united these two peoples. He then extended Persia's territory westward by conquering Lydia and Babylonia, and eastward by conquering territories as far as the Indus River. His son conquered Egypt,

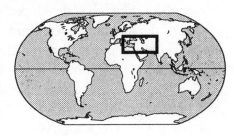

but died while invading Kush. The next ruler, **Darius**, unified the Persian empire by building a network of public roads, introducing uniform weights and measures, and establishing several capital cities.

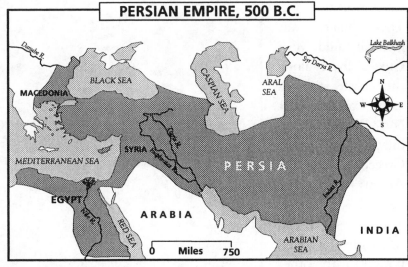

Persia grew larger than any other empire up to that time. It stretched more than 3,000 miles from the Nile to the Indus River. The Persians controlled their vast empire by dividing it into provinces, each of which was ruled by a group of local officials loyal to the Persian king. The Persians collected tribute and taxes from these provinces. The provinces profited under Persian rule by participating in extensive trade throughout the empire.

At first, the Persians worshipped many gods. In 570 B.C., a new faith was introduced into Persia by the religious leader **Zoroaster**. His religion, **Zoroastrianism**, taught that there were only two gods: the god of truth, light, and goodness and the god of darkness and evil. The whole universe was a battleground between these two forces. Those who led life as good people would go to Heaven, while others would be doomed to a fiery Hell.

THE GREEKS (1000 B.C. - 150 B.C.)

SIGNIFICANCE OF THE EARLY GREEKS

The ancient Greeks had an enduring impact on world civilization. They developed the first known system of democratic government. Their belief in the power of human reason and their spirit of free inquiry led to important advances in mathematics, science, art, literature, and philosophy.

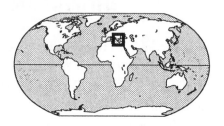

THE IMPACT OF GEOGRAPHY

Ancient Greece consisted of a mountainous peninsula, the hilly coast of Asia Minor (*present-day Turkey*) and many islands in the Aegean Sea. The climate was generally mild. Most Greeks lived along the coast, with its many excellent harbors. Because of its hilly terrain, parts of Greece — especially Athens — came to depend on trade. The Greeks traded wine, olive oil, and pottery with other peoples of the Mediterranean. Through

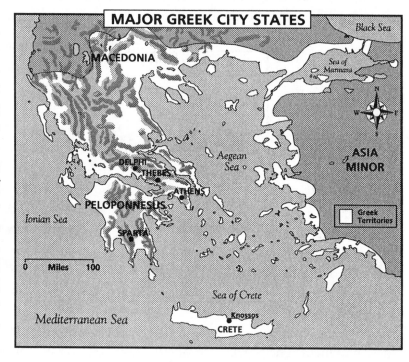

MAJOR GREEK CITY STATES

such contacts, the Greeks learned astronomy, mathematics, navigation, and building techniques. For example, they borrowed the alphabet from the Phoenicians and the use of coined money from the Lydians.

EARLY GREEK CIVILIZATION

Classical Greek culture emerged from two earlier Greek civilizations. The Minoan civilization flourished on the island of Crete from 2000 B.C. to 1400 B.C. The Minoans developed their own form of writing, the use of copper and bronze, and shipbuilding. Their civilization mysteriously collapsed around 1400 B.C. A second ancient Greek civilization thrived around Mycenae on mainland Greece and the coast of Asia Minor from 1400 to 1200 B.C. At the end of this period, the Dorians, a war-like group from northern Greece, conquered the Greek mainland.

THE RISE OF CITY-STATES

Mountains and the sea cut off Greek centers of population from one another. As a result, separate **city-states** developed. Each city-state (*polis*) had its own form of government and system of laws. However, Greeks also shared a common culture, based on their language, religious beliefs, traditions, and economic ties. For example, Greeks from all the city-states participated every four years in Olympic games in honor of Zeus and other Greek gods. Two of the most important city-states were Sparta and Athens:

✦ **Totalitarian Sparta**. Sparta was located in the southern part of Greece, called the Peloponnesus. In 725 B.C., the Spartans conquered their neighbors and forced the people, whom they called **helots**, to farm for them. The Spartans constantly used force to keep control over the helots, who outnumbered them. Due to this threat, Spartan life was organized around military needs. Individualism and new ideas were discouraged. Strict obedience and self-discipline were highly valued. For example, male citizens lived in military barracks from early childhood until the age of 30. If newborn babies were unhealthy, they were left on a hill to die. Spartan women were highly respected, were educated, and could own property.

✦ **Democratic Athens**. Athens developed a unique system of government known as **democracy**. Every citizen could directly participate in government by voting on the issues to be decided by the city-state. However, only a minority of Athenians were citizens. Women, foreigners, and slaves were not considered citizens and could not participate in government. Nevertheless, Athens established a pattern for later democracies.

THE TRIUMPH AND FALL OF THE CITY-STATES

Between 490 and 404 B.C., the Greek city-states first fought together against the invading Persian empire and then fought against each other.

✦ **The Persian Wars (500 B.C. - 479 B.C.).** When the Persian empire pushed westward into Ionia *(the Greek city-states of Asia Minor)*, Athens and other Greek city-states sent military help. To teach the Greeks a lesson, the Persians sent a large army to conquer mainland Greece; however, two attempts failed to defeat the better-armed Greeks. After the Persian Wars, a "Golden Age" in Greece began. Art, literature, and philosophy flourished in Athens. The popular statesman **Pericles** championed democracy. He also used Athenian naval power to force other city-states to pay taxes to Athens.

✦ **The Peloponnesian War (432 B.C. - 404 B.C.).** A rivalry developed between Athens and Sparta. Sparta declared war on Athens, in what became known as the **Peloponnesian War**. After 30 years of fighting, Sparta emerged as the victor, but the war had greatly weakened the Greek city-states.

THE HELLENISTIC PERIOD (338 B.C. - 323 B.C.)

In 338 B.C., the king of Macedonia *(an area north of Greece)* emerged as a powerful ruler. He quickly brought all the Greek city-states under his control. His son, **Alexander the Great**, went on to conquer Persia, Egypt and most of the Mediterranean world. Eventually, Alexander's armies conquered territories as far east as India. Alexander died during

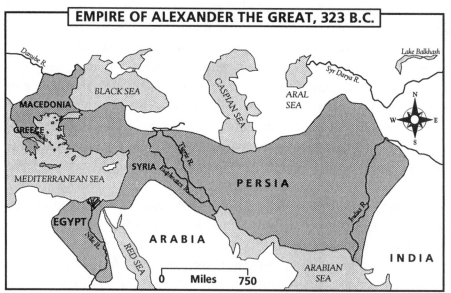

EMPIRE OF ALEXANDER THE GREAT, 323 B.C.

a military campaign. Although his empire collapsed after his early death, his conquests helped spread Greek culture throughout the ancient world. The period in which all of these changes took place is now referred to as the **Hellenistic Period**.

THE LEGACY OF CLASSICAL GREECE

The roots of Western civilization can be traced in part to the enduring contributions of the Greeks. Greek culture was characterized by a questioning spirit and a focus on human achievement.

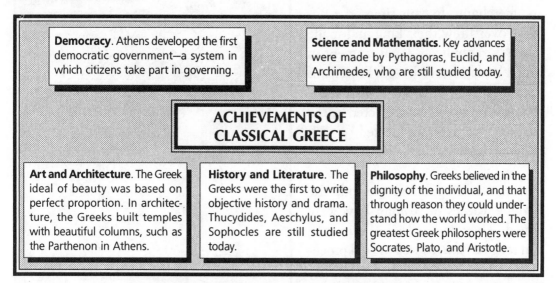

Democracy. Athens developed the first democratic government—a system in which citizens take part in governing.

Science and Mathematics. Key advances were made by Pythagoras, Euclid, and Archimedes, who are still studied today.

ACHIEVEMENTS OF CLASSICAL GREECE

Art and Architecture. The Greek ideal of beauty was based on perfect proportion. In architecture, the Greeks built temples with beautiful columns, such as the Parthenon in Athens.

History and Literature. The Greeks were the first to write objective history and drama. Thucydides, Aeschylus, and Sophocles are still studied today.

Philosophy. Greeks believed in the dignity of the individual, and that through reason they could understand how the world worked. The greatest Greek philosophers were Socrates, Plato, and Aristotle.

THE GRANDEUR OF ROME

THE RISE OF THE ROMAN EMPIRE

One of the cultures most affected by ancient Greece was that of Rome. The Roman empire became a dominant force in the Western world for over 400 years.

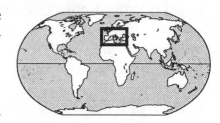

THE IMPACT OF GEOGRAPHY

Italy is a long, narrow, boot-shaped peninsula extending into the Mediterranean Sea. Rome is located in the middle of Italy, on a fertile plain near the west coast. In the north, the Alps Mountains protected the area from invaders. The sea provided further protection against invaders, while serving as a route for Roman trade and expansion.

THE ROMAN REPUBLIC

Rome was founded about 750 B.C. The early Roman city-state contained two main social classes: the **patricians** were wealthy landowning families, while the **plebeians** were small farmers, craftsmen, and merchants. In early times, the Romans overthrew their king and made Rome a **republic** — a government in which leaders were elected. Power was shared between a **Senate** (*a group of patricians*) and two consuls elected by the Senate. The plebeians elected two tribunes to represent their views.

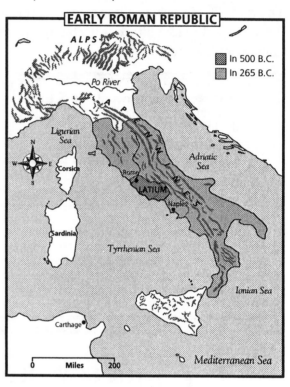

During the Republican period, the **Twelve Tables of Roman Law** were issued. They covered civil, criminal, and religious law, as well as trial procedure, and provided a foundation for later Roman law codes. According to Roman law, all citizens were equal under the law and considered innocent until proven guilty. Roman concepts of justice, equality before the law, and natural law based on reason played a major role in shaping later Western legal systems.

ROME EXPANDS AND BECOMES AN EMPIRE

By 275 B.C. Rome ruled the entire Italian peninsula. Rome then defeated its main rival Carthage, located in north Africa. This victory made Rome the leading power in the Mediterranean. Rome then acquired territories in Spain, North Africa, and the eastern Mediterranean. Roman generals such as **Julius Caesar** completed the conquest of Spain and Gaul (*present-day France*). By 146 B.C., Rome dominated the Mediterranean world.

The expansion of the city-state of Rome into a great power changed its basic character. Instead of being a citizens' army, the Roman army became a professional force completely obedient to its generals. A large number of slaves performed much of Rome's labor. Roman senators became corrupt, while generals with political ambitions — such as Pompey and Julius Caesar — fought against each other.

Caesar's armies eventually defeated Pompey's forces, and Caesar became a dictator in 46 B.C. He instituted the modern calendar, and carried out reforms such as providing municipal constitutions, a jury system, and land grants to veterans and the poor. In 44 B.C. he was assassinated by conspirators in the Senate, who feared he would become king.

Julius Caesar's heir, **Augustus Caesar**, emerged as the next ruler. Although he assumed king-like powers, Augustus also tried to preserve Rome's republican institutions. He removed corrupt officials and attempted to revive the "old" Roman values of responsibility and self-discipline. However, his successors became emperors with dictatorial powers and were worshipped as gods. They made conquests to the north and east, greatly expanding Rome's frontiers.

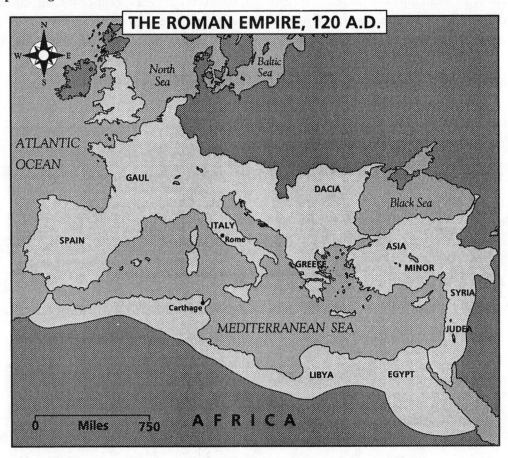

PAX ROMANA: THE "ROMAN PEACE" (27 B.C. - 395 A.D.)

Augustus brought a long period of peace, known as the **Pax Romana**, to Europe and the Mediterranean world. Rome's centralized political authority, trained officials and traditions of law allowed it to rule effectively over this large area. Romans generally respected local customs, provided laws, promoted trade and offered Roman citizenship to peoples throughout the empire. The Romans excelled at building and engineering: they introduced the use of concrete and built stone roads, aqueducts *(systems to carry water for many miles)*, temples, and public baths. New cities became outposts of Roman culture.

THE RISE OF CHRISTIANITY

The Romans allowed many religions to exist throughout their empire, but expected followers of all religions to worship the emperor as a god. Two groups, Jews and Christians, refused to recognize the Roman emperor as divine. The Jews were eventually expelled from their homeland. Christians faced persecution and sometimes death. Despite persecution, Christianity continued to spread. In the 4th century A.D., **Emperor Constantine** proclaimed freedom of worship for Christians and became a Christian himself. By the end of the 4th century, Christianity became the official religion of the Roman empire.

THE DECLINE AND FALL OF THE ROMAN EMPIRE

By the third century A.D., the Roman empire had started to weaken. Historians offer several explanations for this decline.

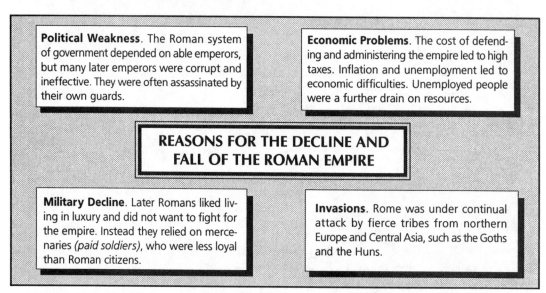

Political Weakness. The Roman system of government depended on able emperors, but many later emperors were corrupt and ineffective. They were often assassinated by their own guards.

Economic Problems. The cost of defending and administering the empire led to high taxes. Inflation and unemployment led to economic difficulties. Unemployed people were a further drain on resources.

REASONS FOR THE DECLINE AND FALL OF THE ROMAN EMPIRE

Military Decline. Later Romans liked living in luxury and did not want to fight for the empire. Instead they relied on mercenaries *(paid soldiers)*, who were less loyal than Roman citizens.

Invasions. Rome was under continual attack by fierce tribes from northern Europe and Central Asia, such as the Goths and the Huns.

Later emperors tried to reverse the decline of the empire. In 284 A.D. **Diocletian** divided the empire in two so it could be governed more efficiently. The eastern part consisted of Greece, Asia Minor, Egypt, and Syria; the western part consisted of Italy, Gaul, Britannia, Spain, and North Africa. Constantine temporarily reunited the empire and moved its capital from Rome to Constantinople in the east. In the late 300s, a nomadic group from Central Asia, known as the **Huns**, began to move westward. This put pressure on the Goths and other tribes, who began entering the Roman empire. A period of great turmoil followed. Some invaders burned estates and seized Roman lands. Rome itself was sacked. In 476 A.D., the last Roman emperor was overthrown in the west. But the eastern empire, later known as the **Byzantine empire**, survived for another 1000 years.

THE ENDURING LEGACY OF ROME

The Romans made many important and lasting contributions:

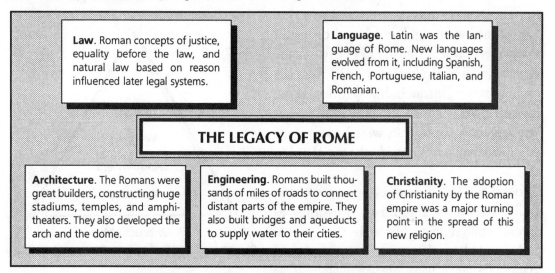

Law. Roman concepts of justice, equality before the law, and natural law based on reason influenced later legal systems.

Language. Latin was the language of Rome. New languages evolved from it, including Spanish, French, Portuguese, Italian, and Romanian.

THE LEGACY OF ROME

Architecture. The Romans were great builders, constructing huge stadiums, temples, and amphitheaters. They also developed the arch and the dome.

Engineering. Romans built thousands of miles of roads to connect distant parts of the empire. They also built bridges and aqueducts to supply water to their cities.

Christianity. The adoption of Christianity by the Roman empire was a major turning point in the spread of this new religion.

THE RISE OF EMPIRES IN INDIA

In the last chapter, you learned how an early civilization developed along the Indus River and then suddenly collapsed. Many historians believe the **Aryans** came from Central Asia, crossed the mountain passes through the Himalayas and arrived in India about 1500 B.C. However, other historians now believe that Aryan culture arose locally.

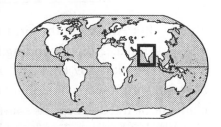

ARYAN CULTURE

The **Aryans** were nomadic peoples who lived by herding cattle and by fighting. They developed iron weapons and horse-drawn chariots which enabled them to conquer their neighbors. After destroying the Indus River cultures, Aryan tribes next moved into the Ganges River valley, pushing the Dravidian people living there farther south.

By 900 B.C., the Aryans had formed city-states in the major river valleys. Each city-state had its own ruler. The Aryans developed their own form of writing, known as **Sanskrit**, and their own religion, Hinduism. (*To learn more about Hinduism, see page 95.*)

NEW BELIEFS EMERGE

The mixing of Aryan and Dravidian peoples led to a new social order known as the **caste system**. Under this system, people were divided into five main castes (*see graphic*):

Caste lines were rigid and based on birth. People were not permitted to marry outside their caste. The **Brahmins** (*priests*) were the highest caste. **Untouchables** performed the lowliest tasks, such as handling dead bodies or sweeping streets. They were looked upon as falling completely outside the social order.

Around 600 B.C., a new religion emerged in India, known as **Buddhism**. Missionaries spread this religion through the rest of India and throughout Southeast and East Asia. (*To learn more about Buddhism, see page 96.*)

THE MAURYAN EMPIRE (321 B.C. - 232 A.D.)

Shortly after Alexander the Great's invasion, one of the greatest Hindu empires rose in northern India. **King Chandragupta** established the powerful Mauryan empire. His grandson **Asoka** (269 B.C. - 232 B.C.) was the next great ruler of India. Asoka began his reign with a series of military campaigns that enlarged the Mauryan empire to include all of India except its southern tip. Asoka eventually became sickened by the bloodshed of battle and converted to Buddhism.

Asoka decided to win his people's loyalty by acts of kindness and by promoting their welfare and happiness. He decreed that people of all religions should live peacefully with one another. Asoka improved roads, built hospitals, and sent teachers throughout his empire to promote education. He built Buddhist shrines throughout India and sent missionaries to other lands to win converts to Buddhism. After Asoka's death, the Mauryan empire began to fall apart.

THE GUPTA EMPIRE (320 A.D. - 535 A.D.)

In 320 A.D., a new ruling family emerged, uniting the territory around the Ganges. The Guptas encouraged peace, prosperity, and trade with foreign lands, especially China. The two centuries of Gupta rule are sometimes referred to as the **Golden Age of Hindu Culture**.

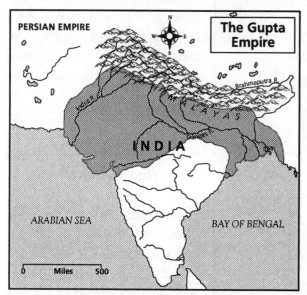

Gupta emperors built universities and supported the arts and literature. Indian scholars excelled in science. Indian mathematicians developed the use of zero, the concept of infinity, and a decimal system. An early form of Arabic numerals was also developed in India during this period. Artists painted colorful murals, while writers created poems and plays in Sanskrit. This period drew to a close around 500 A.D. The **Huns**, a warlike tribe from Central Asia, invaded northeastern India, breaking up the Gupta empire into smaller states.

CHINA'S CLASSICAL AGE

Like the flowering of Greek and Roman culture in the west, China witnessed some of its greatest cultural achievements during this era. Chinese history is generally divided into periods based on the **dynasty** that governed China at that time. From 1027 B.C. to 220 A.D., China was ruled by three dynasties.

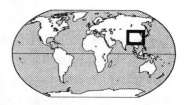

ZHOU DYNASTY (1027 B.C. - 221 B.C.)

In 1027 B.C the Shang were conquered, marking the beginning of the **Zhou dynasty**. The Chinese believed that their ruler was chosen by heaven, and that heaven would also overthrow a bad ruler. The new Zhou ruler therefore justified his rule as the **Mandate of Heaven**. Later Chinese rulers continued to use this mandate as the basis of their authority.

The Zhou dynasty was the longest reigning dynasty in Chinese history. Zhou rulers

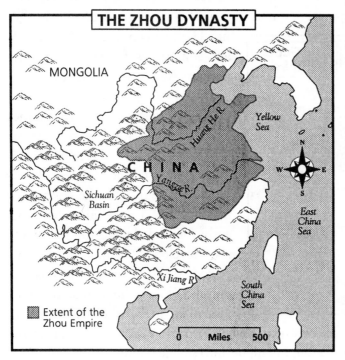

established a system known as **feudalism**, in which land was given to nobles in exchange for military service. Over the centuries, Zhou rulers conquered neighboring peoples and made them a part of China. However, by the 6th century B.C, local nobles became too powerful for the Zhou rulers to control, and China plunged into civil war.

The greatest legacy of the Zhou dynasty was the work of the Chinese philosophers **Confucius** and **Lao-zi** (*Lao Tzu*). Both thinkers were deeply affected by the turmoil at the end of the Zhou dynasty. For Confucius, the preservation of the social order, family, and government became the most important moral values. (You can read more about his philosophy on page 94.)

Daoism is a Chinese philosophy that began in the 5th century B.C, based on the teachings of **Lao-zi**. Its primary focus is the relationship between people and nature. Daoists believe that nature has a "way" in which it moves, and that people should passively accept the way of nature rather than to try to resist it. Daoists have a deep respect for nature and harmony, and accept things as they are rather than trying to change them.

QIN DYNASTY (221 B.C. - 206 B.C.)

Shi-Huangdi began a new dynasty and became the first Chinese ruler to call himself an emperor. He felt that all power should rest in the hands of a single, absolute ruler. **Shi-Huangdi** followed the philosophy of **Legalism**. He believed that people were not necessarily good and needed a strong government to punish those who committed bad acts.

Shi-Huangdi established a central administration and built roads to unite distant parts of China. Uniform systems of writing, weights, and measurement were established throughout the empire. He also joined together several existing protective walls to form the **Great Wall of China**, to protect his empire from invasion by nomadic peoples to the northwest. Stretching 1,500 miles, the wall eventually stood 22 feet high and 15 feet thick, and took thousands of laborers many years to complete.

HAN DYNASTY (206 B.C. - 220 A.D.)

Following Shi-Huangdi's death, people rebelled against his harsh style of rule. After several years of civil war, a new dynasty emerged. The Han emperors kept China unified for over four hundred years.

The Han emperors established official examinations to select candidates for imperial service. Candidates were tested on their knowledge of Chinese history and Confucian philosophy. Only those who passed these rigorous tests were eligible to assist the emperor in government tasks. Examinations were open to all and were viewed as a way for commoners to move up the social ladder. The Han emperors weakened the power of the nobles, and encouraged the spread of Confucian ideas.

Han rulers established overland trade routes such as the **Silk Road** through Central Asia, connecting China to the

Roman empire and other regions. Over these routes, China exported its silk, iron and

bronze in exchange for gold, linen, glass, ivory, animal hides, horses and cattle. Contacts with India led to the introduction of Buddhism, which spread throughout China. The end of the Han dynasty was followed by a period of civil war and disunity.

MAJOR RELIGIONS EMERGE

One of the most important aspects of the classical era was the emergence of major new religions and beliefs that have had a tremendous influence in all parts of the world.

CONFUCIANISM

Confucianism is named for its founder, Kung Fu Zi, also known as **Confucius** (551-479 B.C.). He lived during a time of turmoil and war in China. Confucius established a philosophy based on his belief in the basic order of the universe. He urged people to follow traditional ways that worked well in the past to achieve social peace and harmony.

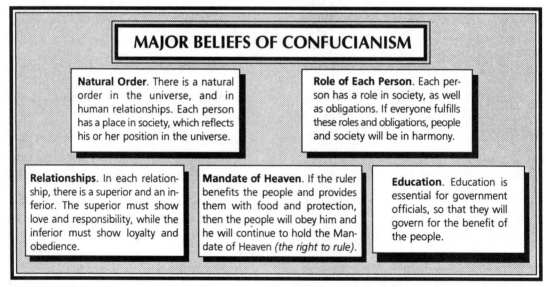

MAJOR BELIEFS OF CONFUCIANISM

Natural Order. There is a natural order in the universe, and in human relationships. Each person has a place in society, which reflects his or her position in the universe.

Role of Each Person. Each person has a role in society, as well as obligations. If everyone fulfills these roles and obligations, people and society will be in harmony.

Relationships. In each relationship, there is a superior and an inferior. The superior must show love and responsibility, while the inferior must show loyalty and obedience.

Mandate of Heaven. If the ruler benefits the people and provides them with food and protection, then the people will obey him and he will continue to hold the Mandate of Heaven *(the right to rule)*.

Education. Education is essential for government officials, so that they will govern for the benefit of the people.

For thousands of years, Confucianism remained the official philosophy of the Chinese empire. Its emphasis on traditional values such as obedience and order helped preserve Chinese civilization. Government officials had to pass a demanding test based on the writings of Confucius in order to be appointed to the emperor's service. Confucianism also strengthened the importance of the family in Chinese life. The family served as a model for society, emphasizing duties, good deeds, and a civilized way of life.

CHRISTIANITY

Christianity began in the Middle East about 2,000 years ago. It was based on the life and beliefs of **Jesus Christ**, who taught brotherhood, charity, and peace. After the death of Jesus, a band of his followers known as the **Apostles** helped to spread the Christian religion. Eventually Christianity became the dominant religion of the Roman empire.

MAJOR BELIEFS OF CHRISTIANITY

The Role Of Jesus. Christians believe Jesus was the son of God. Jesus sacrificed himself to save humans from punishment for their sins. Christians believe that after his death Jesus was resurrected and rose to Heaven.

Christian Conduct. Christians believe they will be saved and will to go to Heaven if they believe in Christ as their saviour and treat others with love and respect.

The Christian Bible. The sacred book of Christianity consists of the **Old Testament** (the Jewish Bible) and the **New Testament**, which describes the life of Christ and the works of the Apostles.

HINDUISM

The period from 1500 B.C. to 500 B.C. saw the formation of the Hindu religion. Hinduism was largely based on the beliefs of the Aryans — invaders who came to the Indus River Valley.

MAJOR BELIEFS OF HINDUISM

Gods. Hindus believe that there are many gods and goddesses. Vishnu is the creator and Shiva is the destroyer. Each of the gods and goddesses is a manifestation (form) of one Supreme Being.

Reincarnation. Hindus believe that at death, a person's soul is reborn as another living thing. There is an endless cycle of rebirth.

Sacred Objects. Hindus believe the Ganges River is sacred and has the power to wash away sin and evil. The cow is also considered sacred, and Hindus will not eat beef.

Karma. Karma refers to a person's behavior in life and determines one's form in the next life. People who have lived a worthy life will be reborn in a higher caste. Those who have not lived up to their duties will be reborn in a lower caste, or as some animal.

Like many religions, Hinduism provides believers with an entire way of life. It serves as a guide, explaining everything a person should do from birth to death. Hinduism has no holy book, but Hindu writings provide guidance and inspiration. Two texts containing the major beliefs of Hinduism are the **Upanishads** and the **Bhagavad-Gita**. Since more than 80% of India's population are Hindus, basic Hindu beliefs affect how most Indians live. There are more than 700 million Hindus in the world today.

BUDDHISM

The religion of Buddhism began in India around 600 B.C. Prince **Siddhartha Gautama** (563-487 B.C.) lived his entire youth in comfort and luxury. One day, he ventured beyond the palace walls and was shocked by all the human suffering he saw. This prompted him to leave his wife, his two children and his wealth and set out in search of truth. After six years of searching, he realized in a flash of insight that all suffering was caused by human desires. To end suffering, people must come to accept the world as it is and to block out their own desires.

Gautama became known as the **Buddha**, or "Enlightened One." Buddhism quickly attracted many followers. For one thing, it rejected the caste system. Missionaries carried Buddhist beliefs throughout India and eventually to China, Korea, and Japan.

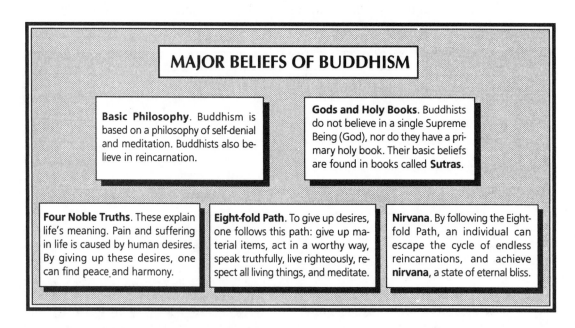

MAJOR BELIEFS OF BUDDHISM

Basic Philosophy. Buddhism is based on a philosophy of self-denial and meditation. Buddhists also believe in reincarnation.

Gods and Holy Books. Buddhists do not believe in a single Supreme Being (God), nor do they have a primary holy book. Their basic beliefs are found in books called **Sutras**.

Four Noble Truths. These explain life's meaning. Pain and suffering in life is caused by human desires. By giving up these desires, one can find peace and harmony.

Eight-fold Path. To give up desires, one follows this path: give up material items, act in a worthy way, speak truthfully, live righteously, respect all living things, and meditate.

Nirvana. By following the Eight-fold Path, an individual can escape the cycle of endless reincarnations, and achieve **nirvana**, a state of eternal bliss.

— STUDY CARDS —

Hinduism

The major religion of India. Beliefs include:

- **Supreme Being:** underlies all reality
- **Many Gods:** Vishnu (creator) and Shiva (destroyer) most important
- **Reincarnation:** endless cycle of death and rebirth
- **Karma:** a person's behavior determines one's level of existence in the next life

Confucianism

The major belief system of China, based on teachings of Confucius (551-497 B.C.). Beliefs include:
- **Virtue:** Each person should cultivate individual virtue through learning, kindness, humility
- **Hierarchy:** Each person in society has specific role and responsibilities to others
- **Mandate of Heaven:** Good rulers have the right to rule as long as they benefit their subjects and enjoy the Mandate of Heaven.

Buddhism

Major religion in China, Japan and Southeast Asia. Based on teachings of Siddhartha Gautama (known as Buddha), a prince who left riches behind in search of enlightenment. Beliefs include:

- **Meditation and self-denial:** all suffering is caused by excessive desire
- **Eightfold Path:** following this way of life, a person eventually achieves nirvana
- **Nirvana:** state of perfection and perpetual bliss

Greek City-States

Each city-state had its own form of government and system of laws. Two of the most noteworthy were:
- **Sparta:** totalitarian organization based on military needs
- **Athens:** first democracy; citizens voted on issues of the day. Citizenship was limited to certain Athenians, denied to many

Art, architecture, philosophy, drama, mathematics and science flourished during Athens' **Golden Age** (Pericles, Socrates, Plato, Aristotle)

Christianity

Major religion of Europe and the Americas. Beliefs include:

- **Jesus:** belief that Jesus was the Son of God and died to save humanity from its sins
- **Conduct:** emphasis on love, forgiveness, respect for human life
- **New Testament:** the Christian addition to the Hebrew Bible; their holy book
- **Major Strands:** Roman Catholic, Eastern Orthodox, various Protestant sects

Ancient Rome

Republic that became an empire, conquered the Mediterranean world and much of Europe. Romans adopted Greek culture and learning.

- **Law: Twelve Tablets, Code of Justinian**
- **Government:** Assembly and Senate adopted by later societies. **Pax Romana** (Roman Peace) ensured stability.
- **Architecture:** developed first domed structures; built stadiums, public baths, roads (**Appian Way**) and aqueducts throughout empire

COMPLETING A TABLE

Test questions about civilizations often focus on their accomplishments. To help you answer such questions, use the table below to organize this information.

NAME OF CIVILIZATION	TIME PERIOD	CONTINENT WHERE LOCATED	MAIN ACCOMPLISHMENTS
PERSIAN EMPIRE			
GREEK CITY-STATES			
ROMAN EMPIRE			
ZHOU DYNASTY			
GUPTA EMPIRE			

TESTING YOUR UNDERSTANDING

1   The political system of the Roman empire was characterized by
    (1) a strong central government
    (2) rule by a coalition of emperors and religious leaders
    (3) universal suffrage in national elections
    (4) national examinations in philosophy and religion

2   One of the greatest contributions of Greek and Roman civilizations to world culture was
    (1) the first alphabet   (3) the decimal system
    (2) monotheistic religion   (4) innovations in government and law

3   In both ancient Babylon and in the Roman republic, an important development was
    (1) a codified set of laws   (3) social and political equality for alll
    (2) aqueducts to provide water (4) acceptance of Christianity

Base your answer to question 4 on the pie chart and on your knowledge of global history.

4   Which is a valid conclusion based on the information in the chart?

(1) The city-state of Athens was a military dictatorship.

(2) Life in Athens was based on the ideal of social equality.

(3) Athens was a limited democracy, granting somecitizens the right to vote.

(4) The majority of Athenians had the right to vote.

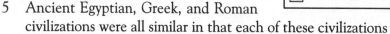

ATHENIAN VOTING AND NON-VOTING POPULATIONS, 450 B.C.

- 15% Male citizens
- 15% Wives of citizens
- 12% Foreigners
- 25% Children of citizens
- 33% Slaves

■ = Voting
▨ = Non-voting

5   Ancient Egyptian, Greek, and Roman civilizations were all similar in that each of these civilizations

(1) failed to develop a system of writing

(2) extended control over nearby peoples

(3) established industrial economies

(4) adopted democratic government

Base your answer to question 6 on the photograph to the right and on your knowledge of global history.

6   Which statement best explains why this structure was built?

(1) China sought to protect itself from invaders.

(2) Rome needed to keep out Germanic tribes.

(3) Persia wanted a highway to other civilizations.

(4) Chinese rulers needed to prevent peasants from escaping their harsh rule.

7   "There are two ends not to be sought by the seeker of truth. The first is the pursuit of desires, which is base, common, and unprofitable, and the second is the pursuit of hardship, which is grievous and unprofitable. The Middle Way avoids both of these. It is enlightened. It brings clear vision and leads to peace, insight, full wisdom, and nirvana."

The ideas contained in this statement reflect the beliefs of which religion?

(1) Buddhism

(2) Christianity

(3) Judaism

(4) Confucianism

INTERPRETING DOCUMENTS

"There are many kinds of government. Our definition of citizen works best for the citizens of a democracy. A citizen is one who shares in political office and in the administration of justice. Whoever has the power to take part in the government or judicial administration of the state is said by us to be a citizen."

—Adapted from Aristotle, *Politics*

1a   What kind of government does Aristotle describe? _____

 b   According to Aristotle, what is the role of the citizen in this kind of state?

THEMATIC ESSAY QUESTION

Directions: Write a well-organized essay that includes an introduction, several paragraphs addressing the task below, and a conclusion.

Theme: Belief Systems

> A people's religious or philosophical beliefs often play a major role in shaping their history and culture.

Task:

- Identify *two* religions or philosophical belief systems that have played a role in shaping the history and culture of a people. You may use a different culture for each belief system.
- Describe *two* basic beliefs of each religion or philosophy you selected.
- Explain how each religion or philosophy had an impact on its people's history and culture.

You may use any examples from your study of global history. Some suggestions you might wish to consider include Judaism, Greek mythology or philosophy, Christianity, Confucianism, Hinduism and Buddhism.

You are *not* limited to these suggestions.

DOCUMENT-BASED ESSAY QUESTION

This question is based on the accompanying documents (1-6). This question is designed to test your ability to work with historical documents. Some documents have been edited. As you analyze the documents, take into account both the source of each document and any point of view that may be presented in it.

Historical Context:
We owe a great debt to ancient civilizations. Their ideas and technologies laid foundations that still influence us today.

Task: Using information from the documents and your knowledge of global history, answer the questions that follow each document in Part A. Your answers to the questions will help you write the Part B essay, in which you will be asked to:

Discuss some of the achievements of ancient civilizations that still influence us today.

Part A — Short-Answer Questions

Directions: Analyze the documents and answer the questions that follow them.

DOCUMENT 1

If a seignior (*person of rank, like a lord*) destroys the eye of a member of the
    aristocracy, they shall destroy his eye.
If he knocks out a tooth of a seignior of his own rank, they shall knock out his
    tooth.
If he knocks out a commoner's tooth, he shall pay one-third mina (*amount*) of
    silver.

— *Code of Hammurabi,* 1750 B.C.

1 What was the significance of the Code of Hammurabi? _____

DOCUMENT 2

Selected letters from the Phoenician alphabet:
    Ҝ [A]   Ⴈ [E]   ↓ [K]   + [T]   O [O]

2 How did the Phoenician alphabet differ from earlier forms of writing? _____

DOCUMENT 3

1. I am the Lord your God. You shall have no other Gods before me.
2. You shall not make an idol (*image of a God*). You shall not bow down to them or worship them.
3. You shall not make wrongful use of the name of the Lord your God.
4. Remember the Sabbath and keep it holy.
5. Honor your father and mother.
6. You shall not kill.
7. You shall not commit adultery.
8. You shall not steal.
9. You shall not bear false witness against your neighbor.
10. You shall not covet anything that belongs to your neighbor.

— *The Ten Commandments*, from the Hebrew Bible

3a Which of these commandments illustrates monotheism? _____

b What is the basic idea behind the last six commandments?

_____

DOCUMENT 4

INDIVIDUAL	ACCOMPLISHMENT
Socrates	He challenged Athenians to question basic assumptions and to examine their own conduct to see if they were leading moral lives.
Plato	He extended Socrates' method of questioning to all areas of human knowledge. In his book *The Republic* he described an ideal society.
Aristotle	An observer of nature, he classified and analyzed plants and animals. He was the "father" of several disciplines, including physics and logic.
Archimedes	He was the first person to make a proof for the area of a circle, to explain the principle of levers, and to measure specific gravity.
Erastothenes	He computed the circumference of the Earth (*the distance around it*) to within 200 miles.
Euclid	He organized the study of geometry into vigorous logical proofs. His "elements" are still taught today.

4 What does this chart show about Greek ways of thinking? _____

_____

DOCUMENT 5

> "Our constitution does not copy the laws of neighboring states. Instead, others copy what we do. Our plan of government favors the many instead of the few; that is why it is called a democracy. As for laws, we offer equal justice to everyone. As for social standing, advancement is open to everyone, according to ability. High position does not depend on wealth."
>
> — *Pericles' Funeral Oration*, Athens, 5th century B.C.

5 In what ways did Pericles indicate that the government of Athens was innovative?

DOCUMENT 6

6a What religious leader is portrayed by this statue?

b State one belief of the religion he founded. ____

Part B — Essay

Directions: Write a well-organized essay that includes an introduction, several paragraphs, and a conclusion. Use evidence from at least **four** documents in the body of the essay. Support your response with relevant facts, examples, and details. Include additional outside information.

Historical Context: We owe a great debt to ancient civilizations. Their ideas and technologies laid foundations that still influence us today.

Task: Using information from the documents and your knowledge of global history and geography, write an essay in which you:

> Discuss some of the achievements of ancient civilizations that still influence us today.

Note: For *Regents Guidelines* for DBQs, re-read page 43.

ANALYZING THE DOCUMENTS

Use the answers you wrote after each document to help you complete the Document Box below. The first document and some related outside information have been provided for you.

— DOCUMENT BOX —

DOCUMENT	MAIN IDEA	CONTRIBUTION
1. (Code of Hammurabi)	• *Earliest known written code of laws* • *Consists of list of crimes and punishments* • *Punishments were based on social class*	*Written laws remain a basis for society today*
2. (Phoenician Alphabet)		
3. (Ten Command-ments)		
4. (Greek Contributions)		
5. (Pericles)		
6. (Statue)		

Analyze these docu-ments

Related outside information:

• *First civilizations developed picture writing to pass down knowledge, beliefs, skills*

•

•

Add related informa-tion

WRITING THE ANSWER

Now you should be ready to write your essay. The opening sentences and the first **part** of the essay have been completed for you. Complete the other parts of the essay. **Use** the information in your Document Box as a guide for your supporting details.

① Opening sentences give the historical context.

The first civilizations began in river valleys thousands of years ago. Their innovations — writing, the use of metals, cities — gradually spread to other regions. During the classical period, civilizations such as Greece and Rome developed high standards of art and learning, many of which still influence us today. The influence of ancient civilizations can be seen in four areas: writing, law, science and philosophy, and religion.

② The fourth sentence is the thesis statement.

③ The fourth sentence also serves as a transition to the four examples.

④ Second paragraph discusses first example. Write information from the documents in your own words.

The ancient world improved on the picture writing of the first civilizations, such as hieroglyphics, cuneiform, and Chinese writing, which had thousands of characters. Document 2 shows some letters from the Phoenician alphabet, which had a smaller number of symbols, each representing a particular sound. This made it easier to learn reading and writing. Over time, the Phoenician alphabet evolved into the alphabet we use in English today.

⑤ Outside information related to the example is added here.

⑥ This sentence ties document to thesis statement.

⑦ Your next three paragraphs should discuss the other examples supporting your thesis statement. Be sure to tie in other documents or related outside information.

A second area in which ancient civilizations still influence us today is in the development of systems of laws. Laws provide a set of rules that members of society must obey. The first known written law was developed in Mesopotamia, and is known as the Code of Hammurabi. Part of this law code is shown in Document 1. Laws further evolved during Roman times, when _____

_____

_____

A third way that ancient civilizations influence us today is by their having introduced science and philosophy. _____

_____

_____

_____

continued...

A fourth area in which ancient civilizations still influence us today is through religion. Several major religions trace their origins to the ancient world. _____

_____

_____

_____

_____

_____

Therefore, we can see that the civilizations of ancient times laid the foundations for many of our beliefs and ways of doing things today. These range from written languages and religions to our system of laws and our scientific and philosophical knowledge.

⑧ Your closing paragraph should restate the thesis statement and refer to your examples: in this case, writing, religions, law, science and philosophy.

NOTE: To further help you answer document-based essay questions, at the end of each later chapter you will find a document-based exercise. Each exercise will require you to relate a sample document to a thesis statement. In addition, you will find complete document-based essay questions at the end of Chapters 12, 13, 14 and 15.

CHAPTER 9

NEW CENTERS OF CULTURE IN AN AGE OF TURMOIL, 500-1200 A.D.

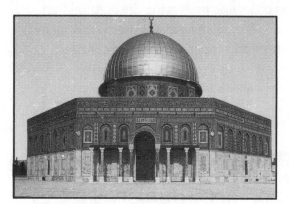

The Dome of the Rock in Jerusalem

KEY TERMS, CONCEPTS AND PEOPLE

• Byzantine Empire	• Manors
• Mohammed	• Serfs
• Islam	• Crusades
• Qu'ran	• Cultural Diffusion
• Middle Ages	• T'ang/Sung Dynasties
• Charlemagne	• Heian Period, Japan
• Feudalism	• Samurai

	500	620	740	860	980	1100	1220
BYZANTIUM	BYZANTINE EMPIRE						
RUSSIA				EMERGENCE OF KIEVAN RUSSIA			
EUROPE	MIDDLE AGES:						
	BARBARIAN INVASIONS	RISE OF FRANKS		VIKING INVASIONS		CHRISTIAN CRUSADES	
MIDDLE EAST		ISLAMIC EXPANSION			ISLAMIC WORLD		
						SELJUK TURKS INVADE	
CHINA		T'ANG DYNASTY			SUNG DYNASTY		
JAPAN			HEIAN PERIOD				

	500	620	740	860	980	1100	1220

WHAT YOU SHOULD FOCUS ON

In the 400s, a period of great turmoil began. In the West, the Roman empire finally collapsed. In the East, civil war followed the fall of the Han dynasty in China. Both empires fell to nomadic invaders. Much of the rest of this period was spent rebuilding systems of law and order and preserving the cultural heritage of the ancient world in the face of constant invasions. After the Roman and Han empires fell, four regions of the world experienced great changes:

Byzantium: The eastern part of the Roman empire continued for another 1,000 years under the name of the Byzantine empire. It preserved much of Roman and Greek culture, and developed its own type of Christianity.

Middle East: A new religion appeared in the 7th century. Arab nomads swept across Southwest Asia and North Africa establishing a new Islamic empire, while absorbing local traditions.

CHANGES AFTER THE FALL OF ROME AND THE COLLAPSE OF THE HAN DYNASTY

Western Europe: Much of the Greek and Roman heritage was lost. Christianity became the main binding force. A new method of social and political organization emerged, known as feudalism.

China: Basic patterns of Chinese culture re-emerged after a long period of civil war. China was also affected by a new religious impulse: Buddhism. Meanwhile, Chinese culture spread into Japan.

In contrast to Western Europe, great centers of culture and urbanization remained in China, the Islamic world, and Byzantium. These areas experienced "Golden Ages" where the arts and technology flourished. By the end of this era, the Crusades brought Europeans into greater contact with these other societies.

In reviewing this era, keep in mind that test writers are most likely to ask you questions about the following:

* What were the main cultural achievements of this era?
* What role did the great religions — Christianity, Islam, and Buddhism — play in the events of this period?
* What was feudalism, and how did it operate?

LOOKING AT GOVERNMENT

The ancient Greek philosopher Aristotle once wrote that "man is a political animal." By this he meant that people are social beings. They cannot live in isolation, but depend on one another and live in communities.

WHAT IS GOVERNMENT?

This need to be with others has important consequences. All communities must make rules to decide disputes among their members and to protect themselves from others who may be hostile. The body given the authority to carry out these functions is known as the **government**. The word "govern" comes from the ancient Greek word for steering a ship. Just as a pilot guides a ship, a government guides the conduct and behavior of the members of a community in their dealings with themselves and outsiders.

WHAT FORMS DO GOVERNMENTS TAKE?

Throughout history, governments have taken many forms. The following presents a chronological survey of some of the more important ones.

TRIBAL GOVERNMENTS
In primitive societies, people were often governed by tribal elders or a chief. Most often the tribal elders or chiefs were respected members of the tribe with skills in warfare or great wisdom. Because there were no written laws, people relied on oral traditions, customs, and the decisions of their leaders.

ANCIENT MONARCHIES
In the ancient civilizations of Mesopotamia, Egypt, India, China, and the Americas, one leader eventually emerged as an all-powerful king. Usually the king claimed to act as a god, combining political and religious powers. The king extended his power over others when his armies conquered their neighbors.

DEMOCRACY

The ancient Athenians were the first to develop **democracy** — rule by the people. Citizens elected their leaders and often made decisions directly by voting in a large assembly. For a democracy to work, citizens must have basic rights such as freedom of speech and the press, the right to organize, freedom from imprisonment without proper cause, and the right to a fair trial.

FEUDALISM

Feudalism was a social and political system that often emerged in areas where central government was weak. The king relied on the services of his loyal nobles, who had almost absolute power over their own local areas.

DIVINE RIGHT MONARCHY OR ABSOLUTISM

Under divine right monarchy, also known as **absolutism,** rulers such as Louis XIV of France controlled their subjects by claiming to derive their authority directly from God. Other monarchs justified their absolutism by declaring that they could provide the fairest and most efficient government when they had total power. Writers such as Machiavelli and Thomas Hobbes believed that human nature was essentially bad, and that a strong ruler was needed to maintain society. Centuries earlier, Shi-Huangdi had taken the same view in China.

THE SOCIAL CONTRACT AND CONSTITUTIONAL MONARCHY

In the late 17th century, John Locke proposed the **social contract theory**. According to Locke, a king ruled with the consent of his subjects. The subjects entered into a contract with the king, promising to obey him as long as he protected their rights. This system, in which the king governs according to a constitution, is known as a **constitutional monarchy**. If the king violated his subjects' rights, Locke said, the people had a right to overthrow him.

TOTALITARIANISM

Totalitarianism is a 20th century system similar to earlier royal absolutism. A dictator claims to rule in the name of the people. Individual citizens have no real rights. The government controls all aspects of public and private life. Modern technology makes totalitarianism far more ruthless than royal absolutism had ever been. Hitler's Germany, Stalin's Soviet Union and Mao's China are examples of 20th century totalitarian states.

MAJOR
HISTORICAL DEVELOPMENTS

NEW CENTERS OF CULTURE

Two new centers of culture emerged during this period. The Byzantines and Arabs controlled large empires in Eastern Europe and the Middle East.

THE BYZANTINE EMPIRE (330 - 1453)

In 330 A.D., Emperor Constantine moved the capital of the Roman empire from Rome to Byzantium, a Greek city in the eastern part of the empire. He renamed it Constantinople. The city was strategically located on the Bosporus Strait, a waterway connecting the Black Sea to the Mediterranean. The city was surrounded on three sides by water and by thick walls, making it almost invulnerable to attack.

THE BYZANTINES DEVELOP A UNIQUE CULTURE

Although the western part of the Roman empire collapsed in the 5th century, the eastern half of the old Roman empire, called the Byzantine empire, survived for another thousand years. The Byzantines maintained the imperial system of government over a diverse population. They also developed their own form of Christianity, known as Eastern

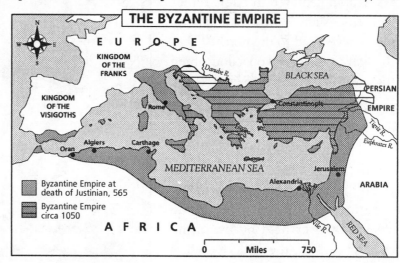

THE BYZANTINE EMPIRE

EUROPE
KINGDOM OF THE FRANKS
Danube R.
BLACK SEA
KINGDOM OF THE VISIGOTHS
Rome
Constantinople
PERSIAN EMPIRE
Tigris R.
Euphrates R.
Algiers   Carthage
Oran
MEDITERRANEAN SEA
Jerusalem
Alexandria
ARABIA
▨ Byzantine Empire at death of Justinian, 565
▨ Byzantine Empire circa 1050
AFRICA
Nile R.
RED SEA
0   Miles   750

Orthodox Christianity, separate from the Roman Catholic Church. Unlike Rome, the main language of the Byzantine empire was Greek.

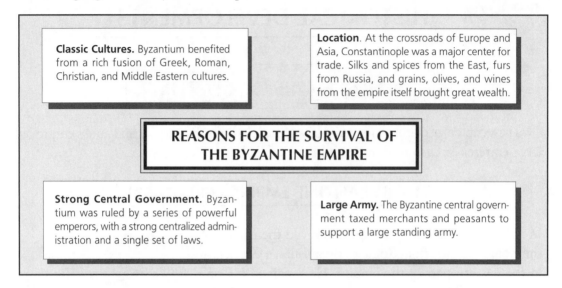

Classic Cultures. Byzantium benefited from a rich fusion of Greek, Roman, Christian, and Middle Eastern cultures.

Location. At the crossroads of Europe and Asia, Constantinople was a major center for trade. Silks and spices from the East, furs from Russia, and grains, olives, and wines from the empire itself brought great wealth.

REASONS FOR THE SURVIVAL OF THE BYZANTINE EMPIRE

Strong Central Government. Byzantium was ruled by a series of powerful emperors, with a strong centralized administration and a single set of laws.

Large Army. The Byzantine central government taxed merchants and peasants to support a large standing army.

BYZANTINE INFLUENCE ON RUSSIA

Russia began as an organized state in the 800s. A group of tribes known as **Slavs** came to dominate the region. Viking raiders organized the Slavs into a kingdom centered in **Kiev**. Other early cities such as Moscow and Novgorod developed to the north. These Russian cities carried on a flourishing trade with the Byzantine empire.

RUSSIA IN THE KIEVAN PERIOD

Extent of Kievan Rus in 1054

Byzantium influenced Russia in significant ways. Byzantine culture — especially Eastern Orthodox Christianity, the Cyrillic alphabet, and Byzantine crafts and products — were introduced into Russia. The absolute power held by Byzantine emperors became the model for future Russian rulers.

DECLINE OF THE BYZANTINE EMPIRE

The size of the empire varied over time. In its early centuries, it ruled over the Balkans, the Middle East, and parts of Italy. Under **Justinian** (527-565), the Byzantines reconquered much of the old Roman empire. But they had to continuously battle the Slavs and Avars to the north, the Persian empire to the east, and the spread of Islam to its south. In the 600s, Muslim Arabs took most of the empire's territory in the Middle East.

The final decline of Byzantium began in the 11th century. City-states in northern Italy began competing with Constantinople for Mediterranean trade. The **Seljuk Turks,** a nomadic people originally from Central Asia, defeated the Byzantines in 1071. They took most of Asia Minor, except for Constantinople itself. But the Byzantines still controlled the Balkans and survived for another 400 years. The empire eventually unraveled under constant attacks. By the 1440s, the great Byzantine empire was reduced to a small area around Constantinople. In 1453, the city was conquered by the Ottoman Turks.

THE LEGACY OF THE BYZANTINE EMPIRE

The roots of Eastern European culture can be traced to the contributions of Byzantium.

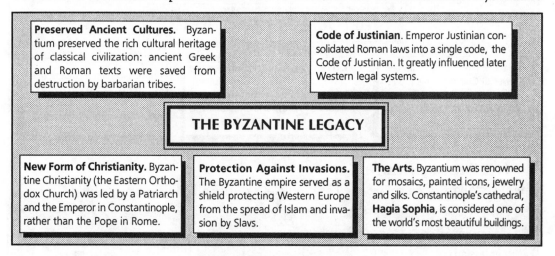

Preserved Ancient Cultures. Byzantium preserved the rich cultural heritage of classical civilization: ancient Greek and Roman texts were saved from destruction by barbarian tribes.

Code of Justinian. Emperor Justinian consolidated Roman laws into a single code, the Code of Justinian. It greatly influenced later Western legal systems.

THE BYZANTINE LEGACY

New Form of Christianity. Byzantine Christianity (the Eastern Orthodox Church) was led by a Patriarch and the Emperor in Constantinople, rather than the Pope in Rome.

Protection Against Invasions. The Byzantine empire served as a shield protecting Western Europe from the spread of Islam and invasion by Slavs.

The Arts. Byzantium was renowned for mosaics, painted icons, jewelry and silks. Constantinople's cathedral, **Hagia Sophia**, is considered one of the world's most beautiful buildings.

THE RISE OF ISLAM

In the 600s, a new religion — Islam — emerged on the Arabian Peninsula. Within a hundred years, Islam controlled an area larger than the Roman empire at its height. The fall of Rome paved the way for the rise of this new force.

Warfare between the Byzantine and Persian empires had interrupted overland trade routes from East Asia. Trade in spices, Chinese silks, and Indian cottons shifted to the sea routes connecting India with Arabia and the Red Sea. Overland caravans carried goods up the western coast of the Arabian peninsula. Cities and towns developed at oases along these caravan routes. **Mecca** was one of the most important of these cities.

MOHAMMED, THE PROPHET OF ISLAM

The Islamic religion was founded by an Arab merchant named **Mohammed.** He was influenced by his contact with Jews and Christians. Mohammed had a vision that an angel commanded him to convert the Arab tribes, who then believed in many gods, to belief in a single God, known in Arabic as "**Allah.**" This was meant to be the same God worshipped by Jews and Christians. After his vision, Mohammed started to preach his beliefs. Merchants in Mecca disliked Mohammed's demand that they donate money to the poor, and feared his growing influence. Afraid for his life, Mohammed fled to the city of Medina in 622. This event, known as the **Hegira,** is the starting point of the Muslim calendar. In Medina, Mohammed became a popular religious leader. He gathered an army and captured Mecca in a **jihad** or "holy war." Two years later, in 632, Mohammed died.

THE FOUNDATIONS OF ISLAM

Allah. Allah is the one all-powerful God who will judge all people at the end of the world. The word *Islam* means "surrendering to God."

Qu'ran. The Qu'ran (*Koran*) is the sacred book. It consists of Mohammed's teachings, including the Five Pillars of Faith, and provides the basis for Islam's legal system.

Jihad. Mohammed taught that anyone who died in a "Holy War" (*jihad*) to spread Islam would go directly to heaven.

THE FIVE PILLARS OF FAITH

The Five Pillars of Faith are the basic religious duties all Muslims must fulfill:

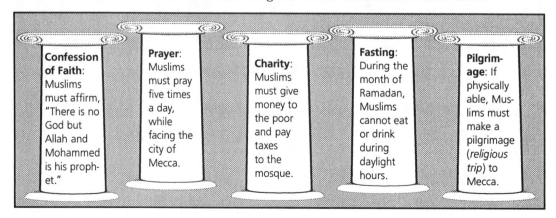

Confession of Faith: Muslims must affirm, "There is no God but Allah and Mohammed is his prophet."

Prayer: Muslims must pray five times a day, while facing the city of Mecca.

Charity: Muslims must give money to the poor and pay taxes to the mosque.

Fasting: During the month of Ramadan, Muslims cannot eat or drink during daylight hours.

Pilgrimage: If physically able, Muslims must make a pilgrimage (*religious trip*) to Mecca.

THE ISLAMIC RELIGION SPREADS (630-800)

Islam united the tribes of Arabia, who shared a common language (*Arabic*). The Arabs then began a "holy war" against non-believers. They were desert fighters who fought with zeal to gain entry into heaven, while the Byzantines and Persians were weak from centuries of war. Within 100 years the Arabs created a vast empire, from Spain to India.

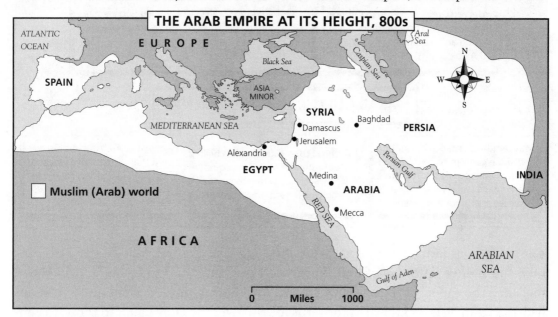

THE ARAB EMPIRE AT ITS HEIGHT, 800s

ARAB METHODS OF RULE

Arabs converted or enslaved conquered peoples who worshipped many gods. At first, non-Arab converts had fewer rights than Arabs, but later all Muslims were treated equally. Jews and Christians were respected as the "People of the Book" (*the Bible*), since Arabs believed they worshipped the same God. However, they were forced to pay special taxes and could not hold many public offices.

When Mohammed died, his followers chose a new leader whom they called the **caliph** or "successor to Mohammed." Caliphs from the Umayyad family moved the capital of the Islamic empire to Damascus (*in present-day Syria*). After 750, a new family called the **Abbasids** took over the caliphate and moved the capital to Baghdad (*in present-day Iraq*). The caliph became an absolute ruler surrounded by a lavish court.

THE GOLDEN AGE OF ISLAMIC CULTURE

During this era, while learning had declined in Western Europe, a **Golden Age of Islamic Culture** occurred — a period of great advances in culture and technology. The

Arabs absorbed the cultural achievements of the Greeks, Persians, Romans, Jews, and Byzantines. They also controlled a vast trading area — larger than the old Roman empire. The Islamic empire, like Byzantium before it, became a crossroads of trade. Goods from India, China, Africa, Spain, and the Mediterranean criss-crossed Arab territories.

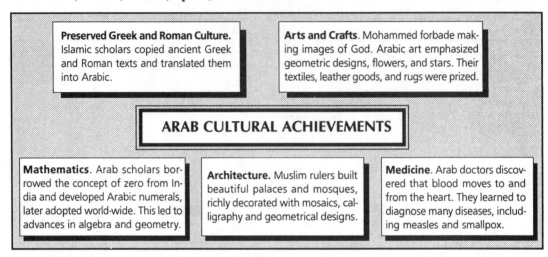

Preserved Greek and Roman Culture. Islamic scholars copied ancient Greek and Roman texts and translated them into Arabic.

Arts and Crafts. Mohammed forbade making images of God. Arabic art emphasized geometric designs, flowers, and stars. Their textiles, leather goods, and rugs were prized.

ARAB CULTURAL ACHIEVEMENTS

Mathematics. Arab scholars borrowed the concept of zero from India and developed Arabic numerals, later adopted world-wide. This led to advances in algebra and geometry.

Architecture. Muslim rulers built beautiful palaces and mosques, richly decorated with mosaics, calligraphy and geometrical designs.

Medicine. Arab doctors discovered that blood moves to and from the heart. They learned to diagnose many diseases, including measles and smallpox.

The prosperous Islamic empire attracted invaders from Central Asia. In the 11th century, the **Seljuk Turks** captured Baghdad. They converted to Islam, and Baghdad remained the capital of their new empire. In the 12th century, Muslims and Christians had a series of wars — known as the **Crusades** — over the Holy Land. In the 13th century, the Islamic world was invaded by the Mongols, who destroyed Baghdad in 1258.

A NEW SOCIETY EMERGES IN WESTERN EUROPE

While the Byzantine and Arab empires emerged as new cultural centers, important changes were occurring in Western Europe. Historians sometimes refer to this era of European history — from the fall of Rome to the 1400s — as the **Middle Ages** or Medieval period.

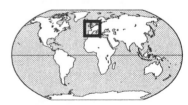

A NEW POLITICAL AND SOCIAL ORDER

Beyond Rome's frontiers lived Germanic tribes such as the Goths, Vandals, Lombards, Burgundians, and Franks. Romans considered these peoples uncivilized "barbarians." In the 300s, a war-like tribe known as the Huns moved from Central Asia to Europe.

BARBARIAN INVASIONS

As the Huns moved into Europe, they forced the Germanic tribes to move westward. These Germanic tribes pushed forward into the Roman empire. The Visigoths defeated a Roman army and sacked the city of Rome in 410. Germanic tribes gradually established kingdoms in many parts of the former Roman empire. The Angles and Saxons invaded England, while the Visigoths occupied Spain. The Lombards occupied northern Italy and the Franks conquered Gaul (*present-day France*). Gradually, these tribes adopted Christianity.

The constant warfare disrupted trade. Travel was not safe because of violence. Bridges and roads fell into disrepair. People stopped using money. Cities and towns were abandoned. People gave up their interest in learning as shortages of food and other goods grew.

BARBARIAN KINGDOMS IN EUROPE, 500 A.D.

THE RISE OF THE FRANKS

The **Franks** established the largest of the new Germanic kingdoms, in present-day France. At first divided into small groups, the Franks were united by **Clovis** in the 490s. After his death, the Frankish kingdom again divided into smaller states. Powerful men became landowners. Peasants built their huts around each landowner's home and grew crops.

Eventually, one of the leading noble families came to power. **Charles Martel** reunited the Frankish kingdom. He created a powerful army by granting lands to the chief Frankish nobles in exchange for their military service. In 732, at the **Battle of Tours,**

Martel stopped the advance of Muslim forces into Western Europe. In 751, his son **Pepin** seized power and made himself King of the Franks. With the support of the Pope, Pepin marched across the Alps and took control of northern Italy.

THE RULE OF CHARLEMAGNE

Pepin's son, known as **Charlemagne** (*Charles the Great*), became king in 768. Charlemagne expanded the practice of giving land to his nobles in exchange for their promises of loyalty and service. Nobles would answer the king's summons by serving in his army with their knights. The chief nobles, in turn, gave land to those below them in exchange for similar promises. Peasants put themselves in service to their local lords in order to gain security. Charlemagne expanded the Frankish kingdom to include present-day France, Germany, Holland, Belgium, and northern Italy.

Charlemagne established his new capital at Aachen, which he turned into a center of learning. Churches and monasteries opened schools. At the request of the Pope, Charlemagne was crowned emperor of the "**Holy Roman Empire**" in 800. In effect, this act announced that Western Europe was independent from the Byzantine emperor. The crowning of Charlemagne also signified the merging of the political and religious unity of Western Europe under the concept of **Christendom** — the unity of all Western Europeans in the Roman Catholic faith. After Charlemagne's death, his empire was divided among his sons. Although his empire did not last, Charlemagne laid the cultural and political foundations for Western Europe for the next several centuries.

EUROPE FACES NEW THREATS

The division of Charlemagne's empire occurred just as Europe faced new threats. From the east, the Slavs and Magyars invaded the lands of present-day Germany, France, and Italy. From North Africa, Muslims attacked southern Italy. However, the greatest new threat came from the **Vikings** — farmers and sailors from Scandinavia, located in the northernmost part of Europe. The Vikings sailed south in search of trade, loot, and land.

Between 800 and 1000, the Vikings launched repeated assaults on the coasts of Western Europe, often committing atrocities. Although spreading fear and destruction in their path, the Vikings also opened up new trade routes. The Vikings shared a common language, religion, and way of life. Their longboats were easy to maneuver and could sail in heavy seas or close to the land. In some places, such as northern England, the Vikings established new settlements; in others, they mixed with local peoples.

FEUDAL SOCIETY IN EUROPE

To protect themselves from violence and provide for basic economic needs, people throughout Western Europe adopted the Frankish system known as **feudalism**. It helped people survive the breakdown of central government and order. Feudalism in Europe was characterized by a number of key social, economic, and political relationships.

SOCIAL

A major characteristic of feudal society was the development of a strict class structure based on the control of land and military power. People born as serfs, knights, or lords could not change their social position. Local nobles (*lords*) were given land by their rulers in exchange for military service. These lords had small armies of their own made up of **knights**, armed warriors on horseback.

ECONOMIC

During the Middle Ages, most people lived on **manors**. A manor consisted of the lord's house, peasant huts on the surrounding land, and fields for planting. Each manor produced its own food, clothing, and shelter. **Serfs** (*peasants*) gave their lord part of their harvest in return for the use of land and other services they needed. In exchange, the lord protected the serfs from attacks by outsiders. Each lord had almost complete power over the serfs who lived on his manor. He could pass laws, impose taxes, and act as a judge. Serfs were bound to the land and had no voice in most matters.

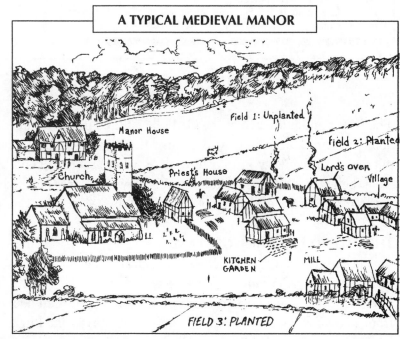

A TYPICAL MEDIEVAL MANOR

Field 1: Unplanted

Manor House

Field 2: Planted

Lord's oven

Village

Priest's House

Church

KITCHEN GARDEN

MILL

FIELD 3: PLANTED

POLITICAL

Under the feudal system, the king and his leading nobles controlled political life. The king relied on the nobles for his armies, and the nobles often fought among themselves or challenged the king's authority. Civil wars were frequent, and powerful nobles often grabbed the throne for themselves.

THE AGE OF FAITH

During the Middle Ages, the Catholic Church remained the single most powerful organization in Western Europe. There were many reasons for this:

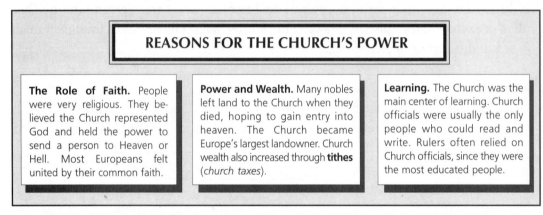

REASONS FOR THE CHURCH'S POWER

The Role of Faith. People were very religious. They believed the Church represented God and held the power to send a person to Heaven or Hell. Most Europeans felt united by their common faith.

Power and Wealth. Many nobles left land to the Church when they died, hoping to gain entry into heaven. The Church became Europe's largest landowner. Church wealth also increased through **tithes** (*church taxes*).

Learning. The Church was the main center of learning. Church officials were usually the only people who could read and write. Rulers often relied on Church officials, since they were the most educated people.

THE CRUSADES (1096 - 1291)

The power and influence of the Catholic Church in the Middle Ages can be seen in its ability to carry out a "holy war" against the Muslims. For hundreds of years, Christian pilgrims had regularly visited Jerusalem, where sacred events described in the Bible were believed to have taken place. However, in the 11th century the Seljuk Turks took control of the "Holy Land" and drove out Christian pilgrims.

THE CALL TO FREE THE HOLY LAND

Shocked and angered, in 1095 Pope **Urban II** called on all Christians in Europe to unite and fight a holy **Crusade** — a war to recapture the Holy Land from its Muslim rulers. Seven Crusades, fought over two centuries, resulted. The Crusades brought together people from all over Europe in a common cause; even kings, like England's **Richard the Lionhearted**, participated. Although the Crusaders never regained permanent control of the Holy Land, the Crusades had important effects:

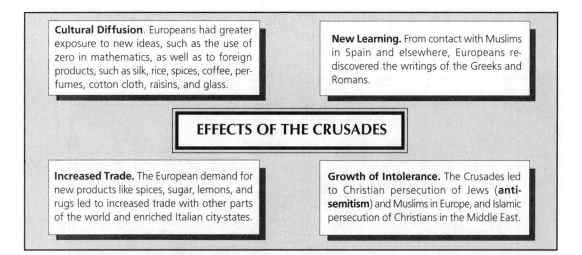

Cultural Diffusion. Europeans had greater exposure to new ideas, such as the use of zero in mathematics, as well as to foreign products, such as silk, rice, spices, coffee, perfumes, cotton cloth, raisins, and glass.

New Learning. From contact with Muslims in Spain and elsewhere, Europeans rediscovered the writings of the Greeks and Romans.

EFFECTS OF THE CRUSADES

Increased Trade. The European demand for new products like spices, sugar, lemons, and rugs led to increased trade with other parts of the world and enriched Italian city-states.

Growth of Intolerance. The Crusades led to Christian persecution of Jews (**anti-semitism**) and Muslims in Europe, and Islamic persecution of Christians in the Middle East.

SURVIVAL OF THE CHINESE TRADITION

Like Western Europe after the fall of the Roman empire, China entered a long period of turmoil and unrest after the collapse of the Han dynasty in 220. As in the West, the advance of the Huns helped plunge China into disarray. Several warring kingdoms arose, while science, art, and culture declined. In these years, Buddhism spread through much of China. This period of China's history is known as the **Six Dynasties**. It was several hundred years before China re-emerged as a leading world civilization under the T'ang.

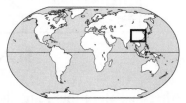

T'ANG DYNASTY (618-907)

During the **T'ang dynasty**, China experienced a **Golden Age**. T'ang rulers reunited China and brought peace and prosperity. They ruled over an immense empire of more than 50 million people. T'ang rulers expanded China into Korea, Manchuria, and parts of Central Asia. The government took careful censuses (*population counts*), gave examinations to candidates for government service, and built public works.

There were also great advances in architecture, sculpture, painting, and porcelain. The Chinese developed unique methods of gardening — with streams, rocks, and trees —

designed for peaceful contemplation. T'ang China also developed block printing, so that copies of Confucian texts could be printed to help candidates for government service prepare for their examinations. During these centuries, China benefited from contact and trade with Arabs, Persians, Japanese, and Byzantines.

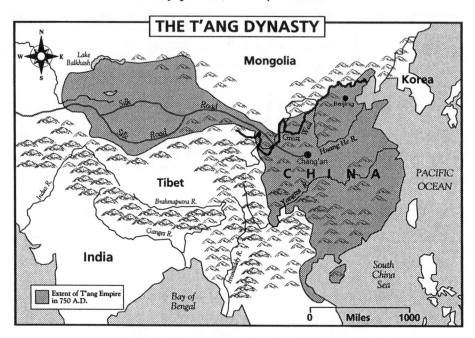

SUNG DYNASTY (960-1279)

After the fall of the T'ang dynasty in 907, China again decreased in size. In 960, the **Sung dynasty** was founded. A rival dynasty was later established in the north, with its capital at Beijing. Despite this further reduction in size and power, Sung China continued to build upon the cultural achievements of the T'ang.

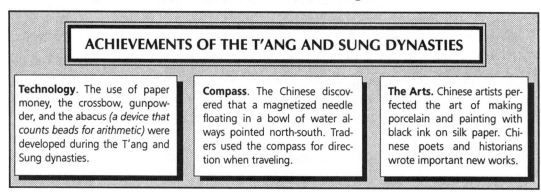

ACHIEVEMENTS OF THE T'ANG AND SUNG DYNASTIES

Technology. The use of paper money, the crossbow, gunpowder, and the abacus *(a device that counts beads for arithmetic)* were developed during the T'ang and Sung dynasties.

Compass. The Chinese discovered that a magnetized needle floating in a bowl of water always pointed north-south. Traders used the compass for direction when traveling.

The Arts. Chinese artists perfected the art of making porcelain and painting with black ink on silk paper. Chinese poets and historians wrote important new works.

Sung China was the most populous and advanced civilization of its time. Merchants, craftspeople, and scholars lived in the larger towns and cities. The Sung capital housed more than a million people. The Chinese engaged in trade with many other parts of the world. Caravans carried Chinese silks across Central Asia. Large ships brought Chinese goods to Korea, Japan, Southeast Asia, India, and Africa.

JAPAN'S EARLY HISTORY

One of the areas to be most influenced by Chinese culture was Japan. Society in ancient Japan revolved around **clans** — groups of families who had common ancestors and followed the same chief. Early Japanese worshipped **Kami** (*spirits found in nature*), giving rise to a religion called **Shintoism**. By the 5th century, the leader of one clan had unified the country and established himself as emperor. To strengthen his authority, the emperor claimed to be descended directly from the Sun Goddess.

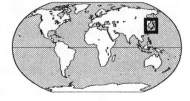

CHINA'S INFLUENCE ON JAPAN
Japan's location close to China encouraged **cultural diffusion**. Scholars and merchants brought many aspects of Chinese culture to Japan, including Confucianism and Buddhism, and the Chinese method of writing. The Japanese were impressed by the quality of Chinese products, like silks and pottery. Chinese music, art, weaving, building, dance and even cooking influenced the Japanese. Chinese ideas of Buddhism, Confucianism, and Daoism interacted with Japanese beliefs to shape new values and beliefs. Confucianism instilled loyalty to the family and ruler. Buddhism taught the Japanese to renounce selfish desires, while Daoism encouraged a love of nature. Japanese rulers deliberately borrowed from China. The Japanese emperor set up an imperial court, similar to the one in China, and declared himself to be an absolute ruler.

Although greatly influenced by China, Japanese society never became an exact copy of China. The Japanese never adopted the Chinese belief that a ruler could be overthrown by the Mandate of Heaven, since they believed their emperor was descended from the gods. The Japanese nobles also rejected the idea of taking examinations for imperial service.

JAPAN'S GOLDEN AGE: THE HEIAN PERIOD (794-1185)

In 794, the Japanese emperor moved his capital to **Heian** (*present-day Kyoto*). His lavish court was supported by a vast system of taxes. All land belonged to the emperor, who lent it to the nobles and peasant farmers for their use. In return, peasants were required to pay a portion of their crops to the imperial tax collectors.

During the Heian period, Japan's **Golden Age**, members of the leading noble families spent much of their time at the emperor's court. Art and literature flourished. *The Tale of Genji*, one of the first novels ever written and a great classic of Japanese literature, was completed around 1008 by **Lady Murasaki** of the imperial court. The novel tells the story of Genji, the emperor's son, and his many romances and adventures.

As time passed, later emperors freed some of the nobles from their tax burdens. Those who brought new lands under cultivation were also allowed to keep them as private lands. Many nobles were able to establish large private estates. By the end of the Heian period, noble landowners began to raise their own private armies of warriors, known as **samurai**. The imperial government, collecting less taxes, grew weaker. In 1156, warfare broke out among Japan's leading noble families.

— STUDY CARDS —

Byzantine Empire	**Middle Ages**
Was a continuation of the Roman Empire in the east. Capital was **Constantinople**. • Preserved Greek and Roman heritage • **Code of Justinian** influenced later legal systems • **Eastern Orthodox Church** spread to Russia and Eastern Europe • Stopped spread of Islam to Western Europe	Time in Western Europe from fall of Rome in the 400s to about 1400. • Barbarian invasions, Viking raids; most Greek and Roman learning was lost • New social, political, and economic order developed, called **feudalism** • **Roman Catholic Church** grew to be most powerful organization in Western Europe
Islam	**Charlemagne**
Religion founded by **Mohammed** in Arabia in 622. Beliefs include: • **Five Pillars of Faith: Allah** (Arabic for God) is the only God, and Mohammed is his prophet; 5 daily prayers; give to charity; fast during month of Ramadan; make at least one pilgrimage to Mecca if possible • **Qu'ran** (Koran): Islam's holy book	King of the Franks; became Holy Roman Emperor in 800. • Extended Frankish practice of feudalism • Expanded the Frankish kingdom, spreading Christianity and countering Islamic influence and power • Revived literacy and learning by establishing church schools

(continued)

Feudalism

A Frankish social organization developed after breakdown of central government in Western Europe; based on use of land for service.
- **Classes**: **Lord** at top; held **manor** and its farmland; **Knights** fought for Lord (loyalty in exchange for being housed, fed, and clothed); **Serfs** were bound to the land from birth, farmed it for the Lord

T'ang and Sung Dynasties (China)

In this period (618-1279) China became world's most advanced civilization. The **T'ang** ruled vast empire (China, Korea, parts of Central Asia). The **Sung** advanced technology and the arts.

T'ang and Sung Achievements:
- Block printing, gunpowder, abacus, compass
- Porcelain, painting on silk paper, gardens

Crusades (1096-1291)

Christians waged series of religious wars against Muslims for control of Holy Land (Jerusalem).

Consequences:
- New products introduced into Europe
- Europe exposed to new ideas
- Christian persecution of Muslims and Jews, Muslim persecution of Christians

Heian Period (Japan)

- **Borrowing from China:** Japan's location next to China led to spread of Chinese culture in Japan: writing, silk, rice cultivation, art, Confucianism, imperial government.
- **Japan's Golden Age:** During Heian Period, art and literature flourished, including the world's first known novel, **The Tale of Genji**, by Lady Murasaki

SUMMARIZING YOUR UNDERSTANDING

COMPLETING A GRAPHIC ORGANIZER

The T'ang and Sung dynasties of China, the Byzantine Empire, and the Umayyad and Abbasid caliphates of the Islamic world made many important contributions. Show how two of these cultures made a lasting contribution to the world.

CULTURES YOU SELECTED

(1)
_____
_____
_____

(2)
_____
_____
_____

TESTING YOUR UNDERSTANDING

Test your understanding of this chapter by answering the following questions

1   An immediate effect of the fall of the Roman empire on Western Europe was
    (1) a renewed interest in education and the arts
    (2) a period of disorder and weak central government
    (3) the growth of cities and the rise of the middle class
    (4) an increase in trade and manufacturing

2   In the Roman and Byzantine empires, an important feature of life was the development of
    (1) a set of codified laws   (3) social and political equality
    (2) the Islamic religion   (4) civil service examinations

Base your answers to questions 3 and 4 on the passage below and on your knowledge of global history.

> **IN THE NAME OF ALLAH**
> **THE COMPASSIONATE, THE MERCIFUL**
>
> Praise be to Allah, Lord of the Creation,
> The Compassionate, the Merciful,
> King of the Last Judgment!
> You alone we worship,
> And to You we pray for help.

3   People who accept the beliefs stated in this passage practice
    (1) polytheism   (3) ancestor worship
    (2) monotheism   (4) animism

4   In which book can this passage be found?
    (1) Old Testament of the Bible   (3) Talmud
    (2) Analects of Confucius   (4) Qu'ran

5   A key characteristic of the Golden Age of Muslim culture was the
    (1) creation of democratic governments
    (2) increased participation of women in government
    (3) restriction of trade and commerce
    (4) toleration of other religions and cultures

6   In Western Europe, which development was a cause of the other three?
    (1) warfare disrupted trade throughout Europe
    (2) travel became unsafe because of violence
    (3) cities, towns and villages were abandoned
    (4) the fall of the Roman empire

7   An important contribution of the Byzantine Empire to Russia was the establishment in Russia of
    (1) Orthodox Christianity
    (2) representative democracy
    (3) a free-market economy
    (4) a jury system

8   The Middle Ages in Europe were characterized by
    (1) the manor system and feudal ties
    (2) absolute monarchies and strong central governments
    (3) decreased emphasis on religion in daily life
    (4) extensive trade with Asia and the Middle East

9   Feudal societies are generally characterized by
    (1) an exchange of land for services
    (2) a representative government
    (3) widespread economic opportunity
    (4) the protection of individual rights

10 Which is the most valid generalization about the Crusades?
    (1) They strengthened the power of the serfs in Europe.
    (2) They led to increased trade between Europe and Asia.
    (3) They brought European influence to Africa.
    (4) They promoted greater religious freedom.

11 Which statement best describes the role of the Roman Catholic Church in Europe during the Middle Ages?
    (1) The Church encouraged individuals to question authority.
    (2) Church leaders were involved solely in spiritual activities.
    (3) The Church gained influence as the world became more secular.
    (4) The Church provided a sense of stability, unity, and order.

Base your answer to question 12 on the map below and your knowledge of global history.

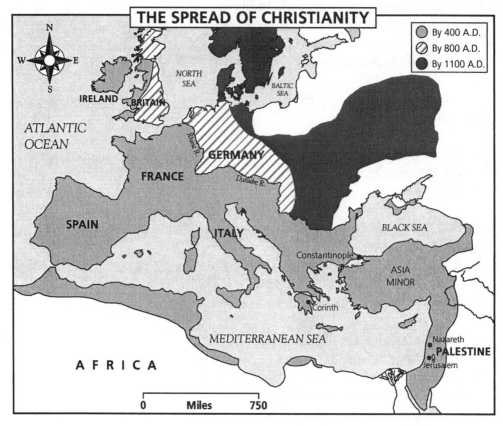

THE SPREAD OF CHRISTIANITY

By 400 A.D.
By 800 A.D.
By 1100 A.D.

12 According to the map, when did Christianity first expand into North Africa?
(1) by 400 A.D.   (3) by 1100 A.D.
(2) by 800 A.D.   (4) after 1100 A.D.

13 What did both the caste system in India and the feudal system in Europe provide?
(1) a growth in trade with neighboring countries
(2) a strong emphasis on the acquisition of wealth
(3) a strong belief in social equality
(4) a set of rules for the conduct of individuals in society

14 One factor that accounts for the Chinese influence on Japanese culture was
(1) several centuries of warfare between China and Japan
(2) the geographic locations of China and Japan
(3) the refusal of Western nations to trade with Japan
(4) the annexation of Japan by China

15 The traditional Japanese concept of the role of the emperor and the Chinese belief in
the Mandate of Heaven were both based on
(1) the democratic election of rulers
(2) a division of power between the nobility and the emperor
(3) the belief that political power comes from a divine source
(4) a constitution that defines individual rights

Base your answer to question 16 on the timeline and on your knowledge of global history.

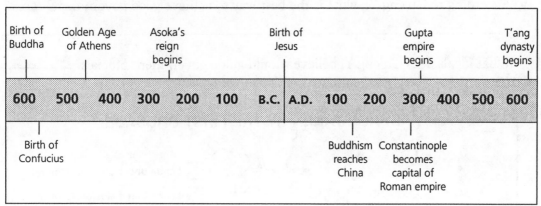

16 According to the timeline, which event occurred during the 2nd century A.D.?
(1) Confucius was born.
(2) Asoka's reign began.
(3) Buddhism reached China.
(4) Constantinople became the capital of the Roman empire.

INTERPRETING DOCUMENTS

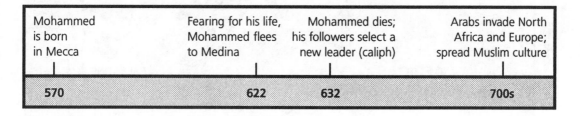

1a The rise of which religion is depicted on the timeline? _____

b Explain **one** effect of the developments shown on the timeline. _____

_____

> "Good government in the empire depends on obtaining worthy men. Misgovernment in the empire derives from the failure to obtain worthy men. The purpose of seeking out worthy men is good government, and the way to govern the empire is the way followed by the Five Emperors and Confucius."
>
> *Ch'eng Yi: To Emperor Jen-tsung*

2a According to Ch'eng Yi, what is the best way to achieve good government? _____

_____

b What ideals does Ch'eng Yi believe should guide government officials? _____

_____

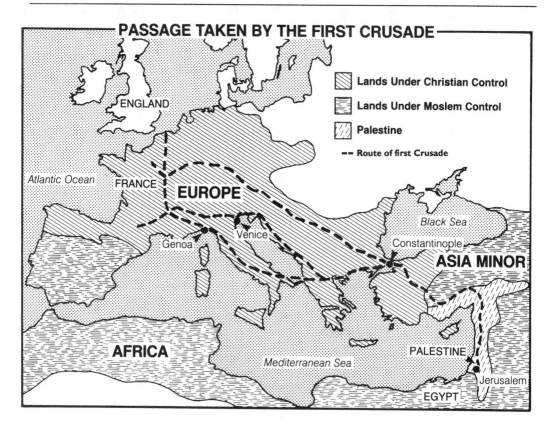

3a Which religious group controlled most of Europe? _____

b What was the purpose of the Crusades? _____

THEMATIC ESSAY QUESTION

Directions: Write a well-organized essay that includes an introduction, several paragraphs addressing the *Task* below, and a conclusion.

Theme: Cultural and Intellectual Life

> Throughout history, many cultures have experienced a "Golden Age."

Task:
  Choose **two** cultures from your study of global history and geography.

  • For *each* culture, describe two achievements of that culture's "Golden Age."
  • Discuss one way in which the two cultures were similar or different.

You may use any examples from your study of global history. Some suggestions you might wish to consider include: Athens in the 5th century B.C., the Gupta empire in India, the Islamic world (700s through 1100s), the T'ang dynasty in China, and the Heian period in Japan.

You are *not* limited to these suggestions.

APPLYING A DOCUMENT TO A THESIS STATEMENT

In this exercise, you will have an opportunity to practice the most challenging part of a document-based essay question — linking a document to a thesis statement. You will recall that in this kind of essay question, you have to support your position with information from the documents provided. Think of yourself as a lawyer, arguing your case by referring to the evidence before the court. Your answer to this practice exercise should have two paragraphs.

  • **First Paragraph.** Your *first sentence* should identify the historical context, setting the time and place for the reader. Next, you should write a *thesis statement*: this states the main idea you are going to discuss. Then write a *transition sentence* that leads the reader to your supporting paragraph.

- **Second Paragraph.** This paragraph should use information from the document to support your thesis statement.

> **Note:** You will find a similar exercise asking you to apply one or two documents to a thesis statement at the end of each later chapter in this book — except for those chapters where there are full document-based essay questions.

QUESTION

Carefully examine the document below and answer the scaffolding questions that follow it. Then write a paragraph showing how the evidence in the document supports the following thesis statement:

European feudalism gave rise to a new system of government based on personal loyalties.

DOCUMENT

> "Since it is known to all how little I have to feed and clothe myself, I have asked for your mercy ... You will aid and nourish me with food and clothing ... And so long as I live, I shall provide service and honor to you."
>
> — *Frankish oath of loyalty by a warrior to a lord, 7th century*

1a In this oath of loyalty, a Frankish warrior is making a pledge to a lord. What is the warrior getting in exchange?

_____

_____

b What is the lord expecting to get as "service" from the Frankish warrior?

_____

_____

(continued)

RELATING THE DOCUMENT TO THE THESIS STATEMENT

①
The two introductory sentences define feudalism and give the historical context.

→ *Feudalism was a political, economic and social system that arose in Europe in the early 800s. After the collapse of the Roman empire, Europe did not have a strong central government. The turmoil of the period gave rise to a new system of government based on personal loyalties. The nature of feudalism can be seen by examining a document from the period.*

②
The thesis statement is the generalization that the rest of the essay will explain.

③
The transition sentence leads into a discussion of the document.

④
In this paragraph, relate the document to the thesis statement. You may add further information about the topic from your knowledge of global history.

→ *In this document,* _____

_____

_____

_____

_____

_____

_____

_____

_____

_____

_____

_____

_____

CHAPTER 10

WARRIORS ON HORSEBACK AND THE REVIVAL OF EUROPE, 1200 - 1500

Martin Luther, leader of the Protestant Reformation

KEY TERMS, CONCEPTS AND PEOPLE

- Chinggis Khan
- Shogun
- Daimyo
- Samurai
- Bushido
- Mali
- Mansa Musa
- Renaissance
- Michelangelo
- Protestant Reformation
- Martin Luther
- Counter-Reformation
- Council of Trent
- Inquisition

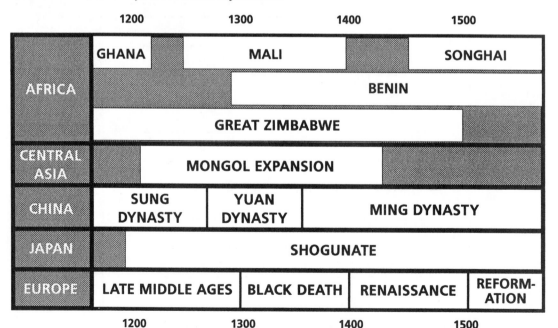

	1200	1300	1400	1500
AFRICA	GHANA	MALI		SONGHAI
		BENIN		
	GREAT ZIMBABWE			
CENTRAL ASIA	MONGOL EXPANSION			
CHINA	SUNG DYNASTY	YUAN DYNASTY	MING DYNASTY	
JAPAN	SHOGUNATE			
EUROPE	LATE MIDDLE AGES	BLACK DEATH	RENAISSANCE	REFORM-ATION

WHAT YOU SHOULD FOCUS ON

This chapter explores the period from 1200 to 1500. During this era, separate civilizations continued along their own unique paths of development but also came to influence one another more than before. As trade increased and ideas spread, the cultures of Eurasia and Africa became more connected.

These were also times of great stress. In the 1200s, the Mongols, fierce nomadic warriors from Central Asia, conquered all the territories from the Black Sea to China. A disease from Central Asia called the Black Death (*plague*) entered Europe during the 1300s, eventually killing a third of the population. In the 1400s, Europe had a revival.

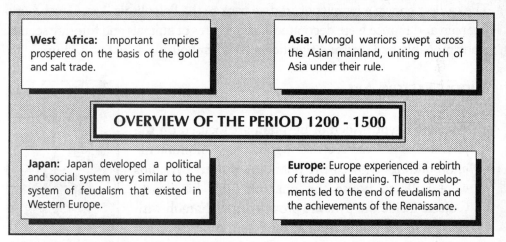

West Africa: Important empires prospered on the basis of the gold and salt trade.

Asia: Mongol warriors swept across the Asian mainland, uniting much of Asia under their rule.

OVERVIEW OF THE PERIOD 1200 - 1500

Japan: Japan developed a political and social system very similar to the system of feudalism that existed in Western Europe.

Europe: Europe experienced a rebirth of trade and learning. These developments led to the end of feudalism and the achievements of the Renaissance.

During these centuries, Islamic civilization continued to spread and began to penetrate India. What was left of the Byzantine empire collapsed. New civilizations arose in Southeast Asia. Important empires also flourished in the Western Hemisphere, which are discussed in the next chapter.

Keep in mind that testmakers are most likely to ask you about the following:

- What led to the rise of the West African kingdoms?
- What were the effects of the Mongol conquests?
- What factors contributed to the decline of feudalism?
- What were the achievements of the European Renaissance?

LOOKING AT
THE ARTS

All cultures have a need to create works of beauty and to express their deepest feelings and beliefs through the arts — painting, sculpture, architecture, literature, music, and dance. Works of art can therefore reveal a great deal about the values of the society that produced them.

A BRIEF SURVEY OF WORLD ART

The earliest known examples of art date back to the Paleolithic Age. Caves found in Spain and France were decorated with pictures of animals and hunting scenes. They probably had spiritual significance — symbolizing a successful hunt.

MIDDLE EASTERN ART

*   **Ancient Egypt.** Much of Egyptian art focused on the pharaoh, who was seen as a god. Huge monuments and buildings showed the pharaoh's power. Pyramids were built to house the pharaoh after his death. Objects inside the pyramid provided the pharaoh with everything he would need in the afterlife.

Pharaoh Tutankhamen

*   **Islamic Art.** Islamic artists generally did not depict people in their art works, since the Qu'ran forbids it. These artists excelled at the decorative arts, using highly complex floral designs and geometric patterns in their architecture, metalwork, glasswork, and textiles. Carpets provided a particularly good way to display their highly developed sense of color, proportion, and intricate design. Each carpet aimed at achieving perfect balance and harmony.

Persian carpet

European Art

- **Ancient Greece and Rome.** Greek art emphasized a sense of proportion and realism. The Parthenon, with its perfect proportions, was the most celebrated building of ancient Greece. The Greeks were also renowned for their superb sculptures of the human figure. Roman artistry was most evident in architecture. The Pantheon, built at the time of Augustus, was known for its perfect dome. One of the most famous buildings of the Roman empire was the Colosseum, an arena built for contests among gladiators. Made of stone and concrete, it held 55,000 people.

Winged Victory, a famous Greek statue

- **Middle Ages.** Medieval paintings and sculptures were largely used for religious purposes. Medieval painters were less concerned with realism than with religious symbolism. The greatest examples of medieval architecture were Gothic cathedrals. They were huge structures with pointed arches, flying buttresses, spires, and high vaulted ceilings built as monuments to God.

Notre Dame Cathedral, Paris

- **Renaissance.** The Renaissance marked a sharp departure from the techniques and content of medieval art. Some Renaissance art even dealt with non-religious themes. Renaissance architecture borrowed heavily from classical Greece and Rome and strove for simplicity and proportion. Renaissance paintings reached new heights of realism, developing techniques such as perspective.

Detail of Botticelli's La Primavera

- **Modern European Art.** European art has gone through many styles since the Renaissance: baroque, romanticism, impressionism, cubism, and surrealism. These styles have fluctuated between increased realism, formal beauty, and depictions of inner emotions. The abstract styles of 20th-century art reflect the excitement and confusion of contemporary life.

Cubist painting by Picasso

AFRICAN ART

Traditional African art often expressed religious beliefs

and rites. Tribal art was a way to communicate with the spirit world and to protect individuals against evil forces. Among traditional African art forms were the masks worn during ceremonial dances and tribal rites. Many tribes also made statues of human or animal figures, often exaggerated in size for symbolic or religious purposes. African music and dance were characterized by great vitality with an emphasis on strong rhythms.

Mask from Benin

ART IN THE AMERICAS

Two civilizations to leave behind significant artworks were the Maya and the Aztec. The Maya constructed pyramids which first served as tombs. Later pyramids were built as vast temples, approaching the size of the Egyptian pyramids. These pyramids were decorated with reliefs *(flattened sculptures)* depicting Mayan gods. The Aztecs also developed free-standing stone sculptures that excelled at portraying human emotions.

Aztec statue

ASIAN ART

- **South and Southeast Asia.** Dancing is an important element of the culture of South and Southeast Asia. Dance first developed in connection with religious ceremonies that told the stories of Hindu gods and goddesses, often portraying the struggle between good and evil. Through the movement of hands and feet and facial expression, dancers communicate emotions and feelings to their audience in the course of telling their stories. Classical Hindu sculpture similarly depicts the human body in various postures representing Hindu gods and goddesses. Later Indian art and architecture were influenced by Persian and Islamic styles.

Indian dancer

- **China**. Chinese paintings, pottery, and porcelains reflect the harmony, symmetry, and perfect balance found

Chinese porcelain teapot

in nature. Painters often illustrated poems written in calligraphy on paper scrolls. China's earliest pottery met religious as well as practical needs. Wealthy people were buried with earthenware dishes, models of animals, and other objects. Later Chinese craftsmen perfected the art of making porcelain. Unlike other pottery, porcelain is shiny, smooth, white, and translucent.

- **Japan**. Japanese art forms emphasize simplicity, harmony, order, and the beauty of nature. For example, the tea ceremony is performed slowly and quietly to promote meditation. Flower arranging emphasizes the symbolism of natural beauty. Origami is the art of folding paper into animal forms and other shapes. Haiku are simple, graceful poems reflecting the beauty of nature.

Japanese origami

QUESTIONS ABOUT THE ARTS

Art questions on global history examinations often will ask you how a work of art reflects the spirit of its culture or times. You must (1) interpret the artwork, and (2) show how it reflects the time or culture in which it was produced. When faced with this type of question, ask yourself the following about the artwork:

- What is being portrayed in the artwork?
- What is the theme or major point of the artwork?
- In which time period and place was the artwork probably created?
- What does it tell us about the culture of the people who produced it?

MAJOR HISTORICAL DEVELOPMENTS

THE KINGDOMS OF SUB-SAHARAN AFRICA

In the last chapter, you read about the expansion of Islam in Arabia, North Africa, Asia, and Europe. South of the Islamic Empire lived the peoples of sub-Saharan Africa.

GEOGRAPHICAL SETTING

For at least 5,000 years, the **Sahara Desert** has covered much of North Africa. Just south of it lies a wide band of grassland known as the **savanna,** stretching from the Atlantic to the Indian Ocean. During the **Bantu migrations**, people spread from West Africa to the east and south. The savanna became home to large numbers of cattle and sheep herders. They learned to smelt iron and grow crops, and developed complex communities with craftpersons, warriors, and traders. South of the savanna are the tropical rain forests of equatorial Africa.

The Sahara was a barrier separating the peoples of sub-Saharan Africa from the Mediterranean world and the rest of Eurasia. But trade was never cut off completely, because the Sahara has oases with fresh water springs. Once merchants knew where these oases were, they could cross the desert on camels, which can go several days without water.

Merchants crossed the Sahara for gold and other riches they could obtain from trade with West Africa. At the same time, West Africans lacked salt. Merchants, moving in caravans across the desert, picked up blocks of salt from desert salt beds along the way to exchange for gold. A thriving trade developed, based on this **gold-salt trade**.

RISE OF THE WEST AFRICAN KINGDOMS

Around the 8th century, a series of powerful kingdoms arose on the West African savanna, based on fine cavalries and control of trade routes. For the next thousand years, these kingdoms dominated West Africa, leading to an exchange of ideas, the rise of cities, and increased wealth.

KINGDOM OF GHANA (750 - 1200)

The kingdom of Ghana was founded around 750. It developed in the region between the Senegal and Niger Rivers. The people of Ghana used their ability to make iron swords, spears, and lances to subdue neighboring peoples and to gain control over West Africa's main trade routes. Caravans brought salt south to Ghana, and returned north with gold from areas southwest of Ghana. The power of the kings of Ghana rested on their ability to tax all trade passing through the region, especially the salt and gold trade. With these rich revenues, they were able to raise a large army and fine cavalry.

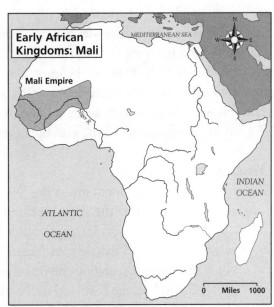

The rulers of Ghana built a capital city and governed a wide area through the use of officials and nobles. The king appointed nobles to govern the provinces in return for paying taxes to the central government. This system had some similarities to European feudalism. Rulers and nobles were further enriched by using captives as slaves. However, in 1076, the Ghanaians were invaded by Muslims from North Africa. Ghana never fully recovered from the invasion and eventually dissolved into several smaller states.

KINGDOM OF MALI (1240 - 1400)

In 1240, the people of Mali conquered the old capital of Ghana and founded a new empire. The rulers brought gold and salt mines under their direct control. Mali's rulers converted to Islam, although most of their people still worshipped spirits (**animism**). The most famous ruler, **Mansa Musa**, expanded his kingdom greatly. He made a religious pilgrimage to Mecca in 1324, also visiting Cairo in Egypt. Mansa Musa brought back Muslim scholars and architects to Mali.

Timbuktu, a flourishing trading city on the Niger River, became a center of learning under Mansa Musa's rule. The city attracted students from Europe, Asia, and Africa. Because of the importance of studying the Qu'ran, many more West Africans learned to read and write. Arab travelers like **Ibn Battuta** were impressed by Mali's wealth, its inhabitants' respect for law, and the power of its ruler. Later rulers proved less capable than Mansa Musa, however, and the kingdom of Mali collapsed in the 1400s.

THE KINGDOM OF SONGHAI (1464 - 1600)

In 1464, Sultan **Sunni Ali,** ruler of the Songhai people, captured Timbuktu and brought

the upper Niger under his control. Songhai grew rich from trade across the Sahara, and soon was the largest of Africa's three trading centers. Songhai expanded trade to Europe and Asia, and established an elaborate system of taxation and communications to govern its large kingdom. Timbuktu continued to flourish as a center of Muslim scholarship.

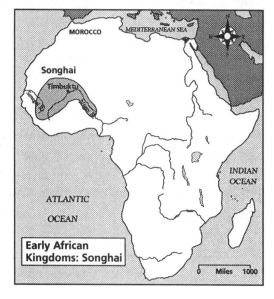

Early African
Kingdoms: Songhai

Despite its riches and power, the kingdom of Songhai lasted only about 100 years. In 1591, the ruler of Morocco, hearing of Songhai's wealth, invaded West Africa. Although the Songhai army was larger, the Moroccans used gunpowder and muskets to defeat the Songhai, who fought with arrows and spears. Despite their military success, the Moroccans were unable to govern Songhai from such a great distance. West Africa again split apart into a large number of independent areas. The fall of Songhai marked the end of the great West African kingdoms.

OTHER AFRICAN STATES

The growth of trading kingdoms in the West African savanna, like Ghana, Mali, and Songhai, was matched by the rise of trading kingdoms in other parts of Africa.

♦ **Benin** developed in the rain forests of West Africa. Benin was famous for its bronze sculptures, among the finest of all African works of art. By the 16th century, Benin became involved in the slave trade. Its rulers traded captured members of other tribes and exchanged them with Europeans for guns and iron goods.

◆ **Great Zimbabwe,** farther to the south, became one of the best known of Africa's trading kingdoms. The existence of gold deposits near Zimbabwe was crucial to its rise. Zimbabwe traded gold, copper, and ivory from Africa's interior to traders coming to Africa's east coast.

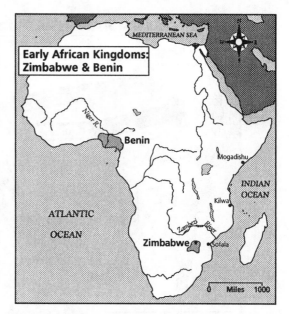

Early African Kingdoms: Zimbabwe & Benin

◆ **Coastal Cities of East Africa,** Along the east coast of Africa, a number of city-states — such as Mogadishu, Kilwa and Sofala — arose around the 900s. Gold from the interior was sent down the Zambia River to these cities and sold to merchants from Arabia and India.

◆ **Ethiopia,** a continuation of the kingdom of Axum, became a Christian state in the 4th century. It remained so despite the rise of Islam, which cut it off from the Christian world until the 1400s.

THE AGE OF MONGOL DOMINANCE

Stretching across Eurasia, from the Carpathian Mountains in Eastern Europe to Manchuria, is an almost unbroken band of treeless grasslands called **steppes.** This band is located between forests to the north and the mountains and deserts to the south. From earliest times nomadic people have lived in the area, relying

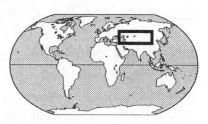

on horses, sheep, camels, and goats, and using these vast grasslands as pastures for their livestock. The steppes provided a unique environment in which these nomadic peoples learned to excel at horsemanship and developed deadly fighting skills. For a thousand years, fierce horsemen from Central Asia threatened neighboring civilizations. The **Huns,** repelled by the Chinese emperors, invaded Europe in the 4th and 5th centuries and contributed to the collapse of the Roman empire. Later, the **Seljuk Turks** and the **Mongols** also came out of Central Asia.

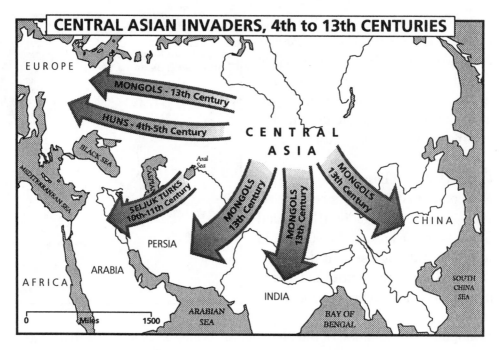

The Mongols lived in the eastern part of Central Asia, northwest of China. Like other Central Asian nomads, the Mongols were excellent horsemen and archers. During the 1200s, the Mongols established the largest empire the world had ever seen.

CHINGGIS KHAN UNITES THE MONGOLS

Like other nomadic peoples, the Mongols were divided into several tribes. A Mongol leader named **Chinggis Khan** (1162-1227), also known as **Ghengis Khan**, united the Mongols by 1206. Chinggis Khan then began attacking neighboring peoples beyond Mongolia. These neighbors had little chance of resisting 200,000 expert Mongol horsemen. Chinggis Khan successfully attacked northern China, taking the city of Beijing. In 1219, he turned westward and captured the Muslim states of Central Asia. Although he was greatly feared as a brutal warrior, Chinggis Khan was tolerant of other religions within his conquered territories. He made use of local administrators and craftspeople. He promoted trade throughout the vast Mongol empire and even ordered the creation of a written script for the Mongol language.

Under Chinggis Khan's successors, Mongol rule extended into Persia, Russia, Iraq, and all of China. The Mongols held sway over one of the largest empires in history — from the Black Sea to the Pacific Ocean. The Mongol empire was so vast that it quickly divided into four kingdoms, called khanates, each ruled by a different descendant of Chinggis Khan. They established a **Pax Mongolia** from the Black Sea to the Pacific Ocean.

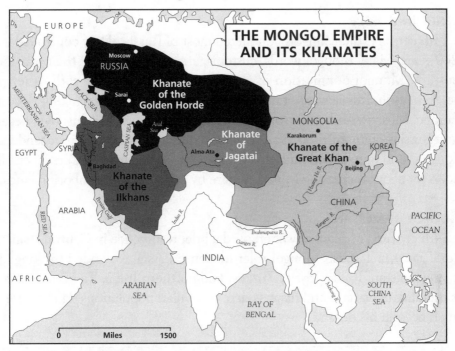

THE YUAN DYNASTY (1279-1368)

Chinggis' grandson, **Kublai Khan** (1215-1294) became emperor of northern China in 1260. In 1279, he reunited northern and southern China. Mongols acted as a military aristocracy, ruling with the help of Chinese officials. Kublai Khan encouraged the Mongols to adopt Chinese ways, and he used the Chinese name Yuan for his dynasty. He claimed to hold the Mandate of Heaven in ruling China.

Marco Polo, a merchant from Venice, visited China in the 1270s. He was astounded at the magnificence of Kublai Khan's court and the technological superiority of the Chinese — for example, the use of gunpowder and coal. After returning home, Marco Polo wrote about what he had seen, inspiring great curiosity in Europe about China. After Kublai Khan's death, weaker Mongol rulers were unable to maintain control; they were overthrown by the Chinese in 1368.

Marco Polo arrives in China

DECLINE OF MONGOL RULE

INFLUENCE IN RUSSIA

In the 13th century, the Mongols conquered most of Russia. They controlled it for the next 200 years. Many Mongol words, customs, and clothing found their way into Russian culture. Mongol domination of Russia limited its contact with other parts of Europe. As a result, Russia was not influenced by important changes taking place in Western Europe. Moscow and its surrounding territories, known as **Muscovy**, became the strongest Russian state. In 1480, **Ivan the Great** declared Muscovy's independence from the Mongols, and proclaimed himself **Tsar** (or *Czar, which means "Caesar" or emperor*). Ivan soon set about increasing Muscovy's size by conquering neighboring lands.

THE RULE OF TAMERLANE

In the 14th century, Mongol power enjoyed a brief resurgence in Central Asia. **Tamerlane** (*or Timur*), a Turkish-Mongol ruler in Central Asia, expanded his kingdom into Persia, Afghanistan, Russia, Syria, Turkey, and northern India. Tamerlane was known for his brutality in warfare and his massacre of civilian populations. His empire did not last much beyond his death.

JAPAN'S FEUDAL PERIOD: 1200 to 1600

In the last chapter we saw that by the late 1100s, the Japanese emperor's power had weakened. Japan then collapsed into civil war. A system of **feudalism**, similar to that in Europe, soon arose. The major feature of Japanese feudalism was the control of government by noble landlords, known as **daimyo**, who owed their loyalty to the Shogun.

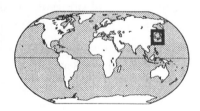

THE SHOGUN

In 1192, one of the nobles, **Minamoto Yoritomo**, defeated the other noble families and became the most powerful person in Japan. Instead of overthrowing the emperor, he had the emperor appoint him as Japan's "Supreme Military Governor," known in Japanese as the **Shogun**. For the next 600 years the Shoguns were the real rulers, with the emperors as mere figureheads. The Shogun was at the top of the Japanese feudal system.

To provide military protection for their lands, noble landowners recruited samurai warriors. **Samurai** were knights on horseback with swords and armor of leather and iron. Each samurai swore an oath of loyalty to the emperor and to his local **daimyo.** A samurai vowed to follow a strict code of honor, known as **Bushido,** "the way of the warrior." Bushido emphasized the loyalty of the samurai to the daimyo. If the samurai dishonored his daimyo, he was expected to take his own life. In return

Samurai warriors

for this loyalty, the daimyo provided the samurai with social status and economic support. The daimyo also protected farmers in exchange for their labor on his lands.

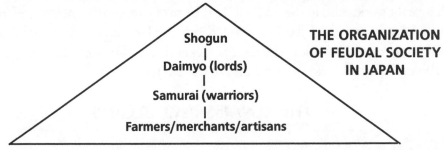

Shogun
|
Daimyo (lords)
|
Samurai (warriors)
|
Farmers/merchants/artisans

THE ORGANIZATION OF FEUDAL SOCIETY IN JAPAN

In 1274, Kublai Khan tried to invade Japan with a massive fleet, but unfavorable winds destroyed his ships. Samurai defeated those enemy soldiers who reached Japan. The defeat of the Mongols reinforced the Japanese belief that their gods protected them. One effect of the attempted invasion was a weakening of the Shogun. Japan again fell into a period of chaos and civil war. For the next century, the daimyos controlled their own lands like absolute rulers, with little interference from the central government. Daimyos raised their own armies, while the Shogun had little power beyond his capital city.

JAPANESE CULTURE BLOSSOMS

Despite the chaos, this was a period of intense cultural activity in Japan. Flower arranging, the tea ceremony, landscape painting, and the art of gardening all developed at this time. Each of these represented an attempt to reflect on life and the beauty of nature. Painting in this period similarly stressed contemplation and spiritual enlightenment.

THE REVIVAL OF EUROPE

THE DECLINE OF FEUDALISM

In the 1100s, life in Europe began to change. New trade led to the growth of towns, a developing middle class, and a greater use of money. New inventions such as clocks, eyeglasses, and the spinning wheel improved the quality of life. Craftspeople began to organize into guilds.

In the mid-1300s, rats with fleas carrying a disease called the **Black Death** (*bubonic plague*) entered Europe on trading ships. Between 1347 and 1351, nearly 25 million people — about a third of Europe's population — died from the disease. This created a labor shortage, allowing peasants to escape from serfdom when landowners offered them freedom in exchange for work. Also in the mid-1300s, the use of gunpowder, introduced from China, made knights on horseback less important. Kings with large armies of foot soldiers gradually gained power over the nobles. The rise of cities and powerful kings, the decline of knights, and the end of serfdom spelled the end of the old feudal order.

THE RENAISSANCE BEGINS

A revival of interest in learning about the classical civilizations of ancient Greece and Rome developed in the city-states of Italy in the 1400s. This was a time of great intellectual and artistic creativity which became known as the **Renaissance**, a French word that means "rebirth." The Renaissance is often considered one of the great advances in civilization. It began in the Italian states because of their

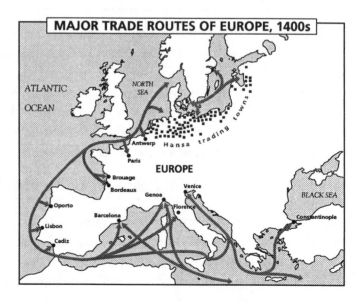

MAJOR TRADE ROUTES OF EUROPE, 1400s

strategic location between Europe and Asia. Italian city-states such as Venice had grown rich from East-West trade. Italian merchants and nobles acted as patrons, supporting artists, writers and scholars. In addition, Italians were influenced by the heritage of ancient Greece and Rome. Gradually, the Renaissance spirit spread to the rest of Europe.

During the Renaissance, the traditional belief in the authority of the Church came under challenge. People showed greater interest in the concerns of this world, rather than in the life hereafter. There was a growth of **secularism**. Scholars used observation and experience to explain the world, rather than looking to Church teachings. Renaissance thinkers had confidence in the powers of human reason. They looked on humankind as the focus of all things. **Humanists** placed great emphasis on the uniqueness and worth of each person. They opened new schools to teach "humanity-related" subjects such as history, philosophy, and classical literature. Some, like Shakespeare and Cervantes (a Spaniard) wrote in **vernacular** languages instead of Latin. Renaissance artists likewise observed nature and people more closely. With new techniques like perspective, paintings became astonishingly lifelike. The arts, literature, music and the sciences all flourished.

ART:

Leonardo da Vinci represented the ideal **"Renaissance man."** He was a painter, sculptor, designer, and inventor. His paintings include the "Mona Lisa" and "The Last Supper."

Michelangelo. His paintings on the Sistine Chapel ceiling in Rome are considered among the greatest works of art of all time. His major sculptures include "David," "Moses," and the "Pieta."

POLITICS AND LITERATURE:

Niccolo Machiavelli wrote *The Prince*, advising rulers to do anything necessary to maintain and increase their power, including deceit and force. He believed "the end justifies the means."

William Shakespeare wrote great plays whose popularity has endured for centuries. His plays *Hamlet*, *Macbeth*, and *Romeo and Juliet* explore the full range of human activities and emotions.

HIGHLIGHTS OF THE RENAISSANCE

SCIENCE AND TECHNOLOGY:

Nicolaus Copernicus stated the earth and other planets revolved around the sun. This went against Church teaching, which said the earth was the center of the universe.

Galileo Galilei and **Francis Bacon** developed the **scientific method** which emphasized careful observation, measurement, and experimentation, and rejected reliance on authorities.

Johann Gutenberg developed a printing press with moveable type. This invention allowed the printing of books in large quantities.

THE PROTESTANT REFORMATION

The spirit of inquiry of the Renaissance, as well as the existence of widespread abuses of the Church, led to new challenges to the Pope's authority. The Church had vast power, but it also suffered from corruption. Some church officials used their positions for self-enrichment. People like Erasmus and Sir Thomas Moore sought reform within the Church.

THE IMPACT OF LUTHER AND HIS IDEAS

In 1517, **Martin Luther** posted his **Ninety-Five Theses** (*statements*) on a church door in Germany. His theses questioned the Catholic Church's teachings and called for reforms. Luther challenged the Pope's right to sell **indulgences** — pardons from punishment for sin. He believed neither priests nor the Pope had the power to grant individual salvation. Luther taught that only through faith could someone be saved and go to Heaven. He believed that people should read and understand the Bible for themselves.

In an attempt to silence Luther, the Pope **excommunicated** (*expelled*) him from the Church. Luther responded by establishing his own church. He was protected by the independent princes of Germany. Luther's ideas quickly spread throughout Europe. Other reformers soon emerged. **John Calvin**, like Luther, was a Protestant theologian who stressed the authority of the Bible and started his own church. Calvin encouraged hard work, supported a strict moral code, and taught

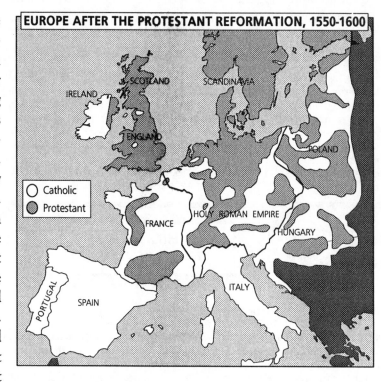

EUROPE AFTER THE PROTESTANT REFORMATION, 1550-1600

IRELAND, SCOTLAND, SCANDINAVIA, ENGLAND, POLAND, FRANCE, HOLY ROMAN EMPIRE, HUNGARY, PORTUGAL, SPAIN, ITALY

○ Catholic
● Protestant

that God had predestined those who would go to Heaven. Calvin's total control of daily life in Switzerland led to the development of a **theocracy** — a form of government based on religious beliefs and controlled by religious leaders.

End of Religious Unity. The religious unity of Western Europe, which had lasted for almost a thousand years, was shattered forever.	**Century of Warfare.** Europe's religious differences caused a century of warfare between Protestants and Catholics, lasting into the mid-1600s.

EFFECTS OF THE REFORMATION

Royal Power. With no powerful central Church, royal power grew. In the 1530s, **King Henry VIII** broke from Rome and established the Church of England.	**Persecution.** Kings tried to ensure that their subjects were all of one faith. This often lead to the persecution of religious minorities.

THE CATHOLIC CHURCH FIGHTS BACK

The Protestant Reformation seriously weakened the power of the Catholic Church. The Church fought back against Protestantism by making limited reforms and halting its previous abuses. This movement was known as the **Catholic Counter Reformation.**

THE CATHOLIC COUNTER REFORMATION

Council of Trent (1545-1563). Called to redefine the Church's beliefs and stop the spread of Protestantism, it ended the sale of indulgences and began an **Index** — a list of banned books.	**Inquisition.** The Inquisition was used by Church officials to end heresy by force. Trials were held to examine, often by torture, those suspected of denying the teachings of the Church.	**Jesuits.** Begun by **Ignatius Loyola** in 1534, the Jesuits were dedicated to defending and spreading the Catholic faith.

— STUDY CARDS —

West African Kingdoms	**Mongols**
Several kingdoms arose in the Sahel region of Africa because of the gold-salt trade. • **Ghana** used iron weapons to subdue neighbors; taxed the gold-salt trade • **Mali** adopted Islam; **Mansa Musa** made the city of **Timbuktu** a center of learning • **Songhai**, under Sultan **Sunni Ali**, grew rich from trade across the Sahara	Tribes of skilled horsemen and warriors from the steppes of Central Asia • **Chinggis (Genghis) Khan** united the Mongols in 1206; conquered Central Asia • Later Mongol rulers extended empire to Russia, parts of China, Persia, Eastern Europe • **Kublai Khan** gained control of all of China and adopted Chinese ways (*Yuan Dynasty*)

(continued)

Shogunate (Japan, 1200-1868)

Shoguns were military governors who controlled Japan with landowners called **Daimyo**.

- **Emperor** became a figurehead with no power; **Shogun** became real ruler
- Social organization was similar to feudalism in Europe
- **Samurai** were warriors who swore allegiance to their local daimyo and followed a strict code of honor known as **Bushido**

Renaissance

Rebirth of classical culture and learning, starting in Italy in the 1400s.

- **Secularism:** Thinkers used observation, instead of Church dogma, to explain world
- **Humanism:** Focused on uniqueness and worth of each person
- **Achievements:** Literature in common languages, scientific method, printing press, perspective in painting, realistic sculpture
- **People:** Leonardo da Vinci, Michelangelo, Galileo, Copernicus, Machiavelli, Gutenberg

Early Russia

Slavs formed first Russian state around 800.
- Strong Byzantine influence: Eastern Orthodox religion, art, Cyrillic alphabet
- Mongols conquered much of Russia in the 1200s
- Moscow and adjacent territories, known as **Muscovy**, became strongest Russian state
- In 1480, **Ivan the Great** declared Muscovy's independence from the Mongols, proclaimed himself **Tsar** (*emperor*), conquered neighboring lands

Protestant Reformation

Martin Luther objected to corruption in Catholic Church, such as sale of indulgences. In his **Ninety-Five Theses** (1517), he challenged the Pope's authority, and shortly afterwards he broke from the Church.

Effects:
- Ended religious unity in Western Europe
- John Calvin and others started Protestant churches of their own
- Led to a century of religious wars between Catholics and Protestants

Decline of Feudalism

Reasons for decline:

- Growth of towns, increased trade, rise in use of money
- Gunpowder, brought from China, made armored knights and castles vulnerable and less important
- **Black Death** (plague, 1300s) killed a third of the population, creating a labor shortage; peasants escaped from serfdom when offered freedom in exchange for work

Catholic Counter-Reformation

Roman Catholic Church fought the rise of Protestantism:

- **Council of Trent**: ended sale of indulgences and began an **Index** of prohibited books
- **Inquisition:** The Church put on trial people suspected of heresy (*non-Catholic beliefs*), frequently executed those found guilty
- **Religious Wars:** Catholic monarchs cooperated with the Pope in fighting Protestantism

SUMMARIZING YOUR UNDERSTANDING

COMPLETING A GRAPHIC ORGANIZER

The Renaissance is considered by many to be one of the Golden Ages of Western civilization. Complete this graphic organizer on the accomplishments of the Renaissance.

Humanism: _____

Science and Technology: _____

ACCOMPLISHMENTS OF THE RENAISSANCE

Art: _____

Literature: _____

TESTING YOUR UNDERSTANDING

Test your understanding of this chapter by answering the following questions.

1   One reason the kingdoms of the West African savanna prospered was that they
    (1) were located along the Tigris and Euphrates Rivers
    (2) had no contact with the rest of the world
    (3) followed the Hindu beliefs of their rulers
    (4) developed an extensive trade in gold and salt

2   Which activity provides the best example of cultural diffusion in Africa?
    (1) weaving kente cloth in Ghana
    (2) using masks in traditional African ceremonies
    (3) the discovery of bronze sculptures in Benin
    (4) the adoption of Islam by Mali's rulers

3   A major impact of the Sahara Desert on the peoples of Africa was that
    (1)   it made them rich from its gold mines
    (2)   it acted as a barrier which separated them
    (3)   it became home to people herding cattle and sheep
    (4)   it cut off Africa completely from the Americas

4   Which phrase best explains the establishment of the West African kingdoms of Ghana, Mali, and Songhai?
    (1)   their large naval fleets   (3)   adoption of feudalism
    (2)   control of the gold and salt trade   (4)   protection provided by rain forests

5   Which characteristic was shared by the kingdom of Mali and the Mongol empire?
    (1)   They thrived on taxing the peasants.
    (2)   They had large cavalries in grassland regions.
    (3)   They adopted the cultural achievements of the Chinese.
    (4)   Their rulers made pilgrimages to Mecca.

6   Why did so many fierce nomadic tribes emerge out of Central Asia?
    (1)   Warm climates encouraged population growth.
    (2)   Diseases like the bubonic plague drove Central Asians into Europe.
    (3)   Vast grasslands supported large numbers of warriors on horseback.
    (4)   The Hindu faith encouraged them to fight.

7   Which was a characteristic of feudalism in both medieval Europe and Japan?
    (1)   The middle classes acquired more power than any other class.
    (2)   Political power was held by a strong central government.
    (3)   The army encouraged strong nationalist feelings among the people.
    (4)   People pledged absolute loyalty to those above them.

Base your answer to question 8 on the diagram and on your knowledge of global history.

8   Merchants appear at the bottom of this social pyramid of feudal Japan because they
    (1)   comprised the majority of Japan's population
    (2)   were viewed as having low status in society
    (3)   were unable to read or write
    (4)   did not share the religious beliefs of the Shogun

Shogun
Daimyos
Samurai
Farmers and Fishermen
Artisans
Merchants

9   In both Europe and Japan, a major reason for the emergence of feudalism was to
    (1) preserve the role of the emperor
    (2) increase foreign trade
    (3) consolidate the power of religious leaders
    (4) provide order in a period of weak central government

10 The Renaissance and the Protestant Reformation were similar in that both were
    (1) stimulated by a spirit of inquiry   (3) limited to Italy and Germany
    (2) supported by the peasantry   (4) marked by the spread of Islam

11 The sale of indulgences and the worldly lives of the clergy were the subject of
    (1) Lady Murasaki's *The Tale of Genji*   (3) William Shakespeare's *Hamlet*
    (2) Martin Luther's *Ninety-Five Theses*   (4) Niccolo Machiavelli's *The Prince*

12 "Christians should be taught that he who gives to a poor man or lends to a needy man
    does better than if he used the money to buy an indulgence."
    This statement was probably made by
    (1) Martin Luther   (3) William Shakespeare
    (2) Niccolo Machiavelli   (4) Ignatius Loyola

Base your answer to question13 on the timeline and your knowledge of global history.

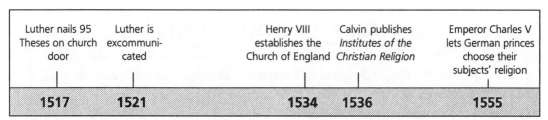

Luther nails 95 Theses on church door	Luther is excommuni-cated		Henry VIII establishes the Church of England	Calvin publishes *Institutes of the Christian Religion*	Emperor Charles V lets German princes choose their subjects' religion
1517	**1521**		**1534**	**1536**	**1555**

13 Which period of European history is represented by this timeline?
    (1) Feudalism   (3) Protestant Reformation
    (2) Renaissance   (4) Catholic Counter-Reformation

14 One reason Italian city-states were able to dominate the trade routes at the start of the
    Renaissance was that they were
    (1) strategically located between Europe and Asia
    (2) situated north of the Swiss Alps
    (3) located on the trade routes of the North Sea
    (4) unified under Mongol rule

15 Which statement best describes a change that occurred during the Renaissance?
    (1) Feudalism became the dominant political system.
    (2) The use of reason and logic was discouraged.
    (3) Technology and science were considered unimportant.
    (4) A new questioning spirit and attitude emerged.

Base your answer to question 16 on the diagram and your knowledge of global history.

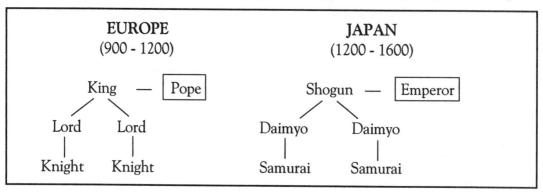

16 What is the name of the system with social structures like those shown in the diagram?
    (1) democracy   (3) feudalism
    (2) shogunate   (4) imperialism

INTERPRETING DOCUMENTS

"A man who wishes to do good in everything must necessarily come to grief among so many who are not good. Therefore it is necessary for a prince, who wishes to maintain himself, to learn how not to be good ... When the prince is with his army, then it is extremely necessary that he should not mind being thought of as cruel; for without this reputation he could not keep his army united and obedient ..."

— Machiavelli, *The Prince*

1a What is the main idea of this quotation? _____

_____

 b How did the views expressed in this quotation differ from Church teachings? _____

_____

THEMATIC ESSAY QUESTION

Directions: Write a well-organized essay that includes an introduction, several paragraphs addressing the *Task* below, and a conclusion.

Theme: Culture and Intellectual Life

> Works of art often express the political, social and economic conditions of the time period in which they were created.

Task:

- Identify **two** works of art that express the political, social or economic conditions of their time period.
- Describe the time period in which each work of art was created.
- Discuss how each work of art expressed the political, social or economic conditions of that period.

You may use any examples from your study of global history. Some suggestions you may wish to consider include the Egyptian pyramids, Greek sculpture, Gothic cathedrals, bronze sculptures of Benin, Chinese porcelain and Renaissance paintings. **You are *not* limited to these suggestions.**

APPLYING A DOCUMENT TO A THESIS STATEMENT

In this exercise, you will practice linking a visual document — in the form of a painting — to a thesis statement. Your answer to this exercise should have at least two paragraphs. The first paragraph should give the historical context, present the thesis statement, and make a transition to your supporting paragraph. The second paragraph should refer to information in the document that supports the thesis statement.

TASK

Examine the document on the next page carefully and answer the short-answer question that follows it. Then write an essay showing how evidence in the document supports the following thesis statement:

Renaissance art often reflected humanist concerns.

1 What characteristics of this painting identify it as a work
   of the Renaissance period?

_____

_____

_____

*Portrait of Cecilia
Gallerani by
Leonardo da Vinci*

WRITING THE PARAGRAPH

In the answer below, the first paragraph has been done for you.
Complete the answer by showing how the painting illustrates
the thesis statement.

①
The intro-
duction →
provides
the histori-
cal context.

②
The thesis
statement
gives the
generaliza-
tion that the
← rest of the
essay will
explain.

③
The transi-
tion sent-
ence men-
tions the
painting.

④ →

This para-
graph
should con-
tain your
interpreta-
tion of the
document,
relating it to
the thesis
statement.
Use infor-
mation from
your answer
to the ques-
tion above,
and other
information
from your
knowledge
of global
history.

*The Renaissance was a period of great change in Europe
that started in Italy in the 15th century. This period is
called the Renaissance, meaning "rebirth," because it
involved a rebirth of classical culture. Among the most
important changes was the way in which people of the
Renaissance viewed themselves and their world. People
began to see humankind as the "focus of all things." Their
art often relected these humanist concerns. This new way
of viewing things can be clearly seen in the painting by
Leonardo da Vinci, "Portrait of Cecilia Gallerani."*

   In this painting, we see that _____

_____

_____

_____

_____

_____

_____

_____

CHAPTER 11

THE BIRTH OF THE MODERN WORLD, 1500-1770

Maya temple pyramids at Chichen Itza, Mexico

KEY TERMS, CONCEPTS AND PEOPLE

- Maya, Aztec, Inca
- Christopher Columbus
- Conquistadors
- Atlantic Slave Trade
- Mercantilism
- Capitalism
- Divine Right
- Absolutism
- Peter the Great
- John Locke
- Martin Luther
- Scientific Revolution
- Enlightenment
- Akbar the Great
- Ming dynasty
- Manchus

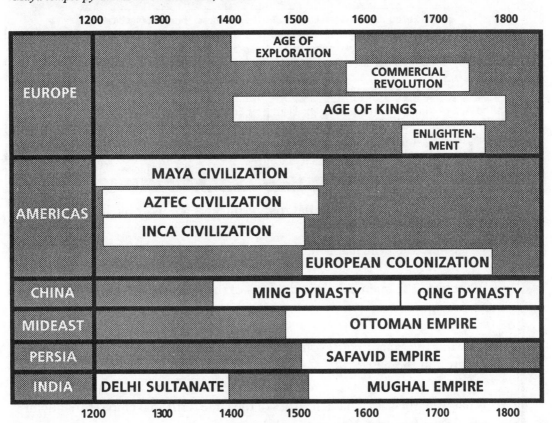

	1200	1300	1400	1500	1600	1700	1800
EUROPE				AGE OF EXPLORATION	COMMERCIAL REVOLUTION / AGE OF KINGS	ENLIGHTEN-MENT	
AMERICAS		MAYA CIVILIZATION / AZTEC CIVILIZATION / INCA CIVILIZATION			EUROPEAN COLONIZATION		
CHINA			MING DYNASTY			QING DYNASTY	
MIDEAST				OTTOMAN EMPIRE			
PERSIA				SAFAVID EMPIRE			
INDIA	DELHI SULTANATE			MUGHAL EMPIRE			

WHAT YOU SHOULD FOCUS ON

The nearly three centuries from 1500 to 1770 witnessed the birth of the "modern world" with the following important developments:

- a greater awareness of other cultures
- the creation of a global economy
- the rise of powerful nation-states
- major technological advances and a deepening reliance on science

In this chapter, you will read about the impact that these developments had on three major areas in the world:

The Encounter Between Europe and the Americas. This encounter brought together all existing centers of civilization and created a truly global economy. By creating colonial empires in the Americas and transporting slaves from Africa, Europeans exerted greater influence on the world than ever before.

The Age of Kings in Europe. European kings built large armies and absolute monarchies by taxing new wealth. Challenges to traditional thinking emerged from the Scientific Revolution and the Enlightenment.

Empires of Asia. Farther east, great empires flourished in the Middle East, Persia, India, and China: the Ottoman, Safavid, Mughal, Ming, and Qing. The pace of change in Asia fell behind that of Europe.

In reviewing this era, keep in mind that testmakers are most likely to ask you:

- What were the principal achievements of the pre-Columbian civilizations?

- What were the main causes and effects of the European encounter with the Native Americans?

- How did the Scientific Revolution and the Enlightenment affect European society and thought?

- What were the basic characteristics of the large territorial empires that dominated Asia from the 16th to the 18th centuries?

LOOKING AT ECONOMICS

Economists study how people produce and use goods and services to meet their needs. They study trade, finance, money, investment, production, and consumption.

THE BASIC PRINCIPLES OF ECONOMICS

THE PROBLEM OF SCARCITY

Most people have unlimited wants. We can never be wholly satisfied because we have only **limited resources** at our disposal to meet these **unlimited wants**. Economists refer to this as the **problem of scarcity**. For example, everyone in your community may want a new home, but there is not enough space, materials or money available to build new homes for everyone.

OPPORTUNITY COSTS

Because of the problem of limited resources, whenever we choose to use resources to satisfy one need, we give up the chance to satisfy other needs. This trade-off, in which we give up the opportunity to meet another need, is known as the **opportunity cost** of an economic choice. For example, if you use your money to buy a new stereo, you give up the opportunity to buy a new computer.

COMPARING ECONOMIC SYSTEMS

THE THREE BASIC ECONOMIC QUESTIONS

Because of the problem of scarcity, all societies must seek answers to three basic economic questions:

What should be produced?

How should it be produced?

Who should get what is produced?

The method that a society uses to answer these questions is known as its economic system. In general, there are three types of economic systems:

TRADITIONAL ECONOMY

In a **traditional economy**, people follow the occupations of their ancestors. They farm and make things based on how their ancestors did. Some families, like nobles, enjoy special benefits when goods are distributed, simply because their ancestors were privileged in the past.

COMMAND ECONOMY

In a **command economy**, the government answers the basic economic questions. Government leaders decide who makes what and who gets it. Communism as it existed in the Soviet Union (1917-1991) was an example of a command economy.

FREE MARKET

The **free market system** is based on individual choice. Individuals invest their money to produce and sell goods and services to gain a **profit**. People are free to produce whatever they wish, and to buy whatever they can afford. Government interference in the economy is limited. The three basic economic questions are answered by the interplay between **consumers** (those who buy and use goods and services) and **producers** (those who make and sell goods and services).

KEY FEATURES OF THE FREE MARKET SYSTEM

Private Property. People have a right to own property and to use it as they see fit.

Profit Motive. The chance to make a **profit** (what remains after the costs of business are paid) is one thing that drives people to risk their money in business.

Supply and Demand. These forces eliminate weak producers, stop production of unwanted goods, and generally determine the prices at which goods are sold.

Free Enterprise. People are free to take part in any business, and buy, sell and advertise any legal product or service. Businesses are free to attract customers with lower prices and better quality.

In a free market economy, the interaction between what consumers will pay and what producers are willing to sell determines what is produced. Consumers will buy more shoes at $25 a pair than at $100 a pair. Shoe manufacturers will make more shoes if they can sell them for $100 a pair instead of $25. The actual prices of most shoes will generally fall somewhere in between.

MAJOR HISTORICAL DEVELOPMENTS

PRE-COLUMBIAN CIVILIZATIONS IN THE AMERICAS

While complex civilizations were emerging in Asia, Africa, and Europe, equally striking developments occurred in the Americas. In this chapter you will review the chain of events set into motion in 1492, when this part of the world first encountered Europeans.

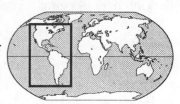

THE FIRST AMERICANS

Scientists believe that during the last Ice Age, Asia and Alaska were attached by a land-bridge where the Bering Straits are today. As long as 25,000 years ago, groups of Asian hunters crossed this land-bridge following the migrations of animals. Over time, these people multiplied and spread throughout North America, Central America, the islands of the Caribbean, and South America. Separated by vast mountains and dense jungles,

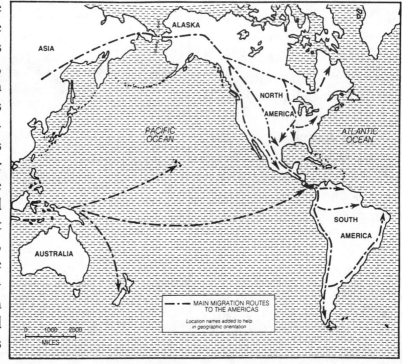

these people developed their own separate languages and cultures.

"Native Americans" had their own Neolithic Revolution, learned to grow corn (*maize*) and other crops, and traded extensively. Several civilizations emerged in **Mesoamerica** (*present-day Mexico and Central America*). Historians call these civilizations **pre-Columbian** because they existed here before the arrival of Columbus in 1492.

Unlike the early civilizations of Africa and Eurasia, the first Native American civilizations did not emerge in river valleys. Native Americans in the warm and humid rain forests of Mesoamerica learned to plant corn, a crop unknown to the peoples of Africa, Asia, and Europe. Corn became the basic food crop in the Americas, supporting the development of permanent settlements and large cities.

THE OLMECS

The earliest known Mexican civilization was the **Olmec**. The Olmecs flourished in the rain forest along the Gulf of Mexico several thousand years ago. They developed a calendar, constructed public buildings and temples, and traded with other groups over long distances.

THE MAYA (1500 B.C. - 1546 A.D.)

Over 3,000 years ago, the Maya developed a complex civilization in present-day Guatemala. Each Maya city had its own chief ruler, who was considered half-man and half-god. Most Maya were peasant farmers who lived in thatched huts and grew corn. There was also a small class of craftsmen, who made luxury goods for their nobles. The nobility were a small hereditary class who performed sacred ceremonies on special occasions and assisted the rulers.

The Maya engaged in frequent wars and practiced human sacrifices. They developed a ball game that became popular throughout the Americas. Two teams competed on a rectangular court, trying to hit a solid rubber ball into wooden rings. Archaeologists believe the game had religious significance and that the losers were sometimes sacrificed.

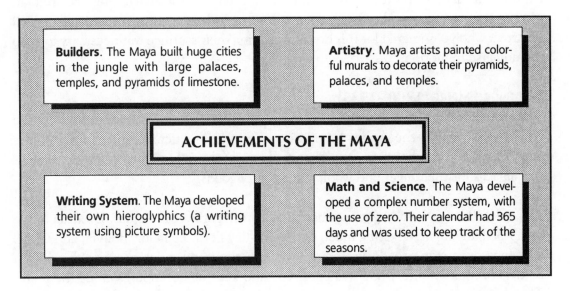

Builders. The Maya built huge cities in the jungle with large palaces, temples, and pyramids of limestone.

Artistry. Maya artists painted colorful murals to decorate their pyramids, palaces, and temples.

ACHIEVEMENTS OF THE MAYA

Writing System. The Maya developed their own hieroglyphics (a writing system using picture symbols).

Math and Science. The Maya developed a complex number system, with the use of zero. Their calendar had 365 days and was used to keep track of the seasons.

Around the 9th century, Maya culture experienced a great crisis. Archaeologists do not know if a food shortage, epidemic, or great war brought an end to the classic period of Maya civilization. The Maya migrated north to the Yucatan peninsula in present-day Mexico, and built a new series of city-states. One of these later Mayan cities is well-preserved at **Chichen Itza**. Constant warfare from the 13th to the 16th centuries and pressures from neighboring peoples led to the final decline of Maya civilization.

THE AZTECS (1200 - 1521)

The Valley of Mexico, in the center of that country, has a high elevation and temperate climate; it is excellent for growing crops. Around 1300, the Aztecs — an alliance of several local peoples — settled on an island in the center of the Valley of Mexico. They learned to grow corn and acquired other skills from their neighbors. Over the next two centuries, they engaged in frequent wars to conquer other peoples in the region. These conflicts continued until the arrival of the first Europeans in the Americas.

The Aztecs developed a highly complex social organization. At the top of their society was the ruler. Below the ruler were the nobles, who often held high positions in the government, army, or priesthood. Most people worked as farmers, fishermen, craftsmen, or as warriors in the Aztec armies. At the bottom of Aztec society were slaves.

Like other Native American cultures, the Aztecs worshipped many gods. The most important was the Sun God. The Aztecs believed the Sun God needed human blood to continue his daily journeys across the sky. For this reason, the Aztecs practiced human sacrifices on a massive scale. Captured warriors from other tribes were sacrificed, as well as Aztecs who volunteered for this honor, believing their sacrifice was necessary to keep the universe in motion.

THE INCA EMPIRE (1200 -1535)

Thousands of miles to the south of Mexico, advanced cultures developed along the Pacific coast and in the Andes Mountains of South America. Peoples in the Andes grew potatoes and other root crops that could resist the cold nights. They kept llamas and alpacas for their meat and wool, and to carry goods.

Around 1400, the Inca began extending their rule across the Andes. Eventually the Inca ruled an empire covering much of present-day Peru, Ecuador, Bolivia, and Chile. The Inca built stone roads stretching over ten thousand miles to unite the distant corners of their empire. Food was preserved and kept in storehouses along the roads. The Inca never developed carts with wheels, possibly because such vehicles were unsuited to the rugged terrain of the Andes Mountains.

The Inca did not develop a system of writing. Instead, they used intricate bundles of knotted and colored ropes to count, keep records, and send messages. Their superb engineering skills allowed them to construct vast stone buildings high in the Andes. They had no cement, but when constructing buildings they fitted the stones together so perfectly that a knife blade could not be inserted into the joints. The ruins of **Machu Picchu**, an ancient fortress city high in the Andes Mountains, provides one of the best surviving examples of Inca building skills.

The ruins of Machu Picchu

THE ENCOUNTER BETWEEN EUROPE AND THE AMERICAS

The Renaissance spirit of inquiry led Europeans to explore the seas. The European encounter with the peoples of the Americas was a world-shaking event. It brought the major civilizations of the world together for the first time and had a profound impact on all peoples.

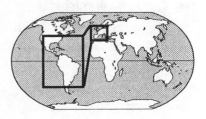

THE AGE OF DISCOVERY

The writings of **Marco Polo** (1254-1324) had stimulated interest in trade with East Asia. Goods were carried overland to Constantinople and then shipped across the Mediterranean Sea by the Italian city-states. The final conquest of the Byzantine empire by the Ottoman Turks in 1453 cut off Europe from trade with East Asia. As a result, there were incentives to find new all-water passages to the East.

Search for New Trade Routes. European rulers correctly believed that control of trade with East Asia would bring them vast wealth.

Technology. Better navigation skills and instruments like the compass and moveable rudder allowed Europeans to sail farther than ever before.

MOTIVES FOR OVERSEAS EXPLORATION

Religion. Christian rulers in Europe wanted to spread their religion through overseas exploration.

Desire For New Products. The Crusades, Marco Polo, and other contacts stimulated interest in East Asian goods like spices, perfumes, and silks.

SPAIN AND PORTUGAL LEAD THE WAY

Spain and Portugal are located at the western end of Europe. Spain has coasts on the Mediterranean Sea and the Atlantic Ocean. Both countries were determined to gain a share of the trade with Asia, and had the resources needed to finance costly overseas exploration. Spain's rulers, Ferdinand and Isabella, had just completed the **Reconquista** (*reconquest*) of Spain's last Muslim areas, reuniting the country under Christian rule in 1492. In the same year, they expelled all Muslims ("Moors") and Jews. Through overseas exploration, Spain hoped to further spread Christianity and glorify the country.

THE GREAT EXPLORERS

Starting in the late 1400s, European monarchs competed with one another in sending out explorers to find new trade routes and seek new lands.

✦ **Christopher Columbus** (1451-1506) was convinced he could reach Asia by sailing westward, and persuaded the rulers of Spain to provide him with three ships in 1492. After two months at sea, he accidentally landed in the Americas instead of reaching the East Indies. His "discovery" of the Americas provided new sources of wealth and raw materials that would forever alter the economy of Europe.

✦ **Vasco Da Gama** (1460-1524), a Portuguese explorer, discovered an all-water route from Europe to India by sailing around the southern tip of Africa in 1497. This made it possible for Europeans to obtain Asian goods without using overland routes. Portugal set up trade routes with the Spice Islands of Southeast Asia.

✦ **Ferdinand Magellan** (1480-1521), another Portuguese explorer, led the first expedition to **circumnavigate** (*circle*) the world in 1519. Sailing around South America and across the Pacific, Magellan confirmed that the world was round.

VOYAGES OF EARLY EUROPEAN EXPLORERS

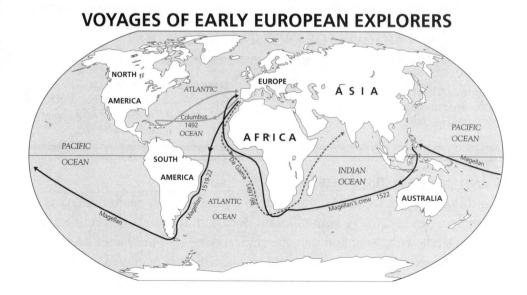

THE EUROPEAN CONQUEST OF THE AMERICAS

The impact of the arrival of the Europeans was especially profound on the Native Americans. Spanish **conquistadors** (*conquerors*) and priests arrived soon after the first explorers. They came to conquer native peoples, seize gold and silver, obtain natural resources, and convert the natives to Christianity. Small numbers of Spanish soldiers using horses and firearms, and acting with local allies, quickly overcame large numbers of indigenous peoples and conquered the two greatest Native American empires of the time: the Aztec and Inca.

THE CONQUEST OF MEXICO
Soon after Columbus' first voyage, the Spanish conquered the main Caribbean islands. In 1519, **Hernando Cortés** sailed from Cuba to Mexico with a small force of soldiers in search of gold and silver. Cortés met the Aztec emperor, **Montezuma**. The Aztecs at first believed the Spaniards were gods, and showered them with gifts. Later, Cortés left the Aztec capital and allied his forces with the enemies of the Aztecs.

With a few hundred Spaniards, and several thousand Native American warriors, Cortés attacked the Aztecs in 1521. Several factors explain his final triumph. The Aztecs fought with clubs, spears, and bows while the Spaniards had guns, steel swords, shields, horses, and cannons. The Spaniards also gathered a large force of native warriors who were hostile to the Aztecs. Finally, the Aztecs were worn down by smallpox, accidentally introduced by the Europeans, against which the Aztecs had no immunity. As a result, Cortés was able to conquer the powerful Aztec empire.

THE CONQUEST OF PERU
In 1530, **Francisco Pizarro** set sail from Panama to conquer the Inca. Pizarro arrived just when they were recovering from a brutal civil war. High in the Andes Mountains, Pizarro and a handful of soldiers faced a much larger force of Inca warriors.

Again, the Native Americans proved to be no match for the more technologically advanced and determined Europeans. Pretending friendship, Pizarro invited the Inca Emperor to visit him. Pizarro and his army ambushed them and murdered the emperor. Pizarro was then able to conquer the Inca capital by 1533. In general, the Spaniards treated the conquered Native Americans harshly. Defeated peoples were forced to accept the Christian religion and to labor for their new rulers.

EFFECTS OF THE ENCOUNTER

The European encounter with the Americas led to an exchange of ideas, customs, and technologies. Such an exchange is known as **cultural diffusion.**

Trade brings people into contact with others, introducing them to new goods and better ways of doing things.

Conquest brings two or more societies together. The conquerors and the conquered often learn from each other.

HOW CULTURAL DIFFUSION OCCURS

Exploration and colonization often causes people to migrate to new areas, bringing them into contact with others who are different.

Warfare often exposes the soldiers of one culture to the ideas and products of another culture.

INCREASED TRADE

Because of the encounter, the European diet was improved by the introduction of new foods like potatoes, corn, and tomatoes. Western Europe quickly became the center of a vast global trading network, with trade shifting away from the Mediterranean

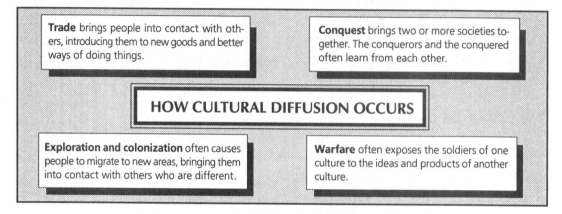

THE EXCHANGE OF GOODS BETWEEN EUROPE AND THE AMERICAS

NORTH AMERICA

EUROPE

Horses, Donkeys, Sheep, Goats, Cattle, Cats, Rats, Mice, Wheat, Onions, Carrots, Lettuce, Grapes, Oranges, Melons

ATLANTIC OCEAN

Corn, Beans, Chocolate, Peanuts, Pineapples, Tobacco Squash, Potatoes, Tomatoes, Chili Peppers

PACIFIC OCEAN

SOUTH AMERICA

to the nations on the Atlantic coast — Portugal, Spain, England, France, and Holland.

Raw materials from the Americas hastened European economic development. Wealth from the "New World" enriched European merchants and their kings.

THE COLONIAL EXPERIENCE IN LATIN AMERICA

The European conquest also brought important changes to Native American society.

COLONIAL GOVERNMENT

In the **Treaty of Tordesillas** of 1494, the Pope divided the Americas between Spain and Portugal by drawing a north-south line that placed Brazil under Portuguese rule. Spain became ruler of an American empire many times larger than Spain itself. Gold and silver from the Americas made Spain the richest power in Europe in the 1500s. Royal governors called **viceroys** were sent to rule the colonies in the king's name.

COLONIAL SOCIETY

The conquered lands were often divided among the soldiers. They forced Native Americans to till the land and work the mines under an arrangement called the **encomienda** *(or hacienda)* **system.** Church leaders were also an elite class and shared in political power. Priests converted many Native Americans to Catholicism. The **Jesuits,** a Catholic religious order established during the Counter-Reformation, built schools, founded hospitals, and taught agricultural skills to Native Americans until the Jesuits were expelled from Latin America in 1767. Meanwhile, native populations rapidly declined because they had no immunity to diseases from Europe like measles and smallpox. As a result, many landowners imported Africans as slaves, particularly to the Caribbean and Brazil.

Peninsulares were Europeans sent from Spain and Portugal to govern the colonies. These European-born nobles held the most power and control in the New World.	**Creoles** were people born in the Americas of European parents. They were wealthy landowners, lawyers, and priests, but were looked down on by the Peninsulares.

SOCIAL CLASSES IN COLONIAL LATIN AMERICA

Mestizos and **mulattos** were people of mixed European and Native American or African ancestry. Their status was only slightly higher than Native Americans and Africans.	**Native Americans** and **Africans** made up the bulk of the population. The Native Americans worked under serf-like conditions, while the Africans were enslaved. Both groups lacked social standing.

THE TRANSATLANTIC SLAVE TRADE

Finding workers able to survive the harsh conditions of working the land became a major problem for the European colonists. The solution led to one of the most serious effects of the European conquest of the Americas: the rise of the slave trade. Slavery had existed in Africa long before European intervention. However, the **Transatlantic slave trade** expanded slavery on a scale unparalleled in human history.

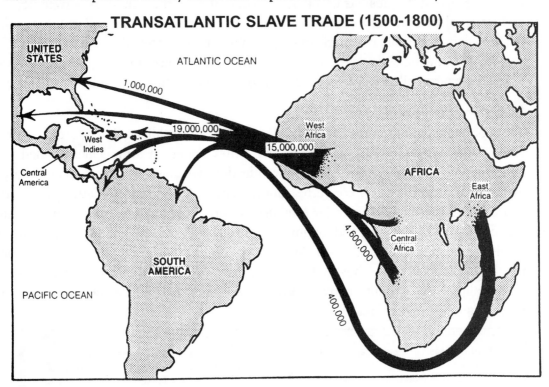

Enslaved people were usually captured by powerful African tribes in raids on less powerful villages. The slaves were brought to the coast where they were traded to European and American slave traders in exchange for guns and other goods.

It is estimated that the slave traders removed as many as 15 million African men and women over a three-hundred-year period. Many died during the **"middle passage"** on the voyage across the Atlantic because of the horrible conditions on board the ships. The survivors worked long hours in the sugar fields of the Caribbean Islands and Brazil, or later in growing tobacco and cotton in North America.

THE LEGACY OF THE TRANSATLANTIC SLAVE TRADE

Encouraged African Warfare. The slave trade encouraged African tribes to go to war with each other to obtain slaves to be traded in exchange for European guns and other goods.

Disrupted African Culture. The slave trade destroyed much of Africa's rich heritage and disrupted its development. It created a legacy of violence, bitterness, and social upheaval, leaving problems still unresolved today.

Increased Cultural Diffusion. The exchange of ideas and goods increased. Slave traders brought new weapons and other goods to Africa, while slaves brought their poems, myths, and music to the Americas.

After three centuries, humanitarian movements against slavery in Europe and America finally brought an end to the Transatlantic slave trade in the early 1800s.

THE COMMERCIAL REVOLUTION (1600-1750)

The creation of colonial empires and the rise of strong national monarchies also had a startling effect on the economies of Europe. Although most European economic activity remained in agriculture, the fastest growing part of the economy was now in trading goods, especially from Asia and the Americas. The **Commercial Revolution**, as it is now called, marked an important step in the transition from the local economies of the Middle Ages to a truly global economy in which goods were produced and exchanged on a world-wide basis. The Commercial Revolution had several important aspects.

MERCANTILISM

European kings hoped to increase their power through the system of **mercantilism**. Rulers tried to increase their supply of gold and silver by achieving a favorable balance of trade — exporting goods of greater value than what they imported. Some European rulers took steps to promote the production of textiles for export. To accumulate greater wealth and power, England, France, and Holland — all countries with coasts on the Atlantic Ocean — established overseas colonies of their own, in imitation of Spain and Portugal. The **Dutch East India Company**, for example, established indirect rule over the Spice Islands of Southeast Asia. Each so-called "mother country" exported expensive finished goods to the colonists and imported less costly raw materials. The competition for colonial empires and control of the seas spilled over into a series of wars between the European powers. Great Britain finally emerged from these wars as the chief victor in the 1760s.

GLOBAL EMPIRES OF EUROPE, 1700

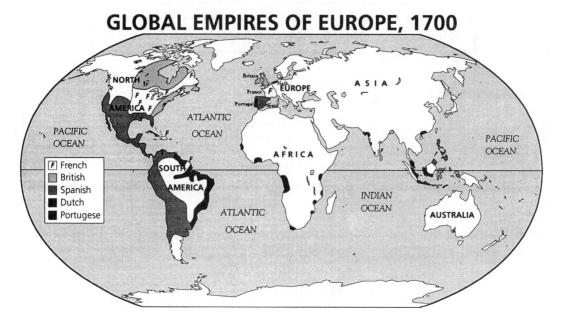

THE EMERGENCE OF CAPITALISM

Merchants and bankers laid the foundations for a new economic system known as **capitalism**. Under this system, **entrepreneurs** (*business owners*) risked their money in new business ventures in order to make a profit. Workers produced goods, but did not share in the profits. The development of new businesses, an increasing number of trading expeditions across the oceans, and the need to finance large armies led to demands for huge sums of money. To raise the money, **joint stock companies** were formed. These privately-owned companies sold stock (*shares in the company*) to investors hoping to make a profit. The new capitalist system and greater wealth from overseas colonies and trade set the stage for the Industrial Revolution, which began in England in the mid-1700s.

THE AGE OF KINGS (1600-1770)

The decline of feudalism, the spirit of the Renaissance, the European encounter with the Americas, the changes of the Reformation, and the Commercial Revolution all served to increase the power of European monarchs (*kings and queens*) while enriching European society.

THE GROWTH OF ROYAL POWER

In the Middle Ages, the power of kings had been limited by nobles, parliaments, and the Catholic Church. In the 16th and 17th centuries, this began to change as kings increased their power and relied less on their nobles.

WARS OF RELIGION

The religious wars that followed the Reformation provided kings with an opportunity to build large standing armies and to increase their wealth through new taxes. The growing middle classes in the towns often allied themselves with kings against the nobility, increasing support for the monarchs. Kings also took control of religion within their own borders, sometimes even appointing themselves leaders of the church. In England, King **Henry VIII** made himself the head of a new national church in the 1530s. His daughter, **Elizabeth I**, defended Protestant England against Catholic Spain.

DIVINE RIGHT THEORY

Monarchs justified their increase in power on the basis of **divine right**. According to this theory, the king was God's deputy on earth, and royal commands expressed God's will. The Englishman **Thomas Hobbes** wrote that monarchs were justified in assuming absolute power because only they could act impartially to maintain order in society.

LOUIS XIV (1638-1715): A CASE STUDY IN ABSOLUTISM

Absolutism refers to a monarch's total control over his subjects. Louis XIV of France provided a model for other absolute monarchs. During his reign, his word was law. Any critic who challenged his authority was punished. To control his nobles, Louis built a large palace at Versailles. Leading nobles were forced to spend most of the year residing with the king at Versailles, so they had little opportunity to plan a rebellion. Louis also interfered in the economic and religious lives of his subjects. Royal regulations established standards for all French industries. Louis demanded that Protestants either convert to Catholicism or leave France. Finally, Louis involved his nation in a series of wars to expand France's frontiers and bring glory to his reign. In the end, Louis XIV and his aggressive actions served to unite Europe against France, leaving his country bankrupt and exhausted.

RUSSIA UNDER THE TSARS

At the eastern end of Europe, the rulers of Russia adopted the system of royal absolutism on a grand scale. In the early 1500s, the rulers of the region around Moscow set about increasing Muscovy's size by conquering neighboring lands and expanding Muscovy into Russia. The bulk of the population were **serfs** — peasants required by law to stay on the land and work for the landowners. Unlike Western Europe, serfom in Russia did not decline at this time. The nobles exercised absolute power over their serfs. In return for their privileges, the nobility pledged absolute loyalty to the Tsar. Two of the most notable monarchs during this period were:

Peter the Great

✦ **Peter the Great** (1682-1725). Peter turned Russia from a backward nation into a modern power by introducing Western ideas, culture, and technology into his country. He defeated neighboring Sweden and Turkey, greatly extending Russia's boundaries. When some of his subjects were reluctant to adopt Western customs, he used force to compel them to do so. Peter moved the capital of Russia from Moscow to St. Petersburg, a city he ordered to be built on the Baltic coast so that Russia would have a "window on the West."

✦ **Catherine the Great** (1762-1796). Catherine continued Peter's policies of expansion and Westernization. She also promoted limited reform at the beginning of her reign and granted the nobles their own charter of rights. However, she refused to part with any of her absolute power. During her long reign the conditions of Russian serfs actually worsened.

ENGLAND BECOMES A LIMITED MONARCHY

In England, monarchs were never able to establish the system of absolute rule that developed in France and Russia. Indeed, as far back as the Middle Ages, strong checks on English royal power were imposed. The most important of these were the Magna Carta and the English Parliament. Later events turned England into a **constitutional monarchy,** in which subjects enjoyed basic rights and power was shared between the monarch and Parliament.

ENGLAND'S ROAD TO CONSTITUTIONAL MONARCHY

Bill of Rights of 1689. The new rulers accepted this bill, which established Parliament's supremacy. Monarchs could not collect new taxes or raise an army without Parliament's consent.

Glorious Revolution (1688-1689). King James II tried to weaken Parliamentary control. Angered by these actions, Parliament asked his daughter and her husband to take James II's place. James II fled and was later defeated in Ireland.

Puritan Revolution (1642-1660). Charles' efforts led to civil war between the King and Parliament. Charles was executed in 1649. When his son was restored to the throne in 1660, he had to agree to accept limits on royal power.

The Early Stuarts. James I became king in 1603. James believed in the divine right of kings and often came into conflict with Parliament. His son, Charles I, tried to establish absolutism and to collect taxes without Parliament's consent.

Tudor Monarchs. In the 1500s, Henry VIII and Elizabeth I created a strong, centralized monarchy based on a sense of national unity, the Church of England, and shared power with Parliament.

Rise of Parliament. Parliament was established as a legislative body made up of nobles in the House of Lords and elected representatives in the House of Commons.

Magna Carta. In 1215, English nobles forced King John to sign the Magna Carta, which guaranteed that Englishmen could not be fined or imprisoned except according to the laws of the land.

Parliament building

One of the most influential writers of this period was **John Locke**. He believed that governments obtain their authority from the consent of people they govern, not from God — as divine right theorists had taught. According to Locke, the main purpose of government was to protect the people's rights to life, liberty, and property. Locke defended people's right to rebel when a government abused its power. His writings were influential beyond the period in which he lived. A century later, Locke's ideas influenced the leaders of both the American and French Revolutions.

THE SCIENTIFIC REVOLUTION

The **Scientific Revolution** began during the Renaissance and continued during the Age of Kings. It rejected traditional authority and church teachings in favor of the direct observation of nature. The revolution in science was largely based on the new **scientific method,** in which men of science observed nature, made hypotheses (*educated guesses*) about relationships, and then tested their hypotheses through experiments. Galileo, for example, conducted tests on the movements of bodies to find general principles of physics. Scientists began to discover that the movements of bodies in nature closely followed what could be predicted by mathematics.

Sir Isaac Newton

The most influential thinker of the Scientific Revolution was **Sir Isaac Newton**. His book *Principia Mathematica* connected the speed of falling objects to the movements of planets. Newton reduced all these patterns to a single formula: the law of gravity. Newton's discovery raised hopes that all of the universe acted according to certain fixed and fundamental laws. It seemed that all scientists had to do was to apply observation, experimentation, and mathematics.

THE INFLUENCE OF THE ENLIGHTENMENT

The **Enlightenment,** also called the **Age of Reason,** refers to an important movement in 18th-century European thought. The spark for the Enlightenment came from the progress made by the Scientific Revolution.

Enlightenment thinkers believed that by applying scientific reasoning, people could better understand both nature and one another. They believed that nature and society operated according to basic universal laws which they called "natural laws." Enlightenment thinkers believed that people could use reason to discover these laws and apply this knowledge to improve the quality of life. They applied the new scientific method to society and its problems. This led them to question the divine right of kings, the hereditary privileges of the nobility, and the power of the Catholic Church.

> **Voltaire (1694-1778)** poked fun at traditional authority. His views on religious toleration and intellectual freedom greatly influenced later leaders of the American and French Revolutions.

> **Jean-Jacques Rousseau (1712-1778)** believed a government should express the "general will" of the people. His book *The Social Contract* helped to inspire the democratic ideals of the French Revolution.

KEY THINKERS OF THE ENLIGHTENMENT

> **Montesquieu (1689-1755)** argued for separation of powers in government as a check against tyranny. His book *The Spirit of Laws* called for a system of checks and balances, which was later used in the U.S. Constitution.

> **Adam Smith (1723-1790)** described capitalism in his book *The Wealth of Nations*. He explained how competition and the division of labor guides a free economic system based on self-interest.

THE ENLIGHTENMENT AND THE AMERICAN REVOLUTION

In 1776, Enlightenment ideas were used by American colonists in their **Declaration of Independence** from England. This document asserted natural human rights such as the right to life, liberty, and the pursuit of happiness. The Declaration argued that the purpose of government was to protect these rights, demonstrating the influence of Locke's theory.

ENLIGHTENED DESPOTISM

Enlightened despots were absolute monarchs who hoped to use Enlightenment ideas to reform their societies "from above." In some cases, they instituted religious tolerance, established scientific academies, and promoted social reform, but they rarely supported a greater sharing of political power. Maria Theresa of Austria, Catherine the Great of Russia, and Charles III of Spain were examples of enlightened despots.

THE TERRITORIAL EMPIRES OF ASIA

While Europeans were creating a new global order affecting Africa and the Americas, large empires continued to flourish further east in Turkey, Persia, India, and China. Like the absolute monarchs of Europe, the rulers of these empires used gunpowder and large armies to impose order on vast territories. But in other ways these 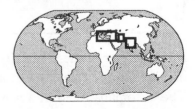 empires did not advance as rapidly in scholarship, science, and technology as the European states did. As a result, these regions later felt the impact of European expansion.

THE OTTOMAN EMPIRE (1453-1918)

In the last chapter, we saw how Arab Muslims created a vast Islamic civilization that eventually covered an area from Spain to the Indus River. The **Ottomans,** a nomadic group of Turkish people originally from Central Asia, emerged as rulers of the Islamic world in the 13th century.

In 1453, they succeeded in capturing Constantinople, the capital of the Byzantine empire. For a time, they cut off European trade with Asia and took control of the Mediterranean. The Ottomans also conquered Egypt and North Africa, uniting all of the Muslim world under their rule, except for Persia and Afghanistan. By the mid-1500s, under **Suleiman the Magnificent,** the Ottoman empire reached its height.

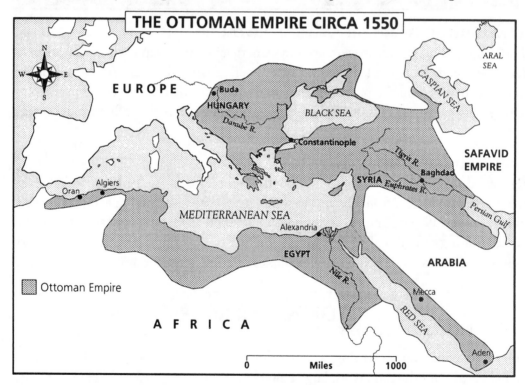

At the center of the Ottoman system was the **Sultan** (*ruler*) and his lavish court. Under the Sultan's rule, the Ottoman empire was well-organized and efficiently governed. The Ottomans ruled in a way that recognized the cultural diversity of their empire. Each of the major religious communities — Muslim, Jewish, and Christian — was represented by its own leaders. Each of these communities was ruled by its own laws and collected its own taxes. At the same time, the Sultan in Istanbul (*Constantinople*) governed over the entire empire as an all-powerful ruler. This unique system of government, combined with Ottoman military power and control of the crossroads of trade, promoted prosperity and stability until the late 18th century.

THE SAFAVID EMPIRE IN PERSIA

The Safavids created a great Islamic empire in Persia in the early 1500s. Members of a Turkish tribe, the Safavids were Shi'ite Muslims. They were hostile to the Ottomans, who followed the Sunni branch of Islam. This association with the Shi'ite branch of Islam gave the Safavids (*the present-day Iranians*) a separate identity from their Turkish and Arab neighbors. Safavid rule eventually extended as far south as the Arabian Sea and east almost to the Indus River.

Safavid rulers, who were known as **Shahs**, used large standing armies to maintain control of their empire. They also did much to encourage trade. Miniature painting flourished and the production of beautiful Persian rugs increased. Literature, medicine, and the study of astronomy thrived. Later Safavid rulers proved less capable, however. High taxes and continuous warfare with the neighboring Ottomans eventually weakened their empire. In 1722, the Safavids were conquered by neighboring Afghanistan.

MUSLIM, MUGHAL, AND BRITISH INDIA

The impact of Islam was felt even farther east than Turkey and Persia. As early as the 8th century, Muslim invaders reached the Indus River Valley by entering the mountain passes to the northwest of the Indian subcontinent.

THE MUSLIM INVASIONS

In the 11th and 12th centuries, Turkish Muslims invaded India's northern plains, destroying Hindu cities. They established independent kingdoms in northern India, known as **Sultanates**. The most important Sultanate was established around 1200 at Delhi. For the next 300 years, the Delhi Sultans ruled much of northern and central India. Unlike prior conquerors, the Muslims never fully adopted Indian ways. For example, Muslim women wore veils and remained secluded, even though Hindu women did not. At the end of the 14th century, Tamerlane destroyed the capital city of Delhi and slaughtered its inhabitants. The Delhi Sultanate never fully recovered from this blow.

THE MUGHAL EMPIRE (1526-1837)

In 1526, **Babur**, a descendant of both Tamerlane and Chinggis Khan, defeated the Sultan of Delhi and founded the Mughal empire. Although their name was taken from the word *Mongol*, the Mughals were Muslims with close ties to Safavid Persia. The most famous Mughal ruler was Babur's grandson, **Akbar the Great** (1542-1605). He conquered neighboring Muslim and Hindu states, uniting all of northern India under his rule. Akbar next set out to unite his Muslim and Hindu subjects through a policy of religious toleration. He ended special taxes paid by Hindus and employed Hindu officials in government. To govern his large empire more efficiently, Akbar divided it into twelve provinces. Well-trained

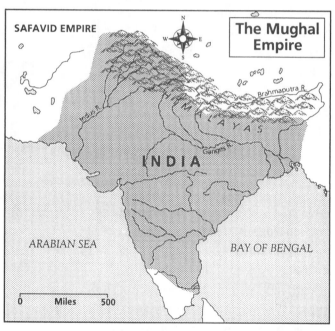

imperial officials were sent to supervise local government, enforce laws, and ensure the collection of taxes. Akbar also encouraged learning, painting, music, and literature.

Akbar's grandson, **Shah Jahan** (1628-1658), had less sympathy for Hindus. He reimposed special taxes on them and ordered the destruction of many Hindu temples. In the northwest and northeast, many people converted to Islam. Some of them changed their religion to avoid special taxes. Others converted because they were from lower castes, and hoped to escape the caste system. Shah Jahan patronized the arts and built palaces, and mosques to glorify his reign. The most famous and beautiful of his buildings, the **Taj Mahal,** was a tomb constructed for his wife. After Shah Jahan's reign, the Mughal empire gradually began to fall apart. Although the Mughals continued to rule in the north, a series of small, independent kingdoms developed in central and southern India.

INDIA UNDER BRITISH RULE

While the Mughals were extending their territories to the north, European countries had established trading posts along the coasts of India. Merchants of the **East India Company** laid the foundation for the rise of the British Empire in India.

At first, the East India Company avoided involvement in rivalries among local kingdoms. However, native rulers often asked the British for protection. In the 1750s, a local ruler attacked the British port of Calcutta. The East India Company recaptured the town with company troops, and became the major military power in India. Soon afterwards, the British defeated their rivals, the French, who had also established outposts in India.

Over time, the East India Company expanded its territories to protect its trading interests. A treaty with the Mughal emperor made the company the imperial tax collector throughout most of India. Gradually, British "residents" were sent to other parts of India to safeguard company interests. Most Indian rulers came under British protection. By the early 19th century, the East India Company had gained control over the entire Indian subcontinent, making it largely a British possession.

THE MING AND QING DYNASTIES IN CHINA

We have already seen how China was reunified under Mongol rule in the 13th century. Despite their achievements, the Mongols remained unpopular. In 1368, they were overthrown by a Chinese monk, who established the Ming dynasty.

MING DYNASTY (1368 - 1644)

During the **Ming dynasty,** China enjoyed nearly 300 years of peace and prosperity. Ming emperors expanded the empire to include Korea, Burma, and Vietnam. The Ming constructed an immense Imperial Palace in Beijing. Known as the Forbidden City, the palace became home to all later Chinese emperors. During the Ming dynasty, Chinese literature and art flourished. Craftsmen excelled at printing and in producing silks and porcelains of great beauty. Urban life and trade prospered, while China exported silk, porcelain, and other luxury goods.

Under the Ming, Chinese society had two main classes. Most people were peasants, barely earning a living. They were mostly illiterate, and their lives centered around their relatives and the village. The other main social group consisted of the scholar-gentry class, who owned the land on which the peasants worked. The gentry greatly respected learning. The Ming restored China's civil service examinations. The gentry studied to pass these demanding tests, which focused on Confucian teachings. In addition to these two main social classes, there were merchants and craftspeople living in China's cities.

Ming China had a large merchant fleet engaged in trade in the South China Sea and Indian Ocean. The Ming launched great naval expeditions in the 1400s in order to spread

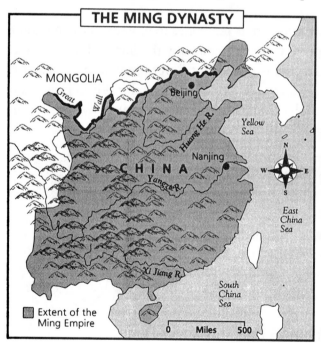

THE MING DYNASTY

MONGOLIA
Great Wall
Beijing
Yellow Sea
Hwang He R.
Nanjing
CHINA
Yangzu R.
East China Sea
Xi Jiang R.
South China Sea
■ Extent of the Ming Empire
0 Miles 500

the news of China's wealth and power. Chinese explorers like **Zheng Ho** sailed to the coasts of India and Arabia. But in the 1430s, the Ming emperor suddenly ordered an end to these voyages because of opposition by noble families. Thus, just as Europe began expanding its horizons, Chinese rulers halted naval exploration.

European contact with China was established in the 16th century. In 1557, Portuguese traders established a settlement on China's southern coast. Catholic missionaries followed the merchants into China in an attempt to convert the people to Christianity. But Christianity had limited appeal for the Chinese, who believed that their culture was far superior to all others, and that China, the "Middle Kingdom," was the center of the universe.

QING (MANCHU) DYNASTY (1644 - 1912)

Population growth, limits on trade, and a series of peasant rebellions weakened the Ming dynasty by the 1600s. In 1644, the Manchus, a nomadic people from Manchuria in the northeast, invaded and conquered Ming China.

THE QING (MANCHU) DYNASTY

Extent of Qing Empire in 1780

Lake Baikal

Lake Balkhash

Mongolia

Japan

Korea

Beijing

Great Wall

Huang He R.

Tibet

C H I N A

PACIFIC OCEAN

Indus R.

Brahmaputra R.

Yangtze R.

Ganges R.

India

South China Sea

0   Miles   1500

The Manchu conquerors founded the **Qing** (*or Manchu*) **dynasty**. Like the Mongols before them, the Manchus adopted Chinese ways for governing their new empire. They continued the traditional civil service examinations and ruled with the help of local officials. However, the Manchus forced Chinese men to shave their heads, leaving a single braided pigtail (*queue*) at the back, as a sign of submission to Manchu rule.

Qing rulers built new roads and canals, cleared additional land for agriculture, and built storehouses for grain. During the 1700s, Qing emperors such as **Kang Xi** and **Qian Long** promoted scholarship and education while reducing taxes.

During these same years, however, European technology gradually surpassed that of China. In later chapters, we will see how the Manchu rulers of China faced new challenges from Europe in the early 1800s.

Duke Obi, the Regent of the Qing Imperial Court in the 17th century

— STUDY CARDS —

Pre-Columbian Civilizations

Before Columbus arrived, three major civilizations flourished in the Americas:
- **Maya:** built cities, pyramids and temples, developed writing, calendar, astronomy
- **Aztec:** ruled in central Mexico; highly developed city planning and art; conquered by **Hernando Cortés** with aid of groups hostile to the Aztecs, guns, horses, smallpox
- **Inca:** ruled large empire across the Andes Mountains; sophisticated builders; overthrown by **Francisco Pizarro**

Europeans in the Americas

Columbus sought new Asian trade routes; **conquistadors** sought wealth, Christian converts.

Effects:
- **Cultural Diffusion:** exchange of ideas and goods between the Americas and the rest of the world; new foods in Europe
- **Colonization:** Europeans defeated natives with horses and guns, established colonial empires
- **Decimation:** millions of Native Americans died from European diseases

Colonial Latin America

Native American cultures were decimated by conquest and European diseases.

Effects:
- Spain and Portugal divided up South America in 1494
- Spain sent governors to rule in the name of the king
- Spanish divided lands into estates (**encomiendas**); Native Americans were forced to work as slaves on the land or in mines; death rate was very high

Transatlantic Slave Trade

Demand for labor in New World led to growth of slave trade. Africans were captured by other tribes, sold to European sea captains and shipped to the Americas under horrendous conditions (many died during the **"Middle Passage"**).

Effects:
- Disrupted African cultures and delayed growth of populations
- Encouraged warfare between African tribes
- Introduced African cultural influences to the Americas

Commercial Revolution

Europe changed from feudal economy to new economy where goods were traded worldwide.

Impact:
- **Mercantilism:** rulers increased their power by amassing gold through colonies and taxes
- **Colonies:** Spain, Portugal, France, Holland and England developed overseas empires
- **Capitalism:** entrepreneurs risked their capital (*money*) in pursuit of profits
- Merchants developed new methods of financing, such as joint stock companies and borrowing

Absolutism

Starting in 1500s and continuing through 1700s, monarchs triumphed over nobles, built powerful central governments through taxation, established standing armies. Monarchs justified their absolute power by claiming they ruled by **Divine Right**.

- **Louis XIV:** built Versailles, patronized the arts, engaged in constant warfare
- **Peter the Great** and **Catherine the Great:** absolute rulers of Russia; sought to expand and "Westernize" their nation

Constitutional Monarchy

Government in which power is shared by king or queen and Parliament. This emerged gradually in Great Britain:

- **Magna Carta (1215):** Limited king's power over subjects' lives and property
- **Rise of Parliament:** Legislative body of nobles and elected commoners
- **Puritan Revolution (1640s)** and **Glorious Revolution (1688)** established Parliament's superiority over the English monarchy

Ottoman Empire (1300-1918)

Ottomans, a nomadic Turkish group, emerged as rulers of the Islamic world:

- Captured Constantinople in 1453, renamed it Istanbul, cut off European trade with Asia for some time
- Sultan ruled empire from Istanbul
- Christians and Jews tolerated, given some limited means of self-government
- Ottoman Empire reached its height in the 1500s under **Suleiman the Magnificent**

Scientific Revolution

Began in Europe during Renaissance and continued into the 1700s.

- Based on the **scientific method** — observe nature, make hypotheses, and test hypotheses through experiments
- Applied mathematics to science to reveal laws of nature — for example, Isaac Newton's law of gravity
- **Key People:** Copernicus, Kepler, Galileo, Bacon, Newton

Mughal and British India

- Muslims had invaded India in the 11th century and established **sultanates**
- In the 16th century, descendants of Mongols founded the **Mughal Empire** in India
- **Akbar the Great** united India and reconciled Hindus and Muslims
- Akbar's grandson, **Shah Jahan,** ended religious toleration, built the **Taj Mahal**
- Starting with trading posts and eventually raising an army, Britain's **East India Company** gained control of most of India by the late 1800s

Enlightenment (1700s)

Intellectual movement in France, England, Scotland and Germany, also known as the **Age of Reason**.

- Thinkers tried to apply scientific reasoning to understand people and to improve society through reform
- Challenged Divine Right of Kings, noble privilege, power of Roman Catholic Church
- **Key People:** John Locke, Voltaire, Montesquieu, Rousseau, Adam Smith

Ming and Qing Dynasties

- **Ming Dynasty** overthrew Mongol rule in 1368; China enjoyed 300 years of peace. Empire expanded to Korea, Burma, Vietnam; "Forbidden City" built; Ming halted overseas exploration. Chinese trade, art, urban life flourished.
- **Qing (Manchu) Dynasty:** conquerors from Manchuria. Overthrew Ming in 1640s, established Qing Dynasty. The Manchus mainly adopted Chinese ways. In late 1700s China's technology fell behind Western Europe. Dynasty overthrown in 1911.

SUMMARIZING YOUR UNDERSTANDING

COMPLETING A TABLE

Use the table below to organize the information you have read about major empires of this era in the Americas and Asia.

NAME	TIME PERIOD	LOCATION	MAJOR ACHIEVEMENTS
Maya			
Aztec			
Inca			
Ottoman			
Safavid			
Mughal			
Ming			
Qing			

TESTING YOUR UNDERSTANDING

Test your understanding of this chapter by answering the following questions.

1 One reason European monarchs sought an all-water route to Asia was that
   (1) they needed a place to send their excess population
   (2) Asia represented a place to sell manufactured goods
   (3) the fall of the Byzantine empire in 1453 cut off Europe from trade with East Asia
   (4) Muslims had gained control of the Holy Land

2 Which characteristic was common to both the ancient Egyptian and Maya civilizations?
   (1) monotheistic religion   (3) influence of European cultures
   (2) nomadic lifestyle   (4) the development of writing

3 During the colonial period in Latin America, a major reason for the importation of enslaved Africans was the
   (1) scarcity of Native American labor   (3) development of advanced farming
   (2) need for skilled industrial workers   (4) desire to promote Christianity

Base your answer to question 4 on the line graph and on your knowledge of global history.

4 Which statement is best supported by the information in the graph?

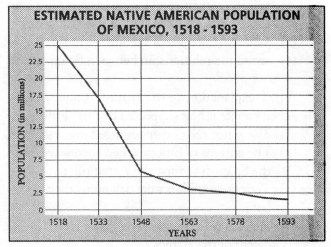

(1) Mexico's Native American population steadily increased between 1500 and 1600.
(2) The effects of the Spanish conquest on the Native American population of Mexico were most severely felt between 1518 and 1548.
(3) The Spanish conquest of Mexico improved standards of living for the Native Americans in Mexico.
(4) Spanish influence in Mexico ended by 1593.

---

5 • Suleiman held complete religious and political power.
   • Charles I stormed the English Parliament.
   • Peter the Great expanded serfdom in Russia.

The actions of these leaders reflect the concept of

(1) scientific theory   (3) mercantilism
(2) natural rights   (4) absolutism

Base your answer to question 6 on the pie chart and your knowledge of global history.

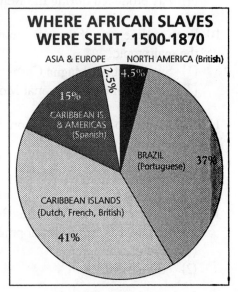

6 Which is a valid conclusion based on the information in the pie chart?
(1) Most slaves were destined for the cotton fields of North America.
(2) Europe and Asia did not participate in importing African slaves.
(3) The largest number of slaves were sent to various Caribbean islands.
(4) African slaves came mostly from the west coast of Africa.

7   The concept of mercantilism is best illustrated by the
    (1) political structure of China during the Zhou dynasty
    (2) social kinship system of the Kushite people
    (3) military strategies of the armies of the Roman empire
    (4) economic relationship between Spain and its "New World" colonies

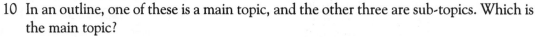

8   Which explanation for the Spanish conquest of the
    Aztec Empire is best supported by this illustration?
    (1) The Aztec religion encouraged non-violence.
    (2) The nations of Europe allied themselves with
        the Spanish against the Aztec rulers.
    (3) The conquistadors were defending their home-
        land.
    (4) Spanish technology was a major factor in the
        defeat of the Aztecs.

9   Which statement concerning the Renaissance in
    Europe is based on opinion rather than fact?
    (1) Literature began to appear in languages other
        than Latin.
    (2) The art of the Northern Renaissance was su-
        perior to that of the Itanlian Renaissance.
    (3) Art reflected the ideas of humanism and in-
        dividualism.
    (4) Art produced during the Renaissance had religious as well as secular themes.

10 In an outline, one of these is a main topic, and the other three are sub-topics. Which is
    the main topic?
    (1) Signing of the Magna Carta   (3) Start of the Glorious Revolution
    (2) Growth of Constitutional Monarchy (4) Rise of Parliament

11 "Kings are God's lieutenants on earth." Which type of government is best character-
    ized by this quotation?
    (1) direct democracy   (3) republic
    (2) limited monarchy   (4) divine right rule

12 The Magna Carta, the Glorious Revolution, and the writings of John Locke all contrib-
    uted to Great Britain's development of
    (1) absolute monarchy   (3) parliamentary democracy
    (2) ethnic rivalries   (4) imperialist policies

13 Which was a result of the Commercial Revolution?
    (1) decline in population growth in Europe
    (2) shift of power from Western Europe to Eastern Europe
    (3) spread of feudalism throughout Western Europe
    (4) expansion of European influence overseas

14 The Ottoman, Safavid, and Mughal empires were similar in that they all
    (1) were followers of Islam   (3) were located in Europe
    (2) limited the power of their rulers (4) had very large navies

15 Which statement best describes the effects of the works of Nicolaus Copernicus, Galileo
    Galilei, Sir Isaac Newton, and René Descartes?
    (1) The acceptance of traditional authority was strengthened.
    (2) The scientific method was used to solve problems.
    (3) Funding for education was increased by the English government.
    (4) Interest in Greek and Roman drama was renewed.

16 A major concept promoted by philosophers of the Enlightenment was the need for
    (1) a return to traditional medieval ideas
    (2) the use of reason for rational and logical thinking
    (3) overseas expansion by Western European nations
    (4) strengthening the power of organized religion.

INTERPRETING DOCUMENTS

The diagram below illustrates colonial society in Latin America.

1a Describe the structure of colonial society in Latin America. _____

_____

b Select one group and tell what role they played in Latin American colonial society.

_____

THEMATIC ESSAY QUESTION

Directions: Write a well-organized essay that includes an introduction, several paragraphs addressing the Task below, and a conclusion.

Theme: Movement of Goods and People

> Cultural diffusion often takes place when one society establishes contact with or conquers another society.

Task:

- Choose *three* examples from your study of global history in which one society established contact with or conquered another society.
- For *each* of the three examples, describe *one* way in which one of the societies was changed.

You may use any example from your study of global history. Suggestions you may wish to consider include ancient Greece, ancient Rome, the Islamic empire, the Crusades, the Mongols, and the Age of Discovery.

You are *not* limited to these suggestions.

APPLYING A DOCUMENT TO A THESIS STATEMENT

In this exercise, you will practice linking an illustration to a thesis statement. Your first paragraph should describe the historical context, present the thesis statement, and make a transition to your supporting paragraph. The second paragraph should refer to information in the document that supports the thesis statement.

TASK:

Examine the document on the next page, and answer the question next to it. Then write an essay showing how the evidence in the document supports the following statement:

New contacts between groups of people
often have important consequences.

According to the drawing, what was a consequence of the contact between the Native Americans and the Spanish conquistadors?

_____

_____

_____

16th-century copy of an original illustration showing the Aztecs during the Spanish conquest

Write a short essay relating the document to the thesis statement. The first two sentences have been done for you. Complete the introduction by writing the thesis statement. In the second paragraph, explain how the drawing is connected to the thesis statement.

① Introductory sentences provide the historical context.

③ Discuss → the document and show how it supports your thesis statement.

The Aztecs were a Native American civilization that flourished in the high plateau of central Mexico. In 1519, Spanish conquistadors arrived in Mexico. _____

_____.

_____

_____

_____

_____

_____

_____

← ② Write your thesis statement here.

CHAPTER 12

NEW CURRENTS: REVOLUTION, INDUSTRY AND NATIONALISM, 1770 - 1900

The Storming of the Bastille

	1750	1770	1790	1810	1830	1850	1880	1910
JAPAN	TOKUGAWA SHOGUNATE						MEIJI RESTORATION	
EUROPE	OLD REGIME IN FRANCE		FRENCH REVOLUTION/NAPOLEON		METTERNICH ERA	REVO-LU-TIONS	GERMAN, ITALIAN UNIFIC.	SCRAMBLE FOR COLONIES
	INDUSTRIAL REVOLUTION							
MIDEAST	OTTOMAN EMPIRE							
LATIN AMERICA	COLONIAL RULE			INDEPEN-DENCE	AGE OF CAUDILLOS			
AFRICA				END OF SLAVE TRADE			EUROPEAN IMPERIALISM	
INDIA	MUGHAL RULE WEAKENS		EXPANSION OF EAST INDIA COMPANY		BRITISH EMPIRE			
CHINA	QING (MANCHU) DYNASTY							
	1750	1770	1790	1810	1830	1850	1880	1910

WHAT YOU SHOULD FOCUS ON

A person born during the Middle Ages would not have felt too out of place 300 years later in Renaissance Italy. Likewise, someone from Japan's Heian Period would not have felt uncomfortable in Japan 300 years later. But a European who had lived before the French Revolution, returning just a century later, would have found the dramatic changes that had taken place almost incomprehensible.

In reviewing this period, it is helpful to group these changes into four areas:

The French Revolution was a political event with world-wide impact. It challenged the way people thought about traditional political authority and social divisions.

The Industrial Revolution caused the greatest changes in lifestyles and technology since the dawn of civilization. New sources of power replaced human and animal power. People began mass-producing goods with machines in factories.

NEW CURRENTS EMERGING IN THE WORLD, 1770-1900

Nationalism caused problems for rulers with many nationalities under their control. National groups under foreign rule or divided among several governments tried to acquire their own unified states.

Imperialism changed the map of the world. The new capabilities provided by the Industrial Revolution and the ambitions inspired by nationalism caused the leading European powers to lay claim to areas in Asia, Africa, and the Pacific.

Under the impact of European imperialism, even traditional empires like China began to erode. The country that proved most able to resist European domination was Japan: it succeeded in doing so by copying European ways.

In reviewing this era, keep in mind that testmakers are most likely to ask:

• What were the causes and effects of the French Revolution?

• What were the causes and effects of the Industrial Revolution?

• What factors led to an upsurge in nationalistic feelings in the 19th century?

• What were the benefits and drawbacks of imperialism in areas such as Africa and Asia?

LOOKING AT THE FORCES OF SOCIAL CHANGE

Just as we experience the process of change in our individual lives, societies also undergo change. The political, social, economic, and religious systems of a society are often in a state of development and flux.

MAJOR FORCES OF SOCIAL CHANGE

Historians are especially interested in understanding why and how societies change, and what forces influence the pace and direction of change. The following have been identified as some of the more important causes of historical change:

CONFLICT AMONG GROUPS IN A SOCIETY
Many societies include people of different religious and ethnic groups, of different social classes, and of different sexes, ages and backgrounds. Often these various groups have conflicting interests. These disagreements may be resolved by repression, reform, compromise, or sometimes by violence and revolution.

NEW IDEAS
New ideas can transform a society. These may be new ideas about social and political organization, such as democracy, absolute monarchy, or dictatorship. They may be new religious beliefs, like Islam, Buddhism, or Protestantism, or new ideas about nature, such as the Scientific Revolution of the 1500s-1600s.

CONTACTS WITH OTHER SOCIETIES
Contacts with other societies can lead to the introduction of new ideas and products through cultural diffusion. For example, the Native American encounter with Europeans in the Americas led to the introduction of new foods to Europe, as well as the introduction of horses and cattle to the Americas. Contacts with other societies can also lead to conflict and war. Wars impose powerful demands on every society, often leading to internal changes.

TECHNOLOGICAL INNOVATION
New inventions can be powerful ingredients of historical change. For example, the introduction of gunpowder helped bring an end to feudalism. The invention of the printing press played an important role in causing the Reformation by allowing Church critics to communicate their ideas widely.

CHANGES IN THE ENVIRONMENT
Changes in the biological and physical environment can strongly affect human society. The end of the Ice Age led to the Neolithic Revolution. The Black Death in the 14th-century caused a drastic loss of population. A slightly cooler climate in the 17th century led to bad harvests and major social unrest. Today, pollution is causing a slight warming of the global climate. This has led to droughts in the Sahel region of Africa, threatening the lives of millions of people.

THE PACE OF CHANGE

In traditional agricultural societies, change is often so slow that it almost goes unnoticed. In industrial societies, the pace of change is usually much faster.

EVOLUTIONARY CHANGE VS. REVOLUTIONARY CHANGE
Evolutionary change is gradual: it gives people time to adapt and evolve. *Revolutionary* change is abrupt: sometimes it is economic or social, like the Industrial Revolution, and at other times it is political, like the French Revolution.

PATTERNS OF POLITICAL REVOLUTION
In a political revolution, new groups challenge the existing order. The government collapses or is overthrown by force, and the revolutionaries introduce major changes. Political revolutions often follow a familiar pattern:

First Stage	Intermediate Stage	Final Stage
Strains appear in the existing system, making it ripe for revolution. As the revolution begins, moderate reformers take over.	Moderate attempts at compromise fail. Radicals take over and the revolution grows more violent. Often civil war and conflicts with neighboring nations occur.	The radicals are replaced by the moderates, who may be replaced by a return to the old order, with some concessions made to reform.

MAJOR HISTORICAL DEVELOPMENTS

In the last chapter, we saw how the creation of a new Atlantic economy stimulated economic growth in Europe. Overseas trade and increased wealth led to the strengthening of European governments and the development of new ideas. These same developments created new tensions in European society. The emerging capitalist economy and Enlightenment ideas made the middle classes less willing to accept the divine right of kings and the privileged positions of the Church and nobility. These tensions finally exploded in the French Revolution, shaking Europe and the Americas.

THE FRENCH REVOLUTION AND ITS IMPACT

For centuries, France had been one of the most populous and powerful countries in Western Europe. Several conditions made France ripe for revolution by 1789.

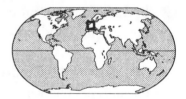

PRECONDITIONS TO REVOLUTION

INEQUALITY AMONG CLASSES

Prior to 1789, French society (*referred to by historians as the "Old Regime"*) was divided into three classes or "estates." The first estate was made up of the clergy; the second was the nobles. The third and largest estate was made up of the common people, including the **bourgeoisie** (*middle class merchants, professionals, and shopkeepers*). French nobles held many special privileges, such as being exempt from most taxes and having the right to collect feudal dues. The bourgeoisie, influenced by their rising wealth and Enlightenment ideas, resented the special privileges of the nobles.

UNFAIR TAX SYSTEM

France's financial system was based on tradition. By the late 1700s, many saw it as outdated and unfair. Different social classes and even various geographical regions paid different tax rates. Towns and provinces taxed each other's goods, restricting trade.

A Bankrupt Government

French kings had bankrupted the government through expensive wars, excessive borrowing, and poor money management. The king's ministers came to believe the only way to solve the government's financial problems was to tax the nobles. But the nobles refused to pay taxes unless the king summoned an **Estates General** — a national assembly in which each of the three social classes was represented. The nobles felt they would be able to control the Estates General. **King Louis XVI** reluctantly gave in to their demands. Elections were held all over France to select delegates for the different estates.

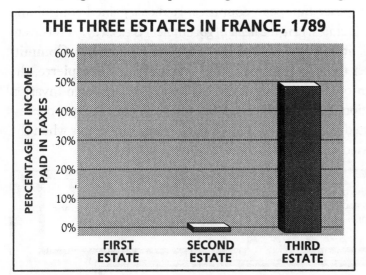

THE THREE ESTATES IN FRANCE, 1789

MAIN EVENTS OF THE REVOLUTION

The revolution began as a contest for power between the king and the nobles. It quickly turned into a struggle in which the king and nobles closed ranks against the bourgeoisie. In the course of the revolution, power shifted first to the moderate bourgeoisie, then to the radical shopkeepers and craftsmen, and finally back to the moderate bourgeoisie.

The Rule of the Moderates

Once the Estates General met, the delegates from the Third Estate declared themselves to be a **National Assembly**. King Louis thought about breaking up the Assembly, but grew afraid when Parisians seized a royal prison known as the **Bastille** on July, 14, 1789. The National Assembly issued a **Declaration of the Rights of Man** proclaiming that government rested on the consent of the people, not on the divine right of the king. The Assembly also announced that all Frenchmen were "free and equal," and abolished the privileges of the nobles. The slogan of the Revolution became "Liberty, Equality, and Fraternity [Brotherhood]." A written constitution was adopted, creating a National Legislature and turning France into a constitutional monarchy.

THE REVOLUTION TAKES A RADICAL TURN

France now posed a threat to monarchs who still claimed to govern by divine right. The French soon were at war with other European countries. Radicals gained control and turned France into a republic (*a state where the head of government is elected*). A return to power by the king was feared, and Louis XVI and his wife were executed. A **Committee of Public Safety** took over the government. Led by **Maximilien Robespierre**, the Committee launched a **Reign of Terror** to save the revolution from foreign invasion and domestic counter-revolution. Catholic priests, former nobles, and other people suspected of treason were executed. Power finally shifted back to the moderates when the threat of foreign invasion passed and the French tired of internal violence.

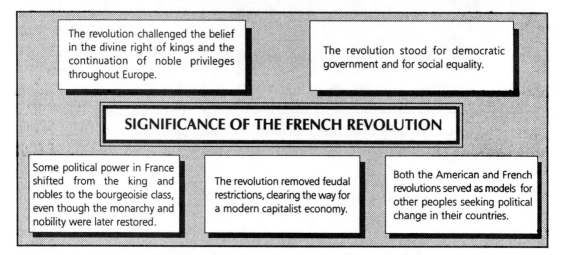

The revolution challenged the belief in the divine right of kings and the continuation of noble privileges throughout Europe.

The revolution stood for democratic government and for social equality.

SIGNIFICANCE OF THE FRENCH REVOLUTION

Some political power in France shifted from the king and nobles to the bourgeoisie class, even though the monarchy and nobility were later restored.

The revolution removed feudal restrictions, clearing the way for a modern capitalist economy.

Both the American and French revolutions served as models for other peoples seeking political change in their countries.

THE RISE AND FALL OF NAPOLEON

Napoleon Bonaparte (1769-1821) came from a family of the lower nobility on the island of Corsica. As a boy, he was sent to military school in France. Napoleon would prove to be one of the most gifted generals of all time.

MILITARISM AND EMPIRE BUILDING

Under Napoleon's leadership, French armies invaded Italy and defeated the Austrians and Russians. In 1799, Napoleon seized power in France. He tried to combine the social reforms of the French Revolution with his own seizure of absolute power. Four years later, he crowned himself emperor. By 1805, Napoleon had defeated all the other European powers except England, and had created a French empire covering much of Europe. He put his relatives in power in Italy, Germany, Holland, and Spain, bringing all of these nations under his influence.

THE DEFEAT OF NAPOLEON

Napoleon's mighty ambitions united most of Europe against him. His inability to invade England, eco-nomic prob-lems in Europe caused by his boycott of Brit-ish goods, and the unpopularity of French rule in the rest of Europe created increasing strains on his empire.

NAPOLEON'S EUROPEAN EMPIRE, 1810

- French Empire
- French satellite kingdoms
- French Allies
- Nations hostile to Napoleon
- Neutrals

NORWAY
SWEDEN
NORTH SEA
DENMARK
BALTIC SEA
RUSSIAN EMPIRE
GREAT BRITAIN
PRUSSIA
Grand Duchy of Warsaw
ATLANTIC OCEAN
CONFEDERA-TION
OF THE RHINE
AUSTRIAN EMPIRE
FRANCE
SWITZ.
KDM. OF ITALY
BLACK SEA
PORTUGAL
SPAIN
KDM. OF NAPLES
OTTOMAN EMPIRE
Sardinia
MEDITERRANEAN Sicily SEA

In 1812, Napo-leon invaded Russia with an army of 422,000 men. The Rus-sians burned their own crops and buildings as they retreated, thus depriving the French of food and shelter. By the time Napoleon reached Moscow, more than 300,000 of his men had either deserted or died. They found Moscow in ruins; it had been set on fire by the Rus-sians as they evacuated the city. The French, forced to retreat in bitter winter weather, lost 90,000 more men to star-vation and cold. Only 10,000 of Napoleon's army survived.

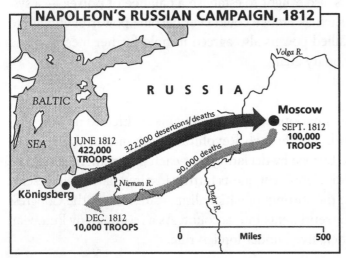

NAPOLEON'S RUSSIAN CAMPAIGN, 1812

Volga R.
R U S S I A
BALTIC SEA
Moscow
SEPT. 1812
100,000
TROOPS
JUNE 1812
422,000
TROOPS
322,000 desertions/deaths
90,000 deaths
Nieman R.
Dnepr R.
Königsberg
DEC. 1812
10,000 TROOPS

0   Miles   500

After Napoleon's failure in Russia, the other European powers combined to overthrow him. These powers then restored the old French royal family to the throne in 1814. The new king, **Louis XVIII,** granted his subjects a charter which guaranteed the people of France their basic civil rights and a national legislature.

THE IMPACT OF NAPOLEON

Although Napoleon ruled France for only fifteen years, he had an important influence on France, Europe, and the rest of the world.

NAPOLEON'S IMPACT ON FRANCE, EUROPE, AND THE WORLD

France. Napoleon created stability by establishing the **Code Napoleon**, a law code which consolidated such achievements of the revolution as social equality, religious toleration, and trial by jury.

Europe. Napoleon introduced the ideas of the French Revolution in the lands he conquered, abolishing serfdom, introducing religious toleration, and reforming local laws.

The World. French rule was greatly resented, fueling the growth of nationalism. Napoleon also weakened Spain, which lost its colonial empire in Latin America to independence movements.

THE RESTORATION OF EUROPE

After Napoleon's defeat, Europe's rulers met in Vienna to redraw national boundaries.

THE CONGRESS OF VIENNA (1814-1815)

At Vienna, Great Britain, Russia, Austria and Prussia restored many former rulers and borders, bringing Europe back in some measure to the way it had been before the French Revolution. But the allied leaders also sought to establish a **balance of power** — a system in which no single country such as France could ever become powerful enough to dominate other countries. The allied powers also agreed to hold further meetings and to cooperate in resisting revolutionary change.

THE SPIRIT OF NATIONALISM

Nationalism is the belief that each nationality (*ethnic group*) is entitled to its own government and national homeland. The French Revolution had ignited the spirit of nationalism throughout much of Europe by declaring that each government should be based on the will of the people. Napoleon's conquests further inspired nationalist resentment against the French. Despite the stirrings of nationalism, statesmen at the Congress of Vienna failed to take these new sentiments into account. As a result, many European peoples were still not united; others lived under foreign rule.

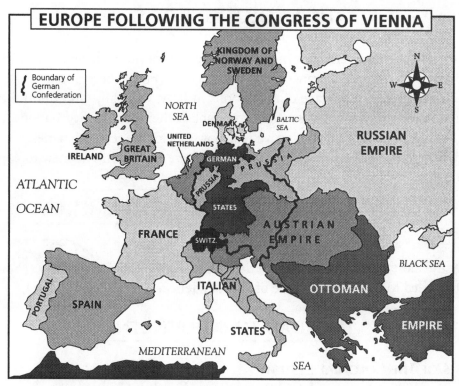

EUROPE FOLLOWING THE CONGRESS OF VIENNA

RANGE OF POLITICAL OPINIONS

In the early 1800s, Europeans were divided into three main political groups about the path countries should follow:

Conservatives were opposed to almost all change, fearing it would lead to social upheaval.

Liberals wanted moderate reforms like giving the middle class a larger say in government.

Radicals favored a revolutionary overthrow of the existing order.

THE METTERNICH ERA (1815-1848)

Prince Metternich of Austria was one of the statesmen at the Congress of Vienna. He helped establish a system that prevented nationalism or liberal political change in Europe. The thirty years following the Congress of Vienna witnessed a series of unsuccessful revolutions in Italy, Germany, and Poland. In each of these countries, national groups sought independence but were defeated. However, in three other cases nationalism triumphed: Greece and Belgium achieved independence in 1830, and the French overthrew the restored monarchy and established a constitutional monarchy in the same year.

THE REVOLUTIONS OF 1848

The year 1848 is considered one of the turning points of the 19th century. In 1848, the constitutional monarchy of France was overthrown and France became a republic. Events in France inspired a new wave of revolutions in Italy, Germany, and Central Europe. Revolutionaries in these places sought to establish their own unified nations. But the Austrians, with Russian support, proved too powerful for the revolutionaries. Each revolutionary regime collapsed, except for France, where Napoleon's nephew took power.

THE INDEPENDENCE OF LATIN AMERICA

One of the most far-reaching effects of the French Revolution was that it led to the independence of Latin America.

THE ROAD TO INDEPENDENCE

ABUSES OF THE COLONIAL SYSTEM

By the late 1700s, the Spanish and Portuguese colonial systems were causing increased unrest in Latin America. Although the Creoles were descended from Europeans, they were denied political power and resented European-born *Peninsulares*.

Europe's Latin American Colonies: 1780

SPANISH
FRENCH
PORTUGUESE
DUTCH

Colonists also resented economic restrictions placed on the colonies that made it difficult for them to trade directly with countries other than Spain, or to manufacture their own goods.

REVOLUTIONARY IDEAS SPREAD TO LATIN AMERICA

Both the American and French Revolutions brought new ideas to Latin America. These revolutions had declared that people were entitled to governments that protected their interests. During the Napoleonic Wars in Europe, the colonists in Latin America had basically governed themselves. When Napoleon was defeated in 1814, the king of Spain was restored to his throne. Once in power, he reimposed the old colonial system, prohibiting the colonists from trading directly with Britain and other countries. Some Latin American leaders refused to return to Spanish rule, and demanded independence.

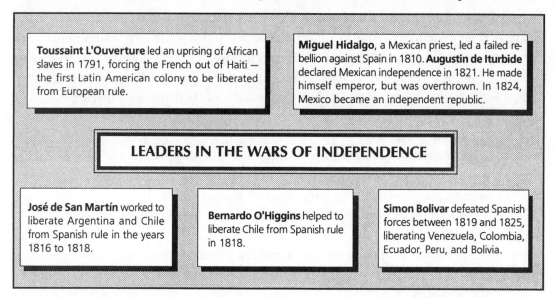

Toussaint L'Ouverture led an uprising of African slaves in 1791, forcing the French out of Haiti — the first Latin American colony to be liberated from European rule.

Miguel Hidalgo, a Mexican priest, led a failed rebellion against Spain in 1810. **Augustin de Iturbide** declared Mexican independence in 1821. He made himself emperor, but was overthrown. In 1824, Mexico became an independent republic.

LEADERS IN THE WARS OF INDEPENDENCE

José de San Martín worked to liberate Argentina and Chile from Spanish rule in the years 1816 to 1818.

Bernardo O'Higgins helped to liberate Chile from Spanish rule in 1818.

Simon Bolivar defeated Spanish forces between 1819 and 1825, liberating Venezuela, Colombia, Ecuador, Peru, and Bolivia.

Meanwhile, a division in the Portuguese royal family led Brazil declare independence from Portugal in 1823. Thus, by 1824, Latin American independence was firmly established.

THE MONROE DOCTRINE (1823)

The United States recognized the independence of the new Latin American nations, but feared that Spain might try to reconquer them. To prevent this, President James Monroe issued the **Monroe Doctrine**. It declared that the United States would oppose any attempt by European powers to establish new colonies in the Western Hemisphere or to reconquer former colonies that had achieved their independence. President Monroe also agreed not to interfere with existing European colonies. At the time, the Monroe Doctrine announced to the rest of the world that the United States had a special interest in the Western Hemisphere.

LATIN AMERICA IN THE NINETEENTH CENTURY

After independence, very few real democratic governments were established in Latin America. Nations throughout Latin America continued to have sharp divisions between rich and poor. After living under strict Spanish and Portuguese rule, people in these countries lacked experience in political participation. As a result, military dictators and unstable governments flourished in Latin American for most of the 19th century.

CONTINUING ECONOMIC DEPENDENCE ON EUROPE

Despite independence, land and wealth remained in the hands of a small elite, supported by the military and the Catholic Church. Most Latin American countries continued to specialize in the production of a few cash crops, like sugar or coffee, for export. They remained dependent on Europe for most of their manufactured goods.

THE ROLE OF THE CAUDILLOS

Several Latin American countries came under the rule of powerful military leaders or political bosses, known as **caudillos**. The caudillo usually came to power by force. Many of the common people supported these leaders because of their concern for law and order and their promises of reform. The power of the caudillos also rested on divisions among the ruling elite. Conservative landowners generally opposed change. Young, well-educated members of the elite often wanted to reform their societies to be more like Great Britain or the United States. The caudillos took advantage of this conflict.

THE INDUSTRIAL REVOLUTION

While the French Revolution encouraged political change, a second revolution occurred in Europe, causing rapid economic and social change. In many respects, its effects were even more far-reaching and significant than the effects of the political revolution in France. The **Industrial Revolution** brought about a fundamental change in society by introducing **mass production**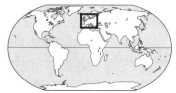
(*the large-scale production of goods*) and the use of new sources of power to meet human needs. Science became more closely linked to technology, resulting in a stream of constant innovations. Agricultural society changed into a modern industrial society.

THE REVOLUTION STARTS IN GREAT BRITAIN

The Industrial Revolution began in Great Britain in the 1750s. It soon spread to the United States and other parts of Europe, and later to the rest of the world. Several factors help explain why the Industrial Revolution first occurred in Great Britain.

Geographical Advantages. Great Britain had many harbors and navigable rivers, and plentiful coal. As an island, it was well protected from invasion. It was close to European markets and well-located for trade with other parts of the world.

Large Colonial Empire. Britain's far-flung colonial empire brought valuable raw materials to her ports. The experience of running a colonial empire contributed to the development of sophisticated financial and commercial skills.

WHY THE INDUSTRIAL REVOLUTION BEGAN IN GREAT BRITAIN

Transportation and Communications. Great Britain had a well-developed coastal trade, canals, port towns, an excellent postal service, daily newspapers, and the most powerful navy in the world.

Agricultural Revolution. British farmers introduced scientific methods to agriculture to boost productivity. Fewer people were needed to work on farms and more were available to work in industry.

Two important British inventions helped trigger the Industrial Revolution — one in textiles, and the other in mechanical power. The **spinning jenny** (1764) spun several threads at once, allowing large quantities of thread to be made quickly and inexpensively. The **steam engine** (1769) made steam power available for mechanical purposes. The steam engine led in turn to the construction of large factories, the invention of the steamboat, and the development of railroad trains.

THE INDUSTRIAL REVOLUTION BRINGS CHANGES

Before the Industrial Revolution, weavers and craftspeople worked in their homes, spinning and weaving wool, cotton, and linen by hand into finished cloth. This method of production was known as the **domestic system.**

THE SHIFT FROM HOME TO FACTORY
With the Industrial Revolution, people began working in factories. There they were supervised, and used machines driven by water or steam power. The rate of production in these factories was astonishing by the standards of the time. Because of mass produc-

tion, textile prices decreased and the demand for them rose. As demand for these products grew, more and more factories were built, employing greater numbers of workers.

✦ **Working Conditions.** While factory owners grew rich and powerful, the lives of workers often worsened. Early factories were usually appalling places with dangerous working conditions. The workday was long, and workers received barely enough wages to live on. Women and children had to work also. In hard times, factory workers lost their jobs and were left to beg, steal, or die of starvation. Writers like **Charles Dickens** and **Emile Zola** exposed working-class hardships.

✦ **Urbanization.** With the shift of work to factories, large numbers of workers moved from the countryside to the cities. The move away from farms to cities marked the largest shift of population in history. As a result, cities became crowded and often unsanitary. Nineteenth-century city governments were poorly organized and unable to cope with the large numbers of factory workers who moved there.

POPULATION OF SELECTED BRITISH CITIES, 1685-1881

City	1685	1760	1881
Birmingham	4,000	30,000	400,000
Bristol	29,000	100,000	206,000
Liverpool	4,000	35,000	555,000
Manchester	6,000	45,000	394,000
Nottingham	8,000	17,000	112,000

✦ **Growth of Railroads.** Steam engines were used to power locomotives in the early 1830s, creating the first railroads. Railroads unified the economy of a region by linking together cities, factories, towns, and the countryside. At the same time, the construction of railroads required vast amounts of coal, iron, and steel, greatly stimulating the growth of heavy industry.

THE EMERGENCE OF INDUSTRIAL CAPITALISM
A new middle class of capitalists, composed of merchants, factory owners, and bankers emerged. These people helped to develop laissez-faire **capitalism**.

CHARACTERISTICS OF CAPITALISM

Role of the Entrepreneur. The means of production were owned by people known as entrepreneurs. They provided work places *(factories)*, raw materials, mechanical energy, and machinery.	**Role of the Worker.** Workers provided their labor, for which they received wages. All risks were taken by the business owners, who were rewarded with profits for their risks.	**Role of the Government.** The policy of *laissez-faire* (French for "let do") meant that government would not interfere in relations between workers and business owners.

REFORM MOVEMENT

The problems caused by the Industrial Revolution eventually led to important social and political reforms, especially in Great Britain:

✦ **Political Reforms.** The wealthy middle class (factory owners, merchants and bankers) demanded and received more political power. In Great Britain, the **Reform Bill of 1832** gave greater representation in Parliament to the new towns and extended voting rights to the middle class. By the end of the century, subsequent reform bills had extended voting rights to the working classes.

✦ **Social Reforms.** The misery of the working classes and the injustices of capitalism began to disturb the conscience of the new middle class. They also feared working-class violence. **Robert Owens**, an early socialist, urged the creation of new communities in which everything was shared. In Great Britain, Parliament passed laws to restrict child and female labor, limit working hours, and bring about safer working conditions. Municipal reform made cities cleaner and more healthful places to live. Finally, workers organized into **unions** and threatened to strike if they did not obtain better conditions. Even those favoring conservative values — such as Bismarck in Germany — proposed some social reforms, like social security and health insurance, to win the favor of the working classes.

MARX AND COMMUNISM

Two leading critics of the capitalist system were **Karl Marx** (1818-1883) and **Friedrich Engels**. Their ideas were published in the *The Communist Manifesto* (1848). Marx later wrote *Das Kapital* (1867). Their ideas became the basis of the economic and political system known as **Communism**:

Class Struggle. Communists believe every society is divided into social classes in conflict with each other. In an industrial society, the main classes are the **bourgeoisie** *(those who own the means of production)* and the **proletariat** *(workers)*.

Exploitation of Workers. The rich prosper from the labor of their workers, who live in poverty. Owners cheat the workers by taking most of the wealth they produce, leaving them with the barest minimum needed to survive.

THE MAIN IDEAS OF COMMUNISM

Communist Revolution. Communists believe the bourgeoisie will never willingly give up their power. The plight of workers will become so desperate that they will eventually join together and start a violent revolution to overthrow the bourgeosie.

Dictatorship of the Proletariat. Workers will establish a society in which they jointly own the means of production. All citizens will be equal, sharing the fruits of their labor. Class struggles will end. Government will become unnecessary and "wither away."

Marx believed a workers' revolution would first occur in the industrialized countries of Western Europe. However, as reforms were introducd, the conditions of workers improved without a revolution. Contrary to Marx's predictions, Communism was first established in Russia. Communist ideas exercised a tremendous influence over much of the world during the 20th century, and will be discussed again in later chapters.

THE RISING TIDE OF NATIONALISM

In the first half of the 19th century, conservative statesmen had managed to contain nationalist forces. Industrialization further strengthened the influence of the middle classes, who demanded national independence and unity.

THE UNIFICATION OF ITALY AND GERMANY

Following the failure of the revolutions of 1848 in Italy and Germany, statesmen such as Cavour and Bismarck managed to unify these countries through a combination of skillful diplomacy and military force.

ITALY (1859-1870)

For centuries, Italy had consisted of a number of small states. Italian nationalists such as **Giuseppe Mazzini** called for the unification of Italy into a single country.

In 1852, Count **Camillo di Cavour** became Prime Minister of Piedmont (*also known as the Kingdom of Sardinia*). With the help of the French, he defeated the Austrians and drove them out of northern Italy. Cavour then annexed the states of northern and central Italy to Piedmont.

Further to the south, the nationalist leader **Giuseppe Garibaldi** and his secret revolutionary society overthrew the King of Naples. He then joined Naples to Cavour's enlarged Piedmont. By 1860, Italy had become a unified nation. Venice and Rome later joined Italy in 1866 and 1870.

GERMANY (1863-1871)

Like Italy, Germany consisted of a number of small states. Chief rivals for the leadership of Germany were the two largest German states — Prussia and Austria. Austria, however, contained many non-German lands and peoples. The leaders of Austria therefore did not want to see Germany united.

In the revolutions of 1848, German liberals had failed to unite the German states. But under the leadership of Prime Minister **Otto von Bismarck,** Prussia succeeded in uniting Germany by following a policy of "**blood and iron**." He combined skillful diplomacy and Prussian military power to achieve German unification. Prussian military leaders made use of new technologies, like the railroad and the rifle, to build the most powerful army in all of Europe. After a series of successful wars against Denmark, Austria, and France, Prussia finally unified Germany in 1871. The Prussian king became the **Kaiser** (*emperor*) of all Germany.

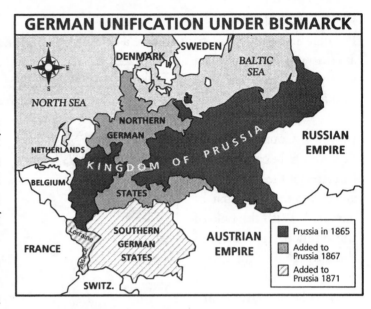

GERMAN UNIFICATION UNDER BISMARCK

SWEDEN
DENMARK
BALTIC SEA
NORTH SEA
NORTHERN GERMAN
NETHERLANDS
KINGDOM OF PRUSSIA
RUSSIAN EMPIRE
BELGIUM
STATES
Lorraine
SOUTHERN GERMAN STATES
AUSTRIAN EMPIRE
FRANCE
Alsace
SWITZ.

- ■ Prussia in 1865
- ▨ Added to Prussia 1867
- ▧ Added to Prussia 1871

AUTOCRATIC RUSSIA IN THE 19TH CENTURY

By 1800, Russia was the largest and most populous country in Europe. The French Revolution and the subsequent unrest in Europe made the Tsars of Russia fearful of introducing new reforms. While the middle classes were demanding and gaining power in Western Europe, the Tsars continued to hold absolute power in Russia.

RUSSIAN SERFDOM

The Tsars were **autocrats** (*absolute rulers*). Using a network of secret police and strict censorship, they repressed new ideas. The vast majority of Russians were illiterate serfs who lived in poverty. They were still bound to the land, long after serfdom had been abolished in Western Europe. A small group of nobles owned thousands of serfs and had vast wealth. Despite earlier efforts to introduce Western ideas and technology, social conditions kept Russia economically undeveloped. Russian reformers, inspired by the example of Western Europe, hoped to abolish serfdom and modernize their country. But the Tsar and leading nobles felt that Russia was not yet ready for such change.

THE EMANCIPATION OF THE SERFS

Acting as "protector of Orthodox Christians," Russia waged a series of wars against the Ottoman empire in the 19th century. Between 1854 and 1856, Russia became involved in the **Crimean War**. Britain and France were concerned that if Russia took over the Ottoman empire, it would have protected access from the Black Sea to the Mediterranean. Finally, Britain and France went to war to reduce Russian influence. Fighting was confined to the Crimean Peninsula. Despite its large army, Russia lost the war due to the advanced weapons of the British and French. After the war, the new Tsar, **Alexander II**, ordered the serfs **emancipated** (*freed*) in 1861. Shortly afterwards, the Tsar was assassinated, putting an abrupt end to reform. The freed serfs remained land-less peasants, paying rents to their former masters. Later Tsars returned to the policy of opposing all change and using repression to maintain the existing social order.

RUSSIAN NATIONALISM

The spirit of nationalism had important effects even on Russia's conservative rulers. They identified their empire with the Russian nationality and the Russian Orthodox Church. The government acted as the protector of new Slav states in the Balkans. The Tsars also adopted the policy of **Russification,** forcing non-Russian people such as the Finns, Poles, and the many peoples of Central Asia to adopt the Russian language and culture. Anti-semitic **pogroms** — officially-encouraged attacks on Jewish areas — caused many Jews to emigrate to the United States in the early 1900s.

OTTOMAN TURKEY, THE "SICK MAN OF EUROPE"

The forces of nationalism also accelerated the decline of the Ottoman empire, which had already begun in the 1700s. Historians attribute the decline of the Ottoman empire to a number of factors:

Disunity. Because of its vast size, the empire was never highly centralized. The Sultan relied on provincial officials to control his large empire.

Failure to Modernize. The Ottoman Turks failed to keep pace with Western technology and science. Muslim religious leaders frequently opposed change.

WHY THE OTTOMAN EMPIRE DECLINED

Warfare. The Ottomans lost important territories to Austria and Russia in the 1700s. Russia, as protector of Orthodox Christianity, continued to wage a series of wars against Turkey in the 1800s.

Nationalism. As nationalism became more widespread, the difficulties of governing different nationalities grew. Serbs, Greeks, and Romanians all gained independence from the Ottomans during the 19th century.

THE CONGRESS OF BERLIN

In spite of these difficulties, the Ottoman empire managed to survive because of disagreements among the European powers. Diplomats considered the Ottoman empire the "sick man of Europe." Great Britain, France, and Austria all feared that Russia would acquire Turkey. In the 1870s, Slav peoples in the Balkans rebelled against Turkish rule. Russia came to the aid of these rebels. European powers met in 1878 at the **Congress of Berlin** to resolve the problem without war. Nevertheless, in the early 20th century most of the Balkans became independent.

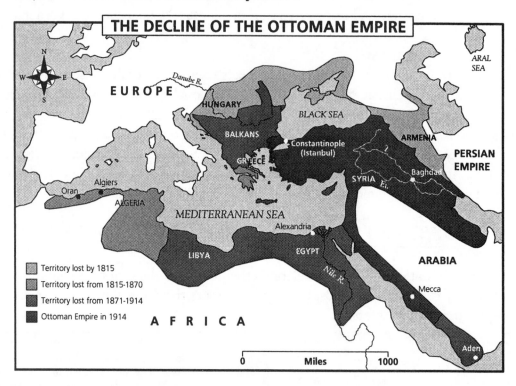

THE DECLINE OF THE OTTOMAN EMPIRE

Territory lost by 1815
Territory lost from 1815-1870
Territory lost from 1871-1914
Ottoman Empire in 1914

EUROPEAN IMPERIALISM TRANSFORMS THE GLOBE

Since ancient times, rulers have built empires by conquering other lands. **Imperialism** refers to the political and economic control of one area or country by another. The area being controlled is known as a "colony," while the controlling imperial power is called the "mother country."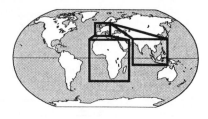

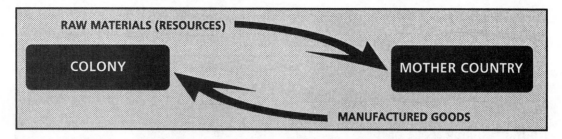

CAUSES OF "NEW" IMPERIALISM

In the 1400s, European nations began developing vast overseas empires. The independence of the Americas by the early 1800s was a severe setback for European imperialism. However, imperialism never wholly died out: it continued in India, South Africa and elsewhere. In the 1880s, European interest in imperialism was renewed. Countries such as Belgium, Germany, and Italy sought colonial empires of their own. Even the older imperial powers, like France and Britain, joined in the new scramble for colonies.

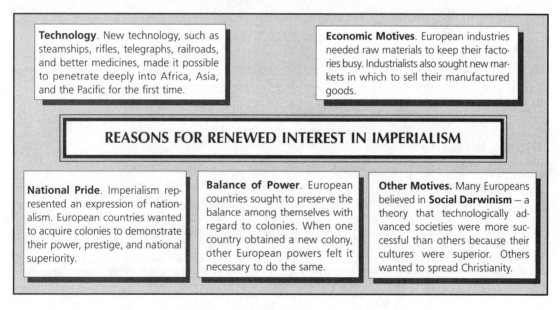

Technology. New technology, such as steamships, rifles, telegraphs, railroads, and better medicines, made it possible to penetrate deeply into Africa, Asia, and the Pacific for the first time.

Economic Motives. European industries needed raw materials to keep their factories busy. Industrialists also sought new markets in which to sell their manufactured goods.

REASONS FOR RENEWED INTEREST IN IMPERIALISM

National Pride. Imperialism represented an expression of nationalism. European countries wanted to acquire colonies to demonstrate their power, prestige, and national superiority.

Balance of Power. European countries sought to preserve the balance among themselves with regard to colonies. When one country obtained a new colony, other European powers felt it necessary to do the same.

Other Motives. Many Europeans believed in **Social Darwinism** – a theory that technologically advanced societies were more successful than others because their cultures were superior. Others wanted to spread Christianity.

THE BRITISH EMPIRE IN INDIA

The British East India Company had gained control over much of the Indian subcontinent by the early 1800s. In the 1830s, the East India Company came largely under the control of the British government. British rule brought many changes. Some older customs, like the forced suicide of women when their husbands died, were stamped out.

European missionaries spread Christianity. The first railway was built in 1853. British schools and colleges opened. English became the official language of government. De-spite some benefits, many In-dians were offended by the chal-lenge to their traditional ways. Imperialists such as the poet **Rudyard Kipling** spoke of the "white man's burden" — the duty of Europeans to spread their civilization.

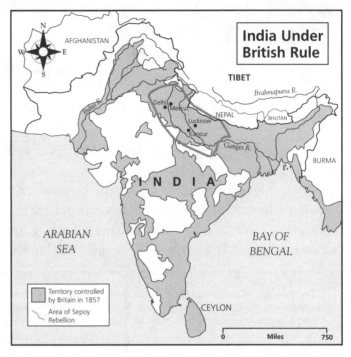

THE SEPOY MUTINY (1857)

The British army included many Indian soldiers, known as **sepoys**. In 1857, a large num-ber of sepoys rebelled against their British officers. The mutiny spread quickly, but the British were able to crush it with loyal Indian soldiers. Afterwards, the British government took official control of India and abolished the East India Company.

THE BRITISH RULE OF INDIA

During the two centuries of British rule, many aspects of Indian life changed:

Government. The British provided a single sys-tem of law and government, unifying India. They provided jobs in the British army and civil service, increased educational opportunities, and made English a unifying language.

Economic. The British built canals, roads, bridges, railroads, and set up telegraph systems. How-ever, India's **cottage industries** *(products made at home)* were destroyed by competition from British manufactured goods.

IMPACT OF BRITISH RULE IN INDIA

Health. The British built hospitals, introduced new medicines, and provided famine relief. At the same time, health care improvements led to a huge popu-lation explosion without an increase in economic opportunities.

Social. Natives were treated as if they were inferior to Europeans. The rich and ancient Indian culture was considered merely exotic. Indian workers provided the British with inexpensive labor, for long hours, often under terrible working conditions.

THE BIRTH OF MODERN INDIAN NATIONALISM

Nationalist ideas from Europe were already spreading to India by the end of the 19th century. Some Indians were sent to Great Britain for an education. When they returned to India, they demanded a greater role in governing their country. In 1885, a group of educated Indians formed the **Indian National Congress**. Its Muslim members broke away from this group in 1906 to form the **Muslim League**. The nationalist movement remained weak, however, because it focused entirely on the needs of the educated middle class. It had no program to improve the lives of India's millions of peasants.

EUROPEAN IMPERIALISM IN AFRICA (1870-1890)

In 1870, Europeans controlled very little territory in Africa. Except for South Africa and Algeria, most European activity was limited to coastal trading ports. African communities in the interior remained isolated. They represented an immense diversity of cultures with many different types of political structures.

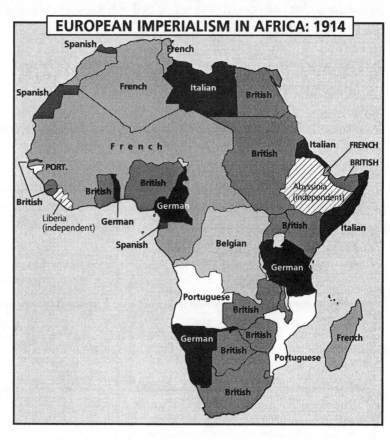

EUROPEAN IMPERIALISM IN AFRICA: 1914

RENEWED EUROPEAN INTEREST IN AFRICA

Over the next twenty years, due to renewed interest in imperialism, the picture changed dramatically. The European powers engaged in a "Scramble for Africa" (1870-1890), during which most of the continent came under their control. By 1890, only Ethiopia (called Abyssinia at the time) and Liberia remained independent. The scramble had begun in earnest in 1882, when a local revolt threatened the **Suez Canal**, the lifeline for ships sailing between Europe and India. The British quickly moved in to take over Egypt. Next, British troops took over the Sudan. Then they defeated the **Zulu** nation to expand British South Africa. Other powers such as France, Germany, and Belgium, eyed British actions jealously. They also wanted parts of Africa. At the **Berlin Conference** of 1884-1885, Bismarck and other European leaders divided up the remaining parts of Africa.

MAJOR IMPERIAL POWERS IN AFRICA

The major European powers to acquire African colonies were Great Britain, France, Germany, Belgium, Portugal, and Italy. The French acquired much of northwest Africa above the Sahara, and Central Africa. Belgian King Leopold ran the Belgian Congo like a private estate. The British established colonies in West Africa and along the length of East Africa down to South Africa. **Cecil Rhodes**, one of the leading British imperialists, hoped to build a railway that would run from Cairo, Egypt to Capetown, South Africa.

THE BALANCE SHEET OF EUROPEAN IMPERIALISM IN AFRICA

In carving up Africa, European powers paid no attention to existing tribal boundaries. They claimed ownership of the land, and wherever possible established mining operations or cultivated cash crops to be sold in Europe. Africans were used as a cheap workforce. On the other hand, Europeans introduced Western technology and ideas. Therefore, colonization had both positive and negative effects on Africa:

POSITIVE EFFECTS ON AFRICA	NEGATIVE EFFECTS ON AFRICA
European medicine and improved nutrition increased the life span of Africans. This also led to an expansion of the population.	European domination often led to an erosion of traditional African values and destroyed many existing social relationships.
Europeans introduced modern transportation and communications, such as telegraphs, railroads, steamships, and telephones.	African peoples were treated as inferior to Europeans. Native peoples were forced to work long hours for low pay.
A small minority of Africans received improved educations and greater economic opportunities. Some served as administrators or in the army.	Europeans divided up Africa artificially, ignoring tribal, ethnic, and cultural boundaries. These divisions have led to ongoing tribal clashes in many African countries.

EUROPEAN POWERS AND CHINA

In China, the European powers faced a situation different from India or Africa. For thousands of years, China had enjoyed an advanced culture and unity under powerful emperors. Nevertheless, China had been isolated from the world for too long. It had fallen behind Europe and now lacked the military technology to prevent European imperialism. Europeans were interested in China because its huge population offered a new market for manufactured goods. China also had valuable raw materials.

THE OPIUM WAR (1839-1842)

In the 1800s, Great Britain began selling opium in China to obtain money to buy tea. When the Chinese government tried to stop this trade, the British declared war. China was defeated in the **Opium War** and forced to allow the sale of opium under the **Treaty of Nanking**. The Chinese were also forced to open "treaty ports," giving the British new trading privileges. Thus the British established several **spheres of influence** — areas of China under British economic control. Other European countries then followed the British example in China.

Increasing European interference in China was extremely unpopular and weakened the Qing dynasty. Manchu rulers faced a series of major revolts, the most important of which was the **Taiping Rebellion** (1851-1864), which they put down with European help. Millions of Chinese died during this uprising.

SINO-JAPANESE WAR (1894-1895)

Sensing China's weakness, Japan also went to war with China and quickly defeated it. Japan then annexed Korea and created its own sphere of influence in China.

OPEN DOOR POLICY

In 1899, fearing it would be shut off from China's profitable trade, the U.S. proposed equal trading rights for all nations in China.

American policy discouraged European powers from further dividing up China, and kept it "open" to trade with all nations.

BOXER REBELLION (1899-1900)

Most Chinese resented the growing foreign interference in their nation. A Chinese group known as the "**Boxers**," with the help of the Manchu Empress, rebelled against Western influence in China. Hundreds of foreigners were killed by angry mobs. An international police force composed of troops from imperialist powers, including the United States, finally crushed the Boxer rebellion. These events further weakened the power of the Qing dynasty.

THE OPENING OF JAPAN

Another Asian country to encounter Westerners in the late 19th century was Japan.

THE TOKUGAWA SHOGUNATE (1603-1868)

In 1603, **Tokugawa Ieyasu** had seized power and founded the **Tokugawa Shogunate**. Unlike European-style feudalism where political power was divided among many lords, Japanese feudalism became more centralized in the hands of a few daimyos. Fearing the influence of foreigners, Japan cut itself off from European trade in 1639, becoming almost totally isolated. Japanese citizens were forbidden to travel to other countries, and foreigners were banned from Japan.

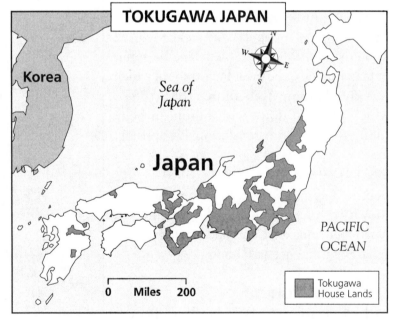

Despite more than two centuries of seclusion, Japan's internal trade grew, its urban areas increased in size, and the arts flourished.

THE UNITED STATES "OPENS" JAPAN

In 1853, the U.S. government sent a naval squadron to Japan under the command of Commodore **Matthew Perry**. The mission was motivated by mistreatment of American sailors who were shipwrecked in Japan. In addition to requesting better treatment for its sailors, the United States sought to develop new markets and to establish a port where American ships could get supplies on their trips to China. Aware of the results of the Opium War in China, Japanese leaders opened their doors to American trade. Within a few years, the British, Russians, and Dutch negotiated similarly favorable treaties.

Commodore Perry arrives in Japan

The opening of Japanese ports in 1854 had a profound effect on Japan's development.

THE MEIJI RESTORATION (1868-1912)

The Japanese samurai and daimyos criticized the Shogun severely for opening Japan to the West. Under the impact of this criticism, the Shogunate collapsed. The emperor, whose ancestors had been mere puppets for over a thousand years, was suddenly "restored" to power. However, **Emperor Meiji** was convinced that Japan had to adopt Western ways if it was to escape European domination. Under Emperor Meiji, Japan became the first non-Western country to successfully imitate and adapt Western ways.

Feudalism Abandoned. Feudalism and serfdom were abolished. The samurai lost their special social status.

Western Technology Adopted. Industrial development based on Western technology, such as the building of railroads and factories, was promoted.

CHANGES DURING THE MEIJI RESTORATION

Government Changes. Japan was given a written constitution, although the emperor kept his full powers. A Western-style army and navy were formed.

Educational Changes. Universal compulsory education was introduced. Students were sent abroad to study European and American economic policies, politics, and technological innovations.

— STUDY CARDS —

French Revolution (1789-1799)

Causes: Inequality among Estates (*social classes*), unfair taxes, bankrupt government, spread of Enlightment ideas.

- Louis XVI summoned **Estates General** (clergy, nobles, commoners) to vote on new taxes
- **Third Estate** declared itself a **National Assembly**, issued **Declaration of Rights of Man**
- Citizens seized **Bastille** prison, revolution began; noble privileges ended; king executed
- **Robespierre** launched revolutionary **Reign of Terror** against all dissenters

Industrial Revolution

Began in Great Britain in 1750s, based on inventions such as James Watt's steam engine.

Effects:
- Shifted production from making goods by hand at home to **mass production** in factories
- Applied new sources of power like steam to manufacture of textiles, ships, railways
- **Urbanization:** people moved from countryside to cities, seeking factory work
- Rise of **capitalists** and **working class** as important new groups in society

Napoleon Bonaparte

General during French Revolution; seized power in 1799; declared himself emperor in 1804.
- **Napoleonic Code:** combined traditional codified law with principles of the Revolution; most legal systems in Europe today are based on the Code
- Introduced French revolutionary ideas to other European countries
- Conquered most of Europe; attack on Russia ended in catastrophe; his army defeated by coalition of European rulers, 1814-1815; French king restored to throne

Communism

Workers in the 1800s labored under horrible conditions for very low wages.

- In the *Communist Manifesto* and *Das Kapital*, **Karl Marx** argued that workers should unite and overthrow capitalist class
- Marx urged creation of a Communist society, end to private property; citizens would own the means of production in common

Significance: in the 20th century, several countries adopted Communist systems — Russia, China, Cuba

Restoration Europe (1815-1848)

After Napoleon's defeat, Europe's Great Powers restored old rulers and cooperated in fighting revolutionary ideas.
- **Congress of Vienna** (1814-1815): Statesmen established "balance of power" to keep any one country from being dominant
- **Metternich** encouraged kings to cooperate against nationalism and revolution
- **1848 Revolutions**: Broke out in France, Italy, Germany, Central Europe; all failed except in France, which declared itself a republic

Nationalism

Belief that each nation or ethnic group should have its own state. Ethnic group can be defined by race, religion, language or common ancestry.

- **Unifying Force:** Italian unification (**Garibaldi, Cavour**), German unification (**Bismarck**)

- **Divisive Force:** Ethnic divisions eventually destroyed several large multi-ethnic states: Austria-Hungary (1918), Ottoman Empire (1919), Soviet Union (1991).

(Continued)

— STUDY CARDS (continued) —

"Scramble for Africa"

In the late 1800s, new technologies (**railroads, armaments, telegraph**) enabled Europe's imperial powers to colonize most of Africa. The "Scramble" was completed at the **Berlin Conference** (1884).

*   Great Britain held colonies from South Africa to Egypt, including Suez Canal
*   France held colonies in West and Central Africa
*   Belgium held the Congo in Central Africa

Latin American Independence

*   During Napoleonic Wars, Latin America was self-governing. After Napoleon's defeat, the Spanish king was restored to the throne. He tried to reimpose colonial rule on Latin Americans, but they wanted to govern themselves
*   Colonists resented economic restrictions and exploitation; ideas of American and French Revolutions influenced Latin American leaders such as **Simón Bolivar**. By early 1800s, most of Latin America had won struggle for independence from Europe

New Imperialism

Revival of imperialism in 1870s. Europe's Great Powers gained colonies in Africa, Asia, the Pacific. U.S. and Japan also participated in Asia.

Impact:
*   Led to flow of raw materials from the colonies to the imperial powers
*   Brought advanced technology, medicines and Christian beliefs to the colonies
*   Native populations treated as inferior; local boundaries and traditions disregarded; local people forced to work mines, plantations

Resistance to Colonialism

*   **Sepoy Mutiny** (1857): Mutiny of Indian soldiers in British army; crushed by Britain, which took control of India from the East India Company
*   **Opium War** (1840s): Chinese tried to end imports of opium; British used gunboats to defeat them and forced Chinese to open "treaty ports" controlled by Westerners
*   **Boxer Rebellion** (1899): Mass Chinese uprising against Western influence; finally put down by international expeditionary force

Meiji Restoration

*   **Tokugawa Shogunate** (1603-1868) had closed Japan to foreign trade , people, and ideas
*   In 1853, Commodore **Matthew Perry** used threat of naval force to "open" Japan
*   Shogunate collapsed; **Emperor Meiji** was "restored" to power
*   Meiji emperor adopted Western technology, education, and military tactics; Japan became first non-western nation to successfully adopt Western ways

Decline of Ottoman Empire

From the 18th century to the early 20th century, the Ottoman Empire gradually declined:
*   **Failure to Modernize:** Ottomans did not keep up with Western technology; Muslim leaders frequently opposed change
*   **Disunity:** Empire was too decentralized; Sultan relied on provincial officials to govern
*   **Nationalism**: Parts of empire were Christian and sought independence
*   **Russia:** Russia took some Ottoman territories and championed Slav peoples in others

SUMMARIZING YOUR UNDERSTANDING

COMPLETING A TABLE

Use this table to organize information on the developments you have just read about.

Event	When it Began	Where it Began	Description
French Revolution			
Industrial Revolution			
Rise of Nationalism			
"New" Imperialism			

TESTING YOUR UNDERSTANDING

Base your answer to question 1 on the pie charts and on your knowledge of global history.

1   Based on the charts, which statement is most accurate?
    (1) The three estates in France owned land equally.
    (2) The second estate was the most numerous of the three.
    (3) The first two estates had landholdings out of proportion to their population size.
    (4) The combined population of the first and second estates was larger than the third estate.

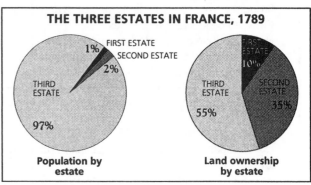

THE THREE ESTATES IN FRANCE, 1789

Population by estate

Land ownership by estate

2   The Renaissance, the French Revolution, and the Industrial Revolution all contributed to the development of
    (1) utopian societies
    (2) a powerful Catholic Church
    (3) divine right monarchies
    (4) a growing middle class

3   The main purpose of the Congress of Vienna (1814-1815) was to
    (1)   restore Europe to peace after the Napoleonic Wars
    (2)   create a European Court of Justice
    (3)   promote the ideas of the French Revolution
    (4)   establish strategies necessary to rebuild the economy of the Ottoman empire

4   Which quotation best reflects the spirit of nationalism?
    (1)   "An eye for an eye and a tooth for a tooth."
    (2)   "Do unto others as you would have others do unto you."
    (3)   "For God, King, and Country."
    (4)   "Opposition to evil is as much a duty as is cooperation with good."

5   The invention of spinning and weaving machinery increased the number of workers in
    the textile industry in Europe because
    (1)   early textile machinery could not produce goods as efficiently as hand labor
    (2)   laws prohibited women and children from working with machinery
    (3)   the demand for textiles increased as they became cheaper to produce
    (4)   unions required that more workers be hired to maintain the machines

Base your answer to question 6 on this illustration and your knowledge of global history.

6   The drawing illustrates workers' reaction to
    which development of the Industrial Revo-
    lution?
    (1)   machines replacing workers
    (2)   rise of labor unions
    (3)   slum housing conditions
    (4)   profit sharing by workers

7   "The average worker can never obtain more
    than a minimum standard of living. Each
    worker is deprived of the wealth he himself
    has created. The state is simply a committee
    of the bourgeoisie for the exploitation of the people."

    The ideas in this quotation would most likely be expressed by a
    (1)   Renaissance humanist   (3)   mercantilist trader
    (2)   laissez-faire capitalist   (4)   communist sympathizer

8   "All great nations ... desire to set their mark upon barbarian lands, and those who fail to enlist in this great rivalry will play a pitiable role in times to come."
This quotation supports the doctrine of
(1) socialism   (3) revolution
(2) human rights   (4) imperialism

9   What did Karl Marx and Friedrich Engels believe would be the result when communism emerged as the dominant political and economic system?
(1) Only two classes would exist in society.
(2) All the evils of industrial society would disappear.
(3) The Soviet Union would become the world's only superpower.
(4) Citizens would own their individual homes and farms.

10 Both the Sepoy Mutiny in India and the Boxer Rebellion in China attempted to
(1) end foreign domination   (3) promote imperialism
(2) halt the trading of illegal drugs (4) overturn Mongol control

11 Which statement best describes events in Japan during the period of the Meiji Restoration?
(1) Japan sought to isolate itself from world affairs.
(2) Rapid industrialization and economic growth occurred.
(3) Local lords increased their power over the Japanese emperor.
(4) Agriculture was taken over by the government.

Base your answer to question 12 on this graph and on your knowledge of global history.

12 Which statement is best supported by the data in the graph?
(1) Most European nations had colonial empires in 1870.
(2) Europe's high birth rate led to overseas expansion.
(3) European colonial empires increased between 1870 and 1914.
(4) By 1914, Germany controlled the greatest land area.

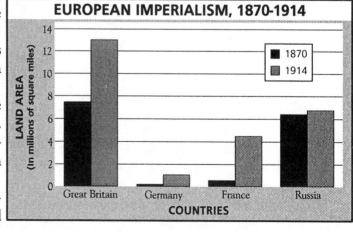

EUROPEAN IMPERIALISM, 1870-1914

LAND AREA (In millions of square miles)

Great Britain   Germany   France   Russia
COUNTRIES

■ 1870
▨ 1914

13 Simón Bolívar, José de San Martín, and Toussaint l'Ouverture were important to Latin
    American history because they were
    (1) twentieth-century caudillos
    (2) leaders of liberation movements
    (3) members of the Organization of American States (OAS)
    (4) winners of the Nobel Peace Prize

14 During the 19th century, one effect of European imperialism on Africa was the
    (1) exploitation of natural resources by colonial powers
    (2) improvement of working conditions in Africa
    (3) African dependence on exportation of manufactured goods
    (4) African acceptance of the doctrine of the "White Man's Burden"

15 Which period of European history do the terms "Scramble for Africa" and the Berlin
    Conference refer to?
    (1) Middle Ages   (3) Age of Discovery
    (2) Protestant Reformation   (4) The New Imperialism

INTERPRETING DOCUMENTS

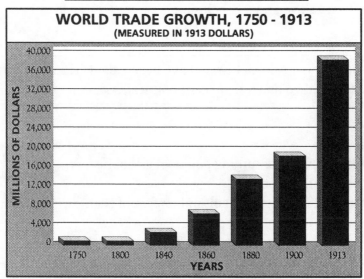

WORLD TRADE GROWTH, 1750 - 1913
(MEASURED IN 1913 DOLLARS)

1a What was the value of world trade in the year 1913? _____

 b What does this graph tell us about the effects of the Industrial Revolution? _____

2a What areas of the world are represented by the two people pulling the cart?

_____

_____

b Explain the historical situation that led to the events shown in this cartoon.

_____

_____

_____

"Learning civilized ways is hard work!"

THEMATIC ESSAY QUESTION

Directions: Write a well-organized essay that includes an introduction, several paragraphs addressing the *Task* below, and a conclusion.

Theme: Change

> Some events in global history have been called "turning points" because they have had a significant political, social or cultural impact.

Task:

- Identify **two** examples of turning points in global history.
- Describe each turning point.
- Explain the political, social or cultural impact of each turning point.

You may use any examples from your study of global history. Some examples you might wish to consider include the Neolithic Revolution, the fall of Rome, the Arab conquest of the Middle East, the rise of kingdoms in West Africa, the encounter between Europe and the Americas, the French Revolution, and the Industrial Revolution.

You are *not* limited to these suggestions.

DOCUMENT-BASED ESSAY QUESTION

This question is based on the accompanying documents (1-6). This question is designed to test your ability to work with historical documents. Some of these documents have been edited for the purposes of this question. As you analyze the documents, take into account both the source of each document and any point of view that may be presented in the document.

Historical Context:
Throughout history, societies have met the economic needs of their members in a variety of ways.

Task: Using information from the documents and your knowledge of global history, answer the questions that follow each document in Part A. Your answers to the questions will help you write the Part B essay, in which you will be asked to:

- Describe some of the ways that societies have met the economic needs of their members.
- Evaluate the advantages and disadvantages of the way in which one of the societies discussed in the documents met those needs.

Part A — Short Answer Questions
Directions: Analyze the documents and answer the scaffolding question that follows each document.

DOCUMENT 1

"The rich, getting possession of the greater part of undistributed lands, and being emboldened by the lapse of time to ... add to their holdings the small farms of their poor neighbors, partly by purchase and partly by force, came to cultivate vast tracts instead of single estates, using for this purpose slaves as laborers. Thus the powerful ones became enormously rich and the race of slaves multiplied, while the Italian people dwindled in numbers and strength, being oppressed by poverty, taxes, and military service."

— Appian of Alexandria, a Roman historian,
discussing the rise of slavery in ancient Rome

1   What impact did the use of slaves have on ancient Roman society? _____

_____

DOCUMENT 2

"I work very hard. I go out at dawn, driving the oxen to the field, and I yoke them to the plough. However hard the winter, I dare not stay home for fear of my master. Having yoked the oxen and made the ploughshare fast to the plough, I have to plough a whole acre or more every day."

— A serf's account of his typical day,
recorded by an English monk (circa 1000 A.D.)

2   What role did this serf play in meeting the economic needs of his society? ———

DOCUMENT 3

"The caliph (*ruler*) takes care of the poor, widows and orphans; pays them special pensions ... does the same for the blind. And, provided this does not overburden the treasury, builds hospitals for sick Muslims, with physicians and attendants who will cure them and minister to their needs ... The caliph distributes taxes in a fair, just and equitable manner; not exempting anyone because of his noble rank or great riches. He does not levy a tax on anyone which is beyond his capacity to pay."

— Provincial Muslim governor Tahir Ibn al Hussein (775-822),
describing the government's economic responsibilities

3   How were the less fortunate cared for in 8th and 9th century Muslim society? ____

DOCUMENT 4

"When we arrived at the great square we were struck by the throngs of people and the amount of merchandise displayed. There were dealers in gold, silver and precious stones, feathers, cloth and embroidered goods, and other merchandise in the form of men and women to be sold as slaves. The slaves were tied to poles with collars around their necks so they couldn't escape. There were merchants who sold homespun clothing, and others who sold cocoa ... There were people who sold rope and shoes. In another location they had skins of lions, deer and other animals."

— A conquistador reveals an aspect of Aztec life (early 1500s)

4   How did this market help to meet the economic needs of the Aztecs? _____

DOCUMENT 5

Photo taken in 19th century England.

5a What does this photograph tell us about England in the 1800s?

_____

b What evidence in the photo supports your answer?

_____

Library of Congress

DOCUMENT 6

MAJOR INVENTIONS OF THE INDUSTRIAL REVOLUTION

Invention	Inventor	Date	Invention	Inventor	Date
Spinning jenny	James Hargreaves	1764	Power loom	Edmund Cartwright	1785
Water frame	Richard Arkwright	1769	Cotton gin	Eli Whitney	1793
Steam engine	James Watt	1769	Steamboat	Robert Fulton	1807
Spinning mule	Samuel Crompton	1779	Telegraph	Samuel Morse	1837

6   Explain how one of these inventions helped meet people's economic needs. _____

_____

Part B — Essay

Directions: Write a well-organized essay that includes an introduction, several paragraphs, and a conclusion. Use evidence from at least **four** documents in the body of the essay. Support your response with relevant facts, examples, and details. Include additional outside information.

Historical Context: Throughout history, societies have met the economic needs of their members in a variety of ways.

Task: Using information from the documents and your knowledge of global history, write an essay in which you:

- Describe some of the ways in which societies have met the economic needs of their members.
- Evaluate the advantages and disadvantages of the way in which one of the societies discussed in the documents met those economic needs.

CHAPTER 13

THE WORLD AT WAR, 1900 - 1945

Fascist dictators Mussolini and Hitler, 1940

	1905	1915	1925	1935	1945
EUROPE		WORLD WAR I	RISE OF FASCISM	WORLD WAR II	COLD WAR
RUSSIA	TSAR NICHOLAS II	REVOLUTION: LENIN	STALIN		
AFRICA	EUROPEAN CONTROL				INDEPENDENCE MOVEMENTS
TURKEY	SULTANATE	YOUNG TURK GOVT.	MODERN TURKEY		
MIDEAST	OTTOMAN EMPIRE	EUROPEAN PROTECTORATES			INDEPENDENCE MOVEMENTS
MEXICO	DIAZ	REVOLUTION	REPUBLIC OF MEXICO		
CHINA	MANCHU DYNASTY	REPUBLIC OF CHINA			
JAPAN	JAPAN'S RISE TO POWER			WORLD WAR II	U.S. OCCUPATION
INDIA	INDIAN NATIONALIST MOVEMENT DURING BRITISH RULE				INDEPENDENCE
S.E. ASIA	EUROPEAN COLONIZATION				INDEPENDENCE MOVEMENTS
	1905	1915	1925	1935	1945

WHAT YOU SHOULD FOCUS ON

In this chapter, you will review how the forces of industrialization and nationalism led to the rise of new political systems like Communism and Fascism. You will also review how in the first half of the 20th century the world experienced two major wars, causing greater devastation than at any other time in human history. European rule over much of the world was shattered as the United States and the Soviet Union emerged as superpowers. It is helpful to think of the developments in this time period as occurring in four main stages:

Pre-War Years (1900-1914): In countries outside of Europe, educated elites, frustrated by their nations' problems, sought change through revolution. Meanwhile, European countries armed themselves for war. In Asia and Africa, European powers controlled vast colonial empires.

World War I (1914-1918): A crisis between Austria-Hungary and Serbia led to war in Europe. In 1917 a Communist revolution took Rus-sia out of the war. After the war, imperial governments in Austria-Hungary, Germany, and Turkey ended. New states formed in eastern Europe.

FOUR KEY STAGES FROM
1900 THROUGH THE WORLD WARS

Inter-War Years (1919-1939): Except for Germany, the 1920s saw general prosperity, followed by the worldwide Great Depression of the 1930s. Economic crises gave rise to Fascist dictators such as Hitler in Germany. Meanwhile, Stalin ruled the Communist Soviet Union as a dictator.

World War II (1939-1945): German and Japanese aggression plunged the world into war. The war resulted in the atomic bomb, the United Nations, and the end of imperialism in Africa and Asia. The U.S. and the Soviet Union became military superpowers.

In reviewing this era, keep in mind that test writers are most likely to ask questions about the following:

• What conditions led to revolutionary changes in Turkey, Mexico, China, and Russia in the early 20th century?

• What factors contributed to the rise of Fascism in Europe and Japan?

• What were the main causes and effects of both World War I and II?

• What changes did Lenin and Stalin introduce to the Soviet Union?

LOOKING AT INFLUENTIAL PEOPLE IN HISTORY

Each of us touches the lives of those around us. However, a number of exceptional people have had an important impact on the lives of millions. In studying these individuals, the key question to focus on is:

How has the world been changed by the actions or ideas of this person?

Two groups of people who often have had a significant impact on others have been leaders and thinkers:

✦ **Leaders** are usually people who rule a country, head a political party or religious movement, or lead an army. They affect history because they are able to persuade or influence millions of people to follow their commands.

✦ **Thinkers** are philosophers, religious thinkers, writers, inventors, scientists, or artists. They affect history because their ideas stimulate others to act, or lead to technological or artistic breakthroughs.

WHAT TO DO WHEN ANSWERING A QUESTION

Essay questions dealing with the impact of individuals often begin with a statement about the influence of key people on history. You are then asked to discuss their accomplishments and significance. The content of your answer will depend in part on whether the individual was a *leader* or a *thinker*.

WHAT YOU SHOULD DISCUSS FOR A LEADER
(1) What country or group did he or she lead?
(2) What problems did the country or group face?
(3) What policies did this leader favor?
(4) What were the effects of these policies?
(5) How was the world changed by the activities of this leader?

WHAT YOU SHOULD DISCUSS FOR A THINKER
(1) What did people think or know before this thinker appeared?
(2) What were this person's main ideas?
(3) What factors helped this thinker come up with these ideas?
(4) How was the world changed by the activities of this person?

KEY LEADERS AND THINKERS IN GLOBAL HISTORY

ASIAN POLITICAL LEADERS:

Shi-Huangdi (200s B.C.)
Asoka (273-238 B.C.)
Kublai Khan (1215-1294)
Akbar the Great (1542-1605)
Sun Yat-sen (1866-1925)

Ho Chi Minh (1890-1969)
Mao Zedong (1893-1976)
Mohandas Gandhi (1869-1948)
Deng Xiaoping (1904-1996)
Indira Gandhi (1917-1984)

AFRICAN POLITICAL LEADERS:

Mansa Musa (1312-1332)
Jomo Kenyatta (1894-1978)

Kwame Nkrumah (1909-1972)
Nelson Mandela, (1918-present)

EUROPEAN POLITICAL LEADERS:

Alexander the Great (356 -323 B.C.)
Constantine (280-337)
Charlemagne (742-814)
Elizabeth I (1533-1603)
Peter the Great (1672-1725)
Catherine the Great (1729-1796)
Napoleon Bonaparte (1769-1821)

Prince Metternich (1773-1859)
Otto von Bismarck (1815-1898)
Vladimir Lenin (1870-1924)
Joseph Stalin (1879-1953)
Benito Mussolini (1883-1945)
Adolf Hitler (1889-1945)
Mikhail Gorbachev (1931-present)

MIDDLE EASTERN POLITICAL LEADERS:

Cyrus the Great (600-530 B.C.)
Kemal Atatürk (1881-1938)

Anwar el-Sadat (1918-1981)
Mohammed Pahlavi (1919-1980)

LATIN AMERICAN POLITICAL LEADERS:

Simón Bolívar (1783-1830)

Fidel Castro (1927-present)

RELIGIOUS LEADERS:

Siddharta Gautama (563 -483 B.C.)
Confucius (551-479 B.C.)
Jesus (1-30 A.D.)

Mohammed (570-632)
Martin Luther (1483-1546)
Ayatollah Khomeini (1900-1996)

THINKERS AND WRITERS:

Socrates (469 -399 B.C.)
Aristotle (384-322 B.C.)
Plato (427-347 B.C.)
John Locke (1632-1704)

Voltaire (1694-1778)
Jean-Jacques Rousseau (1712-1778)
Karl Marx (1818-1883)
Thomas Malthus (1766-1834)

SCIENTISTS AND INVENTORS:

Johann Gutenberg (1398-1468)
Nicolaus Copernicus (1437-1543)
Charles Darwin (1809-1882)

Isaac Newton (1642-1727)
James Watt (1736-1818)
Albert Einstein (1879-1955)

MAJOR
HISTORICAL DEVELOPMENTS

REFORM THROUGH REVOLUTION

In 1900, Europeans were enjoying greater peace and prosperity than ever before. Despite minor conflicts, Europeans had not experienced a major war for almost a century. However, in some places the forces of discontent were brewing. In Turkey, Mexico, China, and Russia, reformers influenced by European ideas of justice and equality were outraged at the sharp social divisions and authoritarian governments that existed in their countries. Unable to achieve reform through moderate means, some reformers turned to forming secret revolutionary movements. Then, shortly after the start of the 20th century, various parts of the world exploded with social revolution.

THE YOUNG TURKS AND THE OTTOMAN EMPIRE

Thirty years earlier, in 1876, Sultan **Abdulhamid II** had granted his subjects the first written constitution in the Islamic world. Almost immediately, he suspended it. Over the following decades, the Sultan built railways, telegraph lines, and increased the strength of his army. Abdulhamid used secret police and brutality against opponents, and ordered the brutal massacre of Armenians in eastern Turkey in 1894-1896.

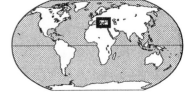

In these same years, young educated members of the Turkish elite became inspired by nationalist ideas. Known as the **Young Turks**, they demanded reform. In 1908, part of the Ottoman army rebelled. The Sultan gave in to their demands, including freedom of the press and the right to form political parties. In the following year, the Sultan was replaced. A new Young Turk government encouraged industrialization, public education, and improved treatment of women. However, the Young Turks could not prevent the further loss of Ottoman territories in Europe. Turkey soon lost Tripoli (*in the Middle East*) and its remaining territories in the Balkans.

THE MEXICAN REVOLUTION OF 1910

Another place to experience rapid social and political change in the early 20th century was Mexico. From 1877 to 1910, Mexico was ruled by General **Porfirio Diaz**, a dictator who limited freedom of the press and used the police to enforce order. Diaz achieved solid economic growth by building 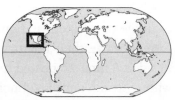 railroads and telegraph lines, and promoting industry and investment. But he also seized lands from villages and left the peasants worse off than before.

REVOLUTION TURNS TO CIVIL WAR

The **Mexican Revolution of 1910** began as a reaction against the Diaz dictatorship. A wealthy liberal, **Francisco Madero**, began the revolt in 1910. When Diaz fled, Madero was elected president of Mexico. Madero soon faced opposition from **Emiliano Zapata** and other peasant leaders, and from **Pancho Villa**, a revolutionary who led a private army in the north. Madero was assassinated in 1913. A period of violence followed.

THE MEXICAN CONSTITUTION OF 1917

Order was finally restored and a new constitution was written. The **Constitution of 1917**, which is still in effect today, made Mexico more democratic. It established an elected president and guaranteed individual rights. The new constitution also divided power between the central government and individual states, much like the U.S. The constitution promoted social and economic reforms. It established public education, universal voting, an eight-hour work day, and gave

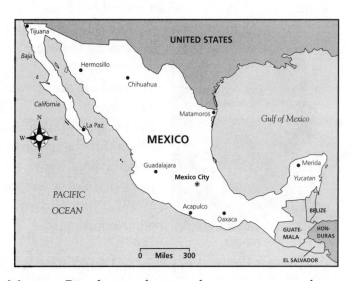

workers the right to strike. The Mexican Revolution also aimed at economic modernization and land reform. For the next twenty years, a series of moderate presidents governed Mexico. They broke up large estates, seized Church lands, and transferred millions of acres of land to peasants. As a result, Mexico became more democratic.

CHINA BECOMES A REPUBLIC (1912)

In China, as in Turkey, younger members of the educated elite were inspired by the example of Western nations. These nationalists hoped to modernize their country. They were especially out-raged at China's repeated humiliation by foreign powers with more advanced technology. Meanwhile, continuing population growth had lowered standards of living. By 1900, millions of peasants lived in starvation and misery.

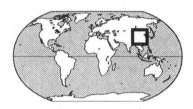

REVOLUTION ERUPTS IN CHINA

China's defeat by Japan in 1894, the foreign intervention against the Boxer rebellion, and the refusal of the Qing dynasty to permit change led to the creation of secret revo-lutionary groups throughout China. In 1911, a mutiny of soldiers in central China quickly led to uprisings in other cities.

SUN YAT-SEN AND THE KUOMINTANG

One of the leading revolutionaries plotting the overthrow of the Qing dynasty was **Sun Yat-Sen**. Sun was in the United States when the uprisings broke out. He quickly returned to China, where an assembly of revolutionaries elected him provisional

president. But the position of Sun and the revolutionar-ies remained insecure.

To ward off the revolutionary challenge, the Manchu government turned itself into a constitutional monar-chy by appointing a military leader as prime minister. When this change proved insufficient, the five-year-old emperor finally gave up his throne. Thus, after 2,500 years of rule by emperors, China became a republic in 1912. Sun also handed over his power to the new prime minister to avoid a civil war.

Sun Yat-Sen

In 1916, Sun returned to power and formed a new political party, the **Kuomintang**. Sun introduced policies based on three principles: "Democracy, Nationalism, and the People's Livelihood." But Sun was never fully able to bring all of China under his con-trol. In many parts of the country, the power of local military commanders — known as warlords — remained too great. Sun died in 1925.

THE OUTBREAK OF WORLD WAR I

WORLD WAR I (1914-1918)

The powerful force of nationalism, which so transformed Turkey, Mexico, and China, had an equally explosive impact on the multi-ethnic empire of Austria-Hungary. There, the challenge of nationalism eventually brought all of Europe into World War I. The war marked a major turning point in global history. New technologies made warfare tremendously more destructive than ever before. The imperial governments and the old class system of Europe were forever shattered. The peace that followed saw the momentary triumph of democracy, national self-determination, and an international peace organization. But the war also paved the way for the rise of totalitarianism.

THE CAUSES OF WORLD WAR I

A complex event like the outbreak of World War I had many causes:

✦ **Nationalism.** Nationalism caused rivalries between France, Britain, Germany, Austria-Hungary, and Russia. The spread of nationalism had also led to the creation of new independent nations in the Balkans—Serbia, Bulgaria, Greece, Albania, and Rumania —where the Ottomans once ruled.

Austria-Hungary still consisted of many ethnic groups including Germans, Hungarians, Czechs, Romanians, Poles, and Serbs. Some wanted their own national states. Their demands threatened to break apart the Austro-Hungarian empire.

✦ **Economic Rivalries and Imperialism**. Behind the nationalistic rivalries of the European great powers lay competing economic interests. German industrialization threatened British economic supremacy. Russian interests in the Balkans threatened both Austria-Hungary and the OrromanTurks. Competing colonial claims in Africa and Asia created an atmosphere of tension between the major powers.

✦ **The Alliance System**. By 1914, Europe was divided into two large camps by a series of secret alliances. On one side stood Germany, Austria-Hungary, and Ottoman Turkey *(the Central Powers)*. On the other stood Russia, France, and Great Britain *(the Allies)*. Although these alliances sought to preserve the existing balance of power, disputes involving any two of these countries threatened to involve all the others.

✦ **Militarism**. Military planning and arms races played key roles in the outbreak of World War I. Germany and Britain competed to build the largest, most powerful navy. Military leaders thought it better to attack first, rather than wait to be attacked.

THE FLASHPOINT THAT IGNITED THE WAR

In 1914, **Archduke Francis Ferdinand** was assassinated in Sarajevo by a member of a Slav nationalist group. Austrian leaders rightly believed that Serb officials had secretly helped the assassins. The Austrians wanted to teach Serbia a lesson, and German leaders encouraged the Austrians to act. Austria-Hungary invaded Serbia, setting off a chain reaction. Because of its alliance treaty, Russia came in to protect Serbia. Next, Germany entered to fulfill its treaty obligations to protect Austria. Finally Britain and France intervened to honor their alliance with Russia. Thus, Russia, Germany, Austria, Britain, and France were suddenly at war. What began as a minor regional crisis in the Balkans had quickly escalated into a major European conflict.

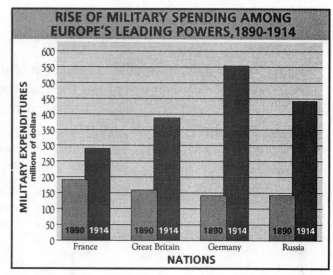

THE MILITARY STRUGGLE

Leaders on both sides thought the war would be over quickly, but in fact the struggle lasted more than four years. New and improved weapons were used, including machine guns, poison gas, submarines, and airplanes. Soldiers dug deep trenches, which they defended with machine guns and barbed wire. Soon these trenches extended hundreds of miles throughout France. It was a new and terrible form of warfare that the world had never seen before.

THE UNITED STATES ENTERS THE WAR (1917)

Although the United States was officially neutral, Americans were sympathetic to Britain and France. When American ships sent supplies to these countries, they were attacked by German submarines. In response, the United States entered World War I in 1917. In the same year, Russia dropped out of the war. President Wilson declared that winning the war would "make the world safe for democracy." America's entry into the war broke the deadlock in Europe. In November 1918, the Germans surrendered.

THE AFTERMATH OF WORLD WAR I

The human and material costs of World War I were staggering. Millions of people had been killed or injured. People in many parts of the world suffered from famine and malnutrition. The imperial governments of both Germany and Russia collapsed.

THE TREATY OF VERSAILLES (1919)

President Wilson announced America's aims in his **Fourteen Points,** demanding national self-determination for the European peoples. He wanted to redraw the map of Europe so that each nationality would have its own nation-state. Wilson also demanded freedom of the seas, an end to secret diplomacy, and the creation of a League of Nations.

Believing that Wilson's offer would be the basis of the peace settlement, the Germans agreed to end the war. They overthrew the Kaiser and became a democratic republic. Nevertheless, the final peace terms turned out to be extremely harsh on Germany. Allied public opinion was eager for revenge. The **Treaty of Versailles** (1919) concluded peace with Germany; related treaties dealt with Austria and Turkey.

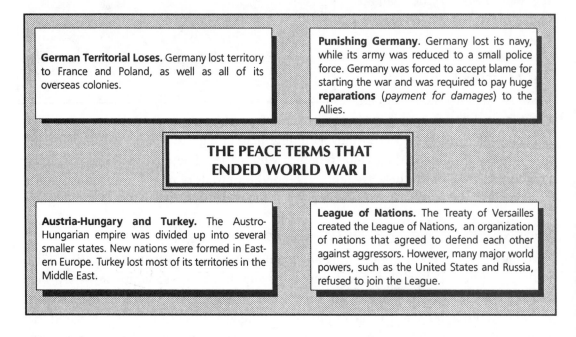

German Territorial Loses. Germany lost territory to France and Poland, as well as all of its overseas colonies.

Punishing Germany. Germany lost its navy, while its army was reduced to a small police force. Germany was forced to accept blame for starting the war and was required to pay huge **reparations** (*payment for damages*) to the Allies.

**THE PEACE TERMS THAT
ENDED WORLD WAR I**

Austria-Hungary and Turkey. The Austro-Hungarian empire was divided up into several smaller states. New nations were formed in Eastern Europe. Turkey lost most of its territories in the Middle East.

League of Nations. The Treaty of Versailles created the League of Nations, an organization of nations that agreed to defend each other against aggressors. However, many major world powers, such as the United States and Russia, refused to join the League.

THE ALLIES AND THE MIDDLE EAST

World War I also led to the end of the Ottoman empire. The Sultan had sided with Germany during the war. Fearing Armenians in the east would ally with Russia, the Ottoman government gave Armenians — who were Christians — the choice of converting to Islam or being exiled in the Syrian desert, where as many as a million of them died. The Ottoman government also committed other wartime atrocities, such as executing Arab nationalists.

After the war, the Allies took away Turkish possessions in Arabia, Syria, and Palestine. To gain the support of Arab groups during the war, the British had promised them independence. But in 1919, instead of becoming independent, these areas were divided between Britain and France. Uprisings broke out in Egypt and Arabia, leading to their independence (1922-1924). The rest of the region remained under foreign control. In 1922, the British divided Palestine in two, creating Palestine and Transjordan.

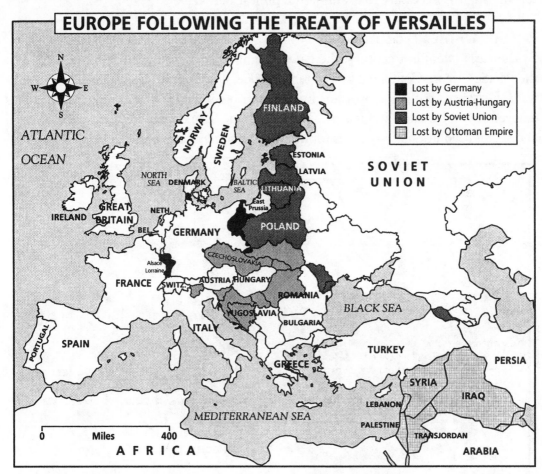

EUROPE FOLLOWING THE TREATY OF VERSAILLES

Lost by Germany
Lost by Austria-Hungary
Lost by Soviet Union
Lost by Ottoman Empire

The Allies also had a plan to take away Turkish lands in Asia Minor. **Mustafa Kemal,** known as **Kemal Atatürk,** was a leading general during the war. He now organized resistance to Allied attempts to further dismember Turkish territory. A new parliament was held, which declared the birth of modern Turkey in 1920. After two years of fighting, Atatürk preserved Turkish territory in Asia Minor and formally abolished the Sultanate in 1923. He introduced sweeping reforms, such as use of the Latin alphabet, to turn Turkey into a Westernized, secular state.

THE RUSSIAN REVOLUTION

One of the most important consequences of World War I was the Russian Revolution. To understand the reasons for the revolution, it is necessary to examine the prewar period.

PRELUDE TO THE REVOLUTION

By the early twentieth century, the Russian empire stretched from Eastern Europe to the Pacific Ocean. Compared to Western Europe, however, Russia was still quite backward. Peasants and factory workers lived in terrible poverty, while landowning nobles enjoyed lives of wealth and leisure. The autocratic Tsars opposed democratic reform, and secret revolutionary societies formed among some of the educated elite.

THE EXPANSION OF RUSSIA

Legend:
- Russia in 1801
- By 1815
- By 1867
- By 1914

THE REVOLUTION OF 1905

Russia was ripe for revolution. The crisis came to a head after Russia was defeated in the **Russo-Japanese War** (1904-1905). When troops shot down unarmed demonstrators in St. Petersburg in 1905, uprisings broke out across the country. Peasants seized nobles' lands, while workers in the cities engaged in demonstrations and general strikes. Tsar **Nicholas II** finally granted limited reforms, creating an elected legislature known as the **Duma.** However, only the very wealthy could vote for the Duma's members.

THE RUSSIAN REVOLUTION OF 1917

The years after 1905 showed some signs of improvement. But Russia was not prepared for the strains of war. In 1914, Nicholas II brought Russia into the war against Austria-Hungary and Germany. In battle, poorly trained and badly equipped Russian soldiers suffered disastrous defeats. In some cases, troops were even sent into battle without ammunition. Mounting defeats in World War I led to widespread discontent in the army. Russian industries were incapable of producing needed weapons and supplies. On the home front, food supplies were dangerously low.

THE REVOLUTION OF 1917 BEGINS
Worker-led food riots broke out in cities all across Russia. When soldiers refused to fire on striking workers in March 1917, Tsar Nicholas realized he was powerless to govern the nation. He gave up his throne, and the leaders of the Duma declared Russia a republic. Once in power, the moderate provisional government refused to withdraw from the war, and soon lost the support of the people.

THE BOLSHEVIKS TAKE POWER
A revolutionary group known as the **Bolsheviks** promised "Peace, Bread and Land" — peace for the soldiers, bread for the workers, and land for the peasants. Led by **Vladimir Lenin,** the Bolsheviks seized power in November 1917. The Bolsheviks changed the name of their political party to the "Communist" party. Russia had become the world's first Communist nation. In 1922, they also changed the name of their country to the Union of Soviet Socialist Republics (U.S.S.R.) or "Soviet Union."

THE SOVIET UNION UNDER LENIN (1917-1924)

Lenin significantly modified Marx's original theory of Communism. He believed that only a small group of dedicated party members could lead a country along the path to Communist equality. Lenin argued that after the revolution, a "temporary dictatorship" of party leaders was needed because the workers could not be trusted to know their own true interests.

CIVIL WAR IN RUSSIA

Once in power, the Communists withdrew from World War I. They declared the transfer of millions of acres of land to poor peasants. Workers were organized to control and operate factories, and all industries were **nationalized** (*taken over by the government*). A civil war followed between those who supported Lenin — known as the "Reds" — and their opponents — known as the "Whites." Foreign powers also intervened, giving some help to the Whites. Parts of the old Russian empire tried to break away. The Red army, with support from peasants and workers, finally defeated the Whites. This victory secured the power of the new Communist government.

THE NEW ECONOMIC POLICY (N.E.P.)

By 1920, Lenin realized that his program needed some modifications. Peasants were not growing enough food, since they feared it would be seized by the government. Lenin instituted the **New Economic Policy** (N.E.P.), in which some private ownership was permit-

Vladimir Ilyich Lenin

ted in agriculture and small factories. However, the government continued to control all major industries. The N.E.P. succeeded in slowly increasing production.

THE EARLY YEARS UNDER STALIN

When Lenin died in 1924, a struggle began between **Joseph Stalin** and other Communist leaders for control of the Party and the government. Stalin eventually emerged as the victor by accusing his rivals of disloyalty and having many of them executed.

STALIN AND THE RISE OF THE MODERN TOTALITARIAN STATE

Totalitarianism is a modern political system in which the government controls all aspects of individual life. Rights of free speech and dissent are denied. Once in charge, Stalin immediately set about turning the Soviet Union into a totalitarian state. Stalin used the government and the secret police to control all phases of Soviet life, including education, ideas, and the economy. He also used censorship to control music and the arts.

Reign of Terror. People lived in dread of being arrested by the secret police. In so-called **purges**, Stalin had other potential leaders arrested and executed. Stalin built enormous slave labor camps in Siberia, known as **gulags**. Tens of millions of people died, victims of his reign of terror.

Collectivization. Private land was taken from the peasants, who were forced to join collective farms owned by the government. When peasants in the Ukraine rejected collectivization, Stalin seized their food supplies and sealed off the entire region. Millions of Ukrainians starved to death.

CHANGES UNDER STALIN

Five-Year Plans. Stalin successfully turned his nation from an agricultural into an industrial country. He introduced a series of goals called **Five-Year Plans** in which all aspects of the economy were controlled. Heavy industries were developed, while consumer needs were ignored.

Glorification of Stalin. Stalin glorified his part in building the nation, portraying himself as Russia's greatest leader. Streets and cities were named after him; his picture appeared everywhere. Statues portrayed him as a gentle, fatherly ruler. Children memorized his sayings in school.

THE WORLD IN PROSPERITY AND DEPRESSION

Life in Europe in 1919 differed in significant ways from what it had been like before the war. The imperial governments of Germany, Russia, Austria-Hungary, and Ottoman Turkey were gone. New countries such as Poland, Czechoslovakia, Hungary, Yugoslavia, and the Baltic states (*Estonia, Latvia and Lithuania*) had reemerged. Russia had overthrown the Tsar and was in the midst of a civil war, which the Communists would win by 1921.

RECONSTRUCTION AND PROSPERITY IN THE 1920S

The first years after the war were not easy ones. The peoples of Central Europe suffered from famine caused by a wartime blockade of food. Returning soldiers faced unemployment. A deadly flu epidemic in 1919 killed as many people as the war itself had. Farms, cities, and railroad lines had been torn up in the fighting. Europeans spent the next five years rebuilding and recovering. Germans had to make huge reparations payments for the war to France and Britain, further slowing down German economic recovery.

The United States had emerged from the war as the world's greatest economic power. During the war, Britain and France had purchased American war goods on credit. Now they were deeply in debt. Americans faced a brief recession when the war ended, but American consumers soon began buying mass-produced goods made in U.S. factories.

One of the most important factors promoting American prosperity was the development of the automobile. Cars first came into widespread use in the United States and Europe after the war. Consumers also benefited from new electric appliances like vacuum cleaners, refrigerators, and toasters. They went to movies and listened to radio.

American bankers and industrialists invested some of their profits overseas, especially in Germany. American prosperity spread to Europe by the late 1920s. As Europeans began to buy more foreign goods, prosperity spread further to Asia, Africa, and Latin America. The 1920s also saw new values emerge, partly an outcome of the war. After working in factories during the war, women in the United States, Great Britain, and other countries won the right to vote and greater freedom. Increased industrialization created new jobs, many filled by women. More women also pursued higher educations.

THE GREAT DEPRESSION (1929)

In 1929, the bubble burst. The stock market crashed in New York, starting a chain reaction that plunged the American economy into the Great Depression. A depression is a deep economic downturn in which large numbers of businesses go bankrupt and workers are unemployed. American banks recalled their loans from Europe, and the depression quickly spread world-wide. About 40 million people were un-

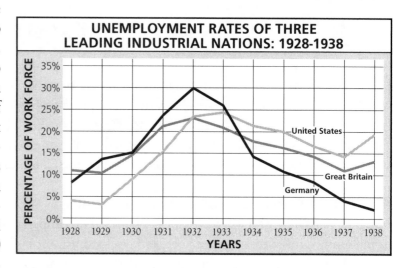

employed in the U.S., Germany, Japan, and other industrialized countries. In Eastern Europe, Asia, Africa, and South America, farmers could no longer sell their cash crops.

THE RISE OF FASCISM

Fascism was a new political movement that appeared in Europe in the unsettled conditions after World War I. The term Fascism is taken from the name of the political party formed by Benito Mussolini in Italy, but is used by historians to identify similar systems like Nazism in Germany. European Fascism had the following characteristics:

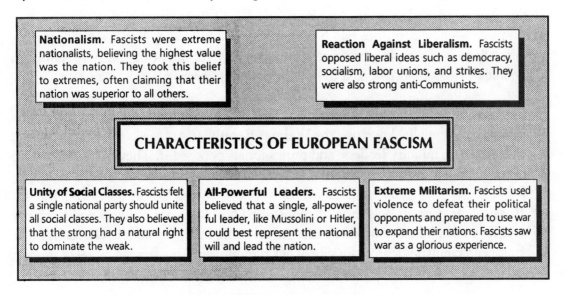

Nationalism. Fascists were extreme nationalists, believing the highest value was the nation. They took this belief to extremes, often claiming that their nation was superior to all others.

Reaction Against Liberalism. Fascists opposed liberal ideas such as democracy, socialism, labor unions, and strikes. They were also strong anti-Communists.

CHARACTERISTICS OF EUROPEAN FASCISM

Unity of Social Classes. Fascists felt a single national party should unite all social classes. They also believed that the strong had a natural right to dominate the weak.

All-Powerful Leaders. Fascists believed that a single, all-powerful leader, like Mussolini or Hitler, could best represent the national will and lead the nation.

Extreme Militarism. Fascists used violence to defeat their political opponents and prepared to use war to expand their nations. Fascists saw war as a glorious experience.

THE ROOTS OF FASCISM

Several earlier currents of European thought, such as anti-Semitism, racism, and Social Darwinism, had helped prepare the way for the rise of Fascism.

✦ **Anti-Semitism** (*hatred of Jews*) was already an established trend in European culture. Jews faced prejudice and persecution because their beliefs and customs made them easy targets in times of social unrest and economic difficulty. This was especially true in the late 1800s, when Jews were blamed for the disruption caused by the rapid industrialization of Europe.

✦ **Racism** is a contempt for other races. This, too, was an established trend in European culture. European racism was strengthened by the experience of overseas imperialism and by the spirit of nationalism.

✦ **Social Darwinism** made racism and anti-Semitism respectable by applying Charles Darwin's theory of evolution to human society. Social Darwinists believed that all human groups competed for survival and that stronger groups had the right to succeed over weaker groups, which deserved to die out.

THE OLD ORDER COLLAPSES

Europe had been shaken to its core by World War I. Immense political changes had taken place — new countries had been created, and old ruling families had lost their power. Often, the people who were running the government in the new European democracies were unaccustomed to holding political power.

✦ **Germany.** In Germany, the Kaiser was forced out when the war was lost. The new democratic republic, known as the **Weimar Republic**, was weak. Many landowners, industrialists, military leaders, and professionals opposed it. They preferred to give all political power to a single leader rather than to entrust it to the common people.

✦ **Russia.** The Russian Bolsheviks demonstrated how to organize a mass political party and how to build a totalitarian state. At the same time, the middle classes in other European countries feared the spread of Communism. This fear led many to support extremists like Mussolini and Hitler, who were strongly anti-Communist.

✦ **Italy.** A mood of dissatisfaction existed in Italy after the war. In 1922, **Benito Mussolini** seized power and began to make Italy into a Fascist state. He copied many Bolshevik practices while denouncing their ideas. Like the Bolsheviks, Mussolini's party had its own newspaper, as well as a private army of party members. Mussolini used violence against his opponents. Unions were abolished, strikes were outlawed, and the press was censored. Within three years, Italy had become a Fascist police state.

THE NAZI DICTATORSHIP IN GERMANY

The leaders of the Weimar Republic were blamed for signing the Treaty of Versailles, which had humiliated Germany and forced it to pay crippling reparations to Britain and France. These reparations had led to a soaring German inflation rate in 1923.

THE WEIMAR REPUBLIC COLLAPSES

By the late 1920s, the Weimar Republic had achieved some stability. This calm ended when the Great Depression spread from the U.S. to Germany in 1930. Six million people lost their jobs — more than a third of the work force. Government leaders could not agree on how to cope with this catastrophe. In the elections, the farmers, the unemployed, and the middle classes turned to the radical solutions offered by the Nazi Party.

RISE OF THE NAZI PARTY

Adolf Hitler (1889-1945) was the leader of the **Nazi** (*National Socialist*) Party. An electrifying speaker, Hitler recorded his main ideas in his book **Mein Kampf** (*My Struggle*):

HITLER'S VISION FOR GERMANY

Condemnation of the Weimar Republic. Hitler blamed Germany's humiliation at Versailles on Weimar leaders. He urged Germans to abandon democracy and return Germany to glory under a strong leader.

Aryan Race. Hitler believed that Germans were a superior "Aryan" race who should rule the world. He planned to wipe out the Slavic peoples to make room ("Lebensraum") for German settlers in Eastern Europe.

Anti-Semitism. Hitler called the Jews an "evil race" that should be destroyed for causing Germany's defeat in the war. He saw Communism as a Jewish plot to control the world.

THE NAZIS COME TO POWER

The Nazis formed a private army of "Brown Shirts" — former soldiers and unemployed workers. They beat up political opponents and Jews, and staged impressive rallies. When the Great Depression hit Germany, support for the Nazis grew. Hitler was appointed chief minister in 1933. He quickly secured complete control by burning down the German legislative building (*the Reichstag*). He then blamed the Communists for the fire and used the incident to obtain emergency powers, becoming an absolute dictator.

GERMANY UNDER NAZI CONTROL

The Nazi Party, like the Fascists in Italy, took over every aspect of German social, economic, and political life. In Hitler's "Third Reich" the following changes took place:

Human Rights Violations. Human rights were suppressed. People were arrested and executed without a trial. Rival political parties, unions, and independent newspapers were closed, and were replaced by pro-Nazi ones.

Control of Education. School children were taught Nazi ideas. Newspapers, radios, and films blared out Nazi propaganda. No other sources of information or organizations were permitted.

HITLER'S NAZI DICTATORSHIP

Persecution of Jews. German Jews lost their citizenship. They were thrown out of government jobs and had to wear yellow stars on their clothes. Jewish shops were vandalized and synagogues were burned.

Economic Changes. Hitler made use of public works projects such as building highways, and military rearmament, to achieve full employment. Economic prosperity returned to Germany.

Secret Police. The Nazis used threats and violence to control society. The **Gestapo** (*secret police*) arrested suspected opponents, who were thrown into **concentration camps** where they were tortured and killed.

WORLD WAR II (1939-1945)

The war that began in Europe in 1939 might be seen as a resumption of World War I. Hitler sought revenge against Britain and France for Germany's humiliating defeat in 1918. His claims for territories in Eastern Europe were apparently meant to satisfy German nationalist desires. But in fact, his vision went far beyond earlier German territorial ambitions. Hitler planned to enslave whole populations and to exterminate others. World War II became a struggle to the death for mastery of the world. The devastating effects of new weapons, and the linkage of German aims in Europe with Japanese ambitions in Asia made this the most destructive war in human history. World War II transformed the world, much as World War I had earlier transformed Europe.

THE ORIGINS OF WORLD WAR II

The rise of Fascist dictators in Italy, Germany, and elsewhere made war almost inevitable. They glorified war and laid plans for conquest. However, the war was postponed for several years while the dictators built up their armaments. Meanwhile, Japan had begun a war in East Asia in 1931. You will learn more about this in a later section.

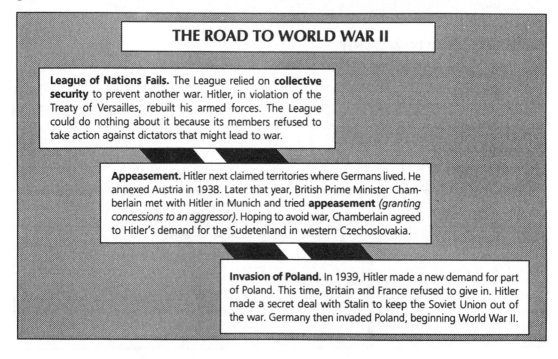

THE ROAD TO WORLD WAR II

League of Nations Fails. The League relied on **collective security** to prevent another war. Hitler, in violation of the Treaty of Versailles, rebuilt his armed forces. The League could do nothing about it because its members refused to take action against dictators that might lead to war.

Appeasement. Hitler next claimed territories where Germans lived. He annexed Austria in 1938. Later that year, British Prime Minister Chamberlain met with Hitler in Munich and tried **appeasement** *(granting concessions to an aggressor)*. Hoping to avoid war, Chamberlain agreed to Hitler's demand for the Sudetenland in western Czechoslovakia.

Invasion of Poland. In 1939, Hitler made a new demand for part of Poland. This time, Britain and France refused to give in. Hitler made a secret deal with Stalin to keep the Soviet Union out of the war. Germany then invaded Poland, beginning World War II.

THE WAR IN EUROPE

THE NAZI BLITZKRIEG AND THE BATTLE OF BRITAIN

Improvements in automobile engines and other technologies made new forms of warfare possible. The Germans developed the **blitzkrieg** (*the use of planes, tanks, and troop carriers to rapidly advance into enemy territory*). Using this tactic, the Nazis quickly overran Poland, Denmark, Holland, Belgium, France, and much of North Africa.

By the end of 1940, Germany controlled most of Western Europe; only Britain held out. Hitler hoped to overcome British resistance by bombing London and other British cities from the air. **Winston Churchill**, the new Prime Minister, rallied the British people. The use of radar, the bravery of the British air force, and Britain's island location helped defend it from German air attacks. Hitler was unable to defeat the British.

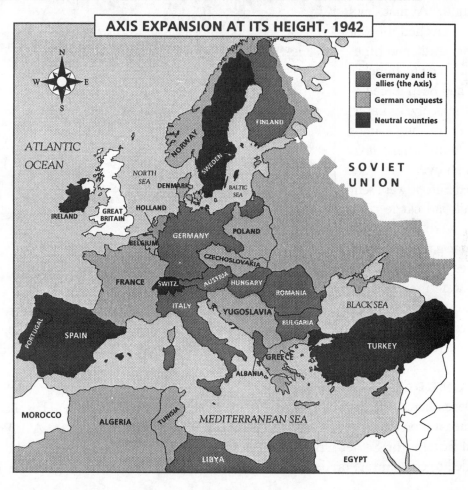

GERMANY INVADES THE SOVIET UNION

In 1941, Hitler betrayed Stalin and attacked the Soviet Union. The bitterly cold winter froze German trucks and tanks before they could reach Moscow. Soviet forces then gradually pushed the Germans back over the next several years, in heavy fighting.

THE HOLOCAUST

The **Holocaust** refers to the genocide of the Jews during World War II. **Genocide** is an attempt to murder an entire race of people. Hitler planned to kill every Jewish man, woman and child in Europe. He called this the "Final Solution." At first, Jews were marched out of towns and machine-gunned next to trenches they had been forced to dig themselves. Later, concentration camps were built where Jews from all over Nazi-controlled Europe were sent in railroad cattle cars. Most were killed with poison gas and their bodies burned. Some Jews were used as slave

labor in nearby weapons factories. Subject to inhumane conditions, few people survived. It is estimated that six million Jews died in the Holocaust. Six million Gypsies, Slavs, political prisoners, and mentally disabled people also died in Nazi concentration camps.

THE UNITED STATES ENTERS THE WAR

In December 1941, Japan attacked American ships at **Pearl Harbor,** Hawaii. Hitler declared war on the United States. Now Germany, Italy, and Japan, called the **Axis Powers,** faced Britain, the Soviet Union and the U.S., called the **Allied Powers.** The Allies decided to concentrate on defeating Germany in Europe before turning against Japan.

THE WAR IN EUROPE ENDS

On June 6,1944 **("D-Day")** U.S. and British troops landed in northern France. They pushed through France and Germany, while to the east the Soviet army advanced through Poland and Eastern Germany. The tide of war turned in favor of the allies because the Soviet Union had greater manpower than Germany, and the United States had greater manufacturing capacity. By 1945, Allied troops occupied all of Germany. Hitler preferred to allow the destruction of his country rather than to surrender. On April 30, 1945, he committed suicide, and in May Germany surrendered.

Several of the most important Nazi leaders were tried and convicted by an international court at Nuremberg, Germany for "crimes against humanity." The **Nuremberg Trials** revealed to the world the full extent and horror of Nazi atrocities — the use of slave labor, barbaric medical experiments on humans, forced starvation, and genocide.

THE WAR IN ASIA

Just as German plans for conquest had triggered the war in Europe, Japan's aggressive ambitions had led to war in Asia. To understand the reasons for Japanese aggression, it is necessary to review developments in Japan following the Meiji Restoration.

JAPAN'S RISE TO POWER

Japan's late 19th century industrialization was remarkably successful. But Japanese leaders needed raw materials and markets for their growing industries. They also wanted to replace European imperialism in East Asia by the imperialism of an Asian power. By the dawn of the 20th century, Japan began its campaign of aggression in mainland Asia.

✦ **First Sino-Japanese War (1894-1895).** China and Japan *("Sino" refers to China)* fought for control of Korea. Japan won, alerting the world to a new military power emerging in Asia. The victory also greatly strengthened the influence of the army in Japanese politics.

✦ **Russo-Japanese War (1904-1905).** Japan saw Russia as a threat to its expansion in Manchuria, and went to war. Japan's victory over Russia startled the world. It was the first time a great European power had been defeated by a non-European nation.

✦ **World War I (1914-1918).** Japan joined the Allies near the close of World War I. Japan's reward for its support was to obtain several German colonies in the Pacific.

✦ **Second Sino-Japanese War (1931-1939).** Japan invaded Manchuria in northern China. After defeating the Chinese, the Japanese set up a puppet government in Manchuria. Because world reaction was mild, Japan invaded the rest of China in 1937. Japanese planes dropped bombs and their army treated civilians brutally in the **Rape of Nanking.**

JAPAN IN WORLD WAR II

When war broke out in Europe, Japan occupied French Indochina. American leaders eyed Japanese expansion with suspicion. When the U.S. threatened to blockade oil shipments to Japan unless it gave up some of its conquests, Japanese leaders decided to go to war. Japan launched a surprise attack on the U.S. fleet at Pearl Harbor on December 7, 1941. Japan's military leaders hoped it would be a "knockout blow," leading to a treaty with the Americans that would give Japan control of East Asia. However, the Japanese had badly miscalculated.

At first, the Japanese achieved sweeping victories on the Asian mainland and in the Pacific. They invaded and occupied the Philippines, Hong Kong, Borneo, the Solomon Islands, Java, and Singapore. However, in 1943 the United States regained naval superiority in the Pacific. American forces began "island-hopping" — liberating Pacif-ic islands from Japanese control one at a time. Japan was slowly forced to retreat back to its home islands. After the defeat of Germany, the United States turned its full military strength on Japan.

In August 1945, the "Atomic Age" began. Rather than risk a full-scale invasion of Japan, the United States dropped an atomic bomb on the Japanese city of **Hiroshima**. Three days later, a second atomic bomb was dropped on **Nagasaki**. Tens of thousands of Japanese were killed. Fearing additional nuclear attacks, Japan surrendered.

THE U.S. OCCUPATION OF JAPAN (1945-1952)

American General **Douglas MacArthur**, who had led the Pacific campaign, was assigned the task of rebuilding and reforming Japan. For almost seven years, Japan's government was under foreign rule. During this time, important changes were made in Japan:

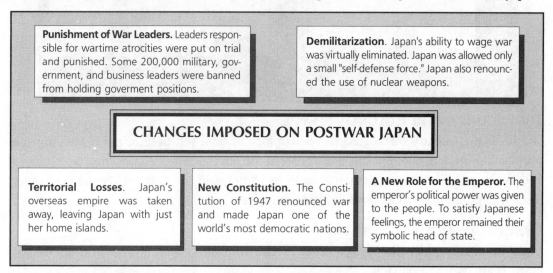

Punishment of War Leaders. Leaders responsible for wartime atrocities were put on trial and punished. Some 200,000 military, government, and business leaders were banned from holding goverment positions.

Demilitarization. Japan's ability to wage war was virtually eliminated. Japan was allowed only a small "self-defense force." Japan also renounced the use of nuclear weapons.

CHANGES IMPOSED ON POSTWAR JAPAN

Territorial Losses. Japan's overseas empire was taken away, leaving Japan with just her home islands.

New Constitution. The Constitution of 1947 renounced war and made Japan one of the world's most democratic nations.

A New Role for the Emperor. The emperor's political power was given to the people. To satisfy Japanese feelings, the emperor remained their symbolic head of state.

THE GLOBAL IMPACT OF WORLD WAR II

World War II dramatically changed the world.

DEFEAT OF DICTATORSHIPS

Hitler's plans to conquer Europe and Japan's plans for dominating Asia were defeated. After the war, Germany, Italy, and Japan were occupied by armies of the victorious nations and turned into democratic, peaceful countries.

UNPARALLELED DESTRUCTION

World War II was a global conflict, fought in Europe, North Africa, East Asia, and on the Pacific and Atlantic Oceans. Its destruction was unparalleled: more than sixty million people died, and much of Europe and Asia lay in ruins.

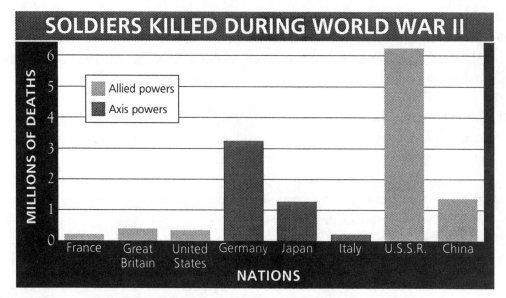

THE DECLINE OF THE COLONIAL POWERS

World War II greatly stimulated the desire for national self-determination among the peoples of Africa and Asia. European colonial powers such as Britain, France, Holland and Belgium had exhausted their resources in fighting the war and could no longer resist independence movements in their colonies.

THE COST OF FIGHTING THE WAR

Some estimates place the direct costs of the war, such as fuel and armaments, at more than two trillion dollars. Spending such a staggering sum brought about the economic collapse of many of the war's participants. Although the United States had shouldered a large share of Allied arms production costs, its economy suffered the least — the war was fought on foreign soil, and the United States was spared the physical destruction and costs of rebuilding.

A view of Warsaw after World War II

THE RISE OF THE SUPERPOWERS AND THE COLD WAR

The collapse of European power left two **superpowers** in command of the world: the United States and the Soviet Union. Their differences in viewpoint and in national interests rapidly led to the Cold War.

BIRTH OF THE UNITED NATIONS

Despite the failure of the League of Nations, the victorious allies launched a new international peace-keeping organization in 1945, known as the **United Nations** (U.N.). Today, the U.N. has more than 180 members — almost every country in the world.

AIMS

The U.N. Charter seeks to maintain peace in the world, while encouraging friendship and cooperation among nations. Members agree to give up the use of force in disputes, except in self-defense. The U.N. also works to eliminate hunger, disease, and ignorance, and promotes human rights and economic development.

ORGANIZATION

To ensure the participation of the major powers, the Charter gave the United States, Soviet Union, Great Britain, France, and China permanent membership on the **Security Council**. Each permanent member has veto power over U.N. military actions. There are also ten elected temporary members, without veto power. The Security Council is responsible for deterring aggression. It can apply economic sanctions or military power to resolve disputes. Since its founding, the U.N. has sent forces to engage in

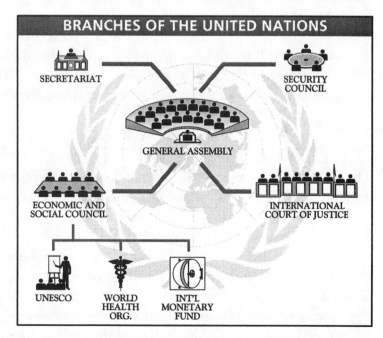

BRANCHES OF THE UNITED NATIONS

SECRETARIAT

SECURITY COUNCIL

GENERAL ASSEMBLY

ECONOMIC AND SOCIAL COUNCIL

INTERNATIONAL COURT OF JUSTICE

UNESCO

WORLD HEALTH ORG.

INT'L MONETARY FUND

"peacekeeping" operations in such places as Korea, Cyprus, Congo, and Iraq.

Every member state has one vote in the **General Assembly**. The Assembly votes on resolutions and makes recommendations to the Security Council. A majority of its members are developing nations. The **Economic and Social Council** cooperates with the General Assembly and specialized agencies like UNESCO (*U.N. Educational, Scientific, and Cultural Organization*) and WHO (*World Health Organization*) to promote economic and social development, world health, and education.

THE DECOLONIZATION OF ASIA AND AFRICA

One of the most significant impacts of World War II was the end of European imperialism in India, Southeast Asia, the Middle East, and Africa. Historians refer to this development as **decolonization**.

Several factors contributed to the end of European imperialism. The aggressions of Nazi Germany and Imperial Japan had largely discredited imperialist beliefs. Having fought for democracy in Europe, it was hard for the Allies to justify denying democracy to the peoples of Asia and Africa. Moreover, after World War II the old colonial powers were exhausted. Most Europeans were not willing to endure further warfare overseas to maintain colonial rule against determined local resistance. Even so, the end of European colonialism was not always bloodless.

INDIA

The first major country to win independence in the post-war period was India. The roots of the Indian independence movement reached back to the late 19th century.

THE INDIAN NATIONALIST MOVEMENT

Since 1885, the **Indian National Congress** had been the main organization dedicated to Indian independence. British officials sometimes reacted harshly. In 1919, peaceful Indian demonstrators were gunned down in the **Amritsar Massacre. Mohandas Gandhi**, the leader of the Congress, developed a large following among India's peasants. His non-violent methods eventually demonstrated the futility of denying Indians their freedom.

INDIA'S STRUGGLE FOR INDEPENDENCE

Non-Violence. Gandhi developed the policy of **passive resistance**. He counseled Indians to peacefully suffer British beatings and violence, and he refused to advocate the use of force against British officials.

Civil Disobedience. Gandhi urged Indians to disobey unjust British laws. In 1930, he led a **Salt March** to protest the British salt tax. His followers also fasted and refused to work for the British. As a result, Indians were jailed in large numbers.

Cottage Industries. Gandhi encouraged Indians to **boycott** (*refuse to buy*) British cotton goods, and to buy homemade goods. He hoped this would rebuild India's cottage industries and raise living standards.

Indian leaders had hoped for independence shortly after World War I, but were disappointed by British opposition. When World War II broke out, Gandhi refused to support Britain. Despite this, many Indian soldiers fought on the British side against Germany and Japan. After World War II, British leaders recognized that they were too weak to resist Indian demands for freedom. In 1947, the British agreed to Indian independence.

THE PARTITION OF INDIA (1947)

One reason for the British delay in granting independence to India was widespread fear of violence between Hindus and Muslims. Muslim leaders, led by **Mohammed Ali Jinnah**, told the British they wanted their own Muslim state. Thus, when the British granted independence in 1947, India was partitioned into two separate nations: India and Pakistan. India was largely a Hindu nation, while Pakistan was Muslim. Because there were large Muslim populations to the east and west, Pakistan became a divided nation, separated by Hindu India and almost a thousand miles. Millions of Hindus and Muslims moved from their homes after independence was granted. Thousands were killed in riots during these migrations.

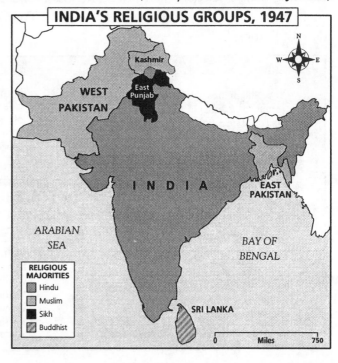

INDIA'S RELIGIOUS GROUPS, 1947

RELIGIOUS MAJORITIES
- Hindu
- Muslim
- Sikh
- Buddhist

SOUTHEAST ASIA

Beginning in the 1500s, most of Southeast Asia had gradually fallen under European control. Europeans were especially attracted by spices such as pepper and cinnamon found on the "spice islands" between the Indian and Pacific Oceans. Spain colonized the Philippines, and the Netherlands colonized the East Indies (*present-day Indonesia*) at the end of the 16th century. In the 19th century, Britain took Burma and the Malay peninsula, while France took most of Indochina — Laos, Cambodia, and Vietnam. In 1898, the Philippines passed from Spanish to American control. In Southeast Asia, only Thailand was able to preserve its independence.

INDEPENDENCE AND WAR

As in India, by the early 20th century, nationalist ideas had spread to members of the educated elite in the colonies of Southeast Asia. During World War II, Japan occupied all of Southeast Asia, driving out the European powers. After the war, nationalist leaders expected to achieve their independence. In some places independence was granted peacefully; in others, it was only achieved through warfare. For example, in 1953, Cambodia won its independence from France. In 1954, the French in Vietnam suffered a crushing defeat at Dien Bien Phu. The loss broke the will of the French to fight for their empire, and they pulled out of Vietnam. That same year, Laos became independent of France.

The Philippines are an archipelago *(group of islands)* in the Pacific. The United States granted the Philippines its independence in 1946.

Burma and Malaya. Myanmar, once called Burma, was for many years a part of British India. Great Britain granted both Burma and Malaya their independence in 1948.

THE NATIONS OF SOUTHEAST ASIA WIN THEIR INDEPENDENCE

Indonesia. Indonesian leaders declared independence in 1945, but they had to fight Dutch troops until 1949, when the Netherlands at last recognized Indonesian independence.

Vietnam. In Vietnam, guerrillas led by **Ho Chi Minh** began a war against the French and won in 1954. At an international conference, Vietnam was split in two: (1) in the north, a Communist state led by Ho Chi Minh; (2) in the south, a pro-Western state.

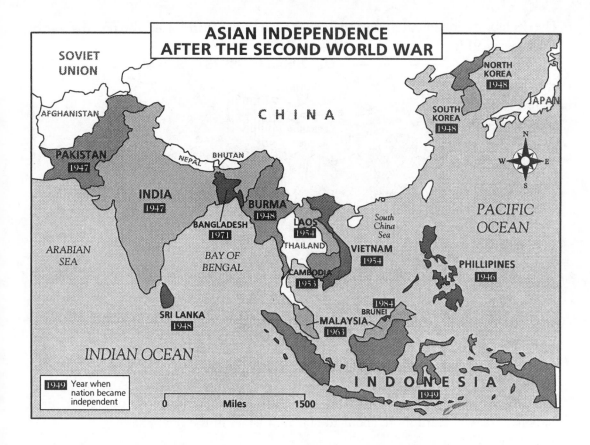

ASIAN INDEPENDENCE AFTER THE SECOND WORLD WAR

THE MIDDLE EAST AND NORTH AFRICA

The British had granted Egypt and Saudi Arabia their independence in 1922. However, the British kept troops in Egypt to protect the Suez Canal. Under this arrangement, the king of Egypt was little more than a British puppet. In 1953, he was overthrown by Colonel **Gamal Abdel Nasser**, an Arab nationalist.

After World War II, the French granted independence to Morocco, Tunisia, and Libya in North Africa, and to Lebanon and Syria in the Middle East. The independence of Algeria, however, posed greater difficulties. Over a million Frenchmen had settled in Algeria. These settlers assumed that one day Algeria would become a part of France. Starting in 1954, Algerian nationalists launched a violent struggle for independence. The French army fought the nationalists for almost eight years. France finally recognized Algerian independence in 1962, and French settlers fled the country.

The decolonization of Palestine and Transjordan under British rule also posed a thorny problem. In 1917, the British had promised to establish a Jewish homeland in Palestine. But the British had limited Jewish emigration to Palestine during and after World War II in order to prevent Arab uprisings. The British feared the end of colonial rule would lead to a full-scale civil war

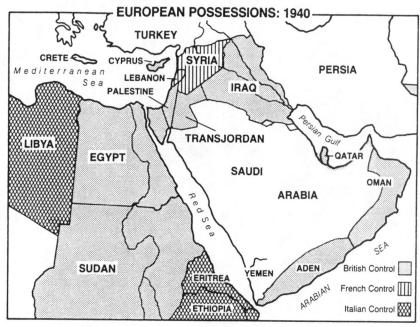

between Jews and Arabs. Finally, the British brought the problem to the new United Nations. You will learn more about the birth of Israel in the next chapter.

SUB-SAHARAN AFRICA

The spirit of nationalism also led to the decolonization of Africa south of the Sahara after World War II. Even before the war, the British and French had offered a European education to some Africans — the British in order to prepare them for self-government, and the French in order to absorb their colonies into France.

Members of this educated African elite became leaders of new nationalist movements. They were greatly impressed by the promises of freedom issued by the United States and Great Britain during World War II, as well as by the decolonization of Asia. **Kwame Nkrumah**, in the British colony known as the Gold Coast, followed the example of Gandhi by staging demonstrations and boycotting British products. At first, Nkrumah was jailed by the British. After his release, he was able to win independence for the Gold Coast in 1957. The Gold Coast changed its name to **Ghana** and became the first black African colony to win its independence.

Over the next decade, almost all of sub-Saharan Africa achieved independence. In some cases violent conflicts arose between European settlers and native Africans. In other cases, individual tribal groups tried to secede from the new nations. But for the most part, the former colonies turned into new states without a major war.

INDEPENDENCE MOVEMENTS IN AFRICA

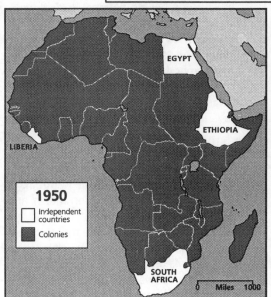

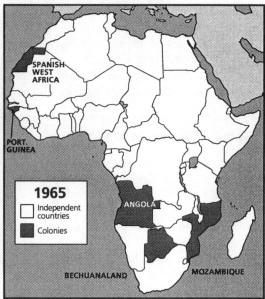

— STUDY CARDS —

Mexican Revolution of 1910

- Dictator **Porfirio Diaz** was overthrown in 1910
- Civil war followed as different factions competed for power
- **Constitution of 1917.** After civil war, government adopted constitution establishing public education, universal voting, 8-hour workday, right of workers to strike
- Large estates were broken up, Church lands seized and given to peasants
- Mexico became more democratic

World War I (1914-1918)

War between **Allied Powers** (Britain, France, Russia, U.S.) and **Central Powers** (Germany, Austria-Hungary, Ottoman Turkey):

- **Causes:** Nationalism, economic rivalries, alliance system, militarism, assassination of **Archduke Francis Ferdinand** in Serbia
- **New weapons and tactics**: machine guns, submarines, airplanes, trench warfare
- **Results:** Versailles Treaty dealt harshly with Germany ; Austria-Hungary and Ottoman Turkey broken up; League of Nations formed; Russian Revolution

(Continued)

Treaty of Versailles (1919)

Treaty ending World War I. Eager for revenge, Allies made treaty very harsh on Germany, which had grave consequences in the 1930s.

- Germany was forced to accept blame for starting the war and to pay huge reparations to the Allies, almost destroying its economy
- Germany lost its colonies and its navy; army was reduced to small police force
- Treaty created **League of Nations**; U.S. and newly-formed Soviet Union refused to join

Fascism

Political system developed in Italy, Germany, Spain and other nations following World War I.

Characteristics:
- **Extreme Nationalism:** Belief that country should unite behind national leaders; glorified violence, racism
- **Devotion to Party Leader:** condemned democracy as feeble; all-powerful leader would embody national ideals
- Instituted in 1930s in Germany under **Adolf Hitler** and in Italy under **Benito Mussolini.**

Russian Revolution (1917)

- Before World War I, most Russians lived in poverty; Tsar and nobles immensely rich
- Russia entered war, lost many battles; supplies to cities cut off; food riots grew
- **Tsar Nicholas II** overthrown; provisional government set up
- Bolsheviks under **Lenin** promised "Peace, Bread, and Land," seized power, pulled out of war, founded first Communist government
- **Civil War** (1919-1921) won by **Reds** (*Communists*) against **Whites** (*Anti-Communists*)

Nazism (National Socialism)

- **Adolf Hitler** became leader of Nazi Party in Germany; condemned **Weimar Republic** (a weak, divided German government) and harshness of the Versailles Treaty
- In *Mein Kampf*, Hitler wrote that Germans were superior race and Jews were major cause of Germany's problems (**anti-semitism**)
- Nazis seized power in 1933, eliminated all political rivals, restricted Jews, rebuilt military, used public projects to stimulate economy; inflicted terror with **Gestapo** (*secret police*)

Joseph Stalin

Lenin died, Stalin took power in Soviet Union by 1925. Brutal regime characterized by:
- **Political purges:** killed opponents or sent them to **gulags** (slave labor camps) in Siberia
- **Collectivization:** land seized from peasant owners, turned into collective farms
- **Five-Year Plans:** Stalin controlled all aspects of economy, tried to move country from an agricultural nation to an industrial power
- **World War II** (1939-1945): Under Stalin, Soviets fought off Nazi invasion; some 20 million Russians died in the war

World War II (1939-1945)

Worldwide war between **Axis** (*Germany, Italy, Japan*) and **Allies** (*Britain, U.S., Soviet Union*).
Causes:
- League of Nations too weak to keep peace; Britain's Neville Chamberlain **appeased** Hitler at **Munich Conference**, giving him part of Czechoslovakia, but failed to avoid war
- **Hitler-Stalin Pact:** This non-aggression pact (1939) led to Nazi conquest of Poland
- **German and Japanese Aggression:** Japan attacked China (1937) and Pearl Harbor (1941); Germans invaded Russia (1941)

(Continued)

Effects of World War II

- **Holocaust:** Six million Jews died in concentration camps such as Auschwitz
- **Atom Bomb:** U.S. dropped atom bombs on Hiroshima and Nagasaki, ending the war
- **Dictatorships Defeated:** Germany, Italy and Japan lost the war. Germany occupied and divided; Japan occupied by U.S.
- **Nuremberg Trials:** Nazi leaders tried for war crimes and genocide at Nuremberg
- **United Nations:** New world peace organization created, to include all nations
- **Decolonization:** Colonial empires dismantled

Gandhi and Indian Independence

- **Mohandas Gandhi:** father of non-violent passive resistance; won independence from British
- **Salt March:** In 1930, Gandhi led huge march to protest British tax on salt
- **Boycotts:** Gandhi urged Indians not to buy British goods
- **Cottage Industries:** Gandhi urged return to homemade goods to raise living standards
- After World War II, Britain was too weak to resist Indian independence. In 1947 British partitioned country into Hindu **India** and Muslim **Pakistan**. Thousands died in riots.

SUMMARIZING YOUR UNDERSTANDING

Use the table below to organize information about important people in this chapter.

PERSON	NATION	SIGNIFICANCE
Kemal Atatürk		
Sun Yat-sen		
Vladimir Lenin		
Joseph Stalin		
Adolf Hitler		
Mohandas Gandhi		
Kwame Nkrumah		

Complete the following graphic organizer.

CAUSES
1 _____
2 _____
3 _____

CAUSES AND EFFECTS OF WORLD WAR II

EFFECTS
1 _____
2 _____
3 _____

TESTING YOUR UNDERSTANDING

1 The harsh conditions imposed by the Allies in the Treaty of Versailles after World War I
   helped lay the foundation for the
   (1) rise of Fascism in Germany
   (2) French Revolution
   (3) downfall of Mexican dictator Porfirio Diaz
   (4) Bolshevik revolution in Russia

2 Which provision of the Treaty of Versailles showed the intent of the Allies to punish
   the Central Powers for their role in World War I?
   (1) All nations shall maintain open convenants of peace.
   (2) Freedom of the seas will be maintained.
   (3) Germany will accept full responsibility for causing the war.
   (4) Territorial settlements shall be based on lines of nationality.

Base your answer to question 3 on the line graph and your knowledge of global history.

3 Which statement is most
   accurate, based on the
   graph?
   (1) German unemploy-
        ment was highest in
        1932.
   (2) Between 1928 and
        1933, German unem-
        ployment remained un-
        changed.
   (3) By 1933, about 6 mil-
        lion German workers
        were unemployed.
   (4) The Nazi Party brought
        German unemployment under control in 1928.

GERMAN UNEMPLOYMENT, 1928-1933

4 Fascism in Europe during the 1920s and 1930s may best be described as a
   (1) demonstration of laissez-faire capitalism that promoted free enterprise
   (2) form of totalitarianism that glorified the nation above the individual
   (3) type of economic system that stressed a classless society
   (4) set of humanist ideals that emphasized an individual's worth and dignity

Base your answers to questions 5 and 6 on the chart and your knowledge of global history.

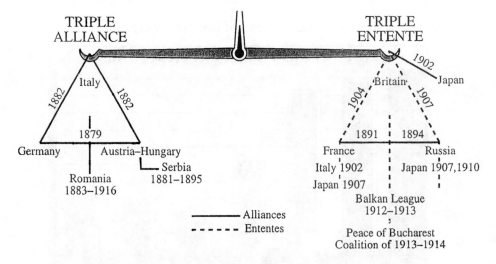

5 Which statement best expresses the main idea of the chart?
   (1) Many nations favor triangular foreign policy relationships.
   (2) Throughout the 20th century, Great Britain, Italy, and Russia were allies.
   (3) Foreign affairs are often based on a balance of power.
   (4) Alliances are stronger than ententes.

6 The Triple Alliance and the Triple Entente were established in the decades just
   (1) before the Congress of Vienna   (3) after the Treaty of Versailles
   (2) before World War I   (4) after the formation of the United Nations

7 The French Revolution of 1789, the Chinese Revolution of 1911-1912, and the Russian Revolution of 1917 were similar in that all these revolutions
   (1) were led by ruthless dictators
   (2) were motivated by a desire to overthrow a monarch
   (3) led directly to the establishment of Communism
   (4) established a higher standard of living for the middle class

8 Which statement best describes a relationship between World War I and the Bolshevik Revolution?
   (1) World War I created conditions in Russia that helped trigger a revolution.
   (2) World War I postponed the revolution in Russia by restoring confidence in the Tsar.
   (3) Opposing Russian forces cooperated to fight the foreign invaders.
   (4) World War I gave the Tsar's army the needed experience to suppress the revolution.

Base your answer to question 9 on the bar graph and your knowledge of global history.

9   According to the graph, which statement is most accurate?

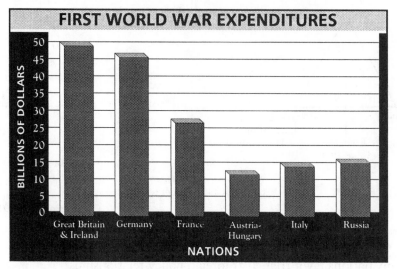

(1) The direct costs of World War I were evenly divided among the warring nations.
(2) Russia spent more in World War I than any other power.
(3) Germany spent more than Austria-Hungary, Italy and Russia combined.
(4) War costs were greatest at the start of the World War I.

10 Which factor contributed most to the rise of totalitarian governments in Europe before
     World War II?
     (1) improved educational systems   (3) increasing political stability
     (2) expanding democratic reforms   (4) worsening economic conditions

11 Stalin's Five-Year Plans and his decision to form collective farms are examples of
     (1) strategies to modernize the Soviet economy through forced Communism
     (2) a more friendly policy toward China
     (3) methods of dealing with the United States during World War II
     (4) programs to Westernize, educate, and enlighten the population

12 The main reason Japan accepted a new constitution after World War II was that
     (1) the new constitution was very similar to the previous one
     (2) Japan's colonial possessions were returned
     (3) the new constitution was imposed by the U.S. military government
     (4) Japan's military forces were allowed to be re-established

13 "It has impoverished the dumb millions by a system of progressive exploitation ... It has reduced us politically to serfdom. It has sapped the foundation of our culture ... and degraded us spiritually."

—Mohandas K. Gandhi, 1930

In the statement, the "It" referred to by Gandhi is
(1) British imperialism in India
(2) India's involvement in World War II
(3) the exploitation of the proletariat by the bourgeoisie
(4) the British endorsement of apartheid in South Africa

14 In 1947, the subcontinent of India became independent and was divided into India and Pakistan. This division recognized the
(1) rivalry between religious groups
(2) strength of Fascism in India
(3) natural geographic boundaries
(4) colonial boundaries of the British

15 Which statement about India is a fact rather than an opinion?
(1) Most Indians are happy with the practice of arranged marriages.
(2) India is fortunate to be a country with religious diversity.
(3) The Mughals ruled India for more than 300 years.
(4) The partition of British India in 1947 helped India prosper.

16 Europeans were able to dominate much of South and Southeast Asia in the 19th century primarily because
(1) Christianity was more appealing to the peoples of the region than their own native religions.
(2) Europeans had considerably more advanced technology, including weapons.
(3) The countries of South and Southeast Asia suffered from a lack of political organization.
(4) There were few natural resources to be found in the region.

17 A foreign policy aimed at preventing any one country from becoming powerful enough to dominate other countries is known as
(1) spheres of influence
(2) encomienda system
(3) balance of power
(4) military blockades

INTERPRETING DOCUMENTS

FIVE-YEAR PLANS IN THE SOVIET UNION
(m=million)

Sector	1928: Before Five-Year Plans	1932: End of lst Five-Year Plan	1937: End of 2nd Five-Year Plan
Industry	18.3m rubles	43.3m rubles	95.5m rubles
Electricity	5.05m kilowatts	13.4m kilowatts	36.6m kilowatts
Steel	4.00m tons	5.90m tons	17.7m tons
Grain	73.3m tons	69.9m tons	75.0m tons
Cattle	70.5m head	40.7m head	63.2m head

1a How much steel was produced in the Soviet Union in 1928? _____

 b What was Stalin's goal in introducing the Five-Year Plans to the Soviet Union?_____

THEMATIC ESSAY QUESTION

Directions: Write a well-organized essay that includes an introduction , several paragraphs addressing the *Task* below, and a conclusion.

Theme: Change

> The ideas and actions of some individuals have had a significant impact on others.

Task:

- Identify *two* influential individuals in global history.
- Explain how each individual's ideas or actions had an important impact.
- Discuss *one* way in which these two individuals were similar or different.

You may use any examples from your study of global history. Some individuals you may wish to consider include Alexander the Great, Mohammed, Martin Luther, John Locke, Catherine the Great, Simón Bolívar, Mohandas Gandhi, Joseph Stalin, Adolf Hitler, and Kwame Nkrumah.

You are *not* limited to these suggestions.

DOCUMENT-BASED ESSAY QUESTION

Historical Context:
The first half of the twentieth century witnessed large-scale human rights abuses. After World War II, important efforts were made to prevent similar abuses in the future.

Task: Using information from the documents and your knowledge of global history, answer the questions that follow each document in Part A. Your answers to the questions will help you write the Part B essay in which you will be asked to:

- Identify and explain two specific human rights abuses that occurred in the first half of the twentieth century.

- Discuss two attempts by nations or international organizations to eliminate human rights abuses at the end of World War II.

Part A — Short-Answer Questions

Directions: Analyze the documents and answer the questions that follow each document.

DOCUMENT 1

> The worst atrocity against defenseless civilians [in World War I] occurred against the Armenian people in 1915 and 1916. The Turks, uncertain of the loyalty of the Armenians, ordered the wholesale deportation of the Armenians from Syria. Armenian historians accuse the Turks of genocide. Turkish historians admit that massacres took place but deny the Turkish government intended them. The forced deportation of men, women, and children caused the deaths of tens of thousands through starvation and disease. Some Turks reverted to outright massacres. There are no reliable figures for those who perished. They vary, according to the whether the source is Turkish or Armenian, from 200,000 to more than 2 million.
>
> —J.A.S. Grenville, *A History of the World in the Twentieth Century* (1994)

1   According to this document, what human rights abuses occurred against Armenians during World War I? _____

DOCUMENT 2

There followed in Nanking a period of terror and destruction that must rank among the worst in the history of modern warfare. For almost seven weeks the Japanese troops, who first entered the city on December 13, unleashed on the already defeated Chinese troops and on the helpless Chinese civilian population a storm of violence and cruelty that has few parallels. Innocent females were abused, many died after repeated assaults, estimated by foreign observers at 20,000. Fugitive soldiers killed were estimated at 30,000; while 12,000 innocent civilians were murdered. Robbery, unjustifiable destruction, and arson left much of the city in ruins. There is no explanation for this grim event nor perhaps can one be found.

—Jonathan Spence, *The Search For Modern China*

2   Identify two human rights abuses committed by Japanese troops during their invasion of Nanking in 1937.

(1) _____

(2) _____

DOCUMENT 3

ARTICLE 9

Aspiring sincerely to an international peace based on justice and order, the Japanese people, forever, renounce war as a sovereign right of the nation, or the threat or use of force, as a means of settling disputes with other nations. For the above purpose, land, sea, and air forces, as well as other war potential, will never be maintained. The right of belligerency of the State will not be recognized.

—*The Japanese Constitution* (1947)

3   How did the Japanese Constitution attempt to curb future abuses by Japanese soldiers?

_____

_____

DOCUMENT 4

"I was ordered to establish extermination facilities at Auschwitz [Poland] in June 1941. I visited Treblinka to find out how they carried out their extermination. The Camp Commandant ... was principally concerned with liquidating the Jews from the Warsaw ghetto. He used monoxide gas which I did not think was very efficient. So at Auschwitz I used Zyklon B. It took from three to fifteen minutes to kill the people in the chamber. We knew when the people were dead because their screaming stopped. We waited a half hour before we opened the doors and removed the bodies. Our special commandos took off the rings and extracted gold from the teeth of the corpses. Another improvement we made over Treblinka was that we built gas-chambers to accommodate two thousand people at one time."
—From an affidavit of Rudolph Hüss, Commandant of Auschwitz

4   According to this passage, how were the human rights of Jewish people in Europe violated during World War II? _____

DOCUMENT 5

With regard to crimes against humanity, there is no doubt that political opponents were murdered in Germany, and many of them were kept in concentration camps in circumstances of great horror and cruelty. The policy of terror was certainly carried out on a vast scale, and in many cases was organized and systematic. The policy of persecution, repression, and murder of civilians in Germany before the war of 1939, who were hostile to the Government, was ruthlessly carried out. The persecution of Jews during the same period is established beyond all doubt. This indictment [bill of criminal charges] charges the defendants with crimes against peace by the planning, preparation, initiation and waging of war crimes; and with crimes against humanity. The defendants are charged with participating in the execution of a common plan or conspiracy to commit all these crimes.
—Judgement by the Tribunal at Nuremberg (1945)

5   List two ways the Nuremberg Trials attempted to prevent human rights abuses in the future.

(1) _____

(2) _____

DOCUMENT 6

Article 1: All human beings are born free and equal in dignity and rights. They are endowed with reason and conscience and should act towards one another in a spirit of brotherhood.

Article 2: Everyone is entitled to all the rights and freedoms set forth in this Declaration, without distinction of any kind, such as race, color, sex, language, religion, political or other opinion, national or social origin, property, birth, or other status.

Article 5: No one shall be subjected to torture or to cruel, inhuman, or degrading treatment or punishment.

Article 9: No one shall be subjected to arbitrary arrest [*imprisonment*], or exile.
—*United Nations Declaration of Human Rights*, approved in 1948

6   Identify two rights in the United Nations Declaration of Human Rights:

(1) _____

(2) _____

Part B — Essay

Directions: Write a well-organized essay that includes an introduction, several paragraphs, and a conclusion. Use evidence from at least **four** of the documents to support your response. Include additional outside information.

Historical Context: The first half of the twentieth century witnessed large-scale human rights abuses. After World War II, important efforts were made to prevent similar abuses in the future.

Task: Using information from the documents and your knowledge of global history, write an essay in which you:

- Identify and explain *two* specific human rights abuses that occurred in the first half of the twentieth century.

- Discuss *two* attempts by nations or international organizations to eliminate human rights abuses at the end of World War II.

CHAPTER 14

FROM THE COLD WAR TO GLOBAL INTERDEPENDENCE, 1945 - PRESENT

Oil fires set in Kuwait by Iraq during the Gulf War

	1945	1959	1973	1987	2001
U.S.S.R	STALIN	KHRUSHCHEV	BREZHNEV	GORBACHEV	C.I.S. / YELTSIN
W. EUROPE	MARSHALL PLAN	COMMON MARKET; NATO; RESISTANCE TO COMMUNISM			EUROPEAN UNION
E. EUROPE	SATELLITES OF THE SOVIET UNION				INDEPEN-DENCE
CHINA		MAO ZEDONG		DENG XIAOPING	JIANG ZEMIN
JAPAN	REBUILDING AFTER WORLD WAR II			ECONOMIC SUPERPOWER	
VIETNAM	FRENCH RULE	DIV. INTO N. & S. VIETNAM	VIETNAM WAR	COMMUNISTS RULE VIETNAM	
S. AFRICA	APARTHEID POLICY				APARTHEID ENDS
ISRAEL	WARS BETWEEN ISRAEL AND ARABS			UNEASY PEACE	
IRAN	RULE OF THE SHAH			ISLAMIC STATE	

1945	1959	1973	1987	2001

WHAT YOU SHOULD FOCUS ON

At the end of the World War II, two superpowers emerged. The Soviet Union had the world's largest army and occupied all of Eastern Europe. The United States possessed unparalleled economic strength and the atomic bomb. Their rivalry unleashed a Cold War that affected nearly every part of the globe. The collapse of the Soviet Union forty years later led to equally monumental changes. Against this background, developing nations struggled to improve their economies, Western Europe and Japan gradually recovered from the war, and ethnic rivalries occasionally erupted. Keep in mind these six major developments in the half-century since World War II:

Birth of the Cold War. Between 1945 and 1950, the wartime alliance between the United States and the Soviet Union broke down and the Cold War began. An "iron curtain" divided Eastern and Western Europe, and China became a Communist nation.

Balance of Terror: The Cold War from the 1950s to the 1970s. Both the United States and Soviet Union avoided head-on confrontation, but engaged in a worldwide competition for influence and in regional conflicts like the Korean and Vietnam wars.

Problems of the Developing World. While the superpowers engaged in the Cold War, the nations of Latin America, Africa, Asia, and the Middle East struggled to overcome poverty, illiteracy, ethnic conflicts, and political instability.

KEY DEVELOPMENTS AFTER WORLD WAR II

End of the Cold War. Gorbachev's attempted reforms led to the collapse of Communism in the U.S.S.R. and Eastern Europe. In China, Communists retained a monopoly of political power but introduced free-market measures.

Progress and Regression in the Post-Cold War Period. The spread of democracy helped move some age-old problems closer to resolution, while new problems — often fueled by ancient ethnic and religious hatreds — have appeared.

New Economic Realities. In an age of global interdependence, people depend more than ever on goods, services, and ideas from other countries. Barriers to world trade have been coming down.

In reviewing this era, keep in mind that test writers are most likely to ask you about the following:

- How did Soviet Communism differ from Western democracy?
- What were the causes and consequences of the Cold War?
- What problems do developing nations face?
- What factors led to the collapse of Communism in Europe?
- What challenges face the world in the post-Cold War era?

LOOKING AT TECHNOLOGY

Technology refers to tools and ways of doing things. Throughout history, people have used existing technologies and tried to improve them. Recently, technological progress has accelerated, giving rise to new hopes but also new problems.

MILESTONES IN THE HISTORY OF TECHNOLOGY

THE NEOLITHIC REVOLUTION (ABOUT 8000 B.C.)
The Neolithic Revolution first occurred in Mesopotamia and Egypt about 10,000 years ago. People learned to grow crops from seeds and to tame animals and use them for work. These developments allowed people to settle down in one place and establish villages.

THE RISE OF CIVILIZATION (ABOUT 3000 B.C.)
Early civilizations invented the sailboat and the wheel, mined metals, irrigated fields, built cities, and developed calendars and forms of writing.

HINDU AND MUSLIM ACHIEVEMENTS (8TH-9TH CENTURIES A.D.)
The concept of zero developed in Hindu India. Muslims developed Arabic numerals and algebra. They also introduced the astrolabe for navigation.

CHINESE ACHIEVEMENTS (1ST-13TH CENTURIES A.D.)
The Chinese invented many things that are still in use today. They created paper and invented water clocks to measure time. They were the first to develop porcelain, silk, the magnetic compass, block printing, and gunpowder.

IMPROVEMENTS IN EUROPE (14TH-EARLY 18TH CENTURIES)
Many key technological advances occurred in Europe during these centuries, including better cannons and guns, telescopes, microscopes, and superior ships. A major new invention was the printing press. During the Scientific Revolution and Enlightenment, thinkers developed the scientific method and calculus.

THE INDUSTRIAL REVOLUTION (LATE 18TH AND 19TH CENTURIES)

The Industrial Revolution began in Great Britain. A series of inventions applied steam power to run machines for spinning and weaving. This allowed British factory-owners to produce more cloth at a much lower price. Steam power was next used to build railroads and steamships. Later the Industrial Revolution brought steel, the chemical industry, and petroleum and electricity to the world.

THE AGE OF RAPID CHANGE (20TH CENTURY)

By the start of the 20th century, there was a major effort to promote scientific research and technology. The result has been a continuous stream of major inventions: the automobile (*at the very end of the 19th century*), the airplane, radio, television, radar, antibiotics, nuclear energy, missiles, and the computer. Each of these has had a major impact on our social and cultural development.

FACTORS IN THE DEVELOPMENT OF TECHNOLOGY

Some of the main factors that sociologists believe affect the pace of technological development are the following:

The Role of Tradition. Some societies pride themselves on following ancient ways. These traditional societies are not interested in technological progress. Instead, they try to preserve the old ways of doing things. In these societies, technological progress is slow.	**Exchange of Thought and Expression.** The free exchange of ideas is crucial to technological development. Societies with no free speech or free press often find progress to be slow. Progress is greatest when a society promotes the work of inventors and scientists with a system of rewards.	**Cultural Diffusion.** During the Crusades, Christians and Muslims exchanged new products and ideas. After Columbus, Europeans and Native Americans learned from each other. In Russia, Peter the Great borrowed Western European technologies. After the Meiji Restoration, the Japanese adapted Western ideas.

THE CHALLENGE OF MODERN SCIENCE AND TECHNOLOGY

Technological developments are not always put to good use. For example, improvements have made weapons much more destructive. Thus, technology can be compared to a hammer. We can use a hammer to build a house, or to damage our neighbor's house — the choice lies with us, not with the hammer.

MAJOR
HISTORICAL DEVELOPMENTS

SUPERPOWER RIVALRY AND
THE BIRTH OF THE COLD WAR

During World War II, the United States and the Soviet Union were allies fighting common enemies, but their political, economic, and social systems were very different. After the war, each superpower attempted to extend its influence, quickly leading to a "Cold War" — first in Europe and then in Asia, Latin America, and Africa. The **Cold War** was "cold" only in the sense that the two superpowers never confronted one another directly in open warfare. But their global competition led to crises and conflicts on every continent, dominating world events for forty years.

ROOTS OF THE COLD WAR

The roots of the Cold War lay in the competing ideological systems of the Western democracies and Soviet Communism. While Western nations hoped to spread democracy and capitalism, Soviet leaders promoted the expansion of Communism. It is therefore essential to understand the basic differences between these two systems.

	WESTERN DEMOCRACIES	SOVIET COMMUNISM
POLITICAL SYSTEM	Citizens elect representatives and national leaders. People have the right to form their own political parties.	The Soviet Union was a dictatorship controlled by Communist Party leaders. The Communist Party was the only political party permitted.
INDIVIDUAL RIGHTS	Citizens have basic rights, such as freedom of speech, freedom of the press, and freedom of religion.	The people had few rights. The government controlled radio, TV, and newspapers. Secret police arrested all critics of the government. Practice of religion was discouraged.
ECONOMIC SYSTEM	Under capitalism, people and corporations own businesses. They provide goods and services in order to make a profit.	Private property was abolished. With state ownership and central planning, the government controlled all production. Private farms became state-owned collective farms.

THE COLD WAR BEGINS

Even before World War II ended, Roosevelt, Churchill, and Stalin met at the **Yalta Conference** in 1944 to make plans for the post-war world. They agreed to divide Germany into four separate zones of occupation, controlled by the U.S., Britain, France, and the U.S.S.R. Stalin pledged to allow free elections in Eastern Europe when the war was over.

AN "IRON CURTAIN" DIVIDES EUROPE

Stalin did not keep his promise to hold free elections. Instead, the Soviet army set up puppet governments in Eastern Europe, headed by local Communists, thereby turning these nations into Soviet **satellites**. Stalin felt that the U.S.S.R. had the right to control Eastern Europe to "protect" the Soviets from invasion. In 1946, Winston Churchill declared that an **"Iron Curtain"** had descended on Europe. Trade and communication between Eastern and Western Europe was cut off. Eastern European governments were forced to adopt Communist economies and to follow policies dictated by the U.S.S.R.

GROWING AMERICAN INVOLVEMENT

Western leaders began to fear that Stalin was another Hitler, bent on world conquest. The United States was the only country powerful enough to resist the Soviet Union, but many Americans wanted to reduce U.S. involvement in world affairs — a policy of **isolation**. President Truman eventually persuaded Americans to take a more active role.

✦ **Military and Financial Aid.** In 1947, Britain withdrew its troops from Greece, where Communist rebels were threatening the government. Truman announced the United States would give aid to Greece and Turkey to prevent a Communist takeover. He offered to support all free peoples resisting Communism. This policy, known as the **Truman Doctrine,** marked the beginning of America's **containment** policy: the United States would not try to overturn Communism where it already existed, but would take steps to prevent it from spreading further. Later that year, the United States announced the **Marshall Plan**. Billions of dollars in aid were given to Western European nations in an effort to help them rebuild their war-torn economies. The aim of the Marshall Plan was to build future trading partners for the United States and to help Europeans resist Communism.

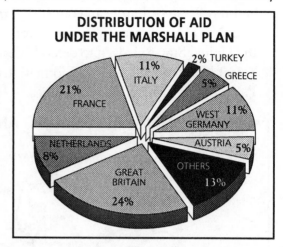

DISTRIBUTION OF AID UNDER THE MARSHALL PLAN

+ **The Berlin Airlift and the Division of Germany.** In 1948, the Western allies took steps to merge their zones of occupation in Germany. The Soviets reacted by closing all highway and railroad links to Berlin, which was in the Soviet sector. The allies began a massive airlift to feed and supply the city. Within a year, the Soviets lifted their blockade. In 1949, the three Western zones of occupation were merged into an independent nation called the **Federal Republic of Germany** (*West Germany*). The Soviets

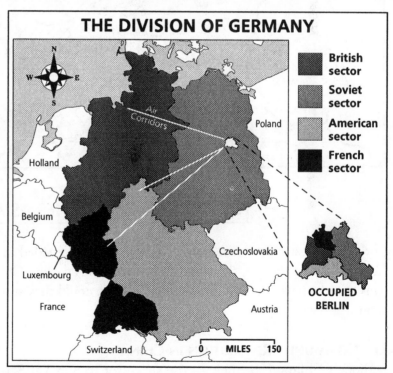

THE DIVISION OF GERMANY

British sector

Soviet sector

American sector

French sector

OCCUPIED BERLIN

responded by turning their zone into a nation known as the **German Democratic Republic** (*East Germany*).

✦ **Formation of NATO and the Warsaw Pact.** In 1949, the United States, Canada, and ten Western European countries formed the North Atlantic Treaty Organization, **NATO,** to protect Western Europe from Communist aggression. With NATO the United States pledged to defend Western Europe with its nuclear weapons. The Soviet Union responded to the formation of NATO in 1955 by creating the **Warsaw Pact** with its Eastern European allies.

MEMBERS OF NATO AND THE WARSAW PACT

THE COLD WAR REACHES ASIA

Just when Western statesmen believed they had succeeded in checking the spread of Communism in Europe, the world's most populous nation, China, turned Communist. This raised a new question for Western leaders: could they stop the spread of Communism worldwide?

THE COMMUNIST REVOLUTION IN CHINA

Although **Chiang Kai-Shek** — the successor to Sun Yat-Sen — had united most of China in 1928, he became engaged in a long struggle against both Chinese Communists and Japanese invaders. **Mao Zedong,** the leader of the Communists, retreated with his

forces to the northwest, in what became known as the **Long March** (1934-1935). In **1937,**
when Japan invaded China, Communist and Nationalist forces agreed to a truce in order to cooperate in defeating the Japanese. After Japan was defeated in 1945, fighting resumed between the Nationalists and Communists.

Soon after World War II, the Communists achieved control over most of the Chinese countryside by winning the support of the peasants through their land-reform programs.

In 1949, Mao Zedong and the Communists finally drove Chiang Kai-Shek and his supporters from mainland China. Chiang retreated to the island of **Taiwan** (*Formosa*). This created **"Two Chinas:"** Mao's Communist China and Chiang's Nationalist China on Taiwan. The United States refused to extend diplomatic recognition to the Communists in China. Using its veto power in the Security Council, the United States continually blocked Communist China's admission to the United Nations.

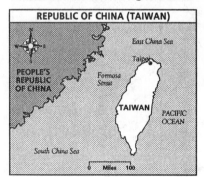

CHINA UNDER MAO ZEDONG

Once Mao took control of China, all aspects of life were brought under the direct control of the Communist Party. Mao dramatically changed traditional ways of life:

CHANGES IN CHINA UNDER MAO ZEDONG

Re-education. Communist beliefs became required learning in all universities and schools. Newspapers and books were controlled by the government and had to promote Communism. Even art and music came under the direct supervision of the government.

Elimination of the "Capitalist Class." Landowners, factory owners, village leaders, and better-off peasants were considered by Communists to be of the "Capitalist Class" which exploited poorer people. These "capitalists" were often killed.

The Family. Family authority was replaced by the authority of the Communist Party. Children were taught to obey the state, not their parents. Ancestor worship, which promoted family tradition, was forbidden. This further weakened the father's role.

THE KOREAN WAR (1950-1953)

After Mao's victory in China, Western leaders feared Communism was on the march in Asia. Like Germany, Korea had been divided in 1945 into two states, one Communist and one non-Communist. In 1950, Communist North Korea invaded South Korea. President Truman and other Western leaders believed it was necessary to take a firm stand. Under a U.N. resolution, the United States and other countries intervened and drove the Communist Koreans back to North Korea. U.N. forces, led by General **Douglas MacArthur,** then invaded North Korea. When they approached the Chinese border, China itself intervened. General MacArthur thought of using nuclear weapons, but President Truman refused. This disagreement led Truman to remove MacArthur from his

MAP 1

A: North Koreans attack, June 25, 1950
B: North Koreans advance, Sept. 1950
C: U.N. landing at Inchon, Sept. 15, 1950
D: U.N. advance, October 27, 1950

MAP 2

E: Chinese advance, Nov. 1950
F: Chinese advance, Jan. 1951
G: Armistice line, July 27, 1953

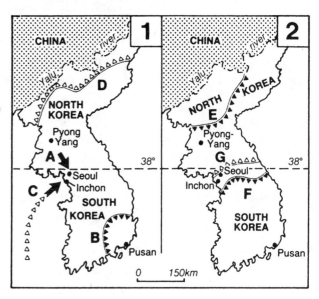

command. In 1953, a compromise ended the war, leaving North and South Korea divided much as they had been before, but with a demilitarized zone between the two countries.

THE GREAT LEAP FORWARD

In 1956, Mao Zedong began forcing Chinese peasants onto cooperative farms where families shared the work and divided the crops. Later these farms were merged into larger communes. In 1958, Mao introduced a **Five-Year Plan** aimed at turning China into an industrial power. China's vast population was used to build dams, bridges, roads, and factories. But poor planning and the high cost of foreign machinery led to an economic crisis.

THE BALANCE OF TERROR: THE COLD WAR FROM THE 1950s TO THE EARLY 1970s

In 1949, the Soviet Union exploded its first atomic bomb. Soon each superpower had also developed far more destructive hydrogen bombs and missiles to deliver them. American and Soviet leaders quickly realized that these weapons could hardly ever be used because of their destructiveness. Instead, nuclear weapons served as **deterrents**, preventing the superpowers from attacking one another. The superpowers became locked in a new "Balance of Terror," which forced them to find other channels for competition. They soon became involved in a number of regional conflicts, sometimes leading to warfare on a limited scale.

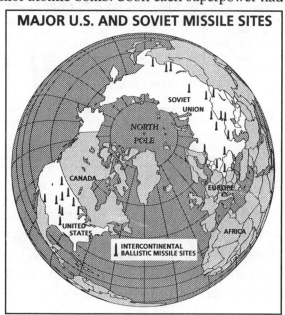

MAJOR U.S. AND SOVIET MISSILE SITES

SOVIET UNION

NORTH POLE

CANADA

EUROPE

UNITED STATES

AFRICA

INTERCONTINENTAL BALLISTIC MISSILE SITES

THE SOVIETS AND EASTERN EUROPE

In 1953, Stalin died. **Nikita Khrushchev** eventually emerged as leader of the Soviet Union. Khrushchev condemned Stalin's atrocities, freed many political prisoners, and attempted to introduce changes into the Soviet Union. But Khrushchev firmly believed that Communism would eventually triumph through peaceful competition with the West. Despite his best efforts, Khrushchev was unable to dramatically increase Soviet economic production. However, he achieved a stunning success when the U.S.S.R. launched the first space satellite, **Sputnik**, in 1957. American leaders feared the Soviets could soon send missiles with nuclear warheads to the United States.

FRICTION BEHIND THE IRON CURTAIN

Khrushchev's condemnation of Stalinism triggered unrest in Eastern Europe, where local populations were unhappy with Communist rule.

Poland. In 1956, workers went on strike for greater freedom. Khrushchev agreed to let Polish reformers handle their own affairs so long as Poland remained Communist and continued to be a member of the Warsaw Pact.

Hungary. Students launched demonstrations in favor of reform. Unlike Poland, Hungarian leaders threatened to leave the Warsaw Pact. Soviet troops were sent into Hungary in 1956 and brutally crushed the reform government.

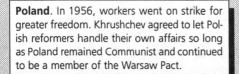

PROBLEMS AND PROTESTS IN EASTERN EUROPE

East Berlin. Many East Germans fled to the West through Berlin. In 1961, Khrushchev had a wall built to seal off East Berlin, and barriers went up along the border of East and West Germany. The **Berlin Wall** became a symbol of the Cold War.

Czechoslovakia. In 1968, after Czech leaders proclaimed a more liberal policy called "Communism with a human face," the Soviets sent tanks into Prague. Czech leaders were replaced by hard-line Communists.

COMMUNISM IN LATIN AMERICA

Since the days of the **Monroe Doctrine** (1823), the United States had banned foreign interference in the Western Hemisphere. The worldwide spread of Communism posed new challenges for the United States. Widespread poverty and political repression made Latin America ripe for the spread of Communist beliefs.

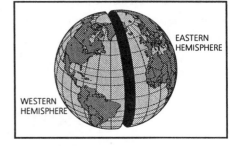

In 1959, **Fidel Castro** and his guerrilla fighters overthrew Cuba's dictatorship. Castro promised the Cuban people democracy, but once in power he nationalized businesses and executed opponents. The United States reacted to the **Cuban Revolution** and the nationalization of American-owned businesses in Cuba by breaking off trade. Castro turned to the

Soviet Union for support, and transformed Cuba into a Communist state. Castro then threatened to export Communism to other Latin America nations.

The Bay of Pigs Invasion. In 1961, Cuban exiles, trained by the U.S. Central Intelligence Agency, invaded Cuba at the Bay of Pigs to overthrow Castro. President Kennedy refused to supply the rebels with air support to carry out the attack, and their effort failed.

The Cuban Missile Crisis. In 1962, American leaders discovered Cuba was secretly building bases to install Soviet missiles with nuclear warheads. Soviet nuclear missiles would now be within easy striking distance of major U.S. cities. In response to this threat, President Kennedy ordered a naval blockade of Cuba, and threatened to invade if the missiles were not withdrawn. The world stood on the brink of nuclear war. Khrushchev finally agreed to withdraw the missiles in exchange for a pledge that the United States would not invade Cuba.

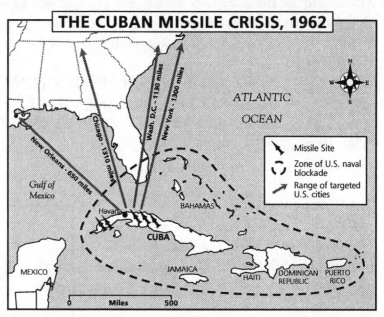

Khrushchev's failure in this risky venture contributed to his removal from power in 1964.

COMMUNISM IN CHINA

THE CHINESE CULTURAL REVOLUTION

By 1962, Mao's condemnation of Khrushchev's reforms in the Soviet Union, as well as border disputes, led to an open disagreement between China and the Soviet Union. Mao used the **Sino-Soviet** split to launch a bid for world leadership of the Communist movement. Mao was also concerned about the loss of revolutionary enthusiasm for Communism among Chinese party officials. Finally, Mao may have wanted to cover up his own mistakes during the Great Leap Forward. He now made a bold attempt to push China towards the ideal Communist society by announcing a **Cultural Revolution**.

In 1966, Mao closed China's universities and schools and invited eleven million students to gather in Beijing as **Red Guards**. Mao hoped to use these young people to revitalize Chinese society. The Red Guards traveled throughout China attacking writers, scientists, doctors, professors, factory managers, and party officials for looking down on the common people and abandoning Communist ideals. Scholars and professionals were sent to work in the fields. Art works from dynastic China were destroyed. Mao's opponents within the Party were removed and punished.

Chinese society eventually became so disrupted by the excesses of the Red Guards that Mao had to use the army to control them. The Cultural Revolution led to shortages of food and goods. In 1969, Mao sent the Red Guards back to the countryside to help with farming. Violence ceased as the Cultural Revolution drew to a close.

THE WAR IN INDOCHINA AND THE ORIGINS OF DÉTENTE

While the Cultural Revolution was raging in China, the Cold War erupted again into open warfare in neighboring Indochina.

THE WAR IN VIETNAM

In 1954, Vietnam had been temporarily divided when the French withdrew from Indochina. Popular nationalist leader **Ho Chi Minh** created a Communist state in North Vietnam, while South Vietnam established ties with the West. However, South Vietnam refused to hold elections to reunify the country, claiming that Northerners would not be free to vote as they wished.

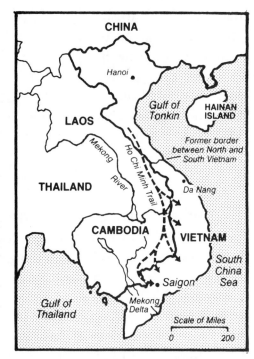

South Vietnamese Communists, called **Viet Cong,** with North Vietnamese support, launched a guerrilla war against the South Vietnamese government. Once again, the United States stepped in to resist Communism. At first, American soldiers acted only as advisors to the South Vietnamese army. However, in 1964 American combat troops were sent to Vietnam. Although the U.S. used extensive bombing, advanced technology, and as many as a half a million troops, it was never able to turn the tide against the Viet Cong and the North Vietnamese. In 1973, American troops withdrew from Vietnam in accordance with an agreement reached in Paris. In 1975, South Vietnam fell to North Vietnamese forces and the country was reunited under Communist rule.

RELAXATION OF COLD WAR TENSIONS

In order to put pressure on North Vietnam, U.S. President Nixon had introduced a policy of **détente** — a relaxation of tensions with the Soviet Union. Nixon signed an agreement with Soviet leaders, known as the **S.A.L.T. Accord**, to limit nuclear missiles. To further pressure the North Vietnamese, Nixon visited Communist China in 1972 and restored diplomatic relations. In 1973, the United States and the Soviet Union also cooperated to end an Arab-Israeli war in the Middle East. These actions did not help the United States to win in Vietnam, but they served to thaw the Cold War.

CAMBODIA (KAMPUCHEA)

The withdrawal of American forces from Vietnam also led to the collapse of the government in neighboring Cambodia. In 1975, Cambodian Communists, known as the **Khmer Rouge,** seized control. **Pol Pot,** the Khmer Rouge leader, carried out a policy of mass murder against city dwellers and political opponents. The Khmer Rouge killed as many as four million Cambodians between 1975 and 1979. They were finally overthrown through Vietnamese intervention.

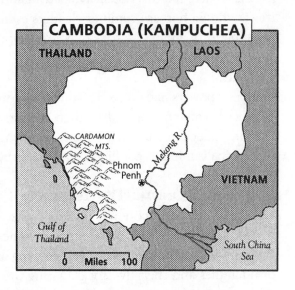

CAMBODIA (KAMPUCHEA)

PROBLEMS OF THE DEVELOPING WORLD

While the superpowers were engaged in a deadly game of global rivalry, the nations of Asia, Africa, Latin America, and the Middle East struggled with age-old problems of political instability and economic underdevelopment. These countries generally followed a policy of **non-alignment** during the Cold War. This policy called for not taking sides with either superpower so that they could receive economic aid from both. Most of these countries had recently been colonies. Despite their achievement of national independence, they often lacked democratic traditions. Frequently, leaders assumed dictatorial powers. In most developing countries a small, highly educated elite controlled national resources, while a majority of the population remained poor and uneducated.

AFRICA

As in most of the developing world, Africans struggled with problems of ethnic disunity and political instability while trying to promote economic development.

THE SINGLE-PARTY STATE

After independence, many African countries allowed only one political party. African leaders argued that this system avoided anarchy and tribal division. In some African countries, national heroes or military leaders established dictatorships. Often they relied on the support of a particular tribe; political opponents were imprisoned or executed.

TRIBALISM

European powers had created colonies without regard for tribal boundaries. When these colonies became nations, often there were rival tribes within them. Many Africans had a greater allegiance to their tribe than to their nation. This is called **tribalism**. Sometimes tribalism led to conflicts or attempts by tribes to withdraw from their nation.

EFFORTS AT ECONOMIC DEVELOPMENT

The need for rapid economic development was the most pressing problem facing new African states. Standards of living and incomes were among the lowest in the world. Most Africans were **subsistence** farmers, growing only enough food to meet the needs of their own families and their livestock. During the colonial period, Europeans had exploited African workers to grow cash crops and to extract minerals, but had done little to develop local African industries. After independence, many Africans began migrating to cities in search of educational and employment opportunities. This rapid urban growth often outstripped employment prospects and public facilities, adding to difficulties.

SOUTH AFRICA AND APARTHEID

One thing that united the new African nations was their hostility to South Africa, which remained under the control of a white minority. In 1948, Dutch-speaking white South

Africans, known as Afrikaners or Boers, instituted **apartheid** *(racial "separateness")*. Under this policy, South Africans were classified by race.

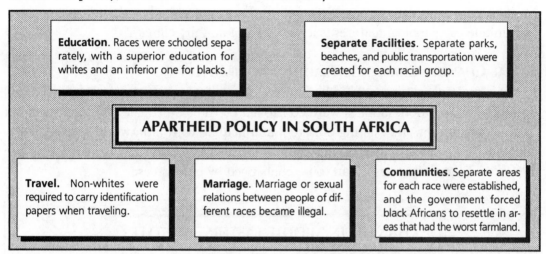

Education. Races were schooled separately, with a superior education for whites and an inferior one for blacks.

Separate Facilities. Separate parks, beaches, and public transportation were created for each racial group.

APARTHEID POLICY IN SOUTH AFRICA

Travel. Non-whites were required to carry identification papers when traveling.

Marriage. Marriage or sexual relations between people of different races became illegal.

Communities. Separate areas for each race were established, and the government forced black Africans to resettle in areas that had the worst farmland.

Many black South Africans resisted apartheid by both violent and non-violent means. In the **Sharpeville Massacre** of 1960, the police killed sixty-nine demonstrators. This massacre led to a general strike by black Africans. In 1976 the government tried to force the use of Afrikaans *(the language of the Afrikaners)* in black schools. This resulted in the **Soweto Uprising**, when rioting spread throughout the country.

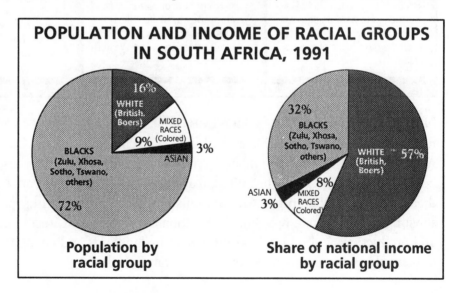

POPULATION AND INCOME OF RACIAL GROUPS IN SOUTH AFRICA, 1991

16% WHITE (British, Boers)
MIXED RACES (Colored)
9%
3% ASIAN
BLACKS (Zulu, Xhosa, Sotho, Tswano, others)
72%

Population by racial group

32% BLACKS (Zulu, Xhosa, Sotho, Tswano, others)
WHITE (British, Boers) 57%
ASIAN 3%
8% MIXED RACES (Colored)

Share of national income by racial group

The economic hardships imposed by apartheid were severe for South African blacks. They were forced to work in mines, farm on poor soils, or take menial jobs, and were denied access to a good education.

THE MIDDLE EAST

Most of the developing nations of the Middle East were united by their Islamic culture and unique geographical features, such as a warm and dry climate.

SOCIAL CHANGES CHALLENGE TRADITIONAL LIFESTYLES

In 1945, most people in the Middle East lived in villages and were farmers or herded livestock. By tradition, families were controlled by the eldest male. Women stayed at home doing housework, bearing children, and helping with farm work. Sons were expected to follow their father's occupation. Marriages were arranged by parents. In the 1960s, traditional lifestyles began to be challenged by new forces:

CHANGES IN MIDDLE EASTERN LIFESTYLES

Modernization. Modern medicine and new conveniences such as electricity, radio, and television began to make inroads into village life. Such changes threatened the basic fabric of traditional life.	**Urbanization.** Young people began moving to the cities in search of new opportunities and a modern way of life. There they often come into contact with a middle class that had Western values.	**Women's Roles.** Modern education led young people to challenge traditional roles and beliefs. Today, many Middle Eastern women go to college, enter professions, and join the work force. Many also adopt Western dress.

NASSER AND THE PAN-ARAB MOVEMENT

Egypt has the largest population in the Middle East. In 1953, Colonel **Gamal Abdel Nasser** seized power in Egypt and set about trying to unite all Arabs under his leadership. The belief that all Arabs should be united in a single state is known as **Pan-Arabism**. Nasser's dream collapsed when other Arab nations refused to unite with Egypt. Nasser tried to solve Egypt's economic problems by nationalizing businesses, regulating wages, prices, and production, and taking land from wealthy landlords and giving it to poor peasant farmers. These programs were known as **Arab Socialism**.

ISRAEL STRUGGLES TO SURVIVE

Zionism was a movement founded by **Theodor Herzl**, calling for a Jewish return to Israel. In 1917, the British issued the **Balfour Declaration**, announcing that a Jewish homeland would be created in Palestine. Jewish immigration to Palestine swelled in the 1930s and 1940s, due to Nazi persecution of Jews in Europe. Palestinian Arabs protested the admission of more Jews, and their immigration was reduced by the British authorities.

In 1948, after years of fighting Jewish guerrilla groups, the British left Palestine. They handed over the question of a Jewish homeland to the United Nations. The U.N. voted to create the new State of **Israel**. Palestinian Arabs were given the West Bank and Gaza Strip. The existence of a Jewish state became a central political issue in the Middle East.

ISRAEL 1967-1974

LEBANON
SYRIA
Golan Heights

0   80 km

Pre 1967

Occupied territory 1967

Territory captured in 1967 and retained after 1982

Tel Aviv

WEST BANK

Jerusalem

Mediterranean Sea

Gaza Strip

ISRAEL

JORDAN

SUEZ CANAL

SINAI

Eilat   Akaba

EGYPT

SAUDI ARABIA

Sharm el Sheikh

◆ **Israel's War For Independence**. Arab nations refused to recognize the new state. They launched an attack on Israel, but were defeated. After the war, Jordan seized the West Bank, Egypt took the Gaza Strip, and Israel took parts of each of these territories. Palestinians fled from Israel and became refugees in neighboring Arab lands.

◆ **Further Wars**. In 1956, Israel, Britain and France attacked Egypt to seize the Suez Canal, but were stopped by the superpowers. In 1967, the **Six-Day War** erupted between Arab states and Israel. Israel won it in six days and acquired the Gaza Strip and Sinai Peninsula from Egypt, the West Bank from Jordan, and the Golan Heights from Syria. In 1973, Egypt and Syria launched a surprise attack on Israel on the holy day of Yom Kippur. Israel again repelled Arab forces in the **Yom Kippur War**, seizing part of the Sinai Peninsula from Egypt.

CAMP DAVID ACCORDS

In 1978, Egyptian President **Anwar el-Sadat** and Israel's Prime Minister **Menachim Begin** were invited by President Carter to a meeting at Camp David. They agreed that Israel would return lands taken from Egypt in exchange for peace between the two countries, ending thirty years of warfare. Other Arab countries denounced the agreement and broke off diplomatic relations with Egypt. In 1981, Sadat was assassinated by Arab extremists who saw the accord as a surrender to Israel. Nevertheless, it was an important first step in the direction of peace in the Middle East.

ISRAEL AND THE PALESTINIANS

Hostility between Palestinian Arabs and Israelis further complicated Israel's relations with its Arab neighbors.

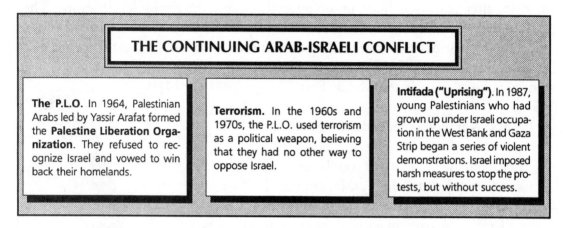

THE CONTINUING ARAB-ISRAELI CONFLICT

The P.L.O. In 1964, Palestinian Arabs led by Yassir Arafat formed the **Palestine Liberation Organization**. They refused to recognize Israel and vowed to win back their homelands.

Terrorism. In the 1960s and 1970s, the P.L.O. used terrorism as a political weapon, believing that they had no other way to oppose Israel.

Intifada ("Uprising"). In 1987, young Palestinians who had grown up under Israeli occupation in the West Bank and Gaza Strip began a series of violent demonstrations. Israel imposed harsh measures to stop the protests, but without success.

CIVIL WAR IN LEBANON

In 1975, civil war erupted in Lebanon between Christians, Sunni Muslims, and Shi'ite Muslims. In 1976, Syria invaded the country. In 1978 and again in 1982, the Israeli army entered Lebanon to destroy P.L.O. camps. Israeli forces occupied Lebanon until 1985.

SOUTH ASIA

Almost one-quarter of the world's population lives on the Indian subcontinent. After independence, this region faced problems typical of developing areas. A large, educated elite helped the nations of this region establish their own unique paths to development.

INDIA

India has had a democratic government since its independence in 1947. With almost one billion people, it is the world's largest democracy. However, one family has headed the government for most of its existence. **Jawaharlal Nehru** was Prime Minister for 17 years, and his daughter **Indira Gandhi** was Prime Minister for 15 years. Her son **Rajiv Gandhi** was Prime Minister for 5 years. Both Indira and Rajiv Gandhi were assassinated.

Economic Development. When India became independent, most Indians were living in villages, farming by hand or with animals. In the 1960s and 1970s, the government tried to improve agricultural production with science and technology — known as the **Green Revolution.** At first, most farmers were too poor to buy the new seeds, fertilizers, and equipment, but by the early 1980s, these "miracle" seeds were producing 35% of India's total grain crop. Leaders also tried to promote industrialization by finding a middle path between central planning and free markets.

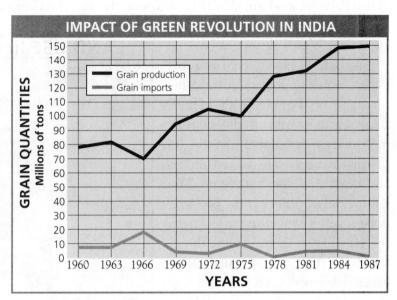

Social Problems. Rapid population growth used up gains in food production and industrial productivity. Rural people streaming into city slums created overcrowding. India now provides benefits to families that limit themselves to two children. The government has also tried to ban discrimination against "untouchables" and the lower castes, with only partial success. India is characterized by deep cultural differences, sometimes causing violence. India's 16 official languages exemplify these differences.

SOUTH ASIAN RELIGIOUS AND CULTURAL CONFLICTS

Hindus and Muslims. Religious differences between Hindus and Muslims continued even after the partition of India and Pakistan. Not all Muslims relocated to Pakistan during the partition; some still live in India, and violent clashes between Muslims and the Hindu majority continue. In addition, India and Pakistan both claim **Kashmir.**

The Sikhs. Sikhism combines Hindu and Muslim beliefs. In 1984, Sikh extremists who wanted their own nation seized a Sikh holy site. Indira Gandhi sent in the army, which dislodged them. In 1984, Prime Minister Gandhi was assassinated by Sikhs, leading to anti-Sikh riots throughout India. Tensions between Sikhs and Hindus still run high.

The Tamils. Sri Lanka (*formerly Ceylon*) is an island southeast of India. Sri Lanka has a Tamil minority which is Hindu. The Sinhalese majority is Buddhist. Many Tamils want their own independent nation, and have staged repeated uprisings. In the first of these clashes, India sent troops to restore order. However, the uprisings still continue.

BANGLADESH

When Pakistan was formed in 1947, it consisted of two parts separated by nearly a thousand miles. In 1971, East Pakistan broke away from West Pakistan to become Bangladesh. A bloody civil war followed, which ended when India intervened on Bangladesh's behalf. Bangladesh is one of the world's most densely populated nations. Its 120 million people are packed into an area the size of New York State. The country also suffers from periodic floods caused by melting snows from the Himalayas. In bad years, three-fourths of the land is flooded, causing crop destruction, property loss, and death. Almost one-third of all children die before their fifth birthday. Most of the people cannot afford basic medical care. Bangladesh continues to be one of the world's most economically troubled nations.

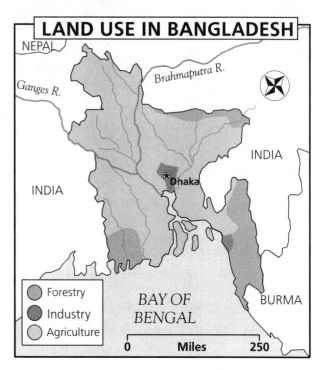

LATIN AMERICA

Although most of the countries of Latin America achieved independence more than a century before World War II, many of them continue to face problems similar to those of other developing countries: a continuing gulf between rich and poor, economic dependence on the West, and political instability.

LATIN AMERICAN POLITICS

As in the 19th century, military governments continued to rule many of these countries in the Cold War era. Often they were supported by the wealthy local elite, who profited by producing raw materials for sale to Europe or the United States. Military leaders sometimes justified their rule by their opposition to Communism. Conflict between social classses sometimes led to violence and civil war.

GOVERNMENTS IN LATIN AMERICA, 1940s-1980s

Argentina. In 1943, **Juan Peron** came to power, but was forced out twelve years later by the military. After an 18-year exile, he returned to power in 1972. He ruled through the military, and was often accused of violating individual liberties. Despite this, Peron was a popular leader, favoring some degree of social reform.

Chile. In 1970, **Salvador Allende**, a Communist, was elected president. He introduced land reform measures and nationalized copper mines, which were largely American-owned. In 1973, Allende was assassinated by the Chilean military, led by General Augusto Pinochet, who established a repressive military dictatorship.

Nicaragua. In 1979, a revolutionary group called the **Sandinistas** seized control of Nicaragua. At first they had popular support, but then they instituted Communist policies. Until 1989, intermittent civil war raged between the Sandinistas and the **Contras**, a U.S.-backed counter-revolutionary group.

HUMAN RIGHTS VIOLATIONS

Military governments in Latin America frequently violated **human rights** — people's civil rights and liberties. In **Argentina**, as many as 20,000 people disappeared during the military rule that ended in 1984. Relatives of the *desaparecidos* — the "disappeared ones" — still demonstrate in Argentina. The **Mothers of the Plaza de Mayo** are a group of mothers searching for their missing children. In **Chile**, the military government tortured and killed suspected opponents. In **Cuba**, Fidel Castro imprisoned and killed opponents of his rule. In **El Salvador,** "death squads" gunned down advocates of reform.

ECONOMIC DEVELOPMENT

Latin American nations were hampered by a lack of capital for investment, an unskilled work force, and foreign competition. Even though Latin America is now industrializing, vast gaps between rich and poor continue. The birth rate is so high that Latin America's population doubles every 25 to 30 years. This growth uses up productivity gains, forcing many Latin American nations to buy imported food, rather than make needed improvements. Local elites often invested their profits overseas instead of in their own countries. In the 1970s and 1980s, some Latin American countries like Mexico and Brazil borrowed heavily from the West to finance improvements. Much of this money was spent unwisely and Western banks later had to excuse some nations from part of their debt.

THE THIRD WORLD AND THE OIL CRISIS

In the 1970s, developing nations began calling themselves the **Third World** to emphasize their separate identity from the West and the Communist bloc. They demanded a new economic order in which industrialized nations would repay them for decades of imperialism and for taking their raw materials at artificially low prices. Only one group of developing nations was ever able to succeed with their demands. Developing nations, especially in the Middle East, contain a large part of the world's oil reserves. These oil-producing countries were able to take control of their resources, demanding and receiving higher prices for their oil.

DAILY OIL PRODUCTION IN THE MIDDLE EAST, 1990s

TUNISIA 100,000

MEDITERRANEAN SEA

SYRIA 500,000

IRAQ 2,600,000

IRAN 3,450,000

ALGERIA 100,000

LIBYA 1,800,000

EGYPT 600,000

KUWAIT 1,700,000

QATAR 500,000

SAUDI ARABIA 10,300,000

UNITED ARAB EMIRATES 1,700,000

OMAN 300,000

RED SEA

Persian

Barrels per day

OPEC AND THE LEAP IN OIL PRICES

In the early 1970s, oil-producing countries formed the **Organization of Petroleum Exporting Countries** (OPEC). In 1973, during a war with Israel, Arab OPEC members used oil as a **"political weapon,"** refusing to sell oil to countries friendly to Israel. Their actions also tripled world oil prices.

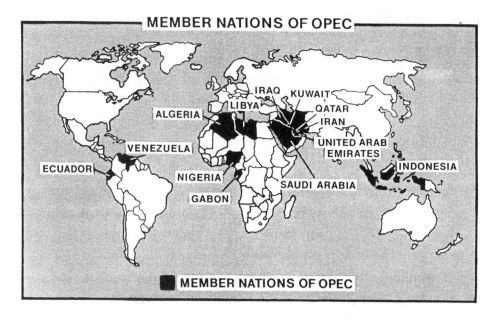

MEMBER NATIONS OF OPEC

IRAQ KUWAIT
LIBYA QATAR
ALGERIA IRAN
VENEZUELA UNITED ARAB EMIRATES
ECUADOR INDONESIA
NIGERIA SAUDI ARABIA
GABON

MEMBER NATIONS OF OPEC

THE IMPACT OF CHANGING OIL PRICES

In the late 1970s, OPEC again raised oil prices sharply. These prices brought a large flow of money into the Middle East, where it financed economic development in the oil-producing nations. But the West and non-oil-producing developing nations suffered high inflation and unemployment throughout the 1970s because of oil price increases. The West took steps such as energy conservation to reduce their vulnerability to OPEC.

THE IRANIAN REVOLUTION AND ISLAMIC FUNDAMENTALISM (1979)

Oil prices further soared because of events in Iran, one of OPEC's largest producers. **Shah Reza Pahlavi,** an absolute monarch, had introduced elements of Western culture and technology into Iran, but had also been guilty of corruption and repression. Iran's religious leaders and massive public demonstrations overthrew the Shah in 1979. **Ayatollah Khomeini,** an Islamic Fundamentalist religious leader, became Iran's new ruler. **Islamic Fundamentalism,** according to its leaders, is a return to the basic values of Islam as spelled out in the Qu'ran. It is also a reaction against the values and culture of the West. Under Khomeini there was no separation of religion and state. Iran instituted a new constitution based on the Qu'ran, sponsored acts of terrorism in the Middle East, and held American embassy personnel hostage in the capital city, Tehran, for more than a year.

THE IRAN-IRAQ WAR (1980-1988)

Iraq attacked Iran in 1980 to seize disputed territory along the Persian Gulf. The war threatened to prevent the shipping of oil needed by Western Europe and Japan. The fighting lasted for eight years, until a cease-fire was finally agreed to in 1988.

THE END OF THE COLD WAR

In 1989, remarkable events began occurring in the Soviet Union, Eastern Europe, and other parts of the world. The Cold War ended as the Berlin Wall came tumbling down and the Soviet Union collapsed. New democracies emerged, and diverse nations moved away from central planning towards free-market economies. The last decade of the 20th century proved to be a time of immense optimism. Philosophers and politicians boldly announced the "end of history" and the birth of a "new world order." Although their predictions now seem to have been overly optimistic, there is no doubt that the 20th century ended on a high note, full of promise for the next millennium.

THE DISSOLUTION OF THE SOVIET UNION

The most dramatic events of this period occurred in the Soviet Union. The sudden and unexpected collapse of Soviet Communism led directly to the end of the Cold War. To understand how this happened, we must return to the years before the collapse.

STAGNATION UNDER BREZHNEV (1965-1982)

After the fall of Khrushchev, **Leonid Brezhnev** eventually emerged as the Soviet leader. Brezhnev's years were marked by a stagnant economy. There was a lack of incentives for employees to work hard. Central planners could not properly foresee economic needs. The economy failed to produce sufficient consumer goods. High tech industries, dependent on the free flow of information, could not develop. Soviet farms failed to produce enough, and the U.S.S.R. was forced to import food.

Brezhnev sought **détente** (*an attempt to ease tensions*) with the United States, but at the same time arrested dissidents (*critics*) and restricted travel. In 1979, Brezhnev ordered troops into Afghanistan to support a pro-Soviet government against Muslim rebels. The Soviet intervention in Afghanistan proved to be costly and divisive, much like the earlier American involvement in Vietnam.

GORBACHEV BRINGS CHANGE (1985-1991)

Three years after Brezhnev's death, **Mikhail Gorbachev** became leader of the Communist Party of the Soviet Union. Gorbachev wanted to preserve Communism, but sought reform through a number of new policies:

✦ **Glasnost** introduced a greater "openness" to Soviet society. Restrictions on speech and the press were lifted. Dissidents were released from prisons and labor camps. Human rights were given greater respect. Restrictions on Soviet Jews emigrating

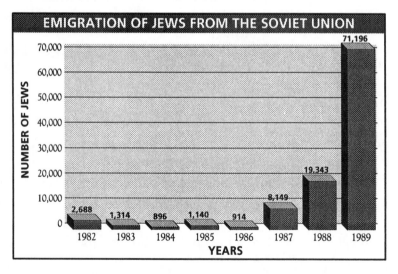

EMIGRATION OF JEWS FROM THE SOVIET UNION

NUMBER OF JEWS

1982	1983	1984	1985	1986	1987	1988	1989
2,688	1,314	896	1,140	914	8,149	19,343	71,196

YEARS

to Israel and the West were lifted. Western contacts were welcomed, and restrictions on foreign travel ended. To counter criticism by party officials, Gorbachev created a **Congress of People's Deputies**, which elected him as Soviet president.

✦ **Perestroika** means "restructuring." Gorbachev introduced reforms to move the economy away from central planning towards individual initiative and freer markets. People were allowed to form small businesses, factory managers were given increased control over production, and foreign companies were invited to invest in the Soviet Union.

✦ **New Foreign Policy**. Gorbachev dramatically reversed earlier Soviet foreign policy. He withdrew Soviet troops from Afghanistan, permitted the breakup of the Warsaw Pact and negotiated with the United States to reduce nuclear arms. He eventually allowed Eastern European states to introduce democratic, non-Communist governments.

GORBACHEV'S REFORMS FAIL

Despite many changes, Gorbachev's policies failed to solve Soviet economic problems. Citizens were not used to the free market system. Party bureaucrats opposed reform. Factory managers did not seize the initiative. Political instability only served to deepen the crisis. Programs announced one day were withdrawn the next. Fearing unemployment and inflation, the government continued to control prices and to delay privatizing state-owned enterprises. Industrial production actually declined.

THE NATIONALITIES PROBLEM

The Soviet Union consisted of fifteen republics, made up of Russian and non-Russian nationalities. Many non-Russian areas had been added earlier by force. Non-Russian groups began to demand independence from the Soviet Union. In 1990, Lithuania declared its independence, despite Soviet efforts to limit the national movement with military action. In 1991, **Boris Yeltsin** was elected president of the Russian Republic, and began to assert Russian authority over Gorbachev's Soviet government. Gorbachev could not stop these nationalistic stirrings without returning to a policy of repression.

THE DISSOLUTION OF THE SOVIET UNION (1991)

As the nationalistic spirit spread to other Soviet republics, Gorbachev sought to end the growing conflict. He began negotiating a new **Treaty of Union** with the leaders of the republics. However, on the eve of signing the treaty, in August 1991, Communist hard-liners staged a **coup d'etat** — an attempt to overthrow the government and halt the reforms. The conspirators sought to return the Soviet Union to its condition before Gorbachev, when the Communist government was in control and the army was used to put down independence movements. However, the coup lacked popular support and quickly collapsed. The Communist Party, which

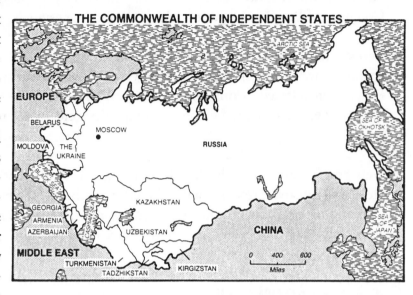

THE COMMONWEALTH OF INDEPENDENT STATES

had supported the coup, was completely discredited. Gorbachev recognized the independence of Lithuania and the other Baltic States. In December of 1991, Russia, Belarus, and Ukraine declared independence and formed the new **Commonwealth of Independent States (C.I.S.)**. Each member state was to be fully independent, while the Commonwealth structure would carry out only limited functions. Other republics also quickly joined the Commonwealth. The former Soviet Union was dead, and Gorbachev resigned at the end of 1991.

THE DISTRIBUTION OF FORMER SOVIET TERRITORIES

RUSSIAN REPUBLIC
76% of former Soviet land

24% of former Soviet land

ARMENIA
AZERBAIJAN
BELARUS
GEORGIA
ESTONIA
LATVIA
LITHUANIA
KAZAKHSTAN
KYRGYZSTAN
MOLDOVA
TURKMENISTAN
TAJIKISTAN
UKRAINE
UZBEKISTAN

RUSSIA UNDER YELTSIN

President Boris Yeltsin quickly took drastic steps to reform the economy of the Russian Republic. He introduced a free market system, ended price controls on most goods, and began to privatize state-owned businesses. Despite these changes, the Russian economy failed to improve. Russians still faced high unemployment, declining health care, malnutrition, and inflation. By 1993, Russia's Parliament feared Yeltsin was moving too fast towards a market economy. Yeltsin suspended the Parliament, which then tried to impeach him. Using military force, Yeltsin disbanded the Parliament and had a new one elected. Another challenge faced him when the Chechens, a non-Russian ethnic group, tried to declare independence. Russian forces became involved in a protracted war in Chechnya, and some Chechan nationalists employed terrorist tactics in Russia.

Because of ill health, Yeltsin resigned at the end of 1999. The new President, **Vladimir Putin,** has taken steps to strengthen state authority, continue pursuing the war in Chechnya, and promote economic growth. He has also cooperated in the global war on terrorism.

THE LIBERATION OF EASTERN EUROPE AND THE UNIFICATION OF GERMANY

Changes in the Soviet Union also had dramatic effects in Eastern Europe. Gorbachev could not reform Soviet society while continuing to repress Eastern Europe. Thus, even before the collapse of the U.S.S.R., Gorbachev had allowed a lifting of the Iron Curtain and the creation of new democracies in Eastern Europe.

✦ **Poland.** In the 1980s, **Lech Walesa** and other labor leaders formed an independent trade union, **Solidarity,** despite the government's attempts to ban it. When Gorbachev took power, the ban was lifted. In free elections in 1989, Solidarity won and formed the first non-Communist government in Eastern Europe since World War II.

✦ **Hungary, Bulgaria, and Czechoslovakia.** In 1989, free elections were permitted in these countries, and non-Communists were elected. In 1990, Czechoslovakia divided peacefully into two nations — the Czech Republic and Slovakia.

✦ **Romania.** A long-time Communist dictator, **Nicolae Ceausescu,** attempted to resist change by force. Thousands of Romanians were killed until a revolution overthrew him. He was tried and later executed by a military tribunal.

✦ **East Germany.** In 1989, thousands of East Germans began leaving for West Germany. To everyone's surprise, the East German Communist government resigned. A new government lifted all travel restrictions. The Berlin Wall, the greatest symbol of the Cold War, was knocked down amid joyous celebrations. Free elections brought a non-Communist government to power that was willing to cooperate with West Germany.

After achieving liberation from decades of Soviet control, Eastern Europeans faced many problems, such as the transition to market economies, fragile democracies, and severe pollution. In addition, with the collapse of the Communist dictatorships, rivalries between nationalist groups resurfaced, causing conflict and violence.

GERMAN REUNIFICATION

Free elections in East Germany resulted in a non-Communist government willing to reunite with West Germany. West Germany's Chancellor **Helmut Kohl** helped negotiate the reunification of Germany, which became official at the end of 1990. In a series of rapid developments, Soviet troops left East Germany, currencies were merged, and the German legislature voted to move the capital of a reunified Germany back to Berlin. Special programs were set up to help East Germans make the transition.

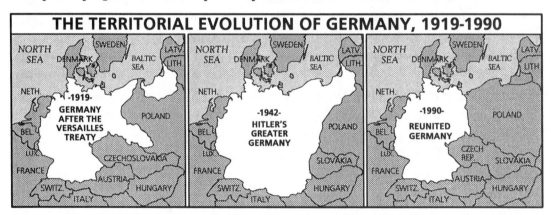

THE TERRITORIAL EVOLUTION OF GERMANY, 1919-1990

CHINA'S ECONOMIC REFORM

As Eastern Europe and the former Soviet Union struggled with drastic changes, Communist China moved gradually towards a free market economy while preserving the Communist Party's political power. Today, the Chinese economy is growing rapidly.

GREATER FREEDOM UNDER DENG XIAOPING

After the death of Mao in 1976, **Deng Xiaoping** became China's leader. Although Deng was a Communist, he sought to "modernize" China by reforming its economy. A new legal code and Constitution went into effect in 1980, giving Chinese people limited rights.

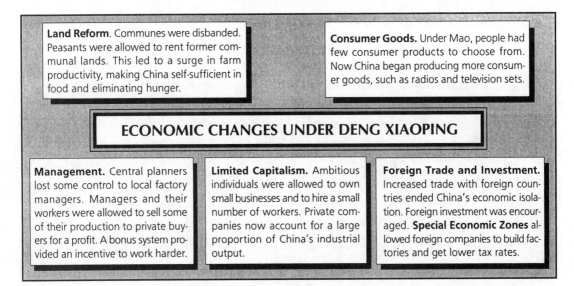

Land Reform. Communes were disbanded. Peasants were allowed to rent former communal lands. This led to a surge in farm productivity, making China self-sufficient in food and eliminating hunger.

Consumer Goods. Under Mao, people had few consumer products to choose from. Now China began producing more consumer goods, such as radios and television sets.

ECONOMIC CHANGES UNDER DENG XIAOPING

Management. Central planners lost some control to local factory managers. Managers and their workers were allowed to sell some of their production to private buyers for a profit. A bonus system provided an incentive to work harder.

Limited Capitalism. Ambitious individuals were allowed to own small businesses and to hire a small number of workers. Private companies now account for a large proportion of China's industrial output.

Foreign Trade and Investment. Increased trade with foreign countries ended China's economic isolation. Foreign investment was encouraged. **Special Economic Zones** allowed foreign companies to build factories and get lower tax rates.

Deng's economic reforms were extremely successful. By the late 1990s, China had the world's fastest growing economy and was selling billions of dollars in exports to the West.

TIANANMEN SQUARE AND THE LIMITS OF REFORM

In 1989, students peacefully demonstrated in Beijing's Tiananmen Square, demanding greater freedom and democracy. When the demonstrators refused to disperse, Deng ordered tanks to fire on them, killing hundreds. Student leaders were arrested and imprisoned or executed. Western leaders were shocked, and briefly reduced trade with China. China has also refused to make concessions regarding **Tibet**, a Buddhist country in the Himalayan Mountains, which China invaded and annexed in 1950. Ever since, Tibet has been ruled as a province of China. An uprising in 1959 was crushed with much bloodshed.

CHINA UNDER JIANG ZEMIN

Deng Xiaoping died in 1997. His successor, **Jiang Zemin**, generally followed Deng's policies. In 1997, the city of Hong Kong, a major financial and industrial center, was returned by Britain to China. Hong Kong continues to enjoy a large degree of self-government, despite its transfer to Communist China. In 2003, **Hu Jintao** became President of China.

NEW DEMOCRACIES EMERGE IN ASIA, AFRICA, AND LATIN AMERICA

Even before the Cold War ended, remarkable changes had begun to take place in Asia, Africa, and Latin America, where many nations started moving towards democracy.

THE PHILIPPINES BECOMES DEMOCRATIC

Once a U.S. colony, the Philippines became independent just after World War II. **Ferdinand Marcos** was president from 1965 to 1986. Ruling as a dictator, Marcos used government funds to enrich his family and friends. In 1986, **Corazon Aquino** was elected. At first Marcos refused to accept his defeat, but mass demonstrations and pressure from the United States forced him to flee. Aquino's success was seen as a triumph for democracy. When her term expired, another election was held and **Fidel Ramos** became president.

LATIN AMERICA AND AFRICA MOVE AWAY FROM DICTATORSHIP

In the late 1980s and 1990s, dictatorial governments around the world transferred power to democratically-elected leaders. Many nations in Latin America became democratic:

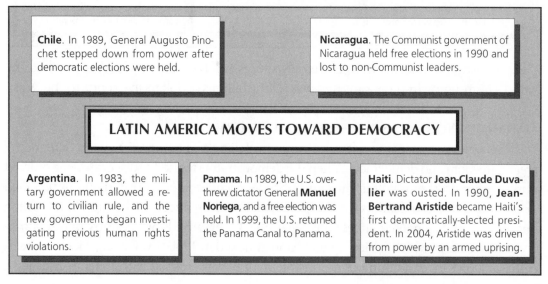

Chile. In 1989, General Augusto Pinochet stepped down from power after democratic elections were held.

Nicaragua. The Communist government of Nicaragua held free elections in 1990 and lost to non-Communist leaders.

LATIN AMERICA MOVES TOWARD DEMOCRACY

Argentina. In 1983, the military government allowed a return to civilian rule, and the new government began investigating previous human rights violations.

Panama. In 1989, the U.S. overthrew dictator General **Manuel Noriega**, and a free election was held. In 1999, the U.S. returned the Panama Canal to Panama.

Haiti. Dictator **Jean-Claude Duvalier** was ousted. In 1990, **Jean-Bertrand Aristide** became Haiti's first democratically-elected president. In 2004, Aristide was driven from power by an armed uprising.

In Africa, dictators were driven from power in Somalia, Liberia, and Ethiopia. Several other African nations moved from single-party to multi-party systems. South Africa's leaders ended apartheid and gave citizens of all races the right to vote.

PROGRESS AND REGRESSION IN THE POST-COLD WAR PERIOD

The end of the Cold War brought some of the world's most stubborn problems back into the spotlight. Despite unexpected progress in some areas of the world, enough trouble spots remain to remind us that the end of human conflict has not been reached.

PROGRESS IN THE RESOLUTION OF OLD DISPUTES

CAMBODIA

After overthrowing the Communist leader Pol Pot and the Khmer Rouge, Vietnamese troops remained in Cambodia until 1989, when they finally withdrew. In 1991, opposing groups in Cambodia signed a peace agreement under the supervision of the United Nations, creating a coalition government.

ISRAEL AND THE MIDDLE EAST

Israel is a nation of 6 million people surrounded by 170 million Arabs in the Middle East. Israelis remain concerned about their security after fifty years of war with neighboring Arab countries. On the other hand, Palestinians feel like a persecuted minority without a homeland of their own. The end of the Cold War saw a period of limited progress in Israeli-Arab relations. In 1991, the United States pressured Arab and Israeli leaders to attend a **Middle East Peace Conference**. The next year, Israeli Prime Minister **Yitzhak Rabin** launched secret negotiations with P.L.O. leader **Yassir Arafat**.

In 1993, Israel and the P.L.O. signed the **Oslo Accords**. Israel recognized the P.L.O. and give Palestinians self-government in the Gaza Strip and Jericho, a city on the West Bank. The Israeli withdrawal was eventually to extend to the entire West Bank, where Jews had established settlements. In exchange, the P.L.O agreed to end its opposition to Israel's existence. In 1995, Rabin was assassinated by a Jewish student who opposed his concessions. Later, Israeli withdrawals from the West Bank were slowed by terrorist attacks. A visit by Israeli Minister **Ariel Sharon** to an Arab holy site sparked a new intifada in 2001. Later, Sharon was elected prime minister. He responded to suicide bombings by attacking Palestinian targets. In 2003, Sharon ordered the building of a high wall along the West Bank to prevent future suicide bombings, and began withdrawing Israeli soldiers and settlers from Gaza and part of the West Bank. In 2004 Arafat died, opening the way for improved Israeli-Palestinian relations. However, Hamas (which Israel considers a terrorist organization) won elections in Gaza in 2006. Then a "Second Lebanon War" occurred when Israel briefly invaded Lebanon in response to militant attacks by Hezbollah. Since then there has been little progress in Israeli-Palestinian relations.

SOUTH AFRICA AND THE END OF APARTHEID

The end of the Cold War also led to the sudden collapse of apartheid. When white South African leaders increased repression against anti-apartheid groups, the United States and other countries adopted economic sanctions against South Africa, creating pressure on South Africa's leaders for change. In 1989, white South Africans elected **F.W. De Klerk** as president. De Klerk repealed all apartheid legislation. He also released **Nelson Mandela** and other political leaders from prison. De Klerk then negotiated a new constitution and a peaceful transition to a democratic multi-racial nation. In 1994, South Africa held its first election in which people of all races were permitted to vote. Nelson Mandela became South Africa's first black president. He faced many problems, including a possible redistribution of the nation's resources, racial reconciliation, and ending disputes among different groups of black South Africans. Mandela pursued economic development, health and educational reforms.

IRELAND AND ITS RELIGIOUS CONFLICT

Another country where strides were made towards the resolution of ancient conflicts was Ireland, a large island west of England. Although brought under English control in the

1500s, the Irish preserved their own culture. During the Reformation, when England became Protestant, the Irish remained Catholic. To maintain control, the English sent Protestant settlers to Ireland in the 1600s. They settled mainly in the north. In 1801, the Irish lost their independent government. In the 1840s, millions of Irish faced starvation during the Potato Famine. Many of them emigrated to the U.S.

In 1922, Ireland was granted its independence from Great Britain. However, in Northern Ireland the Protestant majority chose to remain part of the United Kingdom with Great Britain. Some Catholics objected to the division of Ireland, and formed the **Irish Republican Army (I.R.A.).** Northern Irish Protestants, opposed to unification, formed paramilitary groups. In 1969, fighting erupted in Northern Ireland. The British sent in troops to restore order. Since then, violence and terrorism have often occurred in Northern Ireland. However, in 1993, British leaders began negotiations with Irish leaders and the I.R.A. to reach a compromise. A cease-fire was declared. A broad framework for solving the Irish problem was agreed to in 1995. In 1998, an agreement was reached for the election of the first local assembly in Northern Ireland in over 25 years, and for the creation of several cross-border authorities.

OLD HATREDS IN NEW BOTTLES

YUGOSLAVIA: THE BOSNIAN WAR AND KOSOVO

The liberation of Europe brought a revival of age-old ethnic rivalries in Yugoslavia. The most bitter fighting occurred among Orthodox Christian Serbs, Catholic Croats, and Bosnian Muslims. When Communism collapsed, Croatia and Slovenia declared their independence. Serb-dominated Yugoslavia responded by attacking Croatia. Fighting then erupted in Bosnia between Muslims and Serbs. Yugoslavia intervened on behalf of the Bosnian Serbs. Some Serbs began to murder Muslim civilians, calling this form of genocide **ethnic cleansing**. After several years of civil war, the U.S. and other NATO powers intervened. This led to a truce. Bosnia was divided into two republics: one Muslim and one Serb. Serbs in Yugoslavia then attacked Muslim Albanians in **Kosovo**, still a province of Yugoslavia. NATO powers bombed Serbian

THE BREAKUP OF YUGOSLAVIA

targets in Yugoslavia in 1999 to halt atrocities in Kosovo, and NATO peacekeeping forces were sent in. Yugoslav dictator **Slobodan Milosevic** fell from power in October 2000. He was later captured and put on trial for atrocities committed during his rule.

IRAQ AND THE SECURITY OF THE PERSIAN GULF

Iraq occupies the lands of ancient Mesopotamia, where civilization first began. Today Iraq's 25 million people are divided among Arab Shi'ites (60%), Arab Sunnis (17%) and Kurds (20%).

✦ **Iraq-Iran War, 1980-88.** In 1979, **Saddam Hussein**, leader of the Ba'ath Party, seized power in Iraq. Hussein executed those who opposed his rule, and moved family members into key military and political positions. Hussein had ambitions to become the leader of the Arab world. In 1980, he launched an attack on Iran that led to a bloody 8-year war. When the war ended in a stalemate, Hussein demanded financial aid from Kuwait and other wealthy Persian Gulf states for saving them from Iran's Islamic Shi'ite Fundamentalism.

✦ **Persian Gulf War, 1990.** When Kuwait opposed Hussein's demand, he invaded that small oil-rich nation in 1990 and annexed it. World leaders feared he might try to take over Saudi Arabia next. When Hussein refused to withdraw from Kuwait, a multinational U.N. coalition, led by the United States, attacked. America's superior power pushed the Iraqi forces out of Kuwait. Retreating Iraqi troops set Kuwait's oil wells ablaze. Hussein agreed to pay for the environmental damage, and a cease-fire was declared. A revolt by Kurds in northern Iraq and an uprising by Shi'ites in the south were ruthlessly crushed by Hussein. The coalition established "no-fly zones" in the north and south to protect the civilian population.

✦ **The Iraq War.** As a condition of the cease-fire, Saddam Hussein had agreed to allow U.N. inspectors to monitor Iraq to ensure he did not stockpile nuclear, biological or chemical weapons of mass destruction (WMDs). However, he expelled the inspectors in 1998 when the U.N. refused to lift economic sanctions, which were having a severe impact on the Iraqi economy. After September 11, 2001, Hussein urged Islamic countries to oppose the U.S.-led "war on terrorism." The United States called for a U.N. resolution against Iraq for its failure to disarm. U.N. inspectors sent to Iraq in late 2002 could not locate missing Iraqi biological and chemical weapons, nor evidence of its nuclear arms program. Hussein repeatedly denied that Iraq had WMDs; later it was discovered that he had been telling the truth.

In early 2003, the U.S., Britain and Spain warned Iraq to surrender its WMDs or face invasion. France, Germany and Russia favored a more cautious approach, believing U.N. weapons inspectors in Iraq should be given more time to see if WMDs were really there. American leaders, however, feared Hussein would use the time to hide his weapons. In March 2003, President Bush gave Hussein 48 hours to leave Iraq or face invasion. Hussein rejected the ultimatum, and the U.S. and its allies took military action. In April, U.S. forces entered Baghdad, and Hussein's dictatorship quickly collapsed. Coalition forces now face immense challenges — dealing with widespread guerrilla attacks on the occupying troops by Hussein loyalists and their foreign sympathizers, and trying to restore the Iraqi economy while helping the Iraqis to create a democratic government. Religious and ethnic tensions continue to divide the country. Despite the problems, a transitional Iraqi constitution was adopted in 2004, and popular elections were held in 2005.

AFGHANISTAN

Afghanistan is located in the heart of Central Asia. Once part of the Persian Empire, it was conquered by Alexander the Great. Later Arab invaders introduced Islam, and it became the dominant religion by 900 A.D. Afghanistan became independent in the 1700s.

A century later the British tried unsuccessfully to conquer Afghanistan. In 1978, Afghan Communists seized power with Soviet support. The countryside rebelled, and the Soviets sent in troops. A large number of Afghans fled. Guerrilla fighters known as **mujahideen** fought the pro-Soviet Republic with U.S. and other foreign support until the Soviets withdrew in 1989. Three years later, the Afghan government collapsed. A civil war broke out between ethnic and religious minorities — Pashtuns, Shi'ite Muslims, and other groups.

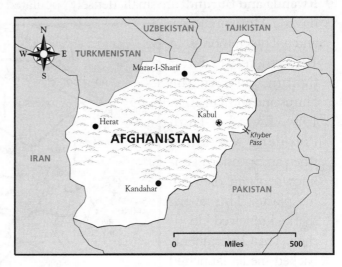

The **Taliban**, a group of Islamic Fundamentalists, gradually took control of most of the country. They imposed their radical religious beliefs on the rest of the nation, often committing atrocities in the process. Women could only appear in public if accompanied by a male family member, and their heads, faces and bodies had to be completely covered. They were barred from working. A woman suspected of adultery could be stoned to death. Females were denied schooling. Men were required to grow beards and attend mosques. Armed religious police patrolled the streets, attacking violators of Taliban rule.

The Taliban sheltered Islamic terrorists, especially the **al-Qaeda** network — groups controlled by Saudi Arabian terrorist **Osama bin Laden**. When the Taliban refused to surrender bin Laden to the U.S. after attacks on the World Trade Center and the Pentagon in September 2001, American air strikes destroyed Taliban and terrorist strongholds throughout Afghanistan. U.S. ground forces then cooperated with opposition Afghan groups and overthrew the Taliban regime. A UN-supported interim government was formed. In 2004, a new constitution was approved, followed by national elections. U.S. and allied troops have remained in Afghanistan to stabilize the new government, help with reconstruction, and defeat a resurgence of the Taliban which began in 2006.

CIVIL WARS IN AFRICA

After the Cold War, renewed ethnic tensions erupted in Rwanda and Burundi, while Somalia suffered from hunger and famine. Africa was also badly hit by the AIDS epidemic.

✦ **Rwanda and Burundi** are small, densely populated countries in Central Africa. Both have a Hutu majority and a Tutsi minority. In 1972, there was bitter fighting between the Hutus and the Tutsis. In 1994, Rwanda's Hutu President was killed when an explosion of unknown origin blew up his plane. This event sparked renewed bloodshed. The Government-backed media launched a propaganda campaign blaming the Tutsi for killing their president and inciting the Hutus to take revenge. The United Nations has estimated that 850,000 people, including about

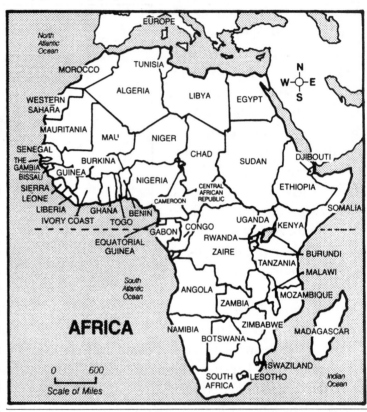

half of the Tutsi population and some moderate Hutus, were slain. The killing ended when Tutsi-dominated forces gained control of the Rwandan government. In December 2003, the International Criminal Tribunal for Rwanda convicted two Hutu radio broadcasters and a newspaper editor of inciting the massacre.

✦ **Somalia,** on the "horn" of Africa, has suffered from drought, destruction of livestock, and famine. In the early 1990s, fighting among local warlords prevented food aid from being distributed, threatening millions of people with starvation. In 1992, the United States and other countries sent troops to Somalia to restore order and distribute food aid. U.S. forces later withdrew when they could not stop the fighting among the warlords.

NEW ECONOMIC REALITIES

Twentieth-century advances in technology, from the airplane to the computer, have made countries world much more dependent on each other for goods, services, and ideas. This mutual reliance is referred to as **global interdependence**. The end of the Cold War again placed an emphasis on economics. Communism became unpopular in the Soviet Union in part because it could not provide the same standards of living as Western capitalism. China and even Cuba have gradually introduced free markets. Without the Soviet military threat, nations were able to focus their energies on economic growth, the production of consumer goods, and the development of new technologies.

ASIA'S NEW ECONOMIC GIANTS: JAPAN AND CHINA

Japan: One nation that profited from the new age of global interdependence was Japan — a country that abandoned military power and concentrated its energies on economic growth. By the 1970s Japan was once again a major economic power. The country became a leader in many high-technology areas, such as electronics, automobiles, and computers. However, economic expansion slowed in the 1990s due to high labor costs and increased foreign competition.

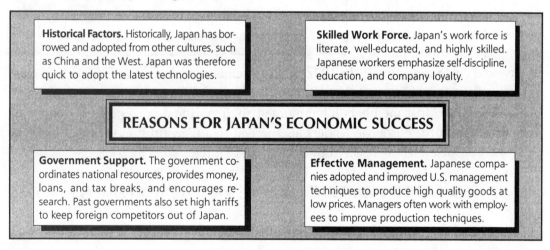

Historical Factors. Historically, Japan has borrowed and adopted from other cultures, such as China and the West. Japan was therefore quick to adopt the latest technologies.

Skilled Work Force. Japan's work force is literate, well-educated, and highly skilled. Japanese workers emphasize self-discipline, education, and company loyalty.

REASONS FOR JAPAN'S ECONOMIC SUCCESS

Government Support. The government co-ordinates national resources, provides money, loans, and tax breaks, and encourages research. Past governments also set high tariffs to keep foreign competitors out of Japan.

Effective Management. Japanese companies adopted and improved U.S. management techniques to produce high quality goods at low prices. Managers often work with employees to improve production techniques.

China: Since opening its economy to foreign investments and technology, China has undergone an economic revolution. After it joined the World Trade Organization, many restrictions on Chinese exports were lifted. China has emerged as the world's fastest-growing economy. Its educated, low-wage labor force has been a key factor in propelling China's economic growth.

FROM COMMON MARKET TO EUROPEAN UNION

Western Europe gradually emerged from the destruction of World War II to become an economic giant. Cooperation among Western European nations helped accelerate economic growth. In 1951, Germany and France began to share their iron and coal resources. This led to the formation of the **European Economic Community** (E.E.C.) or **Common Market** with Italy and the Benelux countries in 1957. In 1973, Great Britain, Ireland, and Denmark joined the Common Market, followed by Greece, Spain and Portugal in the 1980s. The purpose of the Common Market was to eliminate customs duties among its members. This created an immense free trade zone in which goods, money,

and people could move freely. In 1992, E.E.C. members replaced the Common Market with the **European Union (E.U.)**. In May 2004, eight Eastern European countries joined the E.U. Most members have merged their national currencies into a single currency, the **Euro**. European leaders also agreed to a **Constitution for Europe**. However, the constitution was rejected by French and Dutch voters in 2005.

THE NORTH AMERICAN FREE TRADE AGREEMENT

The economic success of the Common Market led the United States to negotiate with its neighbors in North America to form a similar economic bloc. In 1989, the U.S. and Canada signed a free trade agreement to gradually eliminate **tariffs** (*import taxes*) on goods sold to each other. In 1990, Mexico proposed that the U.S. and Canada expand their treaty into a North American Free Trade Agreement (**NAFTA**). By 1992, the agreement was signed. Tariffs between the three countries are gradually being phased out, eventually creating a free trade zone throughout North America.

— STUDY CARDS —

Cold War (1946-1991)

Global competition between the U.S. and the Soviet Union, both armed with atomic weapons.

- **Eastern Europe:** Despite pledge at **Yalta Conference**, Soviet occupiers refused to hold elections after World War II, put Communist puppet governments in power
- **Iron Curtain:** Term used to describe Eastern Europe being cut off from the West
- **NATO:** Alliance formed by Western Europe and U.S. to protect against Soviet Union
- **Warsaw Pact:** Alliance of Eastern European countries and Soviet Union

Cuban Revolution (1959)

- **Fidel Castro** toppled Cuban dictator, formed Communist state supported by Soviet Union
- **Bay of Pigs:** Cuban exiles supported by U.S. failed to incite anti-Castro rebellion in Cuba
- **Cuban Missile Crisis:** In 1962, American spy planes discovered Soviet missiles being placed in Cuba. U.S. President ordered naval blockade, threatened to invade Cuba. World was on brink of nuclear war. Finally Soviet Premier **Krushchev** agreed to withdraw missiles for a "pledge" of no U.S. invasion ot Cuba

Marshall Plan/Truman Doctrine

In 1947, Truman Administration took two important steps to counter its wartime ally (turned adversary), the Soviet Union:

- **Marshall Plan:** Billions of dollars in aid to Western European countries; rebuilt their economies, thwarted Communist revolutions
- **Truman Doctrine:** When Communist rebels arose in Greece and Turkey, Truman announced U.S. would support and aid all free peoples resisting Communism (known as policy of **containment**), and sent military aid

Israel/Palestine

- **Palestine**, home to Arabs and Jews, was under British control until end of World War II
- In 1948, U.N. carved **Israel** out of Palestine as a Jewish nation. Arabs attacked immediately, but were defeated. Hundreds of thousands of Palestinians became refugees.
- **Arab-Israeli Wars** (1956, 1967, 1973): After 1967, Israel occupied West Bank, Gaza.
- **Camp David Accords** (1978): Peace treaty with Egypt; Israel gave Sinai back to Egypt.
- **Oslo Accords** (1993): Israel agreed to a governing Palestinian Authority in West Bank.

Communist China

Communists under **Mao Zedong** drove Nationalists under **Chiang Kai-Shek** from China to Taiwan in 1949. Communists then controlled all aspects of life, killed businessmen and wealthy farmers.

- **Great Leap Forward:** Five-Year Plan that failed to industrialize China. Peasant lands collectivized.
- **Cultural Revolution:** Mao's disastrous attempt to reinvigorate Communism. **Red Guards** (students) forced educated people to work on farms, destroyed ancient works of art.

European Union (E.U.)

- **Common Market**: Formed in 1957, it created a large free-trade zone among its members: France, Germany, Italy, Belgium and the Netherlands. Other Western European nations soon joined.

- In 1991, members agreed to replace the Common Market with the **European Union**. It has expanded to include eight Eastern European countries. Most members have merged their national currencies into a single monetary unit: the **Euro**.

(Continued)

Vietnam War

After French withdrawal in 1954, Vietnam was divided. **Ho Chi Minh** created Communist state in north; south was pro-Western.

- Reunification elections were never held; south believed elections in north would be rigged
- Guerrillas in south (**Viet Cong**) began war with northern help; by 1964, 500,000 U.S. troops were involved to stop spread of Communism. Despite advanced technology, U.S. could not turn the tide. U.S. troops withdrew in 1973. Vietnam was unified under Communism by 1975

South Africa/Apartheid

In 1948, Dutch-speaking white Afrikaners (**Boers**) created **apartheid** policy, persecuted black South Africans, took away their rights.

- Blacks resisted, both peacefully and violently
- In 1989, when years of economic sanctions were wrecking economy, whites elected **F.W DeKlerk**. He repealed apartheid legislation.
- De Klerk and **Nelson Mandela**, a prominent black leader jailed for years, negotiated a constitution and multiracial elections.
- Mandela became free South Africa's first black president and served two terms.

Mikhail Gorbachev

In 1985, **Gorbachev** became leader of Soviet Union. Nation suffered from gross inefficiency, and was losing a war in Afghanistan. To preserve Communism, Gorbachev introduced various reforms.

- **Glasnost**: Greater freedom of expression
- **Perestroika** ("restructuring"): limited economic reforms — allowed small private businesses, gave factory managers greater control
- **Foreign Policy**: Gorbachev withdrew from Afghanistan, held summit talks with U.S.

Islamic Fundamentalism

A belief that Muslims should strictly follow Islamic law and resist Western influences.

- **Iranian Revolution (1979):** Pro-Western Shah overthrown. **Ayatollah Khomeini** established a religious state based on Islamic law. U.S. embassy personnel in Tehran were seized, held hostage for over a year.
- **Afghanistan:** Muslim rebels overthrew Soviet puppet government. The **Taliban** set up an extreme Islamic government, which the U.S. overthrew in 2002 because it was protecting al-Qaeda terrorists.

Collapse of the Soviet Union

Gorbachev's reforms unexpectedly led to demise of Soviet Union:

- **Elections:** In 1989-1990 he allowed free elections in Eastern Europe, and Communists lost
- **Ethnic Nationalism**: Various Soviet ethnic groups began demanding independence
- **Coup of August 1991**: Hardliners tried to seize power, but coup collapsed and Communist Party was discredited
- **Final Breakup:** In late 1991, Russia, Ukraine and Belarus broke away, formed **Commonwealth of Independent States**

Deng Xiaoping

He became China's ruler after Mao died in 1976.
- Deng attacked the leaders of the Cultural Revolution, put the "Gang of Four" on trial
- He sought gradual change to free market, while holding onto Communist Party power
- Deng encouraged private enterprise, passed laws to spur foreign investment, greatly increasing trade with West
- **Tiananmen Square (1989):** When students protesting corruption began to demand democracy and reform, Deng's government brutally crushed the demonstration.

SUMMARIZING YOUR UNDERSTANDING

COMPLETING A GRAPHIC ORGANIZER

Complete the following cause-and-effect graphic organizer on the Cold War.

THE COLD WAR

Cause: _____ _____	Effect: _____ _____
Cause: _____ _____	Effect: _____ _____
Cause: _____ _____	Effect: _____ _____

TESTING YOUR UNDERSTANDING

1 Since the creation of the Organization of Petroleum Exporting Countries (OPEC), member nations have joined together to
   (1) determine the supply of oil on the world market
   (2) establish a policy of independence in trade
   (3) maintain a low price of oil per barrel
   (4) isolate themselves from the rest of the world

2 One similarity between China under earlier dynastic rule and more recently under Communism is that both have stressed
   (1) a state-supported religion   (3) loyalty to leaders
   (2) the importance of women in society (4) limited population growth

3 Mao's Great Leap Forward in China and Stalin's Five-Year Plans in the Soviet Union were similar in that both attempted to increase
   (1) private capital investment   (3) the availability of consumer goods
   (2) individual ownership of land   (4) industrial productivity

Base your answer to question 4 on the table and your knowledge of global history.

NATIONS RECEIVING ECONOMIC AID UNDER THE MARSHALL PLAN
(in millions of dollars)

Country	Amount Received	Country	Amount Received
Great Britain	$2,826	Austria	$561
France	$2,445	Belgium	$547
Italy	$1,316	Denmark	$257
West Germany	$1,297	Norway	$237
Holland	$877	Turkey	$153

4   To which decade of European history does this chart refer?
   (1) 1901-1910   (3) 1941-1950
   (2) 1931-1940   (4) 1971-1980

---

5   The statements below refer to changes in Afghanistan in the 1990s.
   • The Taliban controlled the government.
   • Women had to be clothed from head to toe.
   • Men were required to grow beards.
   • Girls were not allowed to attend school.

   These changes in Afghanistan resulted from a movement toward
   (1) Marxist ideology   (3) constitutional reforms
   (2) liberation theology   (4) Islamic Fundamentalism

6   "We believe in non-aggression and noninterference by one country in the affairs of another and the growth of tolerance between them and the capacity for peaceful coexistence. We seek to maintain friendly relations with all countries, even though we may disagree with their policies."   —*Jawaharlal Nehru, Prime Minister of India*

   This statement describes the foreign policy known as
   (1) imperialism   (3) isolationism
   (2) mercantilism   (4) non-alignment

7   In Africa, South Asia, and Latin America, people have moved from rural villages to urban areas in order to
   (1) avoid the high cost of living in rural areas
   (2) escape the poor climates of rural areas
   (3) find new job opportunities in the cities
   (4) live among people of different ethnic backgrounds in the cities

8   Since World War II, developing nations have experienced great changes in their economies mainly because of
    (1) a greater tolerance of minorities
    (2) the move to Fascism
    (3) the use of modern technology
    (4) the spread of new religions

Base your answer to question 9 on the graph and your knowledge of global history.

9   Which statement is most accurate based on the graph?
    (1) OPEC controls most of the world's oil.
    (2) Algeria, Libya and Kuwait produce most of the oil in the Middle East.
    (3) Saudi Arabia produces more oil than any other Middle Eastern nation.
    (4) Oil production in Saudi Arabia has been rising.

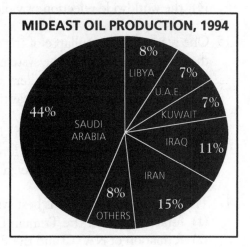

MIDEAST OIL PRODUCTION, 1994

8% LIBYA
7% U.A.E.
7% KUWAIT
44% SAUDI ARABIA
11% IRAQ
15% IRAN
8% OTHERS

10 A major result of increasing urbanization in African nations has been
    (1) decreasing cultural opportunities
    (2) rejection of Western technology
    (3) strengthening of family life
    (4) weakening of ethnic and tribal ties

11 The Kurds, the Sikhs, and the Palestinian Arabs have each attempted to
    (1) establish colonies in Asia
    (2) practice passive resistance
    (3) achieve independent states
    (4) encourage mercantilism

12 Which concept is best illustrated by the formation of new countries by the republics of the former Soviet Union?
    (1) national self-determination
    (2) non-alignment
    (3) imperialism
    (4) Communism

Base your answer to question 13 on the table and your knowledge of global history.

Formerly	Changed	Now Called
Burma	1948	Myanmar
Palestine	1948	Israel

Formerly	Changed	Now Called
Rhodesia	1980	Zimbabwe
Ceylon	1972	Sri Lanka

13 A major factor explaining why these countries changed their names was
    (1) decolonization
    (2) capitalism
    (3) socialism
    (4) nationalism

14 A major factor contributing to terrorist activities in the Middle East has been
   (1) a decrease in crude oil prices on the world market
   (2) the Palestinian effort to establish a national homeland
   (3) the presence of United Nations peacekeeping forces in the area
   (4) the worldwide rejection of violence as a means to end conflict

15 One reason for the collapse of the Communist economic system in Eastern Europe in
   the early 1990s was that the system
   (1) lacked incentives for workers   (3) encouraged laissez-faire practices
   (2) used the principles of mercantilism   (4) relied on laws of supply and demand

16 A major success of the European Union (EU) has been the
   (1) creation of a single military force   (3) adoption of a single language
   (2) rejection of national sovereignty   (4) elimination of trade barriers

17 The end of the Cold War is best symbolized by the
   (1) establishment of the Truman Doctrine and the Marshall Plan
   (2) formation of NATO and the European Common Market
   (3) withdrawal of U.N. forces from Somalia and Kuwait
   (4) destruction of the Berlin Wall and the reunification of Germany

18 The civil war in Lebanon and fighting in Northern Ireland in the 1970s and 1980s both
   demonstrated the
   (1) inability of a command economy to satisfy the needs of citizens
   (2) influence of a peacekeeping organization in resolving national issues
   (3) isolation of these countries from international influences
   (4) difficulties of resolving religious differences

19 A similarity between the goals of Nelson Mandela and Mohandas Gandhi is that both
   leaders wanted to
   (1) secure political power for the majority of their people
   (2) encourage a greater degree of industrialization
   (3) improve the economy by expanding governmental control
   (4) gain independence from the Soviet Union

20 A study of recent civil wars in Cambodia, Bosnia and Rwanda would show that
   (1) ethnic conflict was not a factor in the late 20th century
   (2) the United Nations was successful in resolving these disputes
   (3) genocide was used as a political and military tactic
   (4) civilians were not affected by these disputes

INTERPRETING DOCUMENTS

WORLD COMMUNISM (1960)   **WORLD COMMUNISM (1995)**

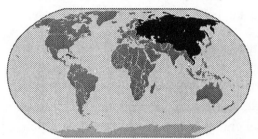
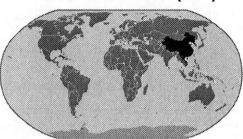

1*a* What trend do these maps indicate about world Communism? _____

 b Provide one reason for the trend indicated by the maps. ─────────────────

THEMATIC ESSAY QUESTION

Directions: Write a well-organized essay that includes an introduction, several paragraphs addressing the *Task* below, and a conclusion.

Theme: Justice and Human Rights

> Throughout human history, certain groups have faced injustice, discrimination and brutality from those in power.

Task:

- Identify *two* groups that have faced injustice, discrimination and brutality.
- Show how each group faced injustice or brutality from those in power.
- Explain how each group or the world community dealt with the injustice.

You may use any example from your study of global history and geography. Some suggestions you may wish to consider include Protestants during the Counter Reformation, Native Americans under European rule, Indians under British rule, Jews in Nazi Germany, black South Africans under apartheid, and Kurds living in Iraq.

You are *not* limited to these suggestions.

DOCUMENT-BASED ESSAY QUESTION

Historical Context: Throughout history, the introduction of new technologies has often been accompanied by significant social, economic and political change.

Task: Using information from the documents and your knowledge of global history, answer the questions that follow each document in Part A. Your answers to the questions will help you write the Part B essay, in which you will be asked to:

- Describe *three* important technological changes in world history.
- Discuss the social, political or economic impact of *two* of these changes.

Part A — Short Answer Questions

Directions: Analyze the documents and answer the question that follows each document.

DOCUMENT 1

"When food production became more efficient, there was time to develop the arts and sciences. Agriculture probably required a far greater discipline than did any form of food collecting. Seeds had to be planted at certain seasons, some protection had to be given to growing plants, harvests had to be reaped, stored and divided. It has been suggested that writing may have come into existence because records were needed by agricultural administrators."

— Charles Heiser, *Seed to Civilization*, 1981

1   How did technological changes in agriculture bring about other changes?_____

DOCUMENT 2

"The most significant invention in the history of warfare prior to gunpowder was the stirrup. In conjunction with a saddle, stirrups welded horse and rider into a single organism. The long lance could now be held at rest under the right armpit. The increase in violence was immense."

— Lynn White, Jr.
The Expansion of Technology, 500-1500

2   How did the invention of the stirrup for mounted knights transform warfare in the Middle Ages?

DOCUMENT 3

3   How did the Industrial Revolution affect the production of
cotton cloth in Britain?

_____

_____

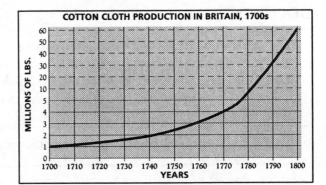

COTTON CLOTH PRODUCTION IN BRITAIN, 1700s

MILLIONS OF LBS.

60 50 40 30 20 10 5 4 3 2 1 0

1700 1710 1720 1730 1740 1750 1760 1770 1780 1790 1800

YEARS

DOCUMENT 4

"Labour in an industrial society ... is overwhelmingly the labour of 'proletarians' who
have no source of income except a cash wage ... mechanized labour imposes a regularity,
routine and monotony quite unlike pre-industrial work ... labour in the industrial
age took place in the unprecedented environment of the big city ... And what cities! It was not merely that smoke hung over them and filth impregnated them, that
elementary public services — water supply, sanitation, street-cleaning — could not
keep pace with the mass migration ... But more than this: the city destroyed society."

— Eric Hobsbawm, *Industry and Empire*, 1969

4 What is Hobsbawm's view of the effect of the Industrial Revolution on workers?

_____

DOCUMENT 5

This photo shows the ruins of a Shinto shrine in
Nagasaki, Japan, after an atomic bomb had been
dropped on the city in August, 1945.

5   What does this picture show about the impact of
atomic weapons? _____

_____

DOCUMENT 6

> "The speed with which computers have spread is ... well known. Costs have dropped so sharply and capacity has risen so spectacularly that, according to one authority, 'If the auto industry had done what the computer industry has done in the last 30 years, a Rolls-Royce would cost $2.50 and would get 2,000,000 miles to the gallon.'"
>
> —Alvin Toffler, *The Third Wave*

6 What does Toffler see as an important achievement of the computer industry?

DOCUMENT 7

7 What two nations produce almost one-third of the world's pollution?

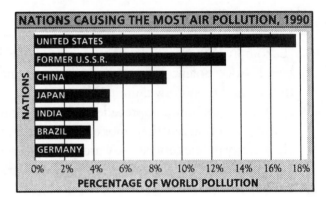

_____

_____

Part B — Essay

Directions: Write a well-organized essay that includes an introduction, several paragraphs, and a conclusion. Use evidence from at least **four** of the documents to support your response. Include additional outside information.

Historical Context:

Throughout history, the introduction of new technologies has often been accompanied by significant social, economic and political change.

Task: Using information from the documents and your knowledge of global history, write an essay in which you:

- Describe *three* important technological changes in world history.
- Discuss the social, political or economic impact of *two* of these changes.

GLOBAL CONCERNS

Deforestation in the Brazilian rain forest

MILESTONES IN THE EVOLUTION OF GLOBAL CONCERNS

1798	Malthus theorizes growing world population will outstrip food supplies
1800	World's population reaches 1 billion people
1960s	Palestine Liberation Organization uses terrorism against Israel
1993	Rio Conference meets in Brazil on world environmental problems
1993	Terrorists try to blow up NY's World Trade Center
1995	U.N. Conference on Women meets to end abuses against women
1996	U.N. reports that 22 million people around the world have AIDS
1997	Kyoto Conference meets in Japan on global warming problem
1998	Terrorists destroy two U.S. embassies in Africa
2000	Three-quarters of world's population now lives in cities
2001	Terrorists destroy World Trade Center, damage Pentagon in Washington

WHAT YOU SHOULD FOCUS ON

Essay questions on the **Global History** Regents Examination may ask about current global concerns, issues, and trends. This section will provide you with an overview of what you need to know in order to answer this type of essay question.

PROBLEMS / CONCERNS

Part of the challenge of the future will be to deal with problems facing the world. Test questions frequently focus on such problems as:

OVERPOPULATION	INTERNATIONAL TERRORISM	POLLUTION
DEFORESTATION	DESERTIFICATION	HUNGER

A GENERAL APPROACH

Although there are many aspects to these problems, test questions will most often require you to do the following:

1. Define the Problem. Define or describe the problem. It will be helpful to go through a mental checklist — *who, what, where, when* — in defining or describing the problem.

3. Explain the Effects. Explain the effects or impact that the problem is having on the world. For example, what has been the impact of deforestation on the peoples of the Amazon?

2. Identify the Causes. Explain why or how something came about. "Causes" are reasons that led to the problem. Why, for example, is pollution increasing? Or why is the world's safety threatened by nuclear weapons?

4. Discuss Possible Solutions. Write about actions that have been taken by government agencies or private institutions to help solve the problem. You can also recommend other steps that would help to provide a solution.

ISSUES

Unlike a *concern*, where most people agree that there is a problem, an **issue** has two or more opposing viewpoints. Questions about issues will usually test your understanding of these viewpoints. Some of the issues on which you might be tested are (1) the role of the United Nations, (2) the best approaches to economic development, and (3) the status of women around the world.

A GENERAL APPROACH

Although there are many aspects to these issues, test questions will most often ask you to do the following:

Define the Issue. First use a mental checklist — *who, what, where, when*. For example, is the most important role of the United Nations to punish aggressive nations, or to resolve disputes peacefully?

Explain the Opposing Viewpoints. Write about the conflicting sides of the issue or controversy. Bring in one or more arguments used in support of each opposing viewpoint.

Deal with the Issue. Discuss or explain some recent action taken by the government or a private group to bring about a resolution of the issue.

TRENDS

A **trend** is a pattern of change that points in some direction. Several trends are visible today that may have an impact on our future. Questions about trends test your understanding of such areas of change as:

TECHNOLOGY	GLOBAL INTERDEPENDENCE	URBANIZATION
MODERNIZATION	SPACE EXPLORATION	POPULATION GROWTH

A GENERAL APPROACH

Although there are many aspects to these trends, test questions will most often require you to do the following:

Define the Trend: Describe the trend or development. Again, go through a mental checklist — *who, what, where, when* — in defining the trend. For example, how has the introduction of computers affected employment and manufacturing processes?

Predict the Effects. Discuss the effects that the trend has had or may have. For example, what impact do you think continued world population growth will have on global resources such as drinking water and farming?

LOOKING AT
ETHNIC DIVERSITY

An ethnic group typically refers to a group of people with a common ancestry and common culture. **Ethnicity** is primarily a social and cultural phenomenon, rooted in the history of a society and the past interactions of the various groups within it. From the standpoint of ethnicity, there are two basic types of society:

✦ In **homogeneous** societies, like Japan and Saudi Arabia, almost everyone is of the same race and shares the same language and traditions.

✦ Other societies are **heterogeneous,** containing a mix of peoples and cultures. Ethnic groups are often mixed throughout the country, as in the United States. Sometimes an ethnic group is connected to a particular region, like the Kurds in northern Iraq.

UNITY OUT OF DIVERSITY

Most countries of the world have heterogeneous populations. Thus a basic problem for most national governments is to create and preserve a single nation-state out of this ethnic diversity. To understand this problem, we must first look at the beginnings of modern nation-states.

THE RISE AND SPREAD OF THE NATION-STATE SYSTEM

The world today is divided into nations, each with a central government and defined boundaries. This system first emerged in Europe when kings established their supremacy. Later, Europeans conquered the Americas, Asia and Africa, and established similar governments. As a result, these colonial governments had to create strategies to deal with the problem of governing different groups living in the same area.

THE EMERGENCE OF NATIONALISM

People often feel more familiar and friendly with those who share common characteristics. It is only natural that many ethnic groups believe in **nationalism** — that each nationality or ethnic group should have its own nation-state. This desire has been a powerful force in world history and can be either unifying or divisive. Because of the rise of nationalism, central governments have often had to devise special strategies to keep their multi-ethnic states together.

PROBLEMS CONFRONTING ETHNIC MINORITIES

Usually there is one dominant ethnic group and several smaller ethnic minorities in a multicultural society. A **minority** is any ethnic group in a nation other than the dominant group. Minorities often face special problems:

Ethnic Prejudice. The dominant group may treat minority group members as inferior, leading minority members to be denied political power. Often the dominant group uses force to keep minorities under control.

Discrimination and Exclusion. In many societies, minorities are denied civil and political rights. In some societies, they have not been allowed to own property, or use public facilities like parks or public transportation.

Expulsion and Genocide. Sometimes actions against minority groups result in the expulsion or extermination of the minority. The most famous example was the Nazi attempt to eliminate the Jews of Europe, murdering more than six million Jews.

THE PROTECTION OF MINORITIES

Human rights have been defined as an individual's right to life, equal protection of the laws, and freedom from arrest, enslavement or torture. Members of minority groups have been frequent targets of human rights violations.

✦ **International Efforts.** Atrocities in World War II led to attempts to protect human rights. In 1948 the United Nations adopted a declaration that everyone has the right to life and liberty, and that slavery and torture are prohibited. In recent times, groups like **Amnesty International** help keep track of human rights violations and publicize them.

✦ **Domestic Efforts.** Minority groups often attempt to overcome their problems themselves. Some are seeking the traditional goal of independence. Other groups resort to terrorism as a desperate measure.

MAJOR PROBLEMS, ISSUES AND TRENDS

Today's rapid changes have made countries more **interdependent** than ever before, "shrinking" the world into a **global village**. As the world grows "smaller," events in any one area have a greater impact on other parts of the world. The effects of pollution or environmental destruction are not limited by national borders. Even poverty in some areas affects other areas because of migration and its impact on the world economy. In this chapter we will look at some key problems, issues, and trends in the world today.

OVERPOPULATION, A CASE OF TOO MANY PEOPLE

In 1798, the English writer **Thomas Malthus** declared that growing populations would always outstrip food supplies. Humans would be condemned to a cycle of population growth and subsequent decline through starvation. In 1800, there were 1 billion people in the world. Today, there are over 6 billion people, and the number almost doubles every 60 years. This threatens to outrun the ability of developing countries to produce enough housing, fuel, and food. Many nations promote family planning. However, people still have large families in areas where children are a source of labor and of future support when parents grow old. Several religions oppose birth control, and many people have no knowledge of or access to modern family planning methods.

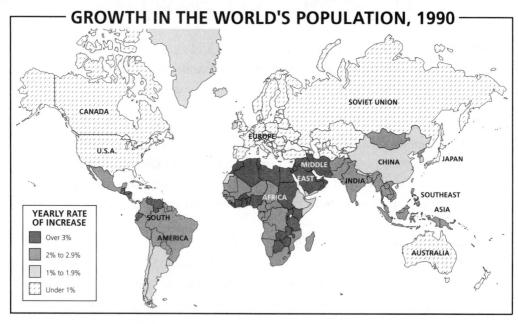

GROWTH IN THE WORLD'S POPULATION, 1990

CANADA

SOVIET UNION

EUROPE

U.S.A.

MIDDLE EAST

CHINA

JAPAN

INDIA

AFRICA

SOUTHEAST ASIA

SOUTH AMERICA

AUSTRALIA

YEARLY RATE OF INCREASE

- Over 3%
- 2% to 2.9%
- 1% to 1.9%
- Under 1%

Possible Solutions. Many developing nations have adopted programs to limit their birth rate, such as China's "one-child" policy. The U.N. and other agencies are promoting family planning — teaching birth control methods and rewarding those who have smaller families.

 ## AIDS AND OTHER NEW EPIDEMICS

Before the discovery of germs and the development of vaccines and antibiotics, people often fell victim to contagious, life-threatening diseases. During the Middle Ages, millions of people in Asia, Europe, and Africa died from **Bubonic Plague**. In the 1500s, a majority of the Native American population was wiped out by smallpox and measles, brought to the New World by European explorers and conquerors. In 1918-1919, more Americans died from influenza (flu) than died in World War I. As many as 50 million died worldwide. Although antibiotics and vaccines have reduced death rates, some bacteria are developing immunity to antibiotics, and they are not effective against diseases like cancer, heart disease, and Alzheimer's (loss of memory).

In recent decades, several new diseases have appeared, the most deadly of which is **AIDS**, a virus that attacks the immune system. People can be infected by sharing hypodermic needles, having unprotected sexual contact, or by blood transfusions. In 2007, about 23 million people had this disease, which killed 2 million people in that year. There is no known cure for AIDS, although some medicines reduce its symptoms. Another deadly virus is **ebola**, which broke out in Central Africa in the 1970s. Ebola causes high fever, vomiting, bleeding and death.

Possible Solutions. These new diseases pose a serious threat to humanity's continued survival. Scientists around the world are working to develop new cures for AIDS, ebola, and drug-resistant bacteria. The U.S. has given millions of dollars in free AIDS drugs to developing nations in order to limit suffering and death from the disease.

 ## HUNGER AND MALNUTRITION

Only a few countries are able to produce more food than their people need. In the rest of the world, hunger and malnutrition are common. In developing nations, about 150 million children under age 5 go to bed hungry every night. Climate changes and soil erosion have worsened the problem in many countries, such as Somalia and Afghanistan. Also, as Malthus predicted, each advance in producing more food is often met with an even greater increase in population.

Possible Solutions. As technology improves, advances are being made in growing more food in shorter periods of time. The **Green Revolution** brought new high-yield crops, and better fertilizers. Environmentally safe insecticides are being perfected. However, hunger and malnutrition cannot be avoided unless population growth is also brought under control.

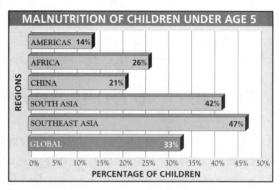

MALNUTRITION OF CHILDREN UNDER AGE 5

REGIONS

AMERICAS 14%
AFRICA 26%
CHINA 21%
SOUTH ASIA 42%
SOUTHEAST ASIA 47%
GLOBAL 33%

0% 5% 10% 15% 20% 25% 30% 35% 40% 45% 50%
PERCENTAGE OF CHILDREN

INTERNATIONAL TERRORISM

Terrorism is the use of violence against civilians for political purposes. It draws attention to the grievances of a group, which tries to frighten governments into making concessions. For example, the I.R.A. used terrorism against the British in an attempt to unify Ireland. Radical groups like **Hamas** and the **Islamic Jihad** use terrorism against Israel, seeing it as self-defense against what they consider Israeli "terrorism"— the occupation of Palestinian lands. Iran, Iraq, Syria and Libya have not only helped Palestinian terrorists, but have used terrorism to silence their own opponents. In Afghanistan, the **Taliban** rulers sheltered international terrorist networks like Osama bin Laden's al-Qaeda, whose aim is to undermine American power. Future terrorists may use biological, chemical or nuclear weapons. Terrorist organizations have made use of the following tactics:

Taking Hostages. Israeli athletes were held hostage at the 1972 Munich Olympic Games. In 1979-1980, Iran held 52 American hostages for 15 months. In 1990, Iraq took hostages at the start of the Gulf War, but then released them.

Bombing. In 1998, U.S. embassies in Kenya and Tanzania were bombed. The I.R.A. used similar tactics against the British. Some groups put bombs on planes, such as Libyans did on the ill-fated Pan Am Flight 103 over Lockerbie, Scotland.

Political Assassination. Egyptian military extremists who opposed President Sadat's peace agreement with Israel assassinated Sadat in 1981. In 1995, an Israeli student opposed to the Mideast peace process assassinated Prime Minister Rabin.

Terrorism reached new levels when commercial airliners were hijacked in the U.S. on September 11, 2001. The terrorists crashed two planes into New York's World Trade Center and one into the Pentagon. More than 3,000 civilians were killed, and the two Trade Towers collapsed. The hijackers belonged to Osama bin Laden's al-Qaeda network. In July 2005, terrorists struck in London, setting off bombs on subway trains and a bus.

Possible Solutions. Governments have various responses to terrorism — negotiation, the use of force, and retaliation. Generally, nations feel it is wrong to negotiate with terrorists because this encourages further acts of terrorism. Some governments have specially trained forces to take direct action in terrorist situations. Governments can also put economic pressure on countries that support terrorism or even attack such countries. In response to the attacks of September 11, 2001, President Bush declared a "war on terrorism." When the Taliban rulers in Afghanistan refused to surrender Osama bin Laden, the U.S. launched air strikes and sent in ground troops, destroying the Taliban regime. Bin Laden escaped into the mountains. The U.S. later invaded Iraq and overthrew the government of Saddam Hussein, partly on the belief that Hussein might have aided terrorist organizations.

ENVIRONMENTAL POLLUTION

As countries become more developed and the world's population grows, pollution of the earth's air, water, soil, and other resources becomes an ever-increasing threat.

✦ **Water Pollution.** Cities have become crowded, straining their ability to handle increased sewage and waste. Often this leads to the dumping of raw sewage into surrounding waters, contaminating drinking water and threatening health and safety.

✦ **Solid Waste**. Modern societies generate millions of tons of garbage, some of which is toxic. It is often dumped into landfills, but these sites are filling up. Burning the waste or dumping it into oceans or rivers also creates pollution.

✦ **Air Pollution.** With industrial growth, more pollutants are released into the air. They cause problems such as **acid rain** and respiratory illnesses. Another threat is the thinning of the **ozone layer**, which protects the earth from harmful effects of the sun's radiation. In addition, increased carbon dioxide and other pollutants in the atmosphere are making the earth warmer. This world-wide warming trend is called the **greenhouse effect**. If **global warming** causes excessive melting of the polar ice caps, the world's ocean levels will rise; low-lying coastal countries could be permanently flooded.

✦ **Nuclear Safety**. Nuclear weapons and power stations pose special dangers to the earth's environment. Nuclear waste can contaminate an area for millions of years. For example, in 1986, a meltdown in **Chernobyl**, a Soviet nuclear power station, caused radiation illness over a wide area and continues to have harmful effects.

Possible Solutions. A greater awareness of the need to preserve and protect the environment has developed. In June 1992, 178 nations met in Brazil at the **Rio Conference**, in an **Earth Summit** devoted to world environmental problems. Participants pledged themselves to the goal of industrial growth without pollution or environmental destruction, and signed a treaty to reduce global warming. In 1997, an international conference on global warming was held in Kyoto, Japan.

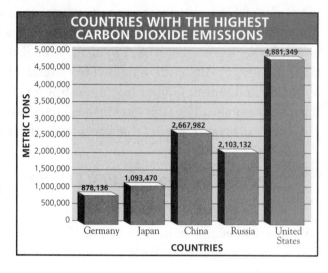

There has also been a move to find alternative energy sources. Since much pollution is caused by burning fossil fuels, there is an effort to harness energy from the sun and wind, to develop safer nuclear reactors, and to tap into other sources of energy. Recently the drastic rise in the price of oil and natural gas has added urgency to efforts to make wind, solar, geothermal and tidal power into practical energy alternatives, while adding millions of good jobs to the economy.

DESERTIFICATION

In some areas, especially on the African continent, attempts have been made to increase food production by clearing large tracts of land. This has combined with several years of drought. In regions like the **Sahel**, just south of the Sahara, this has led to **desertification** — an expansion of desert land. The problem has been aggravated by overgrazing. The United Nations has estimated that in Africa alone, an area half the size of New York State turns into desert each year, putting millions of people at risk of malnutrition and starvation.

Possible Solutions. Reforestation (*planting trees*), restricting cattle grazing, and educating people about how to reduce soil erosion are possible approaches. Also, some inhabitants will have to be relocated to areas where they can grow food and graze cattle.

 # DEFORESTATION

The rainforests of Central and South America, Africa, and South and Southeast Asia provide much of the world's oxygen. Some countries in these areas have been clearing their rainforests. They sell the wood and grow food on the cleared land. However, heavy rains wash away nutrients. The remaining soil is of poor quality, produces few crops, and becomes barren. Loss of rainforests also poses a threat to many **endangered species**.

THE WORLD'S TROPICAL RAINFORESTS

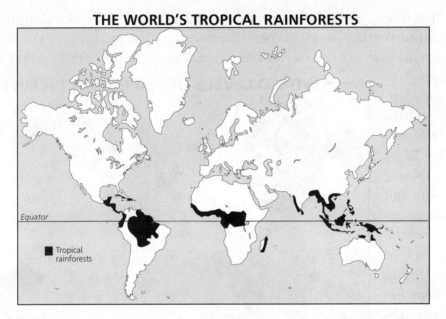

Possible Solutions. An international campaign is taking place to save the world's rainforests. Measures such as educating farmers about soil erosion, replanting trees, and restricting cattle grazing have been adopted.

 # GLOBAL MIGRATION

Economic inequality and political conflict have led to migration on a global scale. After World War II, large numbers of foreign workers migrated to Western Europe to fill low-paying jobs. Turks and Italians migrated to Germany, North Africans to France, and Pakistanis to Great Britain. Many of these "guest workers" were Muslims and were often not accepted as equals by Europeans. Eastern European refugees have flooded into Western Europe. Latin Americans and Asians have similarly migrated to the United States.

Alternative Viewpoints. In times of unemployment, foreign workers and refugees are often resented and attacked by native groups. Extremist politicians even call for them to be forcibly expelled. In industrialized countries, many citizens have condemned violence against immigrants and reaffirmed the principle of equal rights for all. Steps have also been taken to limit the number of refugees and immigrants.

AID TO DEVELOPING NATIONS

More than three-quarters of the world's population live in the **developing nations** of the "**Third World**." People in these countries have low incomes, a short life expectancy, poor medical care and meager education. The gap between rich and poor nations continues to widen. Developing nations have many problems: natural obstacles like deserts, mountains and poor soil; political and social unrest; lack of funds for schools, roads, communications and technology; high

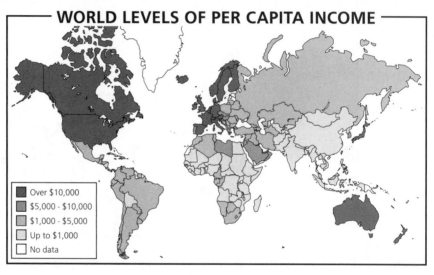

population growth; lack of an educated, skilled workforce; and competition from developed nations in global markets.

Alternative Viewpoints. Some developing countries have made substantial progress by shifting to free markets, limiting population growth, curbing inflation, and creating stable conditions for investment. Industrialized nations have sent aid and advisors to developing countries to improve education, modernize the economy and raise living standards. Private efforts of groups like CARE or individuals like **Mother Teresa** also help; she took care of the sick and homeless in Calcutta, India. But many Third World leaders demand more, in part as reparations for colonialism and other past abuses. They argue that developed countries should cancel the debts they are owed.

THE STATUS OF WOMEN

Throughout history, most societies have been **patriarchal**: men have held power, while women were considered inferior. In these societies, women usually could not own property or participate in government, and had to obey their husbands. In the 19th and 20th centuries, the status of women in the Western world changed. With the Industrial Revolution, many more women entered the workforce. During World War I, women worked in factories while men were fighting overseas, and in most industrialized countries they won the right to vote. Yet women still face inferior status in many parts of the world today. In Africa and Asia, they endure forced mutilation of their bodies when they reach adolescence. In some Islamic countries, women must wear veils from head to toe, refrain from being seen in public, and are not permitted to drive cars. Even in Western countries, women are underrepresented in politics and top corporate jobs, and on average earn less than men. Often, working women must also take care of the children and the home.

Alternative Viewpoints. In the 1960s, the **Women's Liberation Movement** emerged. Laws were passed in many countries guaranteeing women equal rights and outlawing discrimination in education and employment. But some developing nations still claim that treating women equally violates their cultural traditions. Today, international organizations are trying to end the worst abuses against women. An international conference was held in Beijing, China in 1995 to try to enhance women's rights worldwide.

URBANIZATION AND MODERNIZATION

Urbanization refers to the movement of people into cities. In 1850, only England had more than half its people in towns and cities. By the year 2000, three-quarters of the world's population lived in cities. Both poverty and improvements in farming in the Third World have driven

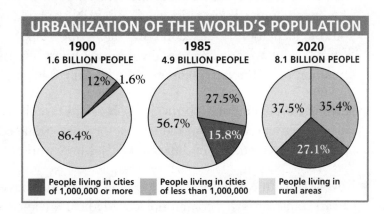

URBANIZATION OF THE WORLD'S POPULATION

1900	1985	2020
1.6 BILLION PEOPLE	4.9 BILLION PEOPLE	8.1 BILLION PEOPLE

1900: 12%, 1.6%, 86.4%

1985: 27.5%, 56.7%, 15.8%

2020: 37.5%, 35.4%, 27.1%

People living in cities of 1,000,000 or more
People living in cities of less than 1,000,000
People living in rural areas

millions to emigrate to cities in search of jobs and education. Once they arrive, rural migrants settle for poorly-paid jobs. Rising urban populations require more food, heat, water, electricity, schools, and medical care than cities can provide. Overcrowding leads to air and water pollution, traffic jams, and mountains of garbage and sewage. Rural newcomers also face new values. **Modernization** refers to the shedding of traditional beliefs and adopting modern methods, ideas, and technologies. Often cities are centers of change and modernization, creating social and psychological conflicts. Citizens in developing nations struggle to combine their traditional beliefs with the modern ideas of the industrialized world.

Future Effects. Urbanization and modernization pose tremendous challenges for the developing world. Third World governments must try to improve conditions in the countryside to slow migration, while providing more services, housing, and education in cities. Reducing population growth will also lessen urban congestion. Adjusting to these changes creates social problems and cultural conflicts. In Iran, for example, Islamic Fundamentalist leaders opposed the effects that Western ideas and modernization had on their local traditions and have tried to suppress many of them.

 # SCIENTIFIC AND TECHNOLOGICAL CHANGE

Because of continuous progress in science and technology, we live in an age of constant change. The pace of technological change can make job skills obsolete well before people have time to adjust.

◆ **The Computer Revolution.** A central feature of the late 20th century has been the computer. Earlier computers required huge buildings to house their memory units. The invention of **silicon chips** made it possible to build computers that perform billions of calculations in a second and fit on one's lap. Some people have had problems adjusting to the computer revolution. Others fear that the vast amounts of information now stored in computers are leading to invasions of individual privacy.

◆ **Automation.** Computer-controlled robots often replace skilled workers. This provides cheaper products, but reduces factory jobs. Some economists believe new jobs are quickly created, but in different fields. Many workers find it hard to adjust.

◆ **Revolutions in Medicine.** Vaccines and antibiotics have wiped out many diseases. Organ transplants are commonplace. Medical advances now seem to occur daily.

The next challenge is to find cures for diseases such as cancer, AIDS, and memory loss in the elderly. But medical costs are rising and developing countries cannot afford proper care; 40,000 childen under five die daily from preventable illnesses.

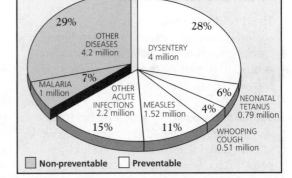

WORLDWIDE CAUSES OF DEATH FROM DISEASE

29% OTHER DISEASES 4.2 million

28% DYSENTERY 4 million

MALARIA 1 million 7%

OTHER ACUTE INFECTIONS 2.2 million

MEASLES 1.52 million

6% NEONATAL TETANUS 0.79 million

4%

15%   11%   WHOOPING COUGH 0.51 million

☐ Non-preventable ☐ Preventable

✦ **Transportation Advances.** When industry developed cars, ships, and planes, the impact on people's lives was enormous. Cars give people the freedom to travel wherever they choose, but increased traffic has caused smog, pollution, and gridlock.

✦ **Communication Advances.** Inventions such as the telephone, radio, television and satellites have made instant communications possible, turning our world into a "global village." The **Internet**, a global network allowing computer users to exchange information quickly and cheaply, is further increasing the knowledge available. People are better informed today, but find it hard to cope with the "information overload."

✦ **Space Exploration.** In 1957 the Soviets launched a satellite, **Sputnik I**, starting a "**space race**" with the U.S. Both countries carried out complex projects, sending astronauts and satellites into space in large numbers. The first humans landed on the moon in 1969. Space exploration continues—costly, but carrying national prestige.

— **STUDY CARDS** —

Overpopulation	Environmental Pollution
The Problem: 200 years ago there were one billion people in the world. Today there are 6 billion, and the number is increasingly rapidly — especially in large countries such as China, India, Pakistan and Bangladesh. This threatens to create shortages of food and resources such as farmland and safe drinking water.	**The Problem:** Industrialization, urbanization and population growth cause increasing air, land and water pollution. Nuclear, biological and chemical wastes pose special problems.
Solutions: Education and family planning help limit population growth. China has adopted a **"one-child" policy**.	**Solutions:** International cooperation and non-polluting sources of energy are needed to solve these problems. **Rio Conference** (1992) and **Kyoto Conference** (1997) were held to develop international strategies to protect the environment.

International Terrorism

The Problem: Terrorism is use of violence against civilians for political purposes. Terrorists hijack planes, bomb buildings, and assassinate people. In the future they may use biological, chemical or nuclear weapons.

Solutions: Negotiating with terrorists is generally considered useless. Undercover agents work to track down terrorist cells, arrest and convict perpetrators. Sometimes attacks are made on countries harboring terrorist groups.

Problems of Developing Nations

The Problem: Three-quarters of the world's people live in developing **Third World** nations. They have low incomes, short life spans, poor education and medical care, low productivity.

Solutions: Developed nations need to make greater investments in Third World economies, and perhaps forgive Third World debts. In addition, developing nations must seek to grow more food, improve education, develop a skilled work force, and limit population growth.

Deforestation

The Problem: Forests provide much of the oxygen humans need in order to breathe. Tropical rainforests also have unique plants that often have medical uses. Deforestation is the clearing of these areas by removing the trees.

Solutions: An international campaign is trying to encourage nations to preserve their forests. Some forest lands are being bought by private groups to prevent the loss of the trees.

The Status of Women

The Problem: In developed nations, women have political and social equality. In many developing nations, women are treated as inferior and have few if any rights.

Solutions: During the **Women's Liberation Movement**, many developed countries passed laws prohibiting discrimination against women. The **Beijing Conference** (1995) addressed the problems of women's rights around the world.

Desertification

The Problem: Changes in the climate, such as **global warming**, are leading to persistent droughts in parts of the world. Regions like the **Sahel**, south of Africa's Sahara Desert, are turning into desert lands, putting millions of people at risk of malnutrition and starvation.

Solutions: International relief efforts are under way, as well as planting trees to reduce soil erosion.

Urbanization/Modernization

Urbanization: Movement of people from countryside to cities. In the Third World, as millions pour into cities, shortages of housing, jobs, transportation, sanitation and other services arise.

Modernization: Shedding traditional beliefs in favor of modern ideas and technology. Adjusting to these changes creates problems and identity conflicts. Islamic Fundamentalism is one way people have reacted to modernization.

SUMMARIZING YOUR UNDERSTANDING

COMPLETING A TABLE

Use the table below to organize information you have read about in this chapter.

Concern	State the Problem	List a Possible Solution
Overpopulation		
Environmental Pollution		
Deforestation		
Desertification		
Status of Women		
Urbanization		

TESTING YOUR UNDERSTANDING

Test your understanding of this chapter by answering the following questions:

MULTIPLE-CHOICE QUESTIONS

1   The global problems of uneven economic development, environmental pollution, and hunger reflect a need for
   (1) a return to policies of economic mercantilism
   (2) increased military spending
   (3) a reduction in foreign aid provided by industrialized nations
   (4) increased international cooperation

2   A valid statement about technology in the 20th century is that it has
   (1) eliminated famine and disease
   (2) delayed economic progress in developing countries
   (3) led to the adoption of free trade policies
   (4) accelerated the pace of cultural diffusion

3   Technological changes in developing countries have often brought about
   (1) mass migrations from urban to rural areas
   (2) fewer educational and employment opportunities
   (3) a weakening of traditional values and family patterns
   (4) the decreased use of natural resources

4   Which is a direct effect of the terrorist attack on the World Trade Center and the Pentagon on September 11, 2001?
    (1) The United States took military action to overthrow the Taliban government of Afghanistan after they refused to turn over terrorist mastermind Osama bin Laden.
    (2) The United States fired missiles at the capital city of Iraq.
    (3) U.S. troops were sent to Somalia to defeat local warlords.
    (4) Osama bin Laden resigned as leader of the al-Qaida terrorist network.

5   Acid rain damage, contamination from nuclear accidents, and the deterioration of the earth's ozone layer indicate a need for
    (1) the elimination of fossil fuels
    (2) greater international cooperation
    (3) high tariffs and a favorable balance of trade
    (4) the nationalization of major industries

6   A major cause of the high birth rates of many developing nations has been
    (1) the need for a large urban workforce
    (2) a desire to counteract an increasing death rate
    (3) the need to replace people killed during civil wars
    (4) traditional beliefs and lack of knowledge about modern birth control methods

7   "People are casting many wary glances at the sky and their surroundings — radioactivity needs no visa and has no respect for national frontiers."

                                                                    Izvestia, May 9, 1986

    This quotation most probably refers to
    (1) the nuclear accident at Chernobyl   (3) deforestation caused by acid rain
    (2) the drought in Africa's Sahel region   (4) monsoon floods in Southeast Asia

8   Russian grain purchases from the United States, sales of Japanese cars in Latin America, and European reliance on Middle Eastern oil are examples of
    (1) the creation of free-trade areas   (3) the rise in economic interdependence
    (2) economically self-sufficient nations   (4) a worldwide spirit of imperialism

9   The main concern about the destruction of the rain forests in Brazil and sub-Saharan Africa is that
    (1) cities will become seriously overcrowded
    (2) it will lead to a decrease of oxygen in the atmosphere
    (3) per capita incomes in developing nations will increase
    (4) the availability of water in these areas will decrease

10 Which statement best describes the status of women today?
    (1) Women have achieved complete equality with men.
    (2) Women have more freedom in developing nations than in developed nations.
    (3) Women's job opportunities have increased in developed nations.
    (4) Women have made no progress in gaining social equality since 1945.

Use the information in the bar graph to answer Question 11.

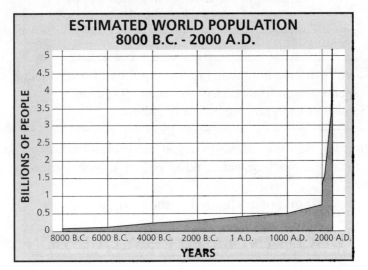

11 What event most likely accounts for the rise in population in the past 200 years?
    (1) Crusades   (3) Cold War
    (2) French Revolution   (4) technological advances

INTERPRETING DOCUMENTS

Study the following quotation from Thomas Malthus.

> "I say that the power of population is indefinitely greater than the power in the earth to produce subsistence for man. Population, when unchecked, increases in a geometrical ratio. Subsistence only increases in an arithmetical ratio. By the law of our nature which makes food necessary to the life of man, the effects of these two unequal powers must be kept equal."

1a What is the main idea of this quotation?_____

 b What does Malthus fear most? _____

THEMATIC ESSAY QUESTION

Directions: Write a well-organized essay that includes an introduction, several paragraphs addressing the Task below, and a conclusion.

Theme: Interdependence

> Changes in the Earth's environment pose
> a danger to the future of all nations.

Task:

- Identify *two* environmental dangers to the future of the Earth.
- Explain why *each* is a danger to the environment.
- Show how each problem might be solved.

Suggestions: You may use any examples from your study of global history. Some suggestions you might wish to consider include water and air pollution, global warming, desertification, and deforestation.

You are *not* limited to these suggestions.

DOCUMENT-BASED ESSAY QUESTION

Historical Context:

As the world looks ahead in the 21st century, it faces many challenges. Three of the most serious challenges are hunger in developing nations, international terrorism, and threats to the environment.

Task: Using information from the documents and your knowledge of global history, answer the questions that follow each document in Part A. Your answers to the questions will help you write the Part B essay in which you will be asked to:

- Identify and describe *two* challenges and explain how each challenge poses a global problem in the twenty-first century.

- Describe *one* effort being made to deal with each of these two challenges.

Part A — Short-Answer Questions

Directions: Analyze the documents and answer the questions that follow them.

DOCUMENT 1

> ### FOOD SHORTAGES IMPERIL 3 MILLION IN SOUTHERN SUDAN
> "Over 3 million people in southern Sudan are facing serious food shortages due to the ongoing civil conflict and an emerging drought. The hardest hit populations are in Darfar, Kordofan, East Equatoria, and Jonglei where continued fighting compounds the drought conditions. Food stocks are rapidly dwindling. The poor harvests have affected 900,000 people."
>
> ### CROPS AND LIVESTOCK HARD HIT BY DROUGHT IN PAKISTAN
> "Prolonged drought in parts of Pakistan has decimated livestock and severely affected fruit and cereal production. Hardest hit are parts of Sindh and Punjab provinces, already in their third consecutive year of drought. Livestock numbers in some districts have been reduced by up to 60 percent of their 1999 levels. Fruit farmers face financial ruin as their fruit trees have dried up."

—Press release of the Food and Agricultural Organization of the U.N., 2001

1 According to this document, what are some of the concerns of the U.N. in Sudan and Pakistan? _____

DOCUMENT 2

> "The key to broad-based growth and reduced poverty is a sound and stable policy that promotes opportunity for all members of society. Since a majority of the people derive their livelihoods from agriculture, the transformation of agriculture is an essential aspect of economic growth. Economic growth leads to reduced poverty, increased food security, and higher standards of living. Broad-based economic growth offers the best chance to enhance political stability and transform societies along the path of reform. It is only by putting resources and decision-making power into the hands of people that true reform can be achieved."

—Statement of the US Agency for International Development (AID), 2001

2 What solution does this agency advocate as the answer to ending hunger in developing countries? _____

DOCUMENT 3

"We declare jihad against the U.S. government, because the U.S. government is unjust, criminal, and tyrannical. It has committed acts that are extremely unjust, hideous, and criminal, whether directly or through its support of the Israeli occupation.

For this and other acts of aggression and injustice, we have declared jihad against America, because in our religion it is our duty to make jihad so that God's word is the one exalted to the heights and so that we drive the Americans away from all Muslim countries. Our jihad is directed against U.S. soldiers in the land of the Two Holy Places (*Saudi Arabia: Mecca and Medina*). In our religion, it is not permissible for any non-Muslims to stay in that country. I have benefited so greatly from the jihad in Afghanistan ... by the grace of God ... the myth of the superpower was destroyed in the minds of all Muslims."

—Osama bin Laden, in an interview with CNN, March 1997

3 What reasons does Osama bin Laden provide for declaring a jihad against the United States?

(1) _____

(2) _____

DOCUMENT 4

4 According to the photograph, what tactics have international terrorists used to increase the damaging effects of terrorism?

_____

_____

_____

_____

DOCUMENT 5

"The year 2001 showed that terrorism continues to pose a clear and present danger to the international community. While the threat continues, the international community's commitment to counter-terrorist measures continues. We base our cooperation with our international partners on four basic policy tenets:

- First, make no concession to terrorists and strike no deals.
- Second, bring terrorists to justice for their crimes.
- Third, isolate and pressure states that sponsor terrorism to force them to change their behavior,
- Fourth, bolster the counter-terrorist capabilities of countries.

—Office of Counter-Terrorism of the U.S. State Department

5 Describe three actions suggested by the U.S. State Department to combat international terrorism:

(1) _____

(2) _____

(3) _____

DOCUMENT 6

Scientists believe that when carbon dioxide gases are released into the atmosphere, they prevent the sun's heat from escaping.

6a What has been the trend of carbon dioxide trapped in our atmosphere?

_____

b Why might this trend be dangerous?

_____

_____

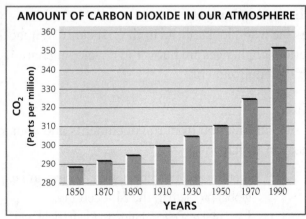

AMOUNT OF CARBON DIOXIDE IN OUR ATMOSPHERE

DOCUMENT 7

Principle 2: States have the sovereign right to exploit their own resources, but also have the responsibility to ensure that activities within their jurisdiction or control do not cause damage to the environment or other states or areas.

Principle 7: States shall cooperate in a spirit of global partnership to conserve, protect, and restore the health and integrity of the Earth's ecosystem.

Principle 10: Environmental issues are best handled with the participation of all concerned citizens, at the relevant level. States shall facilitate and encourage public awareness and participation by making information widely available.

Principle 11: States shall enact effective environmental legislation. Environmental standards, management objectives, and priorities should reflect the environmental and developmental context to which they apply.

—The Rio Declaration on Environment and Development (1992)

7 State two ways the Rio Declaration sought to control environmental pollution:

(1) _____

(2) _____

Part B — Essay

Directions: Write a well-organized essay that includes an introduction, several paragraphs, and a conclusion. Use evidence from at least **four** documents. Support your response with relevent facts, examples, and details. Include additional outside information.

Historical Context:
As the world looks ahead in the 21st century, it faces many challenges. Three of the most serious challenges are hunger in developing nations, international terrorism, and threats to the environment.

Task:
Using information from the documents and your knowledge of global history, write an essay in which you:

- Identify and describe *two* challenges and explain how each challenge poses a global problem in the 21st century.
- Describe *one* effort being made to deal with each of these two challenges.

THE MIDDLE EAST AND NORTH AFRICA

EARLY CIVILIZATION 10,000 BC - 500 BC	NEW CENTERS OF CULTURE 330 - 1257	RELIGIOUS WARS 1096 - 1492	OTTOMAN EMPIRE 1453 - 1918	MIDDLE EAST FROM 1900 - PRESENT

EARLY HUMAN SOCIETY
- Neolithic Revolution

RIVER VALLEY CIVILIZATIONS
- Mesopotamia
  - *Fertile Crescent*
  - *Tigris and Euphrates Rivers*
  - *Sumerians*
  - *Code of Hammurabi*
- Ancient Egypt
  - *Pyramids*
  - *Pharoahs*
  - *Hieroglyphics*
- The Hebrews
  - *Judaism*
  - *Monotheism*
  - *Ten Commandments*
  - *Exodus*
- Phoenicians
  - *First alphabet*

PERSIA (550—100 BC)
- large empire uniting many peoples
- Cyrus the Great
- Zoroastrianism
- attempted conquest of Greek city-states

BYZANTINE EMPIRE
- Continuation of East Roman empire
  - *Emperor Constantine*
  - *Constantinople*
- Legacy of Byzantium
  - *Code of Justinian*
  - *Eastern Orthodox Christianity*
  - *Hagia Sophia*

RISE OF ISLAM
- Arose in Arabia
- Mohammed
  - *Allah*
  - *Qu'ran (Koran)*
  - *Hegira and Jihad*
- Five Pillars of Faith
- Height of Arab Empire
  - *Arabs rule from Spain to western India*
- Golden Age of Islam
  - *Mathematics*
  - *Astronomy*
  - *Architecture*
  - *Greek/Roman learning preserved*

CRUSADES (1096-1291)
- Series of attempts by Christians to free the Holy Land from Muslim rule
  - *Increased trade*
  - *Cultural diffusion*

DECLINE OF ARAB EMPIRE
- Islamic territory invaded and conquered by Mongols; Baghdad destroyed in 1258
- Spain's Catholic rulers expel Muslims and Jews in 1492

OTTOMAN TURK EXPANSION
- Took Constantinople
- Suleiman the Magnificent
- Muslim toleration of Jews and Christians

SAFAVID EMPIRE
- Persia
  - *Ruled by Shahs*

DECLINE OF THE OTTOMAN EMPIRE
- Disunity
- Warfare with Persia, Austria, Russia
- Failure to modernize
- Loss of Territories (Balkans, Egypt)

MODERN TURKEY'S TRANSFORMATION
- Young Turks
- Ottoman Empire sides with Germany in World War I
- Creation of modern Turkey under Kemal Ataürk

RISE OF NATIONALISM
- British and French mandates
- Independent states emerge
- Pan Arab Movement

ARAB-ISRAELI CONFLICT
- Zionism
- War of Independence (1948)
- Further Wars, 1956/67/73
- Continued tensions
  - *Camp David Accords*
  - *P.L.O./Intifada*
- Mideast Peace Conference
  - *Palestinian Authority*
- Sharon and rising violence
  - *Second intifada*
- Hamas founded in Palestine
- Israel attacks Hezbollah in southern Lebanon, 2006

OTHER HOT SPOTS
- OPEC and Middle East Oil
- Iranian Revolution
  - *Islamic Fundamentalism*
  - *Ayatollah Khomeini*
- Iraq and Saddam Hussein
  - *Iran-Iraq War*
  - *Kuwait invaded*
  - *Gulf War, 1990*
  - *Iraq War, 2003, U.S. overthrows Saddam*
- Sept. 11, 2001 terror attacks on U.S. by al-Qaeda
- U.S. overthrows Taliban in Afghanistan, Oct.-Dec. 2001

ASIA

EARLY CIVILIZATIONS 2500 BC - 500 AD	STABILITY AND CHANGE 500 - 1900	TWENTIETH CENTURY 1900 - PRESENT

EARLY CIVILIZATIONS 2500 BC - 500 AD

CHINA
- Huang He Valley (2000–1027 BC)
- Shang Dynasty (1760–1027 BC)
- Zhou Dynasty (1027–221 BC)
  - Mandate of Heaven
  - Confucius
  - Lao Tzu and Daoism
- Qin Dynasty (221 BC-206 AD)
  - Shi-Huangdi was first emperor
  - Great Wall of China built
- Han Dynasty (206 BC-220 AD)
  - Silk Road
  - Examinations for imperial service
- Period of Disunity
  - Warfare among kingdoms for control of China
  - Longest period of disunity in Chinese history

INDIA
- Indus River Valley (2500–1500 BC)
  - Harappans
- Aryan Invasions
  - Hinduism
  - Caste system
  - Buddhism
- Mauryan Empire (321 BC-232 AD)
  - Asoka
- Gupta Empire (320-535)
  - Golden Age of Hindu Culture
  - Hun invasions

STABILITY AND CHANGE 500 - 1900

CHINA
- T'ang Dynasty (618–907)
  - Golden Age: block printing
  - Expansion into Korea and Manchuria
- Sung Dynasty (960–1279)
  - Golden Age: the compass, gunpowder
- Yuan Dynasty (1279–1368)
  - Mongol conquest
  - Kublai Khan
  - Marco Polo visits
- Ming Dynasty (1368–1644)
  - Middle Kingdom
- Qing (Manchu) Dynasty (1644–1912)
  - Opium War
  - Taiping Rebellion
  - Boxer Rebellion (1899)

JAPAN
- Chinese influence on Japan
  - Writing, Confucianism, Buddhism
- Heian Period (794–1185)
  - Golden Age: Tale of Genji
- Shogunates (1200–1550)
  - Japanese feudalism
  - Shoguns, Daimyos, Samurai
  - Tokugawa Shogunate
- Meiji Restoration (1868–1912)
  - Adoption of Western ways

INDIA
- Muslim Invasions
- Mughal Empire (1526–1837)
  - Akbar the Great
  - Shah Jahan, Taj Mahal
- British Rule (1800s–1947)
  - British East India Company

TWENTIETH CENTURY 1900 - PRESENT

CHINA
- Republican Period (1912–1949)
  - Sun Yat-Sen and Three Principles
  - Chiang Kai-Shek and the Kuomintang
  - Japanese invasion (1937–1945)
- Communist Period (1949–Present)
  - Two Chinas: Mainland China and Taiwan
  - Mao Zedong
  - Red Guards and Cultural Revolution
  - Deng Xiaoping
  - Jiang Zemin

JAPAN
- Rise to Power (1900–1930s)
  - Russo-Japanese War
  - Sino-Japanese War
  - World War I
- World War II (1935–1945)
  - Pearl Harbor
  - Hiroshima and Nagasaki
  - U.S. Occupation of Japan
  - Constitution of 1947
- Rise to Economic Power (1970–Present)
  - Economic Superpower

INDIA/SOUTHEAST ASIA
- Independence Movements
  - Mohandas Gandhi, India
  - Ho Chi Minh, Vietnam
- Partition of India (1947)
  - Pakistan & India
  - Bangladesh Independence (1971)
- Cold War in Asia
  - Korean War (1951–1952)
  - Vietnam War (1965–1974)

THE AMERICAS

PRE-COLUMBIAN CIVILIZATIONS 30,000 BC - 1546 AD	EUROPEAN COLONIALISM 1500 - 1850	RECENT HISTORY 1800 - PRESENT

MIGRATIONS FROM ASIA (30,000 B.C.—10,000 BC)
• Settlers cross Bering Strait to the Americas
 	
OLMECS
• One of first known Mexican civilizations
 	
MAYA CIVILIZATION (1500 BC—1546 AD)
• In Guatemala; later Yucatan
• Agricultural, grew corn
• Perfected calendar
• Human sacrifices
 	
AZTEC EMPIRE (1200—1521)
• Controlled Central Mexico
• Rigid social structure
• Human sacrifices to Sun God
 	
INCA EMPIRE (1200—1535)
• Along Andes Mountains
• Rigid class structure
• Grew potatoes, root crops
• Built stone roads and stone buildings
• Developed writing & number systems
• Built large cities with pyramids, palaces
  —*Machu Picchu*
	EUROPEAN CONQUEST (1492—1542)
	• Arrival of conquistadors
	• Cortés defeats Aztecs (1521)
	  —*Montezuma*
	• Pizarro defeats Incas (1535)
	
	EFFECTS OF CONQUEST
	• New foods and products introduced to Europe
	• Diseases devastated native populations
	• Spread of Christianity
	• Spanish and Portuguese culture to Latin America
	
	THE COLONIAL EXPERIENCE
	• Rule of Spain and Portugal
	• Encomienda (hacienda) system
	• Colonial social classes
	  —*Peninsulares*
	  —*Creoles*
	  —*Mestizos, mulattos*
	  —*Natives and Africans*
	• Mercantilism
		INDEPENDENCE MOVEMENTS
		• Causes
		  —*Examples of French and American Revolutions*
		  —*Weakening of Spain*
		• Independence leaders
		  —*Haiti: Toussaint L'Ouverture*
		  —*Venezuela, Colombia: Simón Bolívar*
		  —*Mexico: Miguel Hidalgo*
		
		19TH CENTURY
		• Monroe Doctrine (1823) stopped new colonization
		• Rule of the Caudillos
		
		20TH CENTURY
		• Mexican Revolution of 1910
		  —*Diaz and Pancho Villa*
		  —*Mexican Constitution*
		• Cuban Revolution (1959)
		  —*Castro*
		  —*Communism*
		  —*Bay of Pigs Invasion*
		  —*Cuban Missile Crisis*
		• Nicaraguan Revolution (1979)
		  —*Sandinistas vs. Contras*
		• Military dictatorships
		• Debts to Western banks
		• Problems of economic development

SUB-SAHARAN AFRICA

EARLY HISTORY 750 BC - 1800 AD	RECENT HISTORY 1800 - PRESENT

KUSH (750 BC—350 A.D)
• Important iron producer
• Rich from ivory, ebony
• Egyptian cultural influence
• Developed its own writing
 	
KINGDOM OF GHANA (750-1200)
• Rich from gold-salt trade
• Captives used as slaves
 	
KINGDOM OF MALI (1240-1400)
• Rich from gold-salt trade
• Kings adopted Islam
  —*Mansa Musa*
  —*Timbuktu: center of learning*
 	
KINGDOM OF SONGHAI (1464-1600)
• Founded by Sultan Sunni Ali
• Islamic kingdom
• Grew rich from trade
 	
OTHER AFRICAN STATES
• Benin
• Great Zimbabwe
• Coastal cities of East Africa
• Ethiopia
 	
TRANSATLANTIC SLAVE TRADE
• Greatly expanded slave trade
• About 15 million Africans enslaved in 300 years
• Many died en route
• Disrupted African development
	CAUSES OF NEW IMPERIALISM
	• Expanded technology
	• Economic motives
	• National pride
	• Balance of power
	• Other motives
	  —*Social Darwinism*
	
	SCRAMBLE FOR AFRICA
	• British take Egypt
	• Berlin Conference, 1884-85
	• Boer War in South Africa
	
	DECOLONIZATION
	• Rise of nationalism
	• World War II weakened European control
	• Independence movements
	  —*Kwame Nkrumah*
	  —*Jomo Kenyatta*
	• Single-party states
	• Problems of economic development
	
	MODERN-DAY AFRICA
	• South Africa
	  —*Apartheid*
	  —*Nelson Mandela*
	  —*F.W. DeKlerk*
	• Tribalism
	  —*Rwanda and Burundi*
	• Hunger and famine
	  —*Somalia*
	• Shift to democratic governments

EUROPE

CLASSICAL CIVILIZATIONS 1000 BC - 500 AD	MIDDLE AGES AND RENAISSANCE 500 - 1500	BIRTH OF THE MODERN WORLD 1500 - 1770	NEW CURRENTS 1770 - 1900	THE WORLD AT WAR 1900 - 1945	ATOMIC AGE 1945 - Present

GREEKS
• City-States
  —Sparta
  —Athens
• Persian War
• Golden Age
  —Pericles
  —Democracy
  —Parthenon
• Achievements
  —philosophy
  —sculpture
  —drama
  —history
• Hellenistic Period
  —Alexander the Great
 	
ROMANS
• Roman Republic
  —12 Tables of Roman Law
  —Julius Caesar
• Roman Empire
  —Augustus
  —Pax Romana
  —Rise of Christianity
• Decline
  —slavery
  —economic problems
  —division into East and West Rome
  —barbarian invasions
	BYZANTINE EMPIRE
	• East Roman empire
	• Constantinople
	• Eastern Orthodox Christianity
	• Preserved classical learning
	
	CHAOS IN WEST
	• Barbarian invasions
	• Rise of the Franks
	• Charlemagne
	• Viking Invasions
	
	FEUDAL SOCIETY
	• Lords/knights
	• Serfs/manors
	• Age of Faith
	  —Catholic Church
	  —Crusades
	
	DECLINE OF FEUDALISM
	• Black Death
	• Rise of towns
	• Use of money
	
	RENAISSANCE
	• Italian city-states
	• Humanists
	• Key people
	  —Leonardo da Vinci
	  —Michelangelo
	  —Machiavelli
	  —Gutenberg
		REFORMATION
		• Corruption in Church
		• Martin Luther
		• Wars of religion
		• Catholic Counter Reformation
		  —Jesuits
		  —Council of Trent
		
		AGE OF DISCOVERY
		• Explorers
		• Conquest of Americas
		• New foods to Europe
		
		EUROPE'S CONQUEST OF AMERICAS
		• Cortés/Aztec Civiliz.
		• Pizarro/Inca Civiliz.
		
		COMMERCIAL REVOLUTION
		• Mercantilism
		• Capitalism
		
		AGE OF KINGS
		• Rise of royal power
		• Divine Right
		  —Absolutism
		
		LIMITED MONARCHY
		• Magna Carta
		• Rise of Parliament
		  —English Revolution
		  —Bill of Rights (1689)
			SCIENTIFIC REVOLUTION
			• Scientific Method
			  —Galileo and Newton
			
			ENLIGHTENMENT
			• Belief in natural law
			  —Locke and Voltaire
			  —Rousseau
			
			FRENCH REVOLUTION
			• Causes
			• Highlights
			  —Estates General
			  —National Assembly
			• Reign of Terror
			• Rise of Napoleon
			• Congress of Vienna
			
			INDUSTRIAL REVOLUTION
			• Starts in Britain
			• Reform movement
			• Communism
			  —Marx/Engels
			
			NATIONALISM
			• Revolutions of 1848
			• Italy unified
			  —Count Cavour
			• Germany unified
			  —Otto von Bismarck
			
			IMPERIALISM
			• India, Africa, China, Indochina
				WORLD WAR I
				• Causes
				  —Nationalism
				  —Alliance system
				  —Militarism
				• Major Events
				  —Trench warfare
				• Aftermath
				  —Versailles Treaty
				  —League of Nations
				
				INTERWAR YEARS
				• Prosperity
				• Depression
				• Rise of Fascism
				  —Hitler/Nazis
				  —Mussolini
				
				WORLD WAR II
				• Causes
				  —Nazi aggression
				• Major Events
				  —Blitzkrieg
				  —Battle of Britain
				  —Invasion of Russia
				  —Holocaust
				  —Atom bomb
				• Aftermath
				  —Nuremberg Trials
				  —U.N. created
				  —Germany divided
					SUPERPOWER RIVALRY
					• U.S. vs. Soviet Union
					• Cold War
					  —Truman Doctrine
					  —Marshall Plan
					  —Berlin Wall
					• NATO vs. Warsaw Pact
					
					END OF COLD WAR
					• Policy of détente
					• Freedom for Eastern Europe
					  —Lech Walesa
					  —Solidarity
					• Reunification of Germany
					  —Berlin Wall knocked down
					  —Helmut Kohl
					• Dissolution of USSR
					
					EUROPE TODAY
					• Common Market to European Union
					• Ethnic and religious conflicts
					  —Bosnia
					  —Northern Ireland
					• Immigration policies
					• Pollution
					• Economic problems of Eastern Europe

RUSSIA AND THE COMMONWEALTH OF INDEPENDENT STATES

EARLY HISTORY
800 A.D. - 1917 A.D.

STATE OF KIEV (800s–1240)
- Vikings organized the Slavs into a kingdom

MONGOL CONTROL (1240–1480)

RISE OF MUSCOVY (1480–1598)

ROMANOV RULE (1613–1917)
- Peter the Great (1682–1725)
  - *Westernization*
  - *Expansion*
- Catherine the Great (1762–1796)
  - *Continued Westernization*
  - *Acquisition of Turkish and Polish lands*
  - *Serf conditions worsen*
- Autocratic Russia
  - *Absolute rulers*
  - *Defeat of Napoleon*
  - *Crimean War*
  - *Tsar Alexander II*
  - *Emancipation of the Serfs*
  - *Russification*
  - *Pogroms against Jews*

RUSSIAN REVOLUTION OF 1905
- Nicholas II grants limited reforms

A COMMUNIST STATE
1917 - 1991

RUSSIAN REVOLUTION OF 1917
- Russia unprepared for World War I
- Overthrow of Tsar Nicholas II
- Bolsheviks take power
- Russia withdraws from World War I

RULE BY LENIN (1917–1924)
- Introduces Communism
  - *Civil War: Reds vs. Whites*
  - *New Economic Plan (N.E.P.)*

RULE BY STALIN (1924–1953)
- Totalitarianism: Reign of Terror, purges, gulags
- Economic Changes
  - *Collectivization*
  - *Five Year Plans: from agriculture to industry*
- World War II
  - *Non-aggression treaty with Germany broken*
  - *Joins Allies against Germany*

COLD WAR (1945–1991)
- Democracy vs. Communism
- Occupation of Eastern Europe
  - *Soviet Satellites*
  - *Iron Curtain*
- U.S. Response: Marshall Plan and Truman Doctrine
- Division of Germany
- NATO vs. Warsaw Pact
- Khrushchev (1953–1965)
  - *Denounces Stalinism*
  - *Cuban Missile Crisis*
- Brezhnev (1965–1982)
  - *Stagnation of Soviet economy*
  - *Détente*

MOVE TO DEMOCRACY
1991 - PRESENT

GORBACHEV (1985–1991)
- Reform policies
  - *Glasnost (greater openness)*
  - *Perestroika (restructuring)*
  - *New foreign Policy*
- Gorbachev's reforms fail
  - *unfamiliar with free market system*
  - *opposed by party bureaucrats*
  - *political instability*
  - *declining industrial production*
- Nationalities problem
  - *Baltic States*
  - *Russia*
  - *Treaty of Union*
- Coup of August 1991
- Dissolution of the Soviet Union, December 1991

COMMONWEALTH OF INDEPENDENT STATES (1991–Present)
- Association of independent states
- Importance of the Russian Republic
- Yeltsin introduces changes
  - *Democracy*
  - *Free Market System*
  - *Struggle in Chechnya*
- Putin elected President of Russia, 1999, and re-elected in 2004
- Russia joins in "War on Terror"

CHAPTER 16

PRACTICE REGENTS EXAMINATION #1

AUG. 2007 GLOBAL HISTORY AND GEOGRAPHY REGENTS

PART I: Answer all questions in this part.

1 Which source of information is considered a primary source?
   (1) travel diary of Ibn Battuta
   (2) modern novel about the Golden Age of Islam
   (3) textbook on the history of North Africa
   (4) dictionary of English words adapted from Arabic

2 Which continent's economic and political development has been influenced by the Andes Mountains and the Amazon River?

   (1) Asia   (3) Europe
   (2) Africa   (4) South America

3 • Planting wheat and barley
   • Domesticating animals
   • Establishing permanent homes and villages

   At the beginning of the Neolithic Revolution, the most direct impact of these developments was on
   (1) religion and government
   (2) transportation and trade
   (3) diet and shelter
   (4) climate and topography

4 Which belief system is most closely associated with the terms *Eightfold Path, Four Noble Truths,* and *nirvana?*
   (1) Buddhism
   (2) Christianity
   (3) Judaism
   (4) Shinto

5 • Kushites adapted Egyptian art and architecture.
   • Greeks adopted Phoenician characters for an alphabet.
   • Arabs used the Indian mathematical concept of zero.

   These actions are examples of
   (1) filial piety   (3) scientific research
   (2) cultural diffusion   (4) ethnocentrism

6 ..."If a man has knocked out the teeth of a man of the same rank, his own teeth shall be knocked out. If he has knocked out the teeth of a plebeian(commoner), he shall pay one-third of a mina of silver.". . .
   — Code of Hammurabi

   Which statement is supported by this excerpt from Hammurabi's code of laws?
   (1) All men are equal under the law.
   (2) Fines are preferable to physical punishment.
   (3) Law sometimes distinguishes between social classes.
   (4) Violence must always be punished with violence.

7 Confucianism had a strong impact on the development of China mainly because this philosophy
   (1) established a basic structure for military rule
   (2) provided a basis for social order
   (3) contained the framework for a communist government
   (4) stressed the importance of the individual

Base your answers to questions 8 and 9 on the map below and your knowledge of social studies.

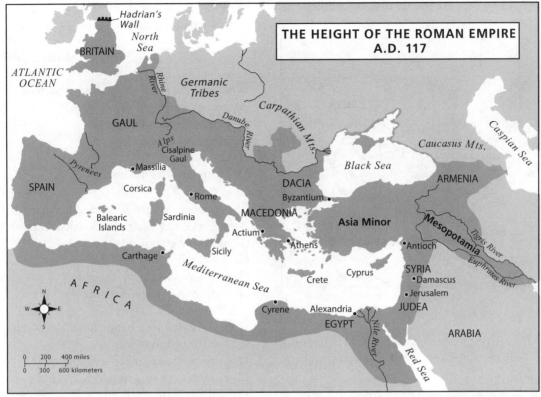

Source: Mazour and Peoples, *World History: People and Nations*, Harcourt Brace Jovanovich (adapted)

8 Which statement is best supported by the information on this map?
  (1) The Roman Empire extended over three continents.
  (2) Rivers kept invaders out of the Roman Empire.
  (3) Alexandria served as the eastern capital of the Roman Empire.
  (4) Carthage was eventually destroyed by the Romans.

9 Based on the information provided by this map, which body of water was most likely the center of Roman trade?
  (1) Red Sea   (3) Atlantic Ocean
  (2) Black Sea   (4) Mediterranean Sea

10 The terms *masters*, *apprentices*, and *journeymen* are most closely associated with the
  (1) encomienda system of Latin America
  (2) guild system of Europe in the Middle Ages
  (3) civil service system of China during the Tang dynasty
  (4) caste system of India

Base your answer to question 11 on the map below and your knowledge of social studies.

Trade about A.D. 1000

Source: Farah and Karls, *World History, The Human Experience*, Glencoe/McGraw-Hill (adapted)

11 Based on the information provided by this map, which statement about Constantinople is accurate?
(1) Africans traded more goods in Constantinople than in any other area.
(2) Constantinople was a city located on the Mediterranean Sea.
(3) Gold was the primary commodity that China sent to Constantinople.
(4) Constantinople was an important trading center.

12 One major characteristic of the Renaissance period is that the
(1) Catholic Church no longer had any influence in Europe
(2) manor became the center of economic activity
(3) classical cultures of Greece and Rome were revived and imitated
(4) major language of the people became Latin

13 "...Therefore those preachers of indulgences are in error, who say that by the pope's indulgences a man is freed from every penalty, and saved; ..."
— Martin Luther

Which period in European history is most directly related to this statement?
(1) Age of Exploration
(2) Scientific Revolution
(3) Crusades
(4) Protestant Reformation

14 The economies of the western African civilizations of Ghana, Mali, and Songhai relied on
(1) industrial growth
(2) shipbuilding
(3) textile production
(4) trans-Saharan trade routes

15 A major reason for Zheng He's voyages during the 15th century was to
(1) promote trade and collect tribute
(2) establish colonies in Africa and India
(3) seal off China's borders from foreign influence
(4) prove the world was round

16 What was one effect of the Columbian exchange?
(1) rapid decline in European population
(2) economic instability in China and Japan
(3) introduction of new foods to both Europe and the Americas
(4) spread of Hinduism into Latin America

17 From the 15th to the 18th centuries, absolute monarchs of Europe and Asia sought to
(1) increase the power of the Catholic Church
(2) centralize their political power
(3) redistribute land to the peasants
(4) strengthen feudalism

Base your answers to question 18 on the map below and on your knowledge of social studies.

Asia — 1294

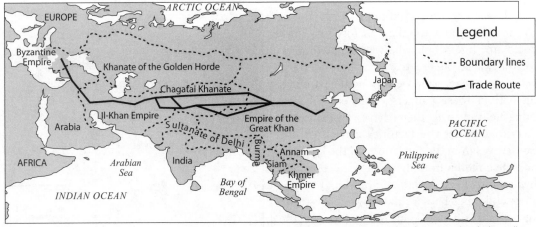

Source: GeoSystems Global Corporation (adapted)

18 Which group of people ruled much of Asia during the period shown on this map?
  (1) Mongol   (3) Japanese
  (2) Indian   (4) European

19 Which person is credited with saying "L'état, c'est moi" (I am the state)?
  (1) Louis XIV   (3) Karl Marx
  (2) John Locke   (4) Queen Isabella

20 Seventeenth-century scholars Galileo Galilei and René Descartes faced serious challenges to their scientific theories because their ideas
  (1) were based on the Bible
  (2) contradicted traditional medieval European beliefs
  (3) relied only on teachings from non-Christian cultures
  (4) were not supported by scientific investigations

21 The breakdown of traditions, increased levels of pollution, and the expansion of slums are negative aspects of
  (1) militarism   (3) pogroms
  (2) collectivization   (4) urbanization

22 Which statement expresses an idea of the Enlightenment?
  (1) The king is sacred and answers only to God.
  (2) History is a continuous struggle between social classes.
  (3) Those who are the most fit will survive and succeed.
  (4) All individuals have natural rights.

23 Which heading best completes this partial outline?

  I._____
    A. Rivalries between powerful countries over colonies
    B. Breakup of large empires
    C. Demand for self-determination by ethnic groups

  (1) Reasons For Communist Revolutions
  (2) Effects of Nationalism
  (3) Methods of Propaganda
  (4) Formation of Democratic Governments

Base your answer to question 24 on the passage below and on your knowledge of social studies.

. . . The factory owners did not have the power to compel anybody to take a factory job. They could only hire people who were ready to work for the wages offered to them. Low as these wage rates were, they were nonetheless much more than these paupers could earn in any other field open to them. It is a distortion of facts to say that the factories carried off the housewives from the nurseries and the kitchens and the children from their play. These women had nothing to cook with and [nothing] to feed their children. These children were destitute [poor] and starving. Their only refuge was the factory. It saved them, in the strict sense of the term, from death by starvation. . . .

— Ludwig von Mises, *Human Action, A Treatise on Economics*, Yale University Press

24 Which statement summarizes the theme of this passage?
(1) Factory owners created increased hardships.
(2) Factory owners preferred to use child laborers.
(3) The factory system allowed people to earn money.
(4) The factory system created new social classes.

25 What was one impact of industrialization on Japan during the Meiji Restoration?
(1) Japan became more isolated from world affairs.
(2) Demand for natural resources increased.
(3) Japan became a colonial possession of China.
(4) Traditional practices of Bushido were re-introduced.

Base your answer to question 26 on the map below and on your knowledge of social studies.

Eastern Asia in 1914

Source: Robert Feeney et al., *Brief Review in Global Studies*, Prentice Hall (adapted)

26 This map illustrates the concept of
(1) ethnocentrism   (3) containment
(2) socialism   (4) imperialism

27 Which region was described as "the powder keg of Europe" prior to World War I?
(1) Iberian Peninsula (3) Balkan Peninsula
(2) British Isles   (4) Scandinavia

28 • Led the Russians in a second revolution (1917)
    • Promised "Peace, Land, and Bread"
    • Established the New Economic Policy (NEP)

Which leader is described by these statements?
(1) Czar Nicholas II
(2) Nikita Khrushchev
(3) Vladimir I. Lenin
(4) Mikhail Gorbachev

Base your answer to question 29 on the following passage and your knowledge of social studies.

. . . In order to obtain Arab support in the War, the British Government promised the Sherif of Mecca in 1915 that, in the event of an Allied victory, the greater part of the Arab provinces of the Turkish Empire would become independent. The Arabs understood that Palestine would be included in the sphere of independence.

In order to obtain the support of World Jewry, the British Government in 1917 issued the Balfour Declaration. The Jews understood that, if the experiment of establishing a Jewish National Home succeeded and a sufficient number of Jews went to Palestine, the National Home might develop in course of time into a Jewish State. . . .

— Summary of the Report of the
Palestine Royal Commission, 1937

29 Which conclusion is best supported by this passage?
(1) The British made no promises to either the Arabs or the Jews.
(2) The Arab-Israeli conflict can be traced in part to British promises.
(3) The United Nations did not try to prevent conflict in the Middle East.
(4) Only the Jews were promised an independent state in Palestine.

Base your answer to question 30 on the following passage and your knowledge of social studies.

. . . A weary, exhausted, nerve-racked group of men it was indeed that, about noon November 1st, assembled in a gully north of Sommerance [France] to rest and dig in for the night. The artillery was still firing furiously, but the enemy's barrage [bombardment] had ceased very suddenly about 10:00 a.m. and now only occasional shells from long-range rifles would explode in the vicinity. The weather was gloomy and the moist air chilled one to the bones. Yet it was with that meticulous [methodical] care that is characteristic of worn-out men, that we prepared our foxholes, carrying boards and iron sheeting from abandoned machine-gunners' dugouts in order to make our "houses" as comfortable as possible, even though only for one night. . . .

Source: William L. Langer,
Gas and Flame in World War I, Knopf/Borzoi

30 Which means of warfare is described in this passage?
(1) guerilla   (3) biological
(2) nuclear   (4) trench

31 A major goal of Joseph Stalin's five-year plans was to
(1) encourage communist revolutions in the colonies of the European powers
(2) transform the Soviet Union into an industrial power
(3) expand the Soviet Union's borders to include warm-water ports
(4) reduce the amount of foreign aid coming from the Western Hemisphere

Base your answer to question 32 on the chart below and on your knowledge of social studies.

NAZI RISE TO POWER

World War I	Weak Government	Economic Problems
• German war debts • Loss of German colonies • Wish for revenge	• Doubts about Weimar Republic • Quarrels among political groups • Wish to return to strong leader like the Kaiser	• Inflation • Worldwide depression • Unemployment

Source: Guide to the Essentials of World History,
Prentice Hall (adapted)

32 Based on the information in this chart, which situation gave rise to Nazi power in Germany?
   (1) global prosperity and trade
   (2) success of the Weimar Republic
   (3) political and economic instability
   (4) expansion of Germany's colonial empire

Base your answer to question 33 on the passage below and on your knowledge of social studies.

. . . "We may anticipate a state of affairs in which two Great Powers will each be in a position to put an end to the civilization and life of the other, though not without risking its own. We may be likened to two scorpions in a bottle, each capable of killing the other, but only at the risk of his own life.". . .
— J. Robert Oppenheimer, July 1953

33 This statement expresses concern about the
   (1) threats to the environment by developed and developing economies
   (2) differences between command and market economies
   (3) economic costs of World War II
   (4) dangers of the Cold War

34 At the end of World War II, the British decided to partition the Indian subcontinent into the nations of India and Pakistan. What was a primary reason for this division?
   (1) India had adopted a policy of nonalignment.
   (2) Religious differences had led to conflicts between Hindus and Muslims.
   (3) Most of India's valuable resources were located in the south.
   (4) British India's Muslim minority controlled most of India's banking industry.

Base your answer to question 35 on the cartoon below and on your knowledge of social studies.

Sending Forth Another Dove

Source: Herblock, May 13, 1941 (adapted)

35 The main idea of this 1941 cartoon is that Japan, Italy, and Germany
   (1) had formed an alliance for peace
   (2) were determined to defeat communism
   (3) had supported a peaceful international solution
   (4) were committed to aggression

Base your answer to question 36 on the graph below and on your knowledge of social studies.

World Petroleum Reserves

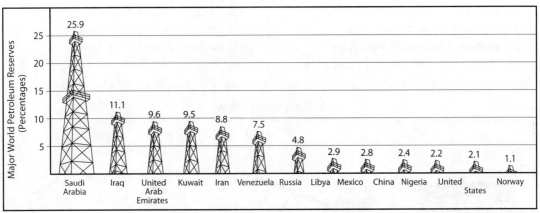

Source: John T. Rourke, *International Politics on the World Stage*, McGraw-Hill, 2003 (adapted)

36 Which conclusion is best supported by the information provided on this graph?
   (1) The United States has adequate petroleum reserves to meet future needs.
   (2) Nations lacking major petroleum reserves cannot industrialize.
   (3) Overproduction of petroleum products has caused inflation in the Middle East.
   (4) Most of the world's largest petroleum reserves are located in the Middle East.

Base your answer to question 37 on the cartoon below and on your knowledge of social studies.

Source: Clay Bennett, *Christian Science Monitor*, 2002

37 What does this cartoon suggest about the introduction of the EURO in Europe?
   (1) Additional countries were created.
   (2) Isolation among nations increased.
   (3) Communist economics policies were adopted.
   (4) Economic barriers between nations decreased.

---

38 The Four Modernizations of Deng Xiaoping in the 1970s and 1980s resulted in
   (1) an emphasis on the Five Relationships
   (2) a return to Maoist revolutionary principles
   (3) a move toward increased capitalism
   (4) the end of the communist system of government

39 One way in which Ho Chi Minh, Fidel Castro, and Kim Jong Il are similar is that each
  (1) set up democratic governments
  (2) used Marxist political principles
  (3) overthrew a ruling monarch
  (4) promoted Confucian principles

40 In the late 20th century, the Green Revolution had the greatest impact on
  (1) grain production in India
  (2) political freedom in Russia
  (3) economic reforms in Cuba
  (4) traditional customs in Japan

Base your answer to question 41 on the illustration below and on your knowledge of social studies.

A European View

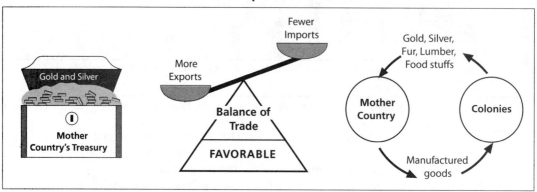

41 Which policy is portrayed in this illustration?
  (1) nonalignment
  (2) laissez-faire capitalism
  (3) perestroika
  (4) mercantilism

Base your answer to question 42 on the cartoon below and on your knowledge of social studies.

Source: Dana Summers, *The Orlando Sentinel* (adapted)

42 What is the main idea of this cartoon?
  (1) The original causes of apartheid have not been eliminated.
  (2) Apartheid improved race relations in South Africa.
  (3) Peace can be achieved by nonviolence.
  (4) Hate is caused by poverty.

43 Ethnic cleansing in Bosnia, the killing fields of Cambodia (Kampuchea), and the dirty war in Argentina are all examples of
  (1) nationalist revolts
  (2) human rights violations
  (3) international terrorism
  (4) religious conflicts

Base your answer to question 44 on the diagram below and your knowledge of social studies.

First Estate	Second Estate	Third Estate
Clergy	Nobles	Middle class, peasants, city workers
1% of the people owned 10% of the land	2% of the people owned 25% of the land	97% of the people owned 65% of the land

Source: Schwartz and O'Connor, *Democracy and Nationalism*, Globe Book Company (adapted)

44 Which revolution resulted from the division of society shown in this diagram?
  (1) Puritan (1642)   (3) Mexican (1910)
  (2) French (1789)   (4) Russian (1917)

45 Which geographic factor had the most influence on the development of Inca society and Japanese society?
  (1) frequent monsoons
  (2) large deserts
  (3) mountainous topography
  (4) tropical climate

46 Studying the architectural features of the Parthenon, Notre Dame Cathedral, and the Taj Mahal provides information about the
  (1) beliefs and values of a given culture
  (2) climatic changes in an area
  (3) 19th-century use of technology
  (4) influence of Chinese design

47 The golden ages of the Roman, Byzantine, and Ottoman Empires can be attributed in part to
  (1) cultural isolation
  (2) stable governments
  (3) command economies
  (4) distinct social classes

48 One way in which Simón Bolívar, Jomo Kenyatta, and Mohandas Gandhi are similar is that each
  (1) led a nationalist movement
  (2) used nonviolent tactics
  (3) supported imperialism
  (4) opposed communism

49 Which factor most hindered the efforts of both Napoleon and Hitler to conquer Russia?
   (1) climate
   (2) fortifications
   (3) advanced technology
   (4) lack of ports

50 One way in which the Sepoy Mutiny in India, the Zulu resistance in southern Africa, and the Boxer Rebellion in China are similar is that each resulted from
   (1) government policies of ethnic cleansing
   (2) attempts by democratic forces to overthrow the monarchy
   (3) native reaction to foreign interference in the region
   (4) government denial of access to fertile farm-land

In developing your answer to Part II, be sure to keep these general definitions in mind:
(a) describe means "to illustrate something in words or tell about it"
(b) discuss means "to make observations about something using facts, reasoning, and argument; to present in some detail"

PART II — THEMATIC ESSAY QUESTION

Directions: Write a well-organized essay that includes an introduction, several paragraphs addressing the task below, and a conclusion.

Theme: Political Systems

Political systems have affected the history and culture of nations and societies.

Task:

Identify *two* different political systems and for *each*
• Describe the characteristics of the political system
• Discuss how the political system has affected the history *or* culture of a specific nation or society

You may use any political systems from your study of global history. Some suggestions you might wish to consider include absolute monarchy, constitutional monarchy, parliamentary democracy, direct democracy, theocracy, communism, and fascism.

You are *not* limited to these suggestions.

Do *not* use the United States as an example of a nation or society.

(continued...)

Guidelines:

In your essay, be sure to
- Develop all aspects of the task
- Support the theme with relevant facts, examples, and details
- Use a logical and clear plan of organization, including an introduction and a conclusion that are beyond a restatement of the theme

---

In developing your answers to Part III, be sure to keep this general definition in mind: <u>discuss</u> means "to make observations about something using facts, reasoning, and argument; to present in some detail"

PART III — DOCUMENT-BASED QUESTION

This question is based on the accompanying documents. This question is designed to test your ability to work with historical documents. Some of these documents have been edited for the purposes of this question. As you analyze the documents, take into account the source of each document and any point of view that may be presented in the document.

Historical Context:

Throughout history, natural resources such as water, coal, oil, and diamonds have both helped and hindered the development of nations and regions.

Task: Using the information from the documents and your knowledge of global history, answer the questions that follow each document in Part A. Your answers to the questions will help you write the Part B essay in which you will be asked to

> - Discuss how natural resources have helped *and/or* hindered the development of specific nations *or* regions

Do *not* use the United States as the specific nation or region

Part A

Short-Answer Questions

Directions: Analyze the documents and answer the short-answer questions that follow each document in the space providedon the next page.

Document 1

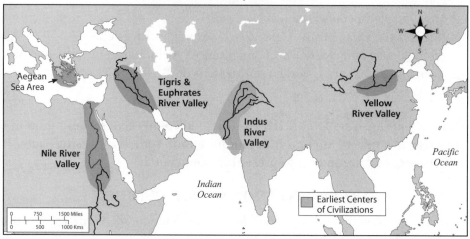

Earliest Civilizations, 3500 – 1500 BC

Source: *Historical Maps on File,* Revised Edition, Facts On File (adapted)

1 Based on this map, identify *one* geographic feature that influenced the location of early centers of civilization. [1]

_____

_____

Score [ ]

Document 2a

"Farmers in India Await the Rains, and Despair"

REWARI, India—When the monsoon rains that sweep across India every year failed to arrive in late June, the farmers here began to worry. Now, as they scan the empty blue skies for signs of clouds, their worry is turning to despair.

Broad swaths [wide areas] of India are seeing the country's worst drought in 15 years. Here in the northern state of Haryana, the level of rainfall until July 24 was 70% below average; for the country as a whole, it was 24% below normal. Since July 24, there has been little relief for the hardest-hit areas.

Under these parched [very dry] conditions, economists say, India's growth could wilt, since agriculture accounts for a quarter of gross domestic product [GDP] and sustains [supports] twothirds of the nation's billion-strong population. Before the drought, economists were expecting agricultural expansion of around 2% and GDP growth of 4.5% to 6% in the current fiscal year, which began April 1. Now they are predicting that agricultural production will remain stagnant or even turn negative, shaving something like half a percentage point off overall economic growth. . . .

Source: Joanna Slater, *The Wall Street Journal,*August 6, 2002

Score ☐

Document 2b

"Indian Monsoon Drenches the Land; Marketers Drench the Consumer"

BOMBAY, India—One year after a crippling drought, plentiful rains are sweeping across India—and delivering a flood of good news for its economy.

Agriculture's contribution to India's gross domestic product [GDP], its total output of goods and services, has declined over the past decade as the service and industrial sectors have grown. Nevertheless, the showers are a relief for farmers, who depend on the monsoon to irrigate theircrops. They are also a boon [benefit] to sales of everything from tractors to shampoo; a good harvest puts more money in the pockets of rural consumers, improving the fortunes of companies ranging from Anglo-Dutch Unilever to Honda Motor Co. of Japan to South Korea's Samsung Electronics Co.

Agriculture still sustains two-thirds of India's billion-strong population and contributes a quarter of its GDP, which economists predict will expand by as much as 6.5% in the fiscal year ending next March, partly because of the abundant rains and the resurgent [recovered] farm sector. . . .

Source: Joanna Slater, *The Wall Street Journal*, July 24, 2003

2b Based on this excerpt by Joanna Slater, state **one** positive impact that abundant levels of rain have had on the economy in India. [1]

Score ☐

Document 3

Great Britain, 1750–1850

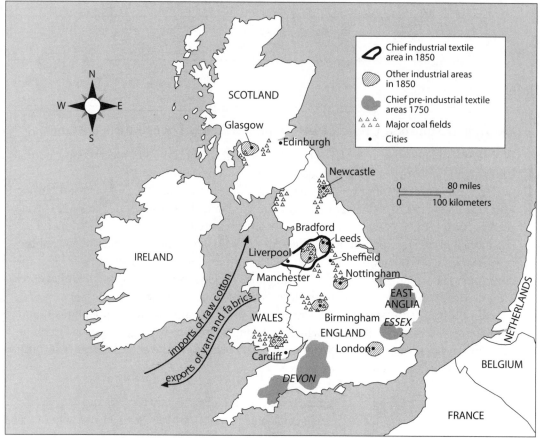

Source: Holt and O'Connor, *Exploring World History Workbook*, Globe Book Company (adapted)

3 Based on this map, state **one** way that coal affected the development of Great Britain between 1750 and 1850. [1]

_____

_____

Score ☐

Document 4

> . . .The lives of factory workers in Manchester, and in the other new industrial cities rising up around Britain, were shaped by the burning of coal just as the coal miners' lives were shaped by the digging of it. Coal made the iron that built the machines the workers operated as well as the factories they worked in, and then it provided the power that made the machines and factories run. Coal gas provided the lights the worked toiled [worked] under, letting their work day start before dawn and end after dusk. When they left the factory doors, they would walk through a city made of coal-fired bricks, now stained black with the same coal soot that was soiling their skin and clothes. Looking up, they would see a sky darkened by coal smoke; looking down, a ground blackened by coal dust. When they went home, they would eat food cooked over a coal fire and often tainted with a coal flavor, and with each breath, they would inhale some of the densest coal smoke on the planet. In short, their world was con-structed, animated, illuminated, colored, scented, flavored, and generally saturated by coal and the fruits [results] of combustion. . . .

Source: Barbara Freese, Coal: A Human History, Perseus Publishing

4 According to Barbara Freese, what are **two** effects that coal had on factory workers in the industrial cities of Great Britain during the Industrial Revolution? [2]

(1) _____

_____

Score ☐

(2) _____

_____

Score ☐

Document 5

Kuwait became a major supplier of oil during the late 1940s and the 1950s. Kuwait made a deal with foreign oil companies in return for payments. This money changed the way many people earned a living in Kuwait and led to a change in Kuwait's economic infrastructure.

> ...The government's efforts to modernize the City of Kuwait resulted in a construction boom, particularly in the period 1952 to 1965. Foreign planning consultants, architects, engineers, construction firms, and labor planned and created a city with the best material and technologies the industrial world could supply. In contrast to the land acquisition program, however, government outlays in this period to create social overhead capital did generate considerable economic activity. In addition to a great many public buildings, commercial centers, apart-ment blocks, and suburban community projects built in the period, the following were also constructed:
> 1. 176 government schools and 32 private schools.
> 2. 8 hospitals, 2 sanatoria [treatment centers], 37 dispensaries and health centers, 148 school dispensaries and 9 centers for preventive medicine.
> 3. 1,100 kilometers of paved roads.
> 4. A number of electric power stations and an expansive network for distribution and street lighting laid; between 1956 and 1965, installed capacity increased from 30,000 kwh to 370,000 kwh. . . .

Source: Jacqueline S. Ismael, "The Economic Transformation of Kuwait,"
The Politics of Middle Easten Oil, Middle East Institute

5 According to Jacqueline S. Ismael, what are **two** ways Kuwait used its oil resources to improve the city of Kuwait? [2]

(1) _____

_____

Score ☐

(2) _____

_____

Score ☐

Document 6

"I can't see a reason to go to war with Iraq...."

Source: Michael Ramirez, *Los Angeles Times,* January, 2003 (adapted)

5 Based on Michael Ramirez's cartoon, in what way did Iraqi oil contracts influence the French government in 2003? [1]

_____

_____

Score ☐

Document 7

> . . . When De Beers discovered diamonds in Botswana in 1969, the government had been independent for three years, and the men running it were traditional chiefs who owned cattle. They came from a desert culture where people have to scrimp and save to survive the long, dry season.
>
> During three decades, Botswana's leaders have carefully guided what became the world's fastest-growing economy. They invested in roads, schools and clinics. In stark contrast to the rulers of Angola and Congo, they created an African nation devoted to improving the lives of its people. In 1965, only about half of primary school-aged children attended school. Today, 90 percent of that group is enrolled. Life expectancy, which was less than 50 at independence, is now near 70.*
>
> Phones work in Botswana, potholes get repaired, garbage gets picked up, and a lively press pokes fun at the government without fear. At $3,600 per year, the gross national product per capita is seven times higher than the average for sub-Saharan Africa. The standard of living is higher than in South Africa, Turkey or Thailand.
>
> "Diamonds are not devils," said Terry Lynn Karl, professor of political science at Stanford and author of "The Paradox of Plenty," (University of California Press, 1997), a book about the poisonous mix of natural resources, big money and thieving elites in developing countries. "What matters is that there be a tradition of good government and compromise in place prior to the exploitation of these resources.". . .
>
> * Correction: The United Nations says that because of AIDS, the figure has fallen sharply and is 41, no longer close to 90.

Source: Blaine Harden, "Africa's Gems: Warfare's Best Friend," *New York Times*, April 6, 2000
Correction published April 17, 2000

7   According to Blaine Harden, what are **two** ways that the sale of diamonds affected Botswana? [2]

(1) _____

_____

Score ☐

(2) _____

_____

Score ☐

Document 8

In 1980, diamonds were discovered at Gope in the Central Kalahari Game Reserve (CKGR). Since 1997, the government of Botswana has been removing the Bushmen from this area. Many wish to return to their traditional homelands.

> . . . In a recent court case concerning the Bushmen's right to return to their ancestral lands, Tombale assured the court that the evictions had nothing to do with diamonds. This was strange, because the Bushmen's lawyers had never mentioned diamonds. They were just defending the Gana and Gwi Bushmen's right to live on lands they had occupied for thousands of years.
>
> And yet when Margaret Nasha said in February 2002 that the relocation of the Gana and Gwi was not unprecedented she cited an example of people being relocated 'to give way for projects of national interest' in Jwaneng. They were, in fact, relocated to make way for a diamond mine.
>
> As Botswana's foreign minister Mompati Merafhe has explained: 'Many Bushmen have been removed because of economic interests. In Orapa, my area, a great chunk of people were removed because of the mine. Botswana is where it is today because of this facilitation. These people are no exception.'. . .
>
> Meanwhile, back in the Kalahari the Botswana government has been parcelling up the CKGR into diamond concessions and sharing them out between De Beers, the Australian-based company BHP Billiton and the Canadian outfit Motapa Diamond Inc. And by November last year virtually the entire game reserve, bar [except for] a small bite-sized chunk in the northwest, had been dished out.
>
> So either the government has pulled off a fat scam by selling dud concessions to three unsuspecting multinationals — or it's lying. . . .

Source: "Why are the Bushmen being evicted?" *The Ecologist*, September 2003

8 Based on this excerpt from *The Ecologist*, state *one* impact the 1980 discovery of more diamonds has had on the people of Botswana. [1]

_____

_____

Score ☐

Part B

Essay

Directions: Write a well-organized essay that includes an introduction, several paragraphs, and a conclusion. Use evidence from *at least five* documents in your essay. Support your response with relevant facts, examples, and details. Include additional outside information.

Historical Context:

Throughout history, natural resources such as water, coal, oil, and diamonds have both helped and hindered the development of nations and regions.

Task: Using information from the documents and your knowledge of global history, write an essay in which you:

> • Discuss how natural resources have helped *and/or* hindered the development of specific nations *or* regions.

Do *not* use the United States as the specific nation or region.

Guidelines:

In your essay, be sure to:
- Develop all aspects of the task
- Incorporate information from *at least five* documents
- Incorporate relevant outside information
- Support the theme with relevant facts, examples, and details
- Use a logical and clear plan of organization, including an introduction and a conclusion that are beyond a restatement of the theme

CHAPTER 17

PRACTICE REGENTS EXAMINATION #2

JAN. 2008 GLOBAL HISTORY AND GEOGRAPHY REGENTS

Part 1: Answer all questions in this part.

Base your answer to question 1 on the map below and on your knowledge of social studies.

Selected World Climate Zones

Tropic of Cancer

Equator

Tropic of Capricorn

■ Desert   ▢ Ice covered   ▨ Mountainous

Source: *Geography on File*, Facts on File, 1994 (adapted)

1 Based on the information provided in this map, which statement is accurate?
   (1) The world's largest icecap is located in northern Europe.
   (2) Most mountainous climates are located on the eastern borders of the continents.
   (3) The largest desert area stretches from western Africa through much of southwestern Asia.
   (4) South America is connected to Antarctica by a narrow land bridge.

2 Slash-and-burn techniques are typically practiced by
   (1) people who live along rivers that deposit rich soil during floods
   (2) subsistence farmers who plant an area until the soil loses its fertility
   (3) farmers who rely on chemical fertilization and pesticides
   (4) nomads who use pastures for their livestock

3 Which feature would most likely be included in an economic system based on traditional agriculture and self-sufficiency?
   (1) banks
   (2) barter
   (3) gold standard
   (4) tariffs

377

4 Which geographic factor had a major influence on the development of both Egyptian and Babylonian civilizations?
   (1) river valleys
   (2) cool temperatures
   (3) locations near a strait
   (4) mountains

5 Which description accurately identifies Socrates, Plato, and Aristotle?
   (1) rulers of the Roman Republic
   (2) artists of the Italian Renaissance
   (3) religious leaders of the Protestant Reformation
   (4) philosophers of ancient Greece

Base your answer to question 6 on the passage below and on your knowledge of social studies.

... The actual journey to Mecca [Makkah] began on the fifth of *Dhu al-Hijjah*, 1393 (the 29th of December, 1973, according to the Gregorian calendar), at Beirut International Airport, but it was not until the afternoon of the seventh that I donned [put on] the *Ihram* [robe] and drove along on the road from Jiddah to Mecca. The road was crowded with cars, buses and trucks all packed with pilgrims chanting the Hajj refrain, the *Talbiyah*: ...
   — Michael E. Jansen, *An American Girl on the Hajj*

6 This passage describes the experience of a follower of
   (1) Christianity   (3) Hinduism
   (2) Islam   (4) Judaism

7 In China, the development of civil service examinations and a belief in filial piety reflect the influence of
   (1) Shinto
   (2) Jainism
   (3) Confucianism
   (4) Buddhism

8 One way in which the Code of Hammurabi, the Twelve Tables, and the Justinian Code are similar is that each
   (1) legalized monotheistic beliefs
   (2) established legal standards
   (3) provided records of economic activity
   (4) supported republican governments

9 Which heading best fits the partial outline below?

I. _____

   A. People become more aware of the outside world.
   B. Merchant and craft guilds help commercial centers grow into cities.
   C. Trade routes develop to supply the growing demand for new products.
   D. Monarchs centralize control and increase their power.

   (1) Seljuk Turks Dominate Europe
   (2) Democracy Ends in Eastern Europe
   (3) Feudalism Declines in Western Europe
   (4) Religion Becomes Powerful Force in Europe

10 One way in which the African kingdoms of Ghana and Mali are similar is that they
   (1) established their wealth through trade
   (2) improved their military strength with the use of gunpowder
   (3) opened trade routes to the Americas
   (4) adopted Christianity as their major religion

11 One way in which the travels of Marco Polo and Ibn Battuta are similar is that they resulted in
   (1) an increased interest in different cultures
   (2) the development of slavery
   (3) a reduction in trade
   (4) the discovery of East Asia

Base your answer to question 12 on the map below and on your knowledge of social studies.

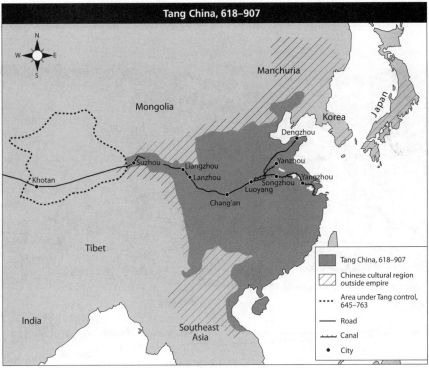

Source: Patrick K. O'Brien, general editor, *Oxford Atlas of World History*, Oxford University Press (adapted)

12 Which statement about the Tang dynasty is best supported by the information on this map?
   (1) It experienced conflict in coastal areas.
   (2) Its boundaries extended to India.
   (3) It gained territory in Tibet and Korea.
   (4) It exchanged goods using overland routes.

13 • Classical Greco-Roman ideas were revived.
   • Wealthy patrons supported the arts and education.
   • Humanism spread throughout western Europe.

Which period in European history is most closely associated with these statements?
   (1) Early Middle Ages
   (2) Industrial Revolution
   (3) Renaissance
   (4) Hellenistic Period

14 One similarity between Martin Luther and Henry VIII is that they
   (1) argued against the establishment of a theocratic state
   (2) protested against the ideas of the Enlightenment
   (3) died during the Reign of Terror
   (4) challenged the teachings of the Catholic Church

Base your answer to question 15 on the drawing below and your knowledge of social studies.

A Typical Medieval Manor

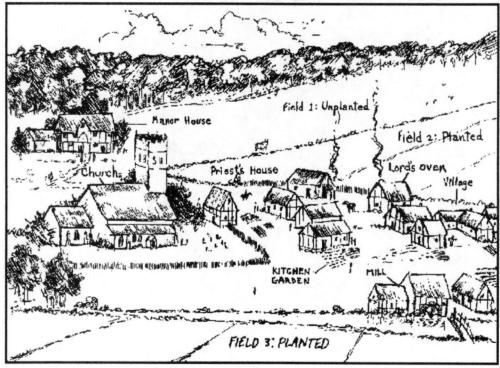

Source: James Killoran et al., *The Key to Understanding Global Studies*, 5th edition, Jarrett Publishing Company (adapted)

15 What inference can be drawn from the location of the church in this drawing?
  (1) The mill was managed by the church.
  (2) Religion played a significant role in the lives of the residents.
  (3) The church controlled trade within the manor.
  (4) The church played a limited role in education.

16 • Literacy rates rise.
   • Shakespeare's sonnets circulated.
   • Secular ideas spread.

Which innovation led directly to these developments?
  (1) printing press
  (2) astrolabe
  (3) paper currency
  (4) caravel

17 Which geographic feature had the greatest influence on the development of the Inca Empire?
  (1) deserts
  (2) irregular coastline
  (3) river valleys
  (4) mountains

18 What was one reason the Spanish conquista-dors were able to conquer the Aztec Empire?
  (1) The Spanish soldiers made effective use of their military technology against the Aztecs.
  (2) Aztec religious beliefs promoted nonvio-lence.
  (3) Spain joined the Incas in their fight against the Aztecs.
  (4) The Spanish cavalry outnumbered the Aztec warriors.

19 Which statement describes an impact of the Columbian exchange on the lives of Europe-ans?
  (1) The combination of new products and ideas promoted economic growth.
  (2) Native Americans immigrated to Europe and competed with Europeans for jobs.
  (3) Millions of Europeans were killed by new American diseases.
  (4) Introduction of the Native American religions resulted in the decline of the Roman Catholic Church.

20 A common goal of Philip II of Spain and Louis XIV of France was to
  (1) spread Calvinism
  (2) promote political revolutions
  (3) maintain absolute power
  (4) isolate their nations

Base your answer to question 21 on the speakers' statements below and on your knowledge of social studies.

Speaker A: My king has brought together the best mapmakers and scientists to study navigation. The expedi-tions he has sponsored will increase Portugal's trade with the East and make us wealthy.

Speaker B: My people lost their land and were forced to work in the mines and fields. They received little economic benefit.

Speaker C: My queen has chartered joint-stock companies to control trade with our colonies.

Speaker D: My people were enslaved and have endured unspeakable hard-ships. Many died during the Middle Passage.

21 Which two speakers would most likely support mercantilism?
  (1) A and B
  (2) A and C
  (3) B and D
  (4) C and D

22 • Parliament offered the throne to King William and Queen Mary.
   • Catholic King James II fled England for France.
   • Parliament agreed to joint rule with the monarch.
These events are most closely associated with the
  (1) Crusades
  (2) French Revolution
  (3) Glorious Revolution
  (4) Reconquista

23 At the Congress of Vienna (1815), the gov-ernments of Europe reacted to the French Revolution and the rule of Napoleon by at-tempting to
  (1) restore old regimes to power
  (2) spread the idea of democracy
  (3) encourage nationalist movements
  (4) promote the European free-trade zone

24 One political objective of both Otto von Bismarck and Giuseppe Garibaldi was to
(1) overthrow divine right monarchies
(2) unify their nations
(3) establish communist systems
(4) form an alliance with Great Britain

25 Karl Marx predicted that laissez-faire capitalism would result in
(1) a return to manorialism
(2) a revolution led by the proletariat
(3) fewer government regulations
(4) an equal distribution of wealth and income

26 Portuguese control of Macao and British control of Hong Kong in China are examples of
(1) collectivization   (3) self-determination
(2) imperialism   (4) containment

27 Commodore Matthew Perry's visits to Japan in 1853 and 1854 resulted in the
(1) colonization of Japan by the United States
(2) transfer of spheres of influence to China
(3) introduction of Christianity to Japanese society
(4) opening of trade and diplomatic relations with Japan

28 The term *militarism* can best be defined as
(1) loyalty to a nation or ethnic group
(2) buildup of armaments in preparation for war
(3) avoidance of military involvement in civil wars
(4) control of territories for economic and political gain

29 A primary reason for Japan's involvement in the Sino-Japanese War and the Russo-Japanese War was to
(1) acquire natural resources in Manchuria and Korea
(2) control trade and markets in Southeast Asia
(3) end Japan's policy of isolationism
(4) remove foreign invaders from Japanese soil

Base your answer to question 30 on the passage below and on your knowledge of social studies.

. . . His Majesty's Government view with favour the establishment in Palestine of a national home for the Jewish people, and will use their best endeavours to facilitate the achievement of this object, it being clearly understood that nothing shall be done which may prejudice the civil and religious rights of existing non-Jewish communities in Palestine, or the rights and political status enjoyed by Jews in any other country. . . .

30 This 1917 passage is taken from a document known as the
(1) Truman Doctrine
(2) Marshall Plan
(3) Fourteen Points
(4) Balfour Declaration

31 Which slogan is associated with the Bolshevik (Russian) Revolution?
(1) "An Eye for an Eye"
(2) "Peace, Land, and Bread"
(3) "Liberty, Equality, Fraternity"
(4) "Take up the White Man's Burden"

32 Which action is most closely associated with Atatürk (Mustafa Kemal)?
(1) beginning the Zionist movement
(2) starting the Palestine Liberation Organization
(3) using Western practices to modernize Turkey
(4) enforcing Islamic law

33 Which aspect of the economy was emphasized in Joseph Stalin's five-year plans?
(1) heavy industry
(2) consumer goods
(3) famine relief
(4) private landownership

34 Mohandas Gandhi is most closely associated with the
(1) support of violence and terrorism to end British rule
(2) desire to strengthen the caste system
(3) use of civil disobedience to gain political freedom
(4) establishment of a national religion in India

35 ". . . Seventy thousand people were killed instantly, and many more would die — 60,000 by November and another 70,000 by 1950. Most of them would be victims of a new method of killing — radiation. . . ."
— Ronald Takai

The situation described in this passage was the direct result of which World War II event?

(1) blitz of London
(2) attack on Pearl Harbor
(3) D-Day invasion of Normandy
(4) bombing of Hiroshima

36 Between 1945 and 1947, the differences between the Hindus and the Muslims in India led to the
(1) Sepoy Mutiny
(2) Salt March
(3) policy of nonalignment
(4) partitioning of the subcontinent

37 What was a major reason for the formation of the North Atlantic Treaty Organization (NATO) in 1949?
(1) to control European trade
(2) to resist Soviet aggression
(3) to support the blockade of Berlin
(4) to strengthen communist governments

38 In Egypt, Gamal Abdel Nasser's seizure of the Suez Canal continued his policy of
(1) attracting investments from Western banks
(2) supporting the rights of British workers
(3) eliminating criticism of political opponents
(4) establishing national control of vital resources

Base your answer to question 39 on the cartoon below and on your knowledge of social studies.

Source: Arcadio Esquivel, Costa Rica, *La Nacion*;
Panama, *La Prensa*

39 Which concept is illustrated in this cartoon?
(1) nonalignment   (3) nationalism
(2) interdependence   (4) socialism

40 The histories of Latvia, Estonia, Lithuania, and Finland have been greatly affected by their
(1) proximity to Russia
(2) abundant oil reserves
(3) aggressive foreign policies
(4) alliances with Israel

41 In 1989, the government of China responded to the protests in Tiananmen Square by
   (1) halting trade with the West
   (2) allowing democratic elections
   (3) sending in tanks and troops to end the demonstrations
   (4) calling for a special session of the United Nations Security Council

42 Which heading best completes the partial outline?

I. _____
   A. Korea remains divided at the 38th parallel.
   B. East and West Berlin are split by a wall.
   C. Strategic arms limitation talks begin.

   (1) Emerging Nations of the World
   (2) Results of the Cold War
   (3) Economic Benefits of World War II
   (4) Ethnic Conflicts in the World

Base your answer to question 43 on the cartoon below and on your knowledge of social studies.

Source: Jonathan Shapiro (Zapiro), *Sowetan*, 1994

43 What is the main idea of this cartoon?
   (1) Nelson Mandela has completed South Africa's reconstruction.
   (2) Although black South Africans have overcome many obstacles to achieve freedom, many struggles lie ahead.
   (3) The mountains of South Africa have hindered black South African participation in national elections.
   (4) The reconstruction of South Africa can only be achieved through violence, treason, and defiance.

44 Which action occurred in the Soviet Union under Mikhail Gorbachev?
   (1) Peasants were forced onto collective farms.
   (2) Citizens experienced more personal freedoms under glasnost.
   (3) The United States and the Soviet Union ended diplomatic relations.
   (4) The Soviet government increased its control over the Orthodox Church.

45 Which statement is a fact rather than an opinion?
   (1) The growing economy of Brazil threatens the economic power of the United States.
   (2) Free trade will lower the standard of living for workers in developed nations.
   (3) The European Union (EU) has issued a common currency called the euro.
   (4) Developing nations will never be able to compete with developed nations.

46 A study of the fall of the Roman Empire (476) and of the collapse of the Soviet Union (1991) shows that powerful empires can
   (1) lose strength when mercenaries enforce reforms
   (2) be threatened only when directly attacked by outsiders
   (3) conquer more than one continent and remain stable
   (4) be weakened by both internal and external pressures

47 A comparison of the feudal system in Europe and the encomienda system in Latin America shows that both systems
   (1) awarded land to the elite
   (2) promoted religious tolerance
   (3) relied on global trade for goods
   (4) used a parliamentary system of government

Base your answer to question 48 on the cartoon below and on your knowledge of social studies.

Russian Economy

Source: Brian Gable, *The Globe and Mail*, Toronto, Canada (adapted)

48 The main idea of this 1990s cartoon is that Russia is
   (1) deciding between a capitalist or a communist system
   (2) attempting to restore military power
   (3) expressing concern about how the rest of the world views its government
   (4) maintaining a balance between a civilian and a military government

49 • Location — included lands surrounding the
     eastern Mediterranean Sea
   • People — Turks, Arabs, Greeks, Muslims,
     Christians, and Jews
   • Nickname during the 19th and early 20th
     centuries — "The Sick Man of Europe"
Which empire is described by these characteristics?

   (1) Gupta   (3) Roman
   (2) Mongol   (4) Ottoman

50 Which sequence of Russian events is in the
   correct chronological order?

A. Catherine the Great westernizes Russia.
B. Ivan III defeats the Mongols.
C. Khrushchev places missiles in Cuba.
D. Czar Nicholas II abdicates the throne.

   (1) $A \rightarrow B \rightarrow C \rightarrow D$
   (2) $B \rightarrow A \rightarrow D \rightarrow C$
   (3) $B \rightarrow C \rightarrow A \rightarrow D$
   (4) $D \rightarrow A \rightarrow C \rightarrow B$

In developing your answer to Part II, be sure to keep these general definitions in mind:
(a) <u>describe</u> means "to illustrate something in words or tell about it"
(b) <u>discuss</u> means "to make observations about something using facts, reasoning, and argument; to present in some detail"

PART II: THEMATIC ESSAY QUESTION

Directions: Write a well-organized essay that includes an introduction, several paragraphs addressing the task below, and a conclusion.

Theme: Change

> Not all revolutions are political. Nonpolitical revolutions have brought important intellectual, economic, and/or social changes to societies.

Task:

> Identify *two* non-political revolutions that brought important intellectual, economic, and/or social changes to societies and for *each*
> • Describe *one* change brought about by this nonpolitical revolution
> • Discuss an impact this nonpolitical revolution had on a specific society or societies

You may use any nonpolitical revolution that brough important intellectual, economic, and/or social changes, from your study of global history. Some suggestions you might wish to consider include the Neolithic Revolution (10,000-6000 B.C.), the Commercial Revolution (11th-18th centuries), the Scientific Revolution (16th-18th centuries), the Enlightenment (17th-18th centuries), the Agricultural Revolution (18th-19th centuries), the Industrial Revolution in Europe (18th-19th centuries, and the Green Revolution (late 20th century).

You are *not* limited to these suggestions.

Guidelines: In your essay, be sure to

• Develop all aspects of the task
• Support the theme with relevant facts, examples, and details
• Use a logical and clear plan of organization, including an introduction and a conclusion that are beyond a restatement of the theme

In developing your answer to Part III, be sure to keep these general definitions in mind:
(a) <u>describe</u> means "to illustrate something in words or tell about it"
(b) <u>discuss</u> means "to make observations about something using facts, reasoning, and argument; to present in some detail"

PART III

DOCUMENT-BASED QUESTION

This question is based on the accompanying documents. It is designed to test your ability to work with historical documents. Some of these documents have been edited for the purposes of this question. As you analyze the documents, take into account the source of each document and any point of view that may be presented in the document.

Historical Context:

Throughout history, governments have sometimes attempted to control the thoughts and actions of their people. Three such governments include **Russia under the rule of Peter the Great, Germany under the rule of Adolf Hitler,** and **China under the rule of Mao Zedong.** The efforts of these governments greatly affected their societies.

Task: Using information from the documents and your knowledge of global history, answer the questions that follow each document in Part A. Your answers to the questions will help you write the Part B essay in which you will be asked to

> Choose *two* governments mentioned in the historical context and for *each*
> - Describe the efforts of the government to control the thoughts *and/or* actions of its people
> - Discuss an impact of this government's efforts on its society

Part A

Short Answer Questions

Directions: Analyze the documents on the following pages, and answer the short-answer questions that follow each document in the space provided.

Document 1a

Peter the Great

Source: Chris Hinton, *What is Evidence?* John Murray, Ltd.

Document 1b

. . . A year later, in January 1700, Peter transformed persuasion into decree [law]. With rolling drums in the streets and squares, it was proclaimed that all boyars [Russian nobles], government officials and men of property, both in Moscow and in the provinces, were to abandon their long robes and provide themselves with Hungarian or German-style caftans. The following year, a new decree commanded men to wear a waistcoat, breeches, gaiters, boots and a hat in the French or German style, and women to put on petticoats, skirts, bonnets and Western shoes. Later decrees prohibited the wearing of high Russian boots and long Russian knives. Models of the new approved costumes were hung at Moscow's gates and in public places in the city for people to observe and copy. All who arrived at the gates in traditional dress except peasants were permitted to enter only after paying a fine. Subsequently, Peter instructed the guards at the city gates to force to their knees all visitors arriving in long, traditional coats and then to cut off the coats at the point where the lowered garment touched the ground. "Many hundreds of coats were cut accordingly," says Perry, "and being done with good humor it occasioned mirth [humor] among the people and soon broke the custom of wearing long coats, especially in places near Moscow and those towns wherever the Tsar came.". . .

Source: Robert K. Massie, *Peter the Great: His Life and World,* Alfred A. Knopf

1 Based on these documents, state *two* ways Peter the Great tried to control the actions of his people.

[1]_____

_____

Score ☐

(2)_____

_____

Score ☐

Document 2a

... Peter's military reform would have remained an isolated incident in Russian military history had it not left a distinct and deep impression on the social and intellectual composition of all Russian society, and even influenced future political developments. The military reform itself made necessary other innovations, first to maintain the reorganised and expensive military forces, and then to ensure their permanency. The new recruiting methods, by spreading military obligations to classes hitherto [up to this time] exempt, and thus affecting all social classes, gave the new army a more varied composition, and completely altered existing social relationships. From the time that noblemens' serfs and servants joined the new army as ordinary recruits instead of only as menials or valets [servants], the position of the nobility, which had been preponderant [dominant] in the old army, was completely changed. . . .

Source: Vasili Klyuchevsky, translated by Liliana Archibald, *Peter the Great,* St. Martin's Press

2a According to Vasili Klyuchevsky, what was *one* way Peter the Great attempted to control the Russian people? [1]

_____

Score ☐

2b According to Vasili Klyuchevsky, what was *one* effect Peter the Great's reform had on the Russian nobles? [1]

_____

Score ☐

Document 3

Emergence of "Dual Russia"

The Petrine [Peter's] Reform is often seen as the main cause and the starting point of the irrevocable [unalterable] split of Russian society into two parts. Peter's reforms transformed the upper levels of Russian society while the masses remained largely unaffected by them. Peter had forced the nobility to acquire technical knowledge of Western Europe and to adopt European styles of dress and manners. An increasingly Europeanized education of the upper classes brought with it a familiarity with the philosophies and theories of the Enlightenment. Soon many Russian nobles even preferred to speak the languages of Western Europe (particularly French and German) to Russian. By the nineteenth century their world was European in dress, manners, food, education, attitudes, and language, and was completely alien to the way of life of the Russian popular masses. . . .

Source: Alexander Chubarov, *The Fragile Empire: A History of Imperial Russia,* Continuum

3 According to Alexander Chubarov, what was *one* long-term effect Peter the Great's reform had on the upper classes of Russian society? [1]

_____

Score ☐

Document 4a

> . . . On the night of May 10, 1933, thousands of Nazi students, along with many professors, stormed universities, libraries, and bookstores in thirty cities throughout Germany. They removed hundreds of thousands of books and cast them onto bonfires. In Berlin alone, more than twenty thousand books were burned. The book burnings were part of a calculated effort to "purify" German culture. Since April 12, the Nazi German Student Association had been purging libraries, working from lists of books deemed "un-German." The authors of some of the books were Jews, but most were not. . . .

Source: Michael Berenbaum, *The World Must Know: The History of the Holocaust as Told in the United States Holocaust Memorial Museum*, Little, Brown and Co.

4a According to Michael Berenbaum, what was *one* way the Nazi Party attempted to control the thoughts of the German people? [1]

_____

_____

Score ☐

Document 4b

> . . . The Hitler Youth Movement was formed for the express purpose of creating loyal subjects to the state. By 1935, over three million boys and girls aged 10 and older were enrolled. "We were born to die for Germany" was one of their popular slogans. In addition to a strenuous physical fitness program, they received training in the use of weapons and heard lexture on Nazi ideology. . . .

Source: Chartock and Spencer, eds., *Can It Happen Again?*, Black Dog & Leventhal

_____

_____

Score ☐

Document 5

In this excerpt Horst Krüger, a German author and prisoner of war, describes his reaction to reading a newspaper account of Hitler's death. He is reflecting on the state of the press while Hitler was in power.

> . . . When I first began to read the newspapers, he was already in power. I knew nothing but a subservient [obedient], bellicose [hostile], boastful press. I always felt it was a proven fact that Hitler had also conquered and occupied the German language, and my parents had always told me, "What you read in the papers isn't true, but you mustn't say so. Outside, you must always act as if you believe everything." The German language and lies had become one and the same thing to me. Home was the only place where you could speak the truth. What you read in the papers was always a lie, but you weren't allowed to say so. And now I was holding a newspaper that was in German and that did not lie. How was it possible? How could language and truth coincide? How did it happen that you could believe something you saw in print? It was the first free German paper of my life. . . .

Source: Horst Krüger, *A Crack in The Wall: Growing Up Under Hitler,* Ruth Hein, tr.,
Fromm International Publishing Corporation

5 According to Horst Krüger, what was *one* impact of the Nazi government on German society? [1]

_____

_____

Score ☐

Document 6

This is an excerpt from the opening statement of Chief Prosecutor Robert H. Jackson at the trial of the major war criminals before the International Military Tribunal given on November 21, 1945.

. . . Germany became one vast torture chamber. Cries of its victims were heard round the world and brought shudders to civilized people everywhere. I am one who received during this war most atrocity tales with suspicion and scepticism [doubt]. But the proof here will be so overwhelming that I venture to predict not one word I have spoken will be denied. These defendants will only deny personal responsibility or knowledge.

Under the clutch of the most intricate web of espionage and intrigue that any modern state has endured, and persecution and torture of a kind that has not been visited upon the world in many centuries, the elements of the German population which were both decent and courageous were annihilated [reduced to nothing]. Those which were decent but weak were intimidated. Open resistance, which had never been more than feeble and irresolute, disappeared. But resistance, I am happy to say, always remained, although it was manifest in only such events as the abortive effort to assassinate Hitler on July 20, 1944. With resistance driven underground, the Nazi had the German State in his own hands.

But the Nazis not only silenced discordant voices. They created positive controls as effective as their negative ones. Propaganda organs, on a scale never before known, stimulated the Party and Party formations with a permanent enthusiasm and abandon such as we, democratic people, can work up only for a few days before a general election. They inculcated [impressed upon] and practiced the Führerprinzip [leadership principle] which centralized control of the Party and of the Party-controlled State over the lives and thought of the German people, who are accustomed to look upon the German State, by whomever controlled, with a mysticism [a power to believe] that is incomprehensible to my people [the United States public]. . . .

Source: *Trial of the Major War Criminals Before the International Military Tribunal,*
Nuremberg, 14 November 1945–1 October 1946

6 According to Chief Prosecutor Jackson, what was *one* effect the Nazi government's actions had on the people of Germany? [1]

_____

_____

Score ☐

Document 7

This is an account of Nien Cheng's experiences during the Cultural Revolution. This excerpt describes what was happening the day she was sent to the Detention House.

> . . . The streets of Shanghai, normally deserted at nine o'clock in the evening, were a sea of humanity. Under the clear autumn sky in the cool breeze of September, people were out in thousands to watch the intensified activities of the Red Guards. On temporary platforms erected everywhere, the young Revolutionaries were calling upon the people in shrill and fiery rhetoric to join in the Revolution, and conducting small-scale struggle meetings against men and women they seized at random on the street and accused of failing to carry Mao's Little Red Book of quotations or simply wearing the sort of clothes the Red Guards disapproved of. Outside private houses and apartment buildings, smoke rose over the garden walls, permeating the air as the Red Guards continued to burn books indiscriminately. . . .

Source: Nien Cheng, *Life and Death in Shanghai*, Penguin Books

7 According to Nien Cheng, what were *two* actions taken by the Red Guards in an attempt to control the thoughts of the people during Mao's rule in China? [2]

(1)_____

_____

Score ☐

(2)_____

_____

Score ☐

Document 8

In Following the Revolutionary Road, Strive for an Even Greater Victory
Mao as the Reddest Red Sun in people's hearts, floating above Tiananmen Square. At the front of the huge, Little Red Book-waving crowd are the figures of a worker, peasant, and soldier, while representatives from other occupations stand just behind. The Book was compiled from Mao's Selected Works by Lin Biao in the early 1960s to be used for propaganda work in the People's Liberation Army. After the Cultural Revolution began, it became an integral part of the ritual of Mao worship. By 1970, this kind of orchestrated adulation [staged praise] and the power of Lin Biao were both at their zenith [height].

Source: *Picturing Power: Posters from the Chinese Cultural Revolution Exhibit,* Indiana University

8 According to this document, what was **one** way that Mao's government attempted to influence the people of China? [1]

_____

_____

Score␣

Document 9

> ... Between 1966 and 1976, a whole generation of teenagers failed to receive a real education; other Chinese came to call them "the lost generation." At least twenty thousand people lost their lives because of the Cultural Revolution.
>
> ... Because of the Cultural Revolution, many Chinese young people grew up with no knowledge of traditional Chinese customs and beliefs. Needing to fill that gap, some of them began looking to the West — especially to the Western ideals of democracy, freedom, capitalism, and individualism. . . .

Source: *Great Events: The Twentieth Century 1960–1968,* Salem Press

9 Based on this excerpt from *Great Events*, state **one** impact the Cultural Revolution had on Chinese society. [1]

_____

_____

Score ☐

Part B
Essay

Directions: Write a well-organized essay that includes an introduction, several paragraphs, and a conclusion. Use evidence from *at least four* documents in your essay. Support your response with relevant facts, examples, and details. Include additional outside information.

Historical Context:

Throughout history, governments have sometimes attempted to control the thoughts and actions of their people. Three such governments include **Russia under the rule of Peter the Great, Germany under the rule of Adolf Hitler,** and **China under the rule of Mao Zedong.** The efforts of these governments greatly affected their societies.

Task: Using the information from the documents and your knowledge of global history, write an essay in which you

(continued on next page)

Choose **two** governments mentioned in the historical context and for **each**

- Describe the efforts of the government to control the thoughts **and/or** actions of its people
- Discuss an impact of this government's efforts on its society

Guidelines:

In your essay, be sure to
- Develop all aspects of the task
- Incorporate information from *at least* **four** documents
- Incorporate relevant outside information
- Support the theme with relevant facts, examples, and details
- Use a logical and clear plan of organization, including an introduction and a conclusion that are beyond a restatement of the theme

INDEX

NOTES

NOTES